Health Technology Assessments and the Right to Health

Global Health, Human Rights and Social Justice

VOLUME 4

The titles published in this series are listed at *brill.com/ghhr*

Health Technology Assessments and the Right to Health

Mobilising and Distributing Resources in Priority-Setting

By

Luciano Bottini Filho

BRILL | NIJHOFF

ISSN 2949-8589
ISBN 978-90-04-73030-4
ISBN 978-90-04-73031-1 (PDF)
DOI https://doi.org/10.1163/9789004730311

Library of Congress Control Number: 2026947982

Brill Nijhoff and Koninklijke Brill BV are part of De Gruyter Brill.
www.degruyterbrill.com

Questions about General Product Safety Regulation: productsafety@degruyterbrill.com

Contents

Foreword

"From the perspective of a more rounded social science, there are so many weaknesses in mainstream economics that it is difficult to know where to begin in laying them out, in offering alternatives and in explaining how the dismal science could have got itself into this state. Even so, despite having spent a working life in criticism of the orthodoxy, I can only be struck by the extent to which the notion of scarcity has attracted so little attention."[1]

1 Ben Fine, 'Economics and Scarcity: With Amartya Sen as Point of Departure' in Lyla Mehta (ed), *The Limits to Scarcity: Contesting the Politics of Allocation* (Routledge 2013) 73.

Figures and Tables

Figures

Tables

PART 1

Scarcity, Law and The Right to Health in HTA

CHAPTER 1

Finding the Right to Health in Health Technology Assessments: An Introduction

Long before countries found themselves on the brink of health systems collapse in the COVID-19 pandemic, several authors had already come to the bitter realisation that the right to health is unrealistic. This criticism has been made on many grounds: vague language and ideology; a morally unenforceable claim; lack of a justifying theory of justice; indeterminacy of content and obligations; and the need for democratic decisions to address scarce resources.[1] Scarcity, above all, defies the ideal of a right to health because not all needs can be met; resources are finite and all countries must be pre-

---

1 For this criticism on the right to health, see e.g.:

a) on ideology and vague language: Laurence Gostin, 'The Ideology of Entitlement: The Contemporary Function of Law and Its Application to Psychiatry', *Psychiatry – Law and Ethics* (Springer 1986); Nikolas Rose, 'Unreasonable Rights: Mental Illness and the Limits of the Law' (1985) 12 Journal of Law and Society 199, 209–215; Baruch A Brody, 'Why the Right to Health Care Is Not a Useful Concept for Policy Debates', *Rights to health care* (Springer 1991)

b) on moral enforceability: Gopal Sreenivasan, 'II – Gopal Sreenivasan: A Human Right to Health? Some Inconclusive Scepticism' (2012) 86 Aristotelian Society Supplementary Volume 239; Carmen E Pavel, 'Healthcare: Between a Human and a Conventional Right' (2019) 35 Economics & Philosophy 499, 507–517.

c) on democratic requirement: John D Arras and Elizabeth M Fenton, 'Access to Health-Related Goods' (2009) 39 Hastings Center Report 27.

d) absence of distributive justice theory: Norman Daniels, 'Rights to Health Care and Distributive Justice: Programmatic Worries' (1979) 4 Journal of Medicine and Philosophy 174.

e) need for public goods justifications: Nicole Hassoun, 'The Human Right to Health: A Defense' (2020) 51 Journal of Social Philosophy 158, 9–13.

f) on foundational problems, lower status than political rights and lack of content: John Harris, 'Taking the "Human" out of Human Rights' (2011) 20 Cambridge Quarterly of Healthcare Ethics 9; Timothy Goodman, 'Is There a Right to Health?' (2005) 30 The Journal of Medicine and Philosophy 643; Nicole Hassoun, 'The Human Right to Health' (2015) 10 Philosophy Compass 275, 278–279; Benedict E Rumbold, 'Review Article: The Moral Right to Health: A Survey of Available Conceptions' (2017) 20 Critical Review of International Social and Political Philosophy 508, 512–513; Madison Powers, 'Health Care as a Human Right: The Problem of Indeterminate Content' (2015) 6 Jurisprudence 138.

 | HTTPS://DOI.ORG/10.1163/9789004730311-002

pared to make hard choices, and so the narrative goes on.[2] An international consensus has been built on this logic of inescapable scarcity and, in the name of Universal Health Coverage (UHC), an international agenda flowing from developed to poor countries was established to disseminate the business of prioritisation in health. Experts held workshops in the Balkans, African countries were trained in setting up their own priority-setting process for UHC and Latin American States started cooperating to support common policies in this area.[3]

To introduce priority-setting to further jurisdictions, it has even been argued (rather boldly) that "all you need is law" to establish formal decision-making procedures and bodies.[4] This particular law revolves less on the right to health and more around institutionalising a specific method through law: Health Technology Assessment (HTA), a multidisciplinary research process to support resource allocation. Since HTA established itself as a policy practice, researchers and health policymakers have wrestled with slightly different definitions, but it seems generally accepted that HTA is a combination of three main components: a formal and transparent procedure; multidisciplinary evidence-based research; and recommendations on the value of health technologies.[5] HTA is now a global health policy, which, after prolonged variations

2 See e.g. Norman Daniels and James E Sabin, *Setting Limits Fairly: Learning to Share Resources for Health* (Oxford University Press, 2nd ed., 2008) 1–2.

3 See e.g.: World Health Organization, 'Current Status of Health Intervention and Technology Assessment in the Balkan Region' (World Health Organization Regional Office for Europe 2020); Samantha Hollingworth and others, 'Implementing Health Technology Assessment in Ghana to Support Universal Health Coverage: Building Relationships That Focus on People, Policy, and Process' (2020) 36 International Journal of Technology Assessment in Health Care 8; Diego Rosselli and others, 'HTA Implementation in Latin American Countries: Comparison of Current and Preferred Status' (2017) 14 Value in Health Regional Issues 20.

4 David Clarke, Gwenaël Dhaene and John Lisman, 'Legal Considerations: Reviewing or Establishing the Legal Framework.' in Melanie Bertram, Gwenaël Dhaene and Tessa Tan-Torres Edejer (eds), *Institutionalizing health technology assessment mechanisms: a how to guide* (World Health Organization 2021) 16–19.

5 Eva Draborg and others, 'International Comparison of the Definition and the Practical Application of Health Technology Assessment' (2005) 21 International Journal of Technology Assessment in Health Care 89; 'WHO | HTA Definitions' (*WHO*) <https://www.who.int/health-technology-assessment/about/Defining/en/> accessed 5 March 2021; Gert Jan van der Wilt, Alric Rüther and Rebecca Trowman, 'Scientific Development of HTA – A Proposal by the Health Technology Assessment International Scientific Development and Capacity Building Committee' (2019) 35 International Journal of Technology Assessment in Health Care 263.

The recommendation for adoption of a new treatment may be called "health technology appraisal" but the term "assessment" will be used for the process of analysis, recommenda-

between organisations, received an international joint-definition in 2020, namely that it is: "a multidisciplinary process that uses explicit methods to determine the value of a health technology at different points in its life cycle. The purpose is to inform decision-making in order to promote an equitable, efficient, and high-quality health system."[6]

While law seems important to HTA, this still requires further elaboration. In the notes of this international HTA definition, "legal issues" are listed as one of its core values.[7] Law is technically as much an essential part of HTA as any other common criterion.[8] Surprisingly, the literature and international community, including in the practice of the World Health Organization (WHO), are almost silent on the application of legal issues relevant to the international right to health in HTA.[9] While HTA institutions depend on law, their growth globally has not been led by the international right to health explicitly (which, as first mentioned, also has a contested role in healthcare policy-making). This book seeks then to address this gap by looking at the role of law and the right to health in HTA, with this particular question: To what extent can the international right to health offer standards for the implementation of HTA policies and criteria?

The argument in this book is that HTA cannot be reduced to a fair procedure, if we are to take seriously the standards set out in the international right to health. As part of a socio-economic rights framework, the right to health makes States responsible for undertaking the best options to mobilise resources and prevent scarcity, just as much as to distribute resources fairly. The right to health, in a socio-economic rights framework, also means that discussions of resource distribution cannot legitimise scarcity, as States should be com-

---

tion and deliberation. See.: Jennifer A Whitty, 'Health Technology Assessment' in Zaheer-Ud -Din Babar (ed), *Equitable Access to High-Cost Pharmaceuticals* (Elsevier 2018) 12.

6 Brian O'Rourke, Wija Oortwijn and Tara Schuller, 'The New Definition of Health Technology Assessment: A Milestone in International Collaboration' (2020) 36 International Journal of Technology Assessment in Health Care 187, 2.

7 Brian O'Rourke and others, 'The New Definition of Health Technology Assessment: A Milestone in International Collaboration' (2020) 36 International Journal of Technology Assessment in Health Care 187, 188.

8 There are many definitions that explicitly or implicitly include law. See e.g. Bryan R Luce and others, 'EBM, HTA, and CER: Clearing the Confusion' (2010) 88 The Milbank Quarterly 256, 271: "a form of policy research that examines short- and long- term social consequences (for example, societal, economic, ethical, legal) of the application of technology)"; David Banta, 'What Is Technology Assessment?' (2009) 25 International Journal of Technology Assessment in Health Care 7, 7: "the systematic evaluation of properties, effects and/or impacts of health technologies and interventions".

9 See chapter 3, pp. 50–59.

mitted to finding solutions for progressive realisation, including building better democratic institutions and coordinating policies for access to new technologies (price negotiation, tax policies, intellectual property agreements, etc.). In essence, the appeal of the right to health is to contest scarcity instead of legitimising inequalities that can be prevented with adequate State interventions. For instance, if funding is unavailable for a hepatitis C medicine solely because patents make the drug prohibitively expensive, can a priority-setting process confer legitimacy on an HTA-based economic recommendation – despite the fact that a powerful determinant of the decision is an unfair overall budget impact, driven by a dysfunctional pharmaceutical market? In this case, the treatment is cost-effective (good value for the investment), but simply not affordable to be made available in many countries.[10]

In this view, HTA represents more than merely a democratic tool for fair decisions. Health systems, as core social institutions, do not amount to merely technical and management services and "communicate and enforce values and norms through many different aspects of their operation".[11] The idea of establishing a health system as a core social institution may often be associated with enforcing rights and citizenship through public participation and accountability.[12] HTA, however, will still be a bureaucratic technical procedure if it is just designed with "added" democracy and citizenship to deliver reports and guidance without being oriented towards the whole range of human rights values and principles that make healthcare realisation possible. A health system as a core social institution may, therefore, uphold equality and dignity with further international socio-economic rights principles, including non-discrimination, maximum available resources, progressive realisation and international cooperation.[13] To embed broader socio-economic rights values principles in a health system, HTA must also engage with policies that address

10 Victoria Charlton and others, 'Cost Effective but Unaffordable: An Emerging Challenge for Health Systems' [2017] BMJ j1402.

11 Lynn P Freedman, 'Achieving the MDGs: Health Systems as Core Social Institutions' (2005) 48 Development 19, 21.

12 See i.e.: Paul Hunt and Gunilla Backman, 'Health Systems and the Right to the Highest Attainable Standard of Health' (2008) 10 Health and Human Rights 81, 82; Alicia Ely Yamin, 'Democracy, Health Systems, and the Right to Health: Narratives of Charity, Markets, and Citizenship' in Silja Voeneky and Gerald L Neuman (eds), *Human Rights, Democracy, and Legitimacy in a World of Disorder* (1st edn, Cambridge University Press 2018) 194–198.

13 Claudia Landwehr, 'Procedural Justice and Democratic Institutional Design in Health-Care Priority-Setting' (2013) 12 Contemporary Political Theory 296, 308–309.

the causes of scarcity and strengthen resource mobilisation to combat economic dynamics of market power and exclusion.

Thus, applying a socio-economic rights lens does not exclusively mean "procedural justice" in resource allocation as a way to achieve fair decisions. In broad terms, procedural justice assumes that a deliberation is fair, not necessarily by applying specific substantive principles but rather by examining how the decision followed the requirements for a fair procedure.[14] This book, in comparison, integrates substantive principles developed from socio-economic rights into the procedure and considers HTA as an essential arm of a health system – functioning as a core social institution – contesting structural flaws in the health market. It means that HTA not only exists to conduct fair procedures but also to adopt policies to combat structural economic barriers that create scarcity and unaffordability. Consequently, the human rights-based approach (HRBA) proposed implies three elements: a) HTA being an instrument for a health system, understood as a core social institution, b) human rights standards in procedural and substantive policies, and c) the right to health, understood as a socio-economic right. What is needed in HTA is a process that translates, into its practice, socio-economic rights standards to make it accountable in both distributing existing resources and enabling their creation, thus preventing undue rationing.

For an HRBA, HTA promotes a principled "deliberative democracy" – it is concerned with procedure while also upholding substantive principles (in this case, through human rights standards).[15] This is comparable to the notion

14 Accountability for reasonableness is the dominant theory of procedural justice devised by Daniels and Sabin. (see chapter 2, 1.1 and 1.2 for a full discussion): Norman Daniels, *Just Health: Meeting Health Needs Fairly* (Cambridge University Press 2007) 108–109.

Procedural justice in health involves a deliberative process, but there might be some variance as to the implementation among authors, such as with Fleck's "rational democratic deliberation", where decisions require those affected by them and are bound to some substantive principles. See: Leonard M Fleck, 'Just Health Care Rationing: A Democratic Decision-making Approach' (1992) 140 University of Pennsylvania Law Review 1597, 1633. For general views on procedural justice, see. Stephen Jan, 'Proceduralism and Its Role in Economic Evaluation and Priority Setting in Health' (2014) 108 Social Science & Medicine 257, 258–260.

15 This is a concept taken from Amy Gutmann, *Why Deliberative Democracy?* (Princeton University Press 2004) 95–124. Other conceptualisations of deliberative democracy do not emphasise substantive principles as a fundamental precondition. See: Jalil Safaei, 'Deliberative Democracy in Health Care: Current Challenges and Future Prospects' (2015) 7 Journal of Healthcare Leadership 123, 124–126.

Procedural justice can be used as a near-synonym of this term, for authors that do not include substantive values in deliberative democracy. See e.g.: Michael D Rawlins, 'Pharmacopolitics and Deliberative Democracy' (2005) 5 Clinical Medicine 471, 472.

presented by Fleck of a "deliberative democracy" bound by "constitutional principles of health care justice", establishing the limits of a legitimate deliberation within multiple appropriate approaches to health justice in the allocation criteria.[16] Fleck considers principles related to the decision-making process, but some of those socio-economic rights constitutive principles, which should be embedded alongside the deliberation, are also responsible for creating and maximising resources in priority-setting.[17] They are, in reality, substantive measures to remedy unfair markets (impacting fair deliberations) such as procurement inefficiencies, price gouging, patient exclusion for lack of clinical data or simply an unregulated pricing system.

Having delimited the central argument of the book, this introduction will briefly answer basic questions about the approach taken to HTA and the right to health. Key terms used will also be considered and defined, such as rationing, priority-setting, scarcity and the right to health. The first section outlines the field of HTA and its importance to priority-setting and the right to health. The second section introduces the scope of resource allocation and scarcity and how it relates to socio-economic rights in this book. Section 3 then sets out the methodological perspective of this research with its original contribution, followed by a summary of the chapters.

1 Why Is HTA Important to the Right to Health?

In facilitating funding decisions, HTA may be a critical process in implementing the right to health. This should seem apparent for those already in the field, but not all human rights lawyers and health advocates may be familiar with this process. HTA supports governments around the world in deciding on the best value policies to expand healthcare, particularly in low- and medium-income countries (LMICs).[18] In some jurisdictions, it has the power to determine the basket of services (health technologies and public health interventions) that comprises a minimal level of healthcare in what is often called

16 Leonard M. Fleck, 'Just Caring: Do We Need Philosophical Foundations?' (2017) 3 Ethics, Medicine and Public Health 221, 229.

17 These principles are elaborated in Chapters 4 to 7.

18 Kalipso Chalkidou and others, 'Health Technology Assessment: Global Advocacy and Local Realities Comment on "Priority Setting for Universal Health Coverage: We Need Evidence-Informed Deliberative Processes, Not Just More Evidence on Cost-Effectiveness"' (2016) 6 International Journal of Health Policy and Management 233, 233–234.

UHC. As an interface between research and policymakers, HTA reports advise health administrators on the uptake or most adequate use of emerging technologies.[19] This practice has implications for how resources are distributed and different patient groups prioritised. As mentioned in the HTA definition, decisions are centred on the "value of a health technology" with a view "to promote an equitable, efficient, and high-quality health system".[20] The concepts of value, equity, efficiency and quality can be interconnected and subjective, but also contradictory because, for instance, some equity choices may reduce the level of efficiency.[21]

HTA-based choices may be designated as rationing and priority-setting and these terms may be used interchangeably herein, but authors do make clear distinctions between those expressions according to the situation. Rationing is more often used with a negative connotation to refer to individual cases (when someone is denied care).[22] By contrast, priority-setting has a somewhat more positive meaning and describes the allocation of resources between concurring options, prioritising courses of action or resource destination to a whole community.[23]

National priority-setting decisions, or macro-allocations, are conducted by HTA governmental agencies such as NICE (National Institute for Health and Care Excellence) in England and Wales, HITAP (Health Interventions and Technology Assessment Program) in Thailand and Conitec (National Committee for Technology Incorporation) in Brazil.[24] A primary function of those institutions is to provide economic and clinical evaluations of healthcare interventions. HTA agencies referred to in this research are typically affiliated to utilitarian approaches that aim to maximise value for money (cost–utility

19 Corinna Sorenson, Michael Drummond and Panos Kanavos, *Ensuring Value for Money in Health Care: The Role of Health Technology Assessment in the European Union* (WHO Regional Office Europe 2008) 6–7.

20 O'Rourke and others (n 7) 2.

21 Ibid.

22 Helen Dickinson and others, 'Resource Scarcity and Priority-Setting: From Management to Leadership in the Rationing of Health Care?' (2011) 31 Public Money & Management 363, 363–364; Guillem López-Casasnovas and Laura Pellisé-Urquiza, 'Resource Allocation and Priority-Setting in Health Care Systems' in RM Scheffler (ed), *World Scientific Handbook Of Global Health Economics And Public Policy (A 3-volume Set)* (World Scientific Publishing Company 2016) 364.

23 Ibid.

24 Wolfgang Greiner and J-Matthias Graf von der Schulenburg, 'HTA in Germany: Very Special and Specific' (2010) 11 The European Journal of Health Economics 1; F Reed Johnson, 'Editorial: Moving the QALY Forward or Just Stuck in Traffic?' (2009) 12 Value in Health S38, S38.

analysis, as ordinarily used by NICE), with Germany being one major exception.[25]

Despite not being the object of this book, HTA has wider usages other than priority-setting that need to be acknowledged. Assessments, for instance, may be used to lay down regulatory frameworks, authorise the registration and marketing of drugs and medical devices or request an independent expert analysis.[26] HTA reports can be issued across the public health system (e.g. private insurance reimbursement, hospital clinical guidelines, pharmaceutical licensing, etc.).[27] In terms of technologies reviewed, in the present empirical research, HTA undertaken to identify policies for social determinants of health or preventive measures (such as addiction or promotion of physical exercise) will be excluded. Similarly, priority-setting for medical research or micro-managing of services at hospitals warrants an examination not possible here.[28] In addition, other types of rationing that are deliberately omitted in this work are queueing (care delivery in a priority order and deferring its cost) or co-payment (cutting costs by sharing the burden of covering some treatments), which have their own moral and legal implications.[29] In brief, for the present study, decisions in HTA concern the public at large by excluding or incorporating medical interventions in the basket of health services, generally adopted at the health system macro level or central government.

25 Economic evaluations can represent different methods, but this thesis will mostly refer to cost–utility analysis (comparing costs to a standard unit of individual health preferences, the utility), cost–benefit analysis, which contrasts costs of a treatment with benefits in monetary terms, and cost-effectiveness, which it uses costs against specific treatment outcomes (thus impeding cross-treatments comparisons). See: Surachat Ngorsuraches, 'Defining Types of Economic Evaluation.' (2008) 91 Journal of the Medical Association of Thailand S21.

26 David Banta, 'The Development of Health Technology Assessment' (2003) 63 Health policy 121, 129.

27 DM Hailey, DE Cowley and W Dankiw, 'The Impact of Health Technology Assessment' (1990) 14 Community Health Studies 223, 224–225.

28 Dan W Brock, 'Broadening the Bioethics Agenda' (2000) 10 Kennedy Institute of Ethics Journal 21, 29.

29 Iman Keliddar, Ali Mohammad Mosadeghrad and Mehdi Jafari-Sirizi, 'Rationing in Health Systems: A CriticalReview' (2017) 31 Medical Journal of the Islamic Republic of Iran 1, 5.

2 Access to Health Technologies and the International Right to Health

The framework argued in this book directly draws on the right to health under international law to provide healthcare interventions using HTA (as opposed to researching a legal or constitutional right to health).[30] This book, however, has a focus on the relationship of human rights with resource allocation and mobilisation element of such a right. Just as economic pressures are a central concern in HTA, this book closely follows the broader principles that have shaped the human rights response to budget constraints (progressive realisation, maximum available resources, affordability and international cooperation, among others). Those are common to all rights in the International Covenant on Economic, Social and Cultural Rights (ICESCR).[31] For the present analysis, it is not necessary to define with precision a philosophical justification for a right to health to be recognised, but rather the obligations involved and its usefulness to policy-making as to resource allocation and priority-setting.[32] Since the focus is on the analysis of human rights on medical interventions, other health-related obligations will be excluded, such as the socio-economic determinants of health, or controversial bodily enhancement interventions sometimes regarded as unnecessary treatments.[33]

Under the Committee on Economic, Social and Cultural Rights (CESCR) General Comment 14, there are several obligations related to the right to health – the most connected to the provision of medical treatments are "to

30 See discussions on moral accounts of the right to health: Rumbold (n 1); Hassoun, 'The Human Right to Health' (n 1). To Sparer, a legal right to health entails "(1) a definable duty on the part of ascertainable medical care providers to give medical care" and (2) the persons who are the beneficiaries of the duty have a legal remedy which they can use to enforce performance of the duty or compensation" Edward V Sparer, 'The Legal Right to Health Care: Public Policy and Equal Access' (1976) 6 The Hastings Center Report 39, 39.
The right to health is a constitutionalised obligation in at least half of the countries in the world. See e.g.: Jody Heymann and others, 'Constitutional Rights to Health, Public Health and Medical Care: The Status of Health Protections in 191 Countries' (2013) 8 Global Public Health 639.

31 International Covenant on Economic, Social and Cultural Rights (ICESCR) (adopted 16 December 1966, entered into force 3 January 1976) 993 UNTS 3, art. 2.

32 John Tobin, *The Right to Health in International Law* (Oxford University Press 2011) 49–50.

33 Norman Daniels, 'Health-Care Needs and Distributive Justice' (1981) 10 Philosophy & Public Affairs 146, 158. Norman Daniels, 'Normal Functioning and the Treatment-Enhancement Distinction' (2000) 9 Cambridge Quarterly of Healthcare Ethics 309, 314–316. For body enhancement, see Søren Holm, 'Natural Talent, Fair Equality of Opportunity, and Therapeutic Use Exemptions' (2018) 18 The American Journal of Bioethics 18.

provide essential drugs" (defined by WHO's Action Programme on Essential Drugs) and "to ensure *equitable distribution* of all health facilities, goods and services".[34] The Covenant itself does not specify a set of health technologies that must be introduced. Rather, it lays out the obligation of "the creation of conditions which would assure to all medical service and medical attention in the event of sickness".[35] The ethos of the Covenant, as to access to healthcare services, has explicit reference to enabling the conditions for medical services, which falls neatly on the idea defended by this book of managing scarcity through an HRBA to HTA. The emphasis in this research will be on obligations to meet the specific needs of curative, preventive or diagnostic therapies and not on public health interventions such as exercise, rest, nutrition and other features of healthy lifestyles. This restriction also allows us to concentrate on the repercussions of the right in one specific policy area of healthcare, instead of trying to assess the effects in supplementary State health programmes (such as preventive measures and social determinants of health, for instance sanitation, access to water and even the right to a healthy environment).[36]

Moreover, the term "health" will be referred to not simply as the biomedical concept of healthcare, even though that may also include patient preferences and human values that will be appropriate to determining the quality and acceptability of interventions. As many scholars agree, however, the right to health does not amount to the right to be healthy, as no State could secure such an end.[37] Nevertheless, framing the right to health as an obligation to provide medical treatments may be criticised as far too conservative. However, in the right-to-health litigation scholarship, as in the empirical analysis undertaken in the present study, access to treatments is the most common theme.[38]

Indeed, it is true that health needs may be justified beyond the mere basic bodily functionalities, and decisions on the allocation of resources in an HRBA for medical treatments can involve other rights-related notions such as equity,

34 ICESCR, (n 31) Article 12; UN Committee on Economic, Social and Cultural Rights "General Comment No. 14. The Right to the Highest Attainable Standard of Health (GC 14)." 12 August 2000 (E/C.12/2000/4), para 43 (d) and (e).

35 ICESCR (n 31), Article 12 (2) d.

36 Manjari Mahajan, 'The Right to Health as the Right to Treatment: Shifting Conceptions of Public Health' (2012) 79 Social Research: An International Quarterly 819, 829–832.

37 GC No. 14 (n 34), para. 8. Jonas Juškevičius and Janina Balsienė, 'On Human Rights in Healthcare: Some Remarks on Limits of the Right to Healthcare' (2010) 122 Jurisprudencija: Mokslo darbu žurnalas 95, 103–105.

38 See chapter 8, 1 for a health litigation overview in Brazil.

social inclusion, dignity or preventing suffering.[39] Thus, though this book will not consider social determinants of health, such as the right for a healthy environment, other rights-related notions to determine the quality of healthcare in resource allocations may be relevant, including the effects of those technologies on well-being, equity, cultural values and other human rights.[40] This book, therefore, does not attempt to cover the full scope of human rights impact assessments that could be applied to any policy decision to identify rights that may be affected or realised in a given context. Instead, its contribution is more modest, focusing specifically on resource-related considerations and the role of human rights principles in economic decision-making within the HTA context.

3 Scarcity, HTA and the Right to Health

By referencing international human rights law, this book proposes a right to health interpretation with a different relationship to scarcity than traditional health economics or public health thinking. HTA methods of value-maximisation may not necessarily reflect the right to health principles, in particular on how to manage scarcity. However, since the 1970s, HTA reports have been devoted to responding to scarcity by measuring cost and quality of life for new health technologies in order to attain cost-effectiveness and scientific robustness in healthcare decisions.[41] Their overall purpose has been to soothe fears about unwise spending, confirming clinical adequacy and gaining control over growing patient demands upon health services.[42] The tension between health economics and rights is seen in priority-setting principles such as consequentialism (morality of conducts by their consequences), utilitarianism (capacity of identifying preferences between alternatives) and wel-

39 For a thorough discussion on health needs, see: Yvonne Denier, *Efficiency, Justice and Care: Philosophical Reflections on Scarcity in Health Care* (Springer Netherlands 2007) 72–75; Maite San Giorgi, *The Human Right to Equal Access to Health Care* (Intersentia 2012) 14–19.

40 The WHO defines health as "a state of complete physical, mental and social well-being and not merely the absence of disease or infirmity". Constitution of the World Health Organization. World Health Organization; 1948, Preamble.

41 Alex Faulkner, "Strange Bedfellows" in the Laboratory of the NHS? An Analysis of the New Science of Health Technology Assessment in the United Kingdom' (1997) 19 Sociology of Health & Illness 183, 189–190. A Stevens, R Milne and A Burls, 'Health Technology Assessment: History and Demand' (2003) 25 Journal of Public Health 98, 98–99.

42 Banta, (n 26) 121.

farism (judging policies by the overall level of utility created by a situation).[43] Such views may dismiss rights, for instance, because only the consequences are relevant to the decision-making and respecting individual rights would not be considered as important as maximising value to society (for a utilitarian, measured by utility indicators).[44]

This utilitarian or consequentialist mindset in HTA aligns with neoliberalism in global health governance, which is devoted to maximum returns on very targeted investments, rather than profound social changes.[45] The ideal of comprehensive health coverage and primary care in the early days of the Alma-Ata Declaration in 1978 gave way to vertical interventions concerned with value for money for donors with regard to a restricted set of diseases (in contrast to horizontal improvements across the health system).[46] Those policies of selected interventions, supported by HTA recommendations, will not always be guided by substantive human rights principles to maximise resources and push the limits of progressive realisation. Cost-effectiveness models work on the premise that scarcity is an inevitable condition. They may even exacerbate the gap between countries, simply because some technologies will be seen as inappropriate in certain parts of the world owing to their unaffordable prices.[47] Often, the prevailing ideas behind fairness in resource allocation can be dominated by attention to just the procedural aspects (how transparent and accountable decisions are in achieving cost-effectiveness) rather than substantive policies to avert scarcity.

---

43 Werner BF Brouwer and others, 'Welfarism vs. Extra-Welfarism' (2008) 27 Journal of Health Economics 325, 327.

44 Christopher P Taggart, 'Fairness Versus Welfare: The Limits of Kaplow and Shavell's Pareto Argument' (2016) 99 Marquette Law Review 662, 670–671; Lanse Minkler, 'Introduction: Why Economic and Social Human Rights?' in Lanse Minkler (ed), *The State of Economic and Social Human Rights: A Global Overview* (Cambridge University Press 2013) 11.

45 Matthew Sparke, 'Neoliberal Regime Change and the Remaking of Global Health: From Rollback Disinvestment to Rollout Reinvestment and Reterritorialization' (2020) 27 Review of International Political Economy 48, 61–67.

46 See: World Health Organization and United Nations Children's Fund, 'Report of the International Conference on Primary Health Care, Alma-Ata, USSR, 6–12 September 1978' (World Health Organization 1978). This document set out values of access to healthcare for all "at a cost that a community can afford" (VI) and emphasise mobilisation of resources domestically and through international cooperation (VIII), even by releasing resources through disarmament policies (X). On global health neoliberalism and verticalisation, post-Alma Ata, see e.g.: Sparke (n 45).

47 Arjun Suri and others, 'Values and Global Health' in Paul Farmer and others (eds), *Reimagining Global Health* (University of California Press 2013) 250.

By contrast, this book argues that human rights obligations place a higher burden on States than simply allocating resources and that States must adopt a constructive mechanism to find solutions for avoidable rationing while containing scarcity. There is an interface between the right to health (which requires expanding resources) and HTA (which rests on resource allocation). HTA as a central policy of resource allocation may pursue a rigid notion of resources and scarcity compared with how socio-economic rights confront the economic status quo. Whenever health rationing is called upon, a common presumption is that resources are limited or constant and expending on one side entails immediate losses for funding of other policies.[48] This research will not attempt to contradict such a view of every possible cause of scarcity entirely, though it must be said that on many occasions, this assumption is by no means indisputable. The inescapability of healthcare constraints is justified by arguments such as that emerging technologies are always escalating costs, ever-lengthening lifespan is pressuring health providers with older patients, and that efficiency in health management is far from saving the resources needed.[49] To rebuke such allegations, it could be argued that technology may spur gains in efficiency as well, that healthcare demand is not absolutely unlimited (people would not want more health treatment indefinitely) and that budgets have a potential to grow. Hence, a commonplace convention is that expenses will indefinitely increase, with the default expectation that resources would not become available via other means, such as by the healthy part of the population contributing more for the ailing minority.[50]

Contrary to the criticism levelled at the right to health as an aspiration without much practical use, this book demonstrates several ways in which this right to health in international law can promote change by managing the conditions of scarcity simultaneously in resource allocation (as with access policies). A difficulty in HTA occurs, therefore, in accepting scarcity universally and incontestably – with no mitigation or remediation through specific policies, including market interventions and price negotiation. A problem of scarcity, observed by behavioural economics, is that it induces a one-track mind that cannot perceive other important aspects of life beneficial to practical

48 Leonard M Fleck, *Just Caring: Health Care Rationing and Democratic Deliberation* (Oxford University Press 2009) 5, 7–8.

49 Greg Bognar and Iwao Hirose, *The Ethics of Health Care Rationing: An Introduction* (Routledge 2014) 14–18.

50 Jürgen Fritze, 'Is Healthcare Budgeting Ethically Justifiable?' (2001) 2 The European Journal of Health Economics 26, 26–27.

solutions or flexible decisions that would generate other resources.[51] Priority-setting also starts from the premise that the current budget is all that can be spent and cannot be expanded.[52] For instance, HTA focused only on resource distribution in developing countries may be insufficient to question those countries that are forced to pay higher prices than richer counterparts (and whether this trend can be challenged).[53] The approach constructed by socio-economic rights runs counter to this tunnel vision by urging flexible policies to identify resources and avoid scarcity as much as possible before non-implementation is justifiable.

Therefore, a social and economic rights position would be to "denaturalise" scarcity, as defended by Schrecker. He claims that "only after resource scarcities have been identified as the consequence of either specific policy choices or more general social arrangements, can appropriate ethical arguments be constructed".[54] The concept of scarcity is, first of all, a social construction, which deems that there will always be a further need of consumption (even if that cannot be quantified). In the modern western world, the idea of scarcity grew from shortage or insufficient supply in a single episode alongside the assumption that resources would inevitably be insufficient and humanity would therefore be perpetually plagued by the curse of limitless needs.[55] The law of scarcity, though, is a classic truism among economists.[56] In reality, scarcity is not always natural (also known as artificial scarcity) and may result from monopolies or market failures, regardless of production capacity or costs.[57] Market failures are a general characteristic of healthcare distribution and require State measures to subdue artificial scarcity.[58] To this effect, policymakers question what causes scarcity of a resource and whether "a decision

---

51 Sendhil Mullainathan and Eldar Shafir, *Scarcity: Why Having Too Little Means so Much* (Macmillan 2013) 20–56.

52 Ted Schrecker, 'Priority Setting: Right Answer to a Far Too Narrow Question? Comment on "Global Developments in Priority Setting in Health"' (2017) 7 International Journal of Health Policy and Management 86, 86–87.

53 Tomasz Zaprutko and others, 'Affordability of Medicines in the European Union' (2017) 12 PLOS ONE e0172753, 8–9.

54 Ted Schrecker, 'Denaturalizing Scarcity: A Strategy of Enquiry for Public-Health Ethics' (2008) 86 Bulletin of the World Health Organization 600, 601.

55 Nicholas Xenos, *Scarcity and Modernity* (Taylor & Francis 2017) 1–27.

56 Martin Bronfenbrenner, 'The Scarcity Hypothesis in Modern Economics' (1962) 21 The American Journal of Economics and Sociology 265.

57 Adel Daoud, 'Scarcity and Artificial Scarcity' in Daniel Thomas Cook and J Michael Ryan (eds), *The Wiley Blackwell Encyclopedia of Consumption and Consumer Studies* (John Wiley & Sons,2015).

58 Anthony Scott and David Kernick, 'Understanding Healthcare Delivery: The Economic Contribution', *Getting Health Economics into Practice* (CRC Press 2018) 11–23.

substantially within the control of that society was made as a result of which the resource was permitted to remain scarce".[59]

4 The Approach of This Book (and Preliminary Answers and Caveats to Scepticism about the Progress of Social Values in HTA beyond Human Rights)

The substantive principles discussed in this book are integral to the very nature of socio-economic rights as they relate to resource allocation. The analysis offers a mapping of how these principles, as developed in international law, might be meaningfully and appropriately applied within HTA practice. While this is not the first attempt to engage with social values in the context of priority-setting, the book aims to undertake a more thorough inquiry into what these particular human rights principles entail for HTA. It is therefore important to dispel the notion that existing discussions of ethical principles or substantive values elsewhere are equivalent to the rights-based framework advanced here.

First, HTA has made significant progress in fostering discussions around the role of social values and substantive principles. But they go in different directions and serve different purposes to international human rights law, because such values are not legally binding principles or necessarily correlated to human rights standards. Considerations about values have gained traction among health economists and policymakers, particularly in relation to a key part of the deliberations: which social values should be taken into account in making fair and legitimate decisions? Within this, such values are part of the engine and the contours of deliberation, both as "procedural values" or "content values" within a deliberation – they inform the process and types of arguments that are considered relevant, but they do not force States to take certain substantive actions; they are parameters for the decision-making and reasons giving in a process agreed upon.[60]

This approach would appear in questions such as "should additional value be assigned in certain circumstances, as with end-of-life treatments?" or "should technologies for patients with no alternative care options be considered more important?". In this view, values may be "elicited" or "agreed

59 Guido Calabresi and Phillip Bobbitt, *Tragic Choices* (Norton 1978) 22.
60 Peter Littlejohns and others, 'Creating Sustainable Health Care Systems: Agreeing Social (Societal) Priorities through Public Participation' (2019) 33 Journal of Health Organization and Management 18.

to" – but not necessarily binding or derived by a State obligation under international law to take substantive steps towards rights implementation.[61] For instance, some research would consider social values elicited through deliberative processes and methods on a case-by-case basis, as explored by Littlejohns et al., or empirically reviewing how certain values emerge across HTA decision-making over time.[62] HTA bodies may have their own declarations or guidance materials setting social values or ethical norms that guide their decisions, which can be produced independently of any human right standards, but on the basis of ethical views, internal decisions or public consultations.[63]

This book, however, focuses on pre-determined legal principles grounded in an economic and social rights-based model of resource allocation in international law – one that would be implemented if international State obligations are observed in the governance of priority-setting. This is particularly relevant for international organisations bound by this framework in their constitution, such as the WHO and States that are party to such international obligations or pursuing them in health policy-making.

There are also practical and conceptual differences as to what values can do in HTA processes from a normative or ethical model, as opposed to a rights-based policy. Within ethical approaches, values are often treated as aspirational ends that society should strive toward.[64] In contrast, this work draws on the right to health to develop principles that emerge directly from State obligations under international human rights law. These human rights principles set out overarching directions for concrete action, outlining general approaches necessary for the fulfilment of State obligations – such as the requirement for States to maximise available resources. They are further translated into specific steps that guide concrete conduct and policy implementation that reduces scarcity levels, for example, negotiating medicine prices with suppliers. Such measures are designed not only to reshape the criteria used for decision-making but also to coordinate the underlying material conditions, ensuring that sufficient resources are actually made available,

61 Yvonne Bombard and others, 'Eliciting Ethical and Social Values in Health Technology Assessment: A Participatory Approach' (2011) 73 Social Science & Medicine 135.

62 Littlejohns and others (n 60); Victoria Charlton, 'NICE and Fair? Health Technology Assessment Policy Under the UK's National Institute for Health and Care Excellence, 1999–2018' (2020) 28 Health Care Analysis 193.

63 Rachel Milstein Breslau and others, 'A Review of HTA Guidelines on Societal and Novel Value Elements' (2023) 39 International Journal of Technology Assessment in Health Care e31.

64 Victoria Charlton and others, 'We Need to Talk about Values: A Proposed Framework for the Articulation of Normative Reasoning in Health Technology Assessment' [2023] Health Economics, Policy and Law 1.

where possible. For the mainstream ethics networks, however, substantive principles are primarily concerned with the social values or normative commitments that ought to be considered in decision-making – that is, the ethical justification for *what* is decided and *why*.[65]

The introduction of evidence-informed deliberative processes (EIDPs) in global health marks a significant step forward in linking procedural fairness with defining the adopted normative considerations (reflecting social values) in priority-setting. EIDP is an approach to decision-making designed to emphasise the role of substantive values in making choices about health policies and resource allocation – yet, the prevailing discourse continues to treat these frameworks predominantly as procedural tools, with values only being used to set the criteria or determine the procedural form.[66] Those substantive principles are not fundamentally the same as substantive principles to resource allocation under the right to health. Thus, ethical values in the EIDP language are not following the same sequence of translating values to specific conducts and standards expected by States within HTA. When such values are acknowledged in EIDPs' frameworks, they are typically expressed in general terms – such as equity, fairness or solidarity – without clear grounding in the specific human rights obligations set out under local or international law.[67] In some cases, the integration of human rights into EIDP frameworks is met with scepticism, particularly due to concerns about the perceived threat of litigation to the integrity of deliberative processes.[68] Even critiques of the overreliance on cost-effectiveness, such as those by Baltussen et al., sidestep questions of integrating into HTA any mode of rights-based resource mobilisation altogether.[69]

Unlike the human rights principles engaged in this book, social values discussed in HTA ethical/social analysis serve to guide how the existing "pie" of resources is divided in a current scenario – determining the ethical angles (criteria) from which decisions are approached. But they do not speak to the bigger picture: the size of the pie itself, nor the forces – such as market dynam-

65 Ibid., 160.

66 Rob Baltussen, Maarten Jansen and Wija Oortwijn, 'Evidence-Informed Deliberative Processes for Legitimate Health Benefit Package Design – Part I: Conceptual Framework' [2021] International Journal of Health Policy and Management 1, 2320.

67 Wija Oortwijn, Maarten Jansen and Rob Baltussen, 'Evidence-Informed Deliberative Processes for Health Benefit Package Design – Part II: A Practical Guide' [2021] International Journal of Health Policy and Management 1, 2332.

68 Chalkidou and others (n 18) 234.

69 Rob Baltussen and others, 'Priority Setting for Universal Health Coverage: We Need Evidence-Informed Deliberative Processes, Not Just More Evidence on Cost-Effectiveness' (2016) 5 International Journal of Health Policy and Management 615.

ics, political power or structural injustice – that determine who wields the "knife of prices and affordability" and what kind of patients hold a better plate to be served for having better evidence of value.

5 An HTA Overreach? Why We Should Embrace Rights-Based Substantive Policies

Now that the concept of substantive principles in this work, under right-to-health obligations, has been set apart from substantive principles applied mainly to the criteria, there is another question that ethicists and HTA experts may immediately ask: are those human rights substantive principles really a matter of HTA (or resource allocation)? Some would react saying that actually HTA operates in a narrow space to provide advice and recommendation on decisions about health technology coverage. It would not be its competence to engage with market interventions and policies that regulate prices or determine procurement strategies. However, more often than not, measures that are called "access policies" are increasingly in the scope of HTA – and may be triggered or facilitated by HTA decisions or recommendations. This book will try to illustrate with examples of how these principles would operate in practice, with an empirical review of HTA decisions in Brazil.

This practice aligns with the broader "whole-of-government" and "whole-of-society" approaches, which call for coordinated action and collaboration across departments and agencies to address major health challenges.[70] Even in public health emergencies, these approaches have been increasingly called upon as the only viable path forward.[71] Therefore, there is growing recognition that public health objectives can only be achieved through concerted efforts across key government sectors and through harmonised policies working towards shared goals. Equally, HTA has been increasingly associated with access-to-medicines policies – and a range of authors and stakeholders have defended that such measures be coupled with or better integrated into deliberations, such as price negotiation, price controls or early access schemes during evidence uncertainty.[72]

70 Flaminia Ortenzi and others, 'Whole of Government and Whole of Society Approaches: Call for Further Research to Improve Population Health and Health Equity' (2022) 7 BMJ Global Health e009972.

71 World Health Organization, 'WHO Director-General's Opening Remarks at the Mission Briefing on COVID-19–9 April 2020' [2020] Geneva, Switzerland: WHO 1502.

72 Verena Stühlinger, 'Health Technology Assessment (HTA) and Access Policies' (2020) 27 European Journal of Health Law 274; Anna-Maria Fontrier, Bregtje Kamphuis and Panos

An understanding of human rights that would separate HTA from other areas of government, which may be associated with the State powers to regulate and mobilise resources, would not be justifiable. From a human-rights obligations perspective, States remain accountable to their implementation, independently of its form or organisation. Internal competences and structures are irrelevant to the implementation of adequate policies because such obligations are binding on the State as a whole in all administrative and policy-making levels.[73]

Additionally, HTA can help uncover the true causes of scarcity and unaffordability, exposing the political choices that shape access. It can highlight when a technology is valued for its intrinsic merits rather than market conditions, and ensure that such technologies are actively pursued through deliberate policy action. There can be no fair procedure in a world of unfair prices, and no procedure will be truly fair so long as hyper-liberal assumptions about how markets ought to function remain unchallenged.

Therefore, during HTA processes, the conditions of scarcity can be exposed and distinguished from unavoidable ones. Australia's path to making new migraine medicines affordable shows how government can step in to keep costs under control while conducting HTA. Three drugs – erenumab (Aimovig), galcanezumab (Emgality) and fremanezumab (Ajovy) – all faced hurdles to receive approval decisions. At first, the Pharmaceutical Benefits Advisory Committee (PBAC, the expert body advising on subsidies) rejected erenumab twice because the company's asking price was not considered cost-effective.[74] Galcanezumab and fremanezumab were only recommended once the companies agreed to bring their prices down to match Botox, an older migraine treatment, and to accept special risk-sharing deals with government.[75] Once

Kanavos, 'How Can Health Technology Assessment Be Improved to Optimise Access to Medicines? Results from a Delphi Study in Europe: Better Access to Medicines through HTA' (2024) 25 The European Journal of Health Economics 935; Amanda Whittal and others, 'Facilitating More Efficient Negotiations for Innovative Therapies: A Value-Based Negotiation Framework' (2022) 38 International Journal of Technology Assessment in Health Care e23; Paul Arora and others, 'The Inflation Reduction Act: An Opportunity to Accelerate Confidence in Real-World Evidence in the United States' (2024) 27 Value in Health 999.

73 See Article 28, ICESCR (note 31): "The provisions of the present Covenant shall extend to all parts of federal States without any limitations or exceptions".

74 Pharmaceutical Benefits Advisory Committee, *Public Summary Document: Erenumab (Aimovig®)* (July 2018) https://www.pbs.gov.au/info/industry/listing/elements/pbac-meetings/psd accessed 16 September 2025.

75 Pharmaceutical Benefits Advisory Committee, *Public Summary Document: Galcanezumab (Emgality®)* (July 2019) https://www.pbs.gov.au/info/industry/listing/elements/

listed on the PBS in 2021, these drugs became affordable for patients. In each case, the government's intervention was decisive: it rejected initial high prices, forced price cuts through "cost-minimisation" rules, required rebate agreements (all confidential) and placed eligibility limits so that the new medicines could be used fairly without overwhelming the budget.

6 This Book's Contributions to HTA Practice and Human Rights Advocacy

In short, in engaging with human rights substantive principles, this book develops multiple contributions to the literature on the right to health, HTA and socio-economic rights at large in resource allocation. The HRBA recommendation gives practical guidance on the right to health in resource allocation, premised on socio-economic rights principles which should inform access policies and criteria in HTA decisions through the use of functional and realistic measures from price negotiation to reformulation of economic methods. It is an alternative framework built on how resource distribution and resource mobilisation are intermeshed within HTA by virtue of the substantive obligations stemming from the right to health. No other research has provided a comprehensive analysis of each of the main principles of resource allocation in HTA as an international law obligation under the ICESCR, including international cooperation, as opposed to UHC in global health governance. The case study confirms that the proposed framework can be satisfactorily employed as a State policy and indicates that traditional procedural fairness is not the only perspective that should be taken into account to manage scarcity.

This study is developed in three stages. Part 1 presents a brief introduction to the theory of resource allocation and the right to health in human rights scholarship and explores the current legal literature in HTA. It provides a framework that functions as the basis for the later sections' examination of what law and the right to health should constitute in HTA. Chapter 2 analyses the meaning of HRBA to resource allocation as a policy framework and explains why the dominant approach (procedural fairness) is insufficient when applied to the right to health in HTA. A second analytical framework

---

pbac-meetings/psd accessed 16 September 2025; Pharmaceutical Benefits Advisory Committee, *Public Summary Document: Fremanezumab (Ajovy®)* (March 2020) https://www.pbs.gov.au/info/industry/listing/elements/pbac-meetings/psd accessed 16 September 2025.

is outlined in Chapter 3, describing the role of law in HTA, both procedurally and substantively, and its possible implications for the right to health.

Part 2 will consider the right to health under international law to question whether it can establish a harmonised set of rules that will steer fair decisions not only related to resource distribution but also resource creation, and regulate standards in the criteria of HTA. Each chapter in Part 2 explores the socio-economic rights principles as pertinent to HTA procedures and substantive policies. Individually, each chapter is also an addition to the literature in its own right. Chapter 4 explains the logic of implementation of socio-economic rights in relation to scarcity and the general principles that differentiate it from traditional procedural approaches: progressive realisation, maximum available resources and the reasonableness standard. The application of human rights principles will be further extended to the criteria of HTA in Chapter 5, in particular with regard to the non-discrimination principle. Chapter 6 considers the application of the role of international cooperation in HTA and its implications for progressive realisation of the right to health. Lastly, Chapter 7 presents a distinct approach to the application of socio-economic rights principles which could be used to simultaneously contain scarcity and enable access policies through the regulation of HTA and the market by means of legislation.

Part 3 is an in-depth case study of the substantive policies and legal issues of HTA deliberations grounded in a socio-economic rights framework in international law. Chapter 8 presents an illustrative analysis that will confirm some points related to the general HRBA framework in international law and what standards it can provide in a local jurisdiction. At heart, the case study helps to illustrate how resource creation and allocation may be interconnected in practice.

In the case study, the unit of analysis will be a public HTA body in charge of appraising new technologies in Brazil (Conitec). A methodological reason for turning to HTA to study priority-setting and human rights is the more explicit public deliberation involved, compared to other situations such as rationing by doctors at the bedside or in private institutions. HTA began precisely because reports were required to provide information to policymakers so they could weigh alternatives in health investment.[76] Thus, it offers documentary evidence of resource allocation decision-making and provides information on how human rights discourse and language are employed in public consultations.

76 Banta (n 26).

The chosen jurisdiction is relevant for numerous reasons, namely because it is a country with a constitutional right to health. HTA is regulated through law and institutionalised through a public agency; data and reports are issued through this process and are publicly available; and, finally, there is a large literature on the right to health in Brazil, also connected with HTA.

In the present study, a case study is an appropriate method and will complement the doctrinal analysis in these circumstances by addressing a "how" question ("How are the law and policies described?") and for the following methodological conditions:

a) research must be conducted in a non-controllable environment;
b) the unit of analysis is available for inspection only in a real-life situation; and
c) there are no other accessible sources that could substitute the method.[77]

Also, as previously mentioned, HTA offers a unique public place for observing discussions on health priorities, while other policies and healthcare rationing occur discreetly or without publicity and documentation.

The type of case study developed is classified as normative, forming the basis of an evaluation of what the law should be (or whether it ever should act upon this matter).[78] Normative cases, as Thacher suggests, have been proposed to canvass ethical principles or study values or the good. In this book, the approach is similar but aims at detecting what should be expected from the law to make the right to health valuable in the HTA context.[79]

Of course, a case study may have its validity challenged as to the criteria for case selection. There might be risks of bias when participants know the research is targeted on them and matters of generalisation (non-reproducibility or limited capacity to make inferences beyond the study itself).[80] Though these concerns are real, I counter those arguments by turning to the positive benefits of the case study. What I suggest is not to make universal claims with a single case, but to offer well-founded insights on how rights are framed in a priority-setting process so we can confirm the potential application of the

---

77 Robert K Yin, *Case Study Research and Applications: Design and Methods* (6th ed., SAGE Publications 2019) 43–47.

78 NK Denzin and YS Lincoln, *The SAGE Handbook of Qualitative Research* (SAGE Publications 2011) 351.

79 David Thacher, 'The Normative Case Study' (2006) 111 American Journal of Sociology 1631, 1665–1667.

80 On empirical legal study limitations, see Aikaterini Argyrou, 'Making the Case for Case Studies in Empirical Legal Research' (2017) 13 Utrecht Law Review 19.

studied human rights standards in other jurisdictions. The proposed model is a solid and replicable transformative framework in response to scarcity, influencing healthcare systems substantively during resource allocation, as opposed to ensuring a mere accountable process that validates pre-existing scarcity conditions.

CHAPTER 2

HRBA and Procedural Approaches to Healthcare Resource Allocation

This chapter seeks to demonstrate that an HRBA to HTA should not be limited to procedural fairness. In pointing out the problems with the predominance of procedural fairness in an HRBA to healthcare priority-setting, this chapter provides the background theory contested in the remaining part of this study to differentiate the procedural model subscribed to by many human rights and public health scholars in resource allocation from the one proposed in this book.[1]

The argument behind this analysis is that procedural approaches are not sufficient to guarantee fair priority-setting in an HRBA. Implementation of State obligations under a socio-economic rights framework requires resource maximisation and progressive realisation, which is a guarantee that best efforts are being made for access to healthcare and not exclusively concentrated on resource distribution. The procedural stance does not directly question the substantive principles in resource allocation. Indeed, obligations regarding the right to health are simply the result of a deliberative process. More significantly, it is not the cause of scarcity that should be addressed but,

---

1 See, e.g.: Audrey Chapman, 'The Foundations of a Human Right to Health: Human Rights and Bioethics in Dialogue.' (2015) 17 Health and Human Rights 16; Norman Daniels and others, 'Role of the Courts in the Progressive Realization of the Right to Health: Between the Threat and the Promise of Judicialization in Mexico' (2015) 1 Health Systems & Reform 229, 229; Sofia Gruskin and Norman Daniels, 'Process Is the Point: Justice and Human Rights: Priority Setting and Fair Deliberative Process' (2008) 98 American Journal of Public Health 1573, 1573–1574; Alicia Ely Yamin and Ole Norheim, 'Taking Equality Seriously: Applying Human Rights Frameworks to Priority Setting in Health' (2014) 36 Human Rights Quarterly 296, 324; Ricardo Perlingeiro, 'Procedural and Substantive Judicial Review of the Right to Health in Brazil' [2014] SSRN Electronic Journal <http://www.ssrn.com/abstract=2481539> accessed 5 April 2018; Siri Gloppen, 'Right to Health in Contexts of Resource Scarcity: Towards Judicial Enforcement of the Right to a Fair Share' [2015] SSRN Electronic Journal <http://www.ssrn.com/abstract=2622779> accessed 28 October 2018; Rui Nunes, Sofia B Nunes and Guilhermina Rego, 'Health Care as a Universal Right' (2017) 25 Journal of Public Health 1, 3; Kristen Hessler and Allen Buchanan, 'Specifying the Content of the Human Right to Health Care' in Rosamond Rhodes, Margaret Battin and Anita Silvers (eds), *Medicine and Social Justice: essays on the distribution of health care* (Oxford University Press 2002) 91–95; Daniel Wang, 'Right to Health Litigation in Brazil: The Problem and the Institutional Responses' (2015) 15 Human Rights Law Review 617, 641.

rather, how to share resources and manage constant deprivation without changing the status quo.

Moreover, as with any method of HRBA, the proceduralisation of the right to health in resource allocation and HTA ought to be critically examined.[2] Increasingly, scholars have developed a research agenda to confirm the effects of HRBA on policies rather than simply identifying potential human rights violations in healthcare provision that need to be redressed by HRBA.[3] This chapter will do so, from a theoretical standpoint, inquiring whether the dominant procedural approach to resource allocation is a satisfactory conceptualisation of an HRBA.

To begin, in contrast to proceduralisation, typically an HRBA, as a form of public policy method, engages with both substance and procedure.[4] Procedural aspects are regarded as the application of certain human rights principles or safeguards for how policies or decisions are delivered (e.g. transparency, accountability, non-discrimination), in contrast to substantive obligations, which are focused on actual realisation of outcomes described by rights.[5] Such a model is followed by the widely accepted UN reference guide known as "UN Common Understanding" (e.g. "monitor and evaluate both outcomes and processes guided by human rights standards and principles").[6]

In an HRBA to health, policies should embed rights both into their substance and procedure – they could "pay equal attention to process (how people's rights are respected within the health system) as well as outcomes

---

2 Sofia Gruskin, 'Rights-Based Approaches to Health: Something for Everyone' (2006) 9 Health and Human Rights 5, 6.

3 Paul Hunt, Alicia Ely Yamin and Flavia Bustreo, 'Making the Case: What Is the Evidence of Impact of Applying Human Rights-Based Approaches to Health?' (2015) 17 Health and Human Rights 1, 3–5; Wouter Vandenhole and Paul Gready, 'Failures and Successes of Human Rights-Based Approaches to Development: Towards a Change Perspective' (2014) 32 Nordic Journal of Human Rights 291, 294–298, 309–311.

4 John Tasioulas, 'Capabilities, Development and Human Rights: A Conversation with Amartya Sen' (*ABC Religion & Ethics*) <https://www.abc.net.au/religion/conversation-with-amartya-sen/10599038> accessed 16 April 2021; Amartya Sen, 'Why Health Equity?' (2002) 11 Health Economics 659, 659–662.

5 This division is drawn from HRBA studies and the report, UN Common Understanding, but the usages may vary according to the policy at hand. See, e.g.: Hannah Miller and Robin Redhead, 'Beyond "Rights-Based Approaches"? Employing a Process and Outcomes Framework' (2019) 23 The International Journal of Human Rights 699, 703–708; United Nations, 'The Human Rights-Based Approach to Development Cooperation towards a Common Understanding among the UN Agencies (UN Common Understanding)' (Workshop on a human rights-based approach in the context of UN reform, 3–5 May 2003) <http://www.undp.org/governance/docs/HR_Guides_CommonUnderstanding.pdf> accessed 1 May 2020.

6 United Nations (n 5).

(the goal of improving health)".[7] Accordingly, in his development of a theory of justice, Sen has argued that "we cannot have an adequate concept of equity if it does not pay sufficient attention to processes in addition to the outcomes".[8] At the WHO level, an HRBA incorporates process and outcomes, "guided by human rights standards and principles and aimed at developing the capacity of duty-bearers to meet their obligations and empowering rights-holders to effectively claim their health rights".[9]

Despite this, even though it can be said that process and substance are entwined in an HRBA, when it comes to healthcare, rights may be narrowly interpreted as a procedure. Murphy has questioned whether the phenomenon of proceduralisation in health, conceived within the field of bioethics to escape dilemmas in health rationing, would spread to human rights.[10] At least in resource allocation, as this chapter shows, proceduralisation has been dominant. Such a trend is not unique to the right to health, as procedural approaches have now gained more popularity in international human rights law, particularly in the context of the European Convention on Human Rights.[11] This jurisprudential movement in the Strasbourg Court is marked by a judicial review which does not engage with the substantive elements of a policy decision accused of being a violation, allowing a large margin of appreciation to the State as long as due process or public deliberation was observed. This approach is made without regard for the actual merit of the State measure (e.g. considering the legislative process instead of the content of the law).

Further, given that the HRBA literature has not been tailored specifically to HTA, an HRBA to resource allocation will be considered to the extent applicable to HTA. HRBA to public health policies, however, are complex not only in resource allocation, but also other fields, and there are variations as to the understanding of human rights principles, the implementation of norms and political influence of stakeholders. To this end, Section 1 provides the meaning of HRBA in general and its problematic application in resource allocation, compared to an exclusively procedural approach. Then, Section 2 considers

7 Lawrence Gostin, 'Health and Human Rights Working Paper Series 2 – The Domains of Health Responsiveness – A Human Rights Analysis' (World Health Organization 2003).

8 Tasioulas, 'Capabilities, Development and Human Rights: A Conversation with Amartya Sen' (n 4).

9 WHO, A Human Rights-Based Approach to Health, http://www.who.int/hhr/news/hrba_to_health2.pdf, accessed in 29 June 2018.

10 Therese Murphy, *Health and Human Rights* (Bloomsbury Publishing 2014) 37.

11 Eva Brems and Laurens Lavrysen, 'Procedural Justice in Human Rights Adjudication: The European Court of Human Rights' (2013) 35 Human Rights Quarterly 176.

the limitations of the proceduralisation movement among health and human rights scholars and its underlying theory of "accountability for reasonableness" (A4R). Section 3 outlines the criticism in relation to such a theory of justice in health and how it is difficult to implement procedural fairness in HTA. Remarkably, as I will show, the right to health has been equipped with guidance on how to create procedural approaches, yet it offers elements of substantive policies to complement procedural fairness.

1 Human Rights-Based Approaches

This section analyses the difficult conceptualisation of an HRBA to public policies, compared to addressing rights as a form of procedural fairness in resource allocation. First of all, it must be reminded that procedural fairness, as a theory of justice in health, is not the same as having procedural elements within an HRBA to resource allocation in healthcare. A procedure in an HRBA, as argued in this book, is governed by substantive principles, such as non-discrimination and priority for the worse-off, and is designed alongside substantive policies to increase resources and reduce scarcity. In this sense, the criteria have to follow preset human rights standards and values in an accountable process. In procedural justice, there is no linkage to a distributive principle and the process serves only to legitimise decisions that have to choose multiple irreconcilable values (without considering the unfairness of scarcity itself).[12] Both HRBA and procedural justice should have procedural safeguards to minimise risks of a deliberation being unfair, through an accountable process. However, only in an HRBA are there extraprocedural values which are reflected not only in the criteria, but in substantive policies beyond priority-setting (e.g. market regulation).

However, a problem in identifying an HRBA to resource allocation is how to establish exactly which principles will govern the substantive criteria and healthcare policies. Principles and outcomes may vary among HRBA in health, yet the procedural elements seem more constant. For instance, the human rights principles set out in the UN Common Understanding are universality and inalienability, indivisibility, inter-dependence and inter-relatedness, equality and non-discrimination, participation and inclusion, accountability and rule of law.[13] Drawing on different documents from NGOs, governments and

12 William R Smith, 'Legitimacy in Bioethics: Challenging the Orthodoxy' (2018) 44 Journal of Medical Ethics 416, 416.

13 Ibid.

international organisations, Gruskin et al. observe different articulations of HRBA, some of which do not provide details on how to transform this discourse into practice or only include rights very broadly. Their proposal is also not minimalistic and "requires the adoption of an approach explicitly shaped by human rights principles", based on the pertinent legal frameworks that acknowledge principles of non-discrimination, participation, transparency and accountability, with health policies measured by availability, accessibility, acceptability, and quality of services.[14]

Alongside poor delineation of principles, the best way to implement an HRBA is also unclear. A very common interpretation of HRBA is the assumption (but not always with proven evidence, as suggested by Gruskin) that joining public health and rights produces synergy between health professionals and the legal framework for health promotion.[15] Some NGOs and civil society may depart from a pure HRBA to a more "framed" or "referenced" relationship with human rights, depending on how central human rights language and concepts are to their advocacy.[16]

Yet, HRBAs in health have been extensively employed and advocated, from sexual minorities to family planning.[17] Their usage has been championed by several public health specialists as a powerful platform to engender transformation in health systems globally, generally grounded in human rights broadly speaking, but with variations not always explicitly centred on the international right to health.[18] In a seminal article of this normative alliance, "Health and Human Rights", Mann et al. proposed a linkage with human rights and public health that inaugurated a whole scholarship on framing health policies under rights that continued in the journal of the same name.[19] Mann et al. argued that human rights and public health ethics are comple-

14 Sofia Gruskin, Dina Bogecho and Laura Ferguson, '"Rights-Based Approaches" to Health Policies and Programs: Articulations, Ambiguities, and Assessment' (2010) 31 Journal of Public Health Policy 129, 129, 138–140.

15 Gruskin (n 22) 6.

16 Hannah Miller, 'Human Rights and Development: The Advancement of New Campaign Strategies' (2019) 23 The International Journal of Human Rights 719, 723–729.

17 See, e.g.: Dina Bogecho and Melissa Upreti, 'The Global Gag Rule: an Antithesis to the Rights-Based Approach to Health' (2006) 9 Health and Human Rights 17; Julie Fish and Susan Bewley, 'Using Human Rights-based Approaches to Conceptualise Lesbian and Bisexual Women's Health Inequalities' (2010) 18 Health & social care in the community 355.

18 See: Paul Hunt, 'Interpreting the International Right to Health in a Human Rights-Based Approach to Health' (2016) 18 Health and Human Rights 109.

19 Jonathan M Mann and others, 'Health and Human Rights' (1994) 1 Health and Human Rights 6.

mentary, as they work towards well-being and in direct correlation: violating human rights impacts negatively on public health; conversely, respecting human rights bolsters public health.[20]

In this sense, HRBA is not static and a set of rules, but rather a political and dynamic instrument to steer public mobilisation towards health promotion and social justice.[21] HRBA is viewed as a catalyst of advocacy, in legal mobilisation and social accountability to empower individuals in their relations with the government.[22] Yamin and Cantor, considering the UN Human Rights Council technical guidance on maternal mortality, have associated HRBA to "circles of accountability", to subvert "structures and practices that systematically condemn certain people".[23] Through an HRBA, stakeholders "convert passive targets of services into active claims holders, which means that there cannot be a static package of services for Universal Health Coverage (UHC) defined by technocrats behind closed doors".[24]

Because of persistent variations in their interpretation, political forms and links with health practice, tying human rights to public health policies is problematic in creating an ambiguous or even contradictory discourse. Gostin notes that human rights for public health professionals may seem indeterminate between moral and legal claims and even the State's obligations from the right to health may distinguish between these two areas.[25] Rights can be summoned in public ethics with very different moral content, with libertarians only agreeing with negative rights, egalitarians seeking a minimum level of healthcare, and others expecting the health services that enable sufficient

20 Ibid., 12–13.

21 Leslie London, 'What Is a Human-Rights Based Approach to Health and Does It Matter?' (2008) 10 Health and Human Rights 65, 70.

22 On social accountability and legal empowerment, see: Vivek Maru, 'Allies Unknown: Social Accountability and Legal Empowerment' in Stephen Golub and Thomas McInerney (eds), *Legal Empowerment: Practitioners' Perspectives* (International Development Law Organization 2010).

23 UN Human Rights Council, "Technical Guidance on the Application of a Human Rights-Based Approach to the Implementation of Policies and Programmes to Reduce Preventable Maternal Morbidity and Mortality", 12 July 2012 (A/HRC/21/22 2012), paras 1–19, Alicia Ely Yamin and Rebecca Cantor, 'Between Insurrectional Discourse and Operational Guidance: Challenges and Dilemmas in Implementing Human Rights-Based Approaches to Health' (2014) 6 Journal of Human Rights Practice 451, 454.

24 Alicia Ely Yamin and Ariel Frisancho, 'Human-Rights-Based Approaches to Health in Latin America' (2015) 385 The Lancet e26, e28.

25 Lawrence O Gostin, 'Public Health, Ethics, and Human Rights: a Tribute to the Late Jonathan Mann' (2001) 29 The Journal of Law, Medicine & Ethics 121, 128.

opportunities to exercise normal life functions.[26] In addition, human rights advocacy, as London suggests, may be used too individualistically and could paradoxically damage principles of equity in health distribution.[27] While public health has increasingly recognised equity needs, this does not mean that practitioners can promptly find in human rights a straightforward obligation to promote equity. As London argues, instead of "assuming that human rights and public health are inevitably consonant, careful analysis should be able to demonstrate why that is the case, and, moreover, what are the specific mechanisms by which human rights can serve to promote equity".[28]

These multiple forms of HRBA may have conflicts with other normative perspectives in public health, which has its own utilitarian and consequentialist roots that are not in harmony with individual rights.[29] In this context, an HRBA associates itself with unsuccessful attempts to find a moral justification to improve justice in health through individual rights, but this has not been enough to sketch out adequate priority-setting solutions, let alone address the inequality dilemmas in health care distribution caused by the social determinants of health, for differences such as income and education.[30] Public health ethics has been recently challenged by the arrival of human rights discourse to bring a new normative framework to health policies, which is less utilitarian and more respectful of equity and individual differences.[31] Authors such as Rothstein, however, reject this HRBA undertaking by arguing that it sets out an impossible task that cannot be subsumed under public health.[32]

In summary, an HRBA in healthcare lends itself to distinct interpretations and usages, which may vary among users. A common view is that it involves substantive and procedural aspects of policies, and must be used to empower citizens and promote rights realisation. Yet, in resource allocation, it appears

---

26 Marc J Roberts and Michael R Reich, 'Ethical Analysis in Public Health' (2002) 359 The Lancet 1055, 1056–1057.

27 Leslie London, *Can Human Rights Serve as a Tool for Equity?* (Regional Network for Equity in Health in Southern Africa (EQUINET) and the University of Cape Town School of Public Health and Family Medicine 2003) 2–3 <http://www.equinetafrica.org/bibl/docs/POL14rights.pdf> accessed 28 June 2021.

28 Ibid., 2.

29 Miguel Ángel Royo-Bordonada and Begoña Román-Maestre, 'Towards Public Health Ethics' (2015) 36 Public Health Reviews 3; Minkler (chapter 1, n 44) 11.

30 Brock (chapter 1, n 28).

31 Kristen Hessler, 'Exploring the Philosophical Foundations of the Human Rights Approach to International Public Health Ethics' in Michael Boylan (ed), *International Public Health Policy and Ethics* (Springer 2008) 32–33.

32 Mark A Rothstein, 'Rethinking the Meaning of Public Health' (2002) 30 The Journal of Law, Medicine & Ethics 144.

that scholarship has moved mainly towards procedural fairness, which is not governed by substantive human rights principles and is flexible to the varying values elected in a deliberation.

Ultimately, proceduralisation in an HRBA to resource allocation in healthcare is unique among socio-economic rights, for having a clear model that is much more precise than that of a fair procedure in international human rights law. A fair procedure generally encompasses broad concepts such as accountability, public participation, and transparency in governance.[33] As a doctrinal and practice convention, a fair procedure is a central plank of human rights implementation and even though it has been more explicitly applied to civil and political rights, international human rights bodies and scholarship recognise the importance of this principle for socio-economic rights.[34] In this context, the UN Convention on the Rights of Persons with Disabilities (CRPD) is the key document among human rights treaties that explicitly embraces the principle of participation in public policy decisions (even applying it during its drafting process).[35]

What has happened with regard to the right to health in resource allocation is much more particular because it equates the right to health with a thorough theory of procedural justice drawn from bioethics, establishing specific conditions deemed sufficient to achieve an HRBA. The next section analyses why procedural justice seems so attractive to human rights scholars in health priority-setting and why it became equivalent to an HRBA for some authors. It introduces the main theory of justice in health underpinning this approach: accountability for reasonableness (hereafter A4R), a theory for health justice based on procedural standards that if followed, would render rationing decisions legitimate.[36]

33 United Nations (n 5).; CESCR, GC 14 (chapter 1, n 34) paras. 11, 17, 34, 54; UNGA "Human Rights to Safe Drinking Water and Sanitation" 16 July 2018 (A/73/162), paras 1–10; HRC, Draft guidelines for States on the effective implementation of the right to participate in public affairs, 20 July 2018 (A/HRC/39/28).

34 Id. See also: Alicia Ely Yamin and Fiona Lander, 'Implementing a Circle of Accountability: a Proposed Framework for Judiciaries and Other Actors in Enforcing Health-Related Rights' (2015) 14 Journal of Human Rights 312.

35 Sarah Arduin, 'Article 3: General Principles' in Ilias Bantekas, Michael Ashley Stein and Dimitris Anastasiou (eds), *The Convention on the Rights of Persons with Disabilities: a Commentary* (Oxford University Press 2018) 2.

36 Norman Daniels and James E. Sabin have worked on A4R over more than two decades and first presented it in 1997, with their ideas culminating in a book, which has since been the main reference on the framework. See Norman Daniels and James E Sabin, 'Limits to Health Care: Fair Procedures, Democratic Deliberation, and the Legitimacy Problem for Insurers' (1997) 26 Philosophy & Public Affairs 303; Norman Daniels and

1.1 Accountability for Reasonableness and Fair Procedure

In priority-setting, procedural justice has become quasi-synonymous with HRBA, especially with the prevailing opinion that courts should only look at whether fair procedures were in place in distributive decisions.[37] In principle, a priority-setting procedure is not in itself inconsistent with human rights, unless this process is the dominant feature of an HRBA.[38] As explained before, the problem is when the emphasis on procedural fairness strips this process of substantive human rights values and measures.

As developed by Daniels, the A4R approach has led to the popularisation of procedural approaches and become the staple element of the theoretical background to priority-setting in many government programmes and in global health policy.[39] It has now been recognised as a source of legitimacy beyond health priority-setting, in far-reaching public health decisions such as restricting behaviour or assessing environmental risks.[40] It is premised on the idea that resource allocation in health is a matter of distributive justice and that such decisions should be determined by the public.

This model contains four main pillars necessary to provide deliberative legitimacy in health prioritisation:

a) decisions are to be made publicly accessible (the Publicity Condition)

James E Sabin, *Setting Limits Fairly: Learning to Share Resources for Health* (2nd edn, Oxford University Press 2008).

The theory builds on Rawls approach of "Fair Equality of Opportunity", which advances that individuals should have same opportunities Though Rawls does not include health, Daniels advocates that people should have equal opportunity in resource allocation and focus his theory in legitimacy of such decisions by a fair procedure rather than substantive values. John Rawls, *A Theory of Justice* (Oxford University Press 1999).

37 See section 2.1.

38 See, e.g. Benedict Rumbold and others, 'Universal Health Coverage, Priority Setting, and the Human Right to Health' (2017) 390 The Lancet 712.

39 See, e.g. efforts in the global agenda: Jens Byskov and others, 'The Need for Global Application of the Accountability for Reasonableness Approach to Support Sustainable Outcomes Comment on "Expanded HTA: Enhancing Fairness and Legitimacy"' (2016) 6 International Journal of Health Policy and Management 115.

In less-developed countries, see, e.g.: Stephen Maluka and others, 'Implementing Accountability for Reasonableness Framework at District Level in Tanzania: A Realist Evaluation' (2011) 6 Implementation Science 11. Or in HTA agencies such as NICE: Rawlins (chapter 1, n 15) 471.

40 David B Resnik, D Robert MacDougall and Elise M Smith, 'Ethical Dilemmas in Protecting Susceptible Subpopulations From Environmental Health Risks: Liberty, Utility, Fairness, and Accountability for Reasonableness' (2018) 18 The American Journal of Bioethics 29, 35–37; Tom R Tyler and Avital Mentovich, 'Mechanisms of Legal Effect: Theories of Procedural Justice' [2011] PHLR Methods Monograph Series 11–14, 19–20.

b) justification for resource constraints founded on reasons of evidence that "fair-minded" people can agree on. "The rationales for limit-setting decisions should aim to provide a reasonable explanation of how the organization seeks to provide 'value for money' in meeting the varied health needs for a defined population under reasonable resource constraint" (the Relevance Condition)
c) there must be a means to challenge and review the conclusion as new knowledge is garnered or more beneficial practices are defined (the Revision and Appeals Condition); and
d) the conditions should be publicly enforced by authorities (the Regulatory Condition).[41]

These pillars are entrenched into a system of procedural justice (following Rawls).[42] In this view, *how* matters more than *what* in health rationing, as it is assumed that there is no predefined universal principle to base such decisions. The core rationale, drawing on democratic theory, is that fair-minded people are able to achieve fair judgements by means of reaching agreement on which factors will be considered in deliberations publicly conducted, even in circumstances of resource shortage.

An HRBA defines the content and outcomes of health policies in a process according to human rights. However, in procedural fairness, there is no precisely predetermined result but rather an intention to allocate resources that may differ according to various outcomes depending upon the local reality. A4R, in contrast to HRBA in general, is measured principally by standards related to the rules of procedure in a decision and not the final decision itself or the facts that should be given weight in the criteria. Hence, procedural fairness seems more easily achievable than a substantive interpretation of rights in resource allocation. Substantive claims in health may collide with priority-setting and may appear to be instituting "rigidities into the health care system as well as committing the government to open-ended expenditure".[43] Yamin holds that "the very notion of priority-setting runs counter to some human rights advocacy regarding the right to health, or certain health issues".[44]

While priority-setting would never be incompatible with the right to health per se, A4R is far from being its direct expression and should not be con-

41 Daniels, *Just Health* (chapter 1, n 14) 118–119.
42 Rawls (n 36) Chapter II, Section 14.
43 Joanne Lenaghan, *Rationing and Rights in Health Care* (Institute for Public Policy Research 1996) iii.
44 Yamin, 'Democracy, Health Systems, and the Right to Health' (chapter 1, n 12) 199.

sidered in isolation of resource mobilisation measures. Indeed, one of the most influential statements of the CESCR, General Comment 14, does acknowledge the need for well-grounded resource allocation decisions and discourages investment in excessively costly technologies at the expense of broader population access to care (as a form of covert discrimination by excluding population needs), reminding the importance of considering cost-effectiveness.[45] However, it does not explicitly endorse the model proposed with A4R, as a way to legitimise rationing, and waives simultaneously resource allocation with obligations of resource maximisation, which are much more strongly emphasised throughout the document: "If resource constraints render it impossible for a State to comply fully with its Covenant obligations, it has the burden of justifying that every effort has nevertheless been made" to maximise resources.[46] This guidance needs to be considered altogether, as priority-setting alone will not fully deliver human rights obligations if there are substantive efforts that can be pursued alongside or within such deliberations.

The emphasis placed on the procedural aspect of resource allocation – rather than on the substantive principles inherent in socio-economic rights – is also evident in the way some scholars adopt the terminology of "substantive principles" as used by ethicists and health economists in HTA. As discussed in the first chapter, this community distinguishes between procedural and substantive principles in terms of process and decision criteria. A similar approach is taken by Wang and Rumbold, who examine the interpretation of rights, judicial review and State obligations in the context of priority-setting, yet do so without engaging with "substantive principles" engaged in this book, in the sense of creating favourable conditions for resource generation or addressing the structural drivers of scarcity.[47] Equally, this approach is taken by Rumbold et al. in developing a consensus statement where substantive principles are the ethical criteria open to decision-makers, and not substantive policies to maximise resources, as prescribed by international socio-economic rights.[48]

Therefore, attempts to connect the right to health with priority-setting have largely concentrated on their procedural compatibility and how human rights

45 GC 14 (note 34) para 19.

46 GC 14 (note 34) para 47.

47 Daniel Wang and Benedict Rumbold, 'Priority Setting, Judicial Review, and Procedural Justice' in Andelka M Phillips, Thana C De Campos and Jonathan Herring (eds), *Philosophical Foundations of Medical Law* (1st edn, Oxford University Press, Oxford 2019) 186.

48 Benedict Rumbold and others, 'Universal Health Coverage, Priority Setting, and the Human Right to Health' (2017) 390 The Lancet 712, 712.

principles are applied to ensure appropriate deliberations, often neglecting the substantive duties of States to mobilise and allocate resources by all available means. While academics such as Rumbold et al. may conclude that the right to health and priority-setting may be mutually reinforcing, this is made to the extent the right supports institutionalisation and application of fair priority-setting procedures. Where resources obligations are mentioned, they are placed as secondary or less central caveat – such as the need of finance ministers to "require resources, whether through taxation or other means" – without exploring what these "other means" represent, beyond financial availability, in particular during priority-setting processes.[49] The authors' selective emphasis on the right to health concluded that it can be "reconciled" with certain aspects of priority-setting, but they do not fully consider how other human rights principles – such as resource maximisation, which are equally central to the right to health – inform the understanding of scarcity in rationing decisions.[50]

As a result, fundamental drivers of resource distribution, including access to medicine regulation and systemic inequities in global markets, are left unaddressed in those priority-setting models where the right to health serves basically to ensure the existence of a deliberative process. This stands in contrast to the more integrated approaches advanced by the Office of the United Nations High Commissioner for Human Rights today, underscoring that priority-setting in health systems is intrinsically linked with the mechanisms that make selected technologies affordable and available. It recommends that national essential medicines lists, developed through transparent and evidence-based processes, should serve not only to guide coverage decisions but also to inform procurement and pricing policies.[51]

1.2 The Right to a Fair Share

Procedural justice ideals, among human rights scholars, have led to a proposed reconceptualisation of the right to health, devoid of substantive claims, as a purely procedural right. The "right to a fair share" (RTFS), as I call this type

49 Benedict Rumbold and others, 'Universal Health Coverage, Priority Setting, and the Human Right to Health' (2017) 390 The Lancet 712, 713.

50 Ibid, 172.

51 Office of the United Nations High Commissioner for Human Rights, *Comprehensive Report on Access to Medicines, Vaccines and Other Health Products in the Context of the Right to the Highest Attainable Standard of Physical and Mental Health*, UN Doc A/HRC/59/29 (7 April 2025) paras 58, 71(c).

of proposition, equates the right to health with an enforceable right to whatever is the allocation out of a fair procedure, or a right to ensure Daniels' A4R conditions in priority-setting, sometimes in response to litigation.[52] The trust in procedural justice may also prompt authors to identify whether countries are implementing A4R conditions, rather than verifying what is really being achieved in terms of fairness and legitimacy by human rights standards in the criteria of those HTA institutions.[53] The procedural model, as Eleftheriadis reminds us, depletes the right of health of fundamental content, since the substantive right to health does not provide criteria for deciding which interests are more important in health or determining other policy decisions.[54]

The RTFS is then a way of denying the direct enforceability of substantive claims and accepting that the only enforceable claims are those resembling a fair procedure or A4R. Daniels himself questions the usefulness of rights when claimants can invoke the same right in a situation where all healthcare needs cannot be provided, limiting the power of rights to highlighting particular needs but not indicating any priority between them.[55] After discarding all common foundations of the right to health to assist in these disputable allocations, Chapman concludes that the best route to interpret the right to health would be to collapse the right with the A4R framework, as alternative interpretations failed to address finite resources.[56]

This association of the right to health with A4R among some scholars is, however, a later development, as Daniels' model was first advanced with specific resistance to HRBA. One of the first caveats posed by Daniels, as he outlined his health justice theory, was to avoid the temptation of misunderstanding the nature of human rights, warning that "the appeal to a right to health or to health care is not an appropriate starting point for an inquiry into just health or just health care".[57] The reasons for this caution are that the claim to human rights is an imprecise concept and thus does not provide adequate rules to determine the extent of the obligations to individuals and how they equate with competing resources and needs. Under Daniels' ideas, instead of a moral

52 Daniels, *Just Health* (chapter 1, n 14) 324.

53 Katharina Kieslich and Peter Littlejohns, 'Does Accountability for Reasonableness Work? A Protocol for a Mixed Methods Study Using an Audit Tool to Evaluate the Decision-Making of Clinical Commissioning Groups in England: Table 1' (2015) 5 BMJ Open e007908, 2.

54 Pavlos Eleftheriadis, 'A Right to Health Care' (2012) 40 The Journal of Law, Medicine & Ethics 268, 276.

55 Daniels, *Just Health* (chapter 1, n 14) 324.

56 Chapman, (n 1) 16.

57 Daniels, *Just Health* (chapter 1, n 14) 15.

obligation justifying the entitlements of the right to health, what is needed is "a systematic theory of distributive justice for health-related needs".[58] While human rights do not arrange themselves in an orderly rank to help decision-makers select between conflicting morally desirable alternatives, procedural justice may deliver informed judgements that will achieve the status of fairness because the procedures have been constructed consciously and democratically.[59] Attempts to find substantive solutions to resource allocation that comply with moral conceptions of rights or derive substantive guidance from HRBA do not solve the problem, in Daniels' view.[60]

However, over time, Daniels has conceded that HRBA has some synergies with A4R or could be useful in bolstering accountability in a health system. He acknowledges elements of the right to health that promote transparency, public involvement, governance and visibility of health needs, in line with A4R conditions.[61] Daniels himself, when commenting on the Mexican Constitution, has propounded that the right to health ought to be interpreted in line with A4R, if made into a legal right.[62]

Alongside Daniels, this proceduralisation of the right to health has been discussed by other authors with varied justifications (and different degrees of association with A4R). Yamin and Norheim conclude that it is impossible for human rights to point to which specific group has more priority over the others, so an HRBA requires more "a process of meaningful democratic deliberation, which includes those who are or will be affected by the decisions taken, with all of the challenges that such deliberation entails".[63] The instinctive need to avoid intractable choices between life and death, as indicated by Schokkaert, makes the RTFS immediately more attractive to scholars than simply the right to health.[64] A procedural right to health is much more flexible, manageable and inexpensive than promoting only substantive claims.[65] It is also a much more clear concept as a procedural approach imposes obligations far more consolidated in human rights principles such as transparency

58 Ibid., 23.

59 Gruskin and Daniels (n 1) 1573–1574.

60 Daniels, *Just Health* (chapter 1, n 14) 316–317, 323.

61 Ibid., 328–329.

62 Daniels and others (n 1) 229.

63 Yamin and Norheim (n 1) 324.

64 Erik Schokkaert, 'Philosophers and Taboo Trade-Offs in Health Care' in A Gosseries and Y Vanderborght (eds), *Arguing about Justice: Essays for Philippe Van Parijs* (Presses universitaires de Louvain 2011) 308–309.

65 Lenaghan (n 43) iii.

and public participation than actually defining substantive principles to resource allocation.

Similarly, in empirical studies, RTFS resonates well with researchers worried about the scale of health litigation in some countries.[66] Gloppen prescribes a RTFS in the accountability function for courts, including enforcing rationing decisions, ensuring the establishment of a priority-setting system and addressing issues of negligence and bad performance of health providers.[67]

In theory, a RTFS also appears suitable for progressive realisation of access to health that allows variations in priorities in each jurisdiction – which would presume, not uncontroversially, that low-income countries have a right to health that is more limited in content than is the case in richer ones.[68] The institutional definition of the right to health, professed by Hessler and Buchanan, rests on the idea that local institutions are better placed to coordinate the best policy choices, establishing how rights are executed and fulfilled under resource pressure – in this case, rights are just a "fundamental social interest" realised by making efforts to achieve them through democratic debate.[69] While an effort has been made to outline some substantive meaning (the social interest), the content of the right totally hinges on the democratic will and such interest is more to promote health in general than actual individual access to healthcare.[70] The content of the right depends then on "varying degrees of scarcity and different priorities in different states".[71] Nunes et al. discussed this idea of varying scarcity, grounded in A4R, arguing that neither development is equally distributed worldwide nor is health spending in each country.[72]

66 See, e.g. Ricardo Perlingeiro, 'Procedural and Substantive Judicial Review of the Right to Health in Brazil' [2014] SSRN Electronic Journal 23–24, Siri Gloppen, 'Right to Health in Contexts of Resource Scarcity: Towards Judicial Enforcement of the Right to a Fair Share' [2015] SSRN Electronic Journal <http://www.ssrn.com/abstract=2622779> accessed 28 October 2018.Rebecca Dittrich and others, 'The International Right to Health: What Does It Mean in Legal Practice and How Can It Affect Priority Setting for Universal Health Coverage?' (2016) 2 Health Systems & Reform 23.

67 Gloppen (n 1).

68 Nunes, Nunes and Rego (n 1) 3.

69 Hessler and Buchanan (n 1) 91–95.

70 Ibid., 94.

71 Arras and Fenton (chapter 1, n 1) 31.

72 Nunes et al. present an allocative model based on an "hierarchy of needs" (physiological, safety, belongingness and love, esteem, self-actualisation and self-transcendence), denominated "Equal Opportunity Function", where poor countries would only meet basic needs. Nunes, Nunes and Rego (n 1) 2.

2 Criticism of A4R and Limitations to a Procedural Approach

Despite the procedural movement in HRBA that influences the reading of the right to health as an RTFS, A4R is not easily achievable or immune to criticism. The first to cast this doubt are Daniels and Sabin themselves, advising that their justice framework should be put to the test in real life, inasmuch as it constitutes in essence "theoretical justifications" and deserves empirical confirmation.[73] Therefore, the first point that needs to be raised is that A4R or procedural justice is not a perfect theory and its application, in the human rights domain, is not a guarantee of justice. After considering this question (the conceptual flaws of A4R as a theory of justice in healthcare), I will turn to the fact that this framework is not sufficient to replace the content of an HRBA (both procedurally and substantively).

The first problem – namely, the shortcomings in the A4R theory – is an important consideration, as human rights scholarship has been converted to the idea of a fair procedure without directly engaging with its weaknesses. Originally, A4R was justified by Rawls' ideal justice, which could only be implemented in a "well-ordered society under conditions of full compliance", different from the real-world circumstances where Daniels applies his theory.[74] More notably, the shortcomings of A4R have been largely condemned by bioethicists and philosophers for not ensuring fair outcomes or being conceptually flawed.[75] Ashcroft advises that efforts to find substantive values in allocating resources should not be abandoned for absolute confidence on the

73 Norman Daniels and James E Sabin, 'Accountability for Priority Setting' in A den Exter and M Buijsen (eds), *Rationing Health Care: Hard Choices and Unavoidable Trade-offs* (Maklu 2012) 23.

74 Smith, 'Legitimacy in Bioethics' (n 12) 418.

75 See, e.g. Richard Ashcroft, 'Fair Process and the Redundancy of Bioethics: A Polemic' (2008) 1 Public Health Ethics 3; Amy Ford, 'Accountability for Reasonableness: The Relevance, or Not, of Exceptionality in Resource Allocation' (2015) 18 Medicine, Health Care and Philosophy 217; Leah Rand, 'Legitimate Priority-Setting: Refining Accountability for Reasonableness and Its Application within NICE' (PhD Thesis, 2016); Michal Stanak, 'Nudging in Neonatology: Practical Wisdom and Accountability for Reasonableness' (2019) 35 International Journal of Technology Assessment in Health Care 5; Samuel J Ujewe and Werdie C van Staden, 'Inequitable Access to Healthcare in Africa: Reconceptualising the "Accountability for Reasonableness Framework" to Reflect Indigenous Principles' (2021) 20 International Journal for Equity in Health 1; Andreas Hasman and Søren Holm, 'Accountability for Reasonableness: Opening the Black Box of Process' (2005) 13 Health Care Analysis 261; Alex Friedman, 'Beyond Accountability for Reasonableness' (2008) 22 Bioethics 101; Taro Okuda, 'Deliberation, Fair Outcome, and Empirical Evidence: An Analogy with Archives' in Akira Akabayashi (ed), *The future of bioethics: international dialogues* (Oxford University Press 2014); Lindsay M Sabik and Reidar K

procedures.[76] The criticism also includes not being able to determine the relevant or appropriate criteria for a decision; being unable to guarantee legitimacy and substantive constraints to a decision; not allowing fair consideration of new reasons provided within the process beyond the agreed criteria; dismissing extra-procedural values for legitimacy; not addressing possible "nudges" in the way questions are formulated and corrupting its original theory of justice principles by indirectly adopting cost-effectiveness or preventing underhanded interests in political decision-making.[77] Additionally, A4R has been said to conflict with communitarian values of shared responsibilities in Africa (potentially imposing a common obligation to organise the healthcare market in a fair way).[78]

Taking into consideration the limitations outlined above, the implementation of A4R must also address inequalities, barriers to public participation and inadequate market organisation responsible for avoidable scarcity. Hence, procedural justice has two main obstacles from a human rights standpoint: a) it is difficult to implement, let alone ensure fair outcomes; and b) it does not provide substantive principles and policies from a socio-economic rights model, in particular to contain unnecessary rationing.

As to the first problem, A4R is an ideal framework that cannot be easily achieved, so the projected legitimacy is rarely attained even if its conditions were sufficient. Authors may take issue with the impossibility of finding common ground on what should be the relevant factors in deliberation; and setting what is a "reasonable" criteria, as Daniels proposes, is already a subjective and contentious point.[79] Friedman has extensively discussed the problem of the relevance condition, and denies that one can "reduce all of our moral disagreements to 'merely' disagreements about weights", so there is also imprecision as to which factors be considered in the first place.[80] Using procedural justice can give the veneer of legitimate outcome, no matter how much the content of the decision could be regarded as objectively unfair.[81] Procedural rules can also be a matter of disagreement as Sabik and Lie note, and the legitimacy of conditions such as the appeal process may not be guar-

Lie, 'Principles versus Procedures in Making Health Care Coverage Decisions: Addressing Inevitable Conflicts' (2008) 29 Theoretical Medicine and Bioethics 73.

76 Ashcroft (n 75).

77 See, e.g.: Ford (n 75); Rand (n 75) 96–113; Stanak (n 75).

78 Ujewe and van Staden (n 75).

79 Andreas Hasman and Søren Holm, 'Accountability for Reasonableness: Opening the Black Box of Process'(2005) 13 Health Care Analysis 261, 266–272.

80 Friedman (n 75) 106.

81 Okuda (n 75).

anteed if they are designed in a way that does not provide effective opportunity of revision.[82]

Procedural approaches are further complicated by the nature of the HTA practice, since the steps to implement a fair procedure in this method of decision-making are not self-evident. The difficulty is that HTA as a policy is not yet fully standardised, with subjective elements that make values a strong influence on the procedures and differences between practice across jurisdictions.[83] The goal of harmonising moral interests and reflecting decisions among stakeholders could be seen more as an art than a well-established hard science, putting the results at the mercy of the competence of the participants.[84] Procedurally, the hurdles in HTA are to determine the methods that ensure participation and accountability and who has the power to influence resource allocation – both A4R and human rights standards are silent in this regard. Although patient involvement is normally understood as a right even in HTA studies, patient powers are not fully described either in the literature or international law guidance.[85] Thus, there are common challenges for a fair procedure in HTA that require substantive policies, such as to implement patient participation and reduce power imbalances in political decisions.

At the very least, an accountable process requires substantive policies to enhance participation and ensure that voices that are not normally heard take part in the process. States would need to actively implement measures, according to their resource availability, to enhance the participation process (e.g. identifying those negatively and positively affected by the decision, allowing participation at different stages and making evidence more easily accessible and understandable by the public).[86] HTA is intrinsically political, and the role patients and laypersons can take may vary from mere consultants to actual representative voters, which also raises questions of mechanisms to

82 Sabik and Lie (n 75).

83 Bjørn Hofmann, 'Health Technology Assessment–Science or Art?' (2013) 9 GMS Health Technology Assessment 7; Rick A Vreman and others, 'Differences in Health Technology Assessment Recommendations among European Jurisdictions: The Role of Practice Variations' (2020) 23 Value in Health 10, 10–11.

84 Ibid.

85 See, e.g. Janet Wale and others, 'Why Patients Should Be Involved in Health Technology Assessment' (2017) 33 International Journal of Technology Assessment in Health Care 1, 1–2.

86 Maarten PM Jansen, Rob Baltussen and Kristine Bærøe, 'Stakeholder Participation for Legitimate Priority Setting: A Checklist' (2018) 7 International Journal of Health Policy and Management 973, 974–975.

make this participation possible.[87] HTA organisations may adopt an institutionalised involvement, but may also engage with the public on an ad hoc basis.[88] For HTA officers, though, it may be difficult to conceptualise what public involvement is and when it is properly realised. In Latin America, countries still struggle to implement participatory process and government officials show concerns about patients' claims beyond resource availability.[89] Some of the more concrete indicators of participation used by HTA agencies include listening to external participants to take their views into account, using mediators to liaise with the public and giving a response that considers those inputs.[90] In reality, patients' involvement in HTA does not normally satisfy what would be a full engagement with human rights standards.[91] Commonly stakeholders complain of inaccessibility and lack of opportunities to be listened to.[92] The timeframe and the consultation may be severely impaired by a quick HTA process (in contrast with the full systematic procedure), where off-the-shelf, much less-detailed studies are used to fast-track the policymaking.[93]

Moreover, there are notable difficulties in managing the diversity of personal interests in HTA. Fleck recognises that competing interests mean that a legitimate procedure is not straightforward to pursue, but must include all individuals (sick or not), rather than only small groups of those affected by a particular medical intervention.[94] The wide spectrum of opinions would need

87 Julia Abelson and others, 'Bringing "the Public" into Health Technology Assessment and Coverage Policy Decisions: From Principles to Practice' (2007) 82 Health Policy 37, 41.

88 Ibid.

89 Andres Pichon-Riviere and others, 'Stakeholder Involvement in the Health Technology Assessment Process in Latin America' (2018) 34 International Journal of Technology Assessment in Health Care 248, 249–250.

90 Kathy K Li and others, 'Conceptualizing the Use of Public Involvement in Health Policy Decision-Making' (2015) 138 Social Science & Medicine 14, 19.

91 For an HRBA to health deliberations, a high level of engagement with the population and transparency are required. See: Helen Potter, 'Participation and the Right to the Highest Attainable Standard of Health' (Human Rights Centre, University of Essex 2003).

92 Edilene Lopes and others, 'Involving Patients in Health Technology Funding Decisions: Stakeholder Perspectives on Processes Used in Australia' (2016) 19 Health Expectations 331.

93 Amber Watt and others, 'Rapid Versus Full Systematic Reviews: Validity in Clinical Practice?' (2008) 78 ANZ Journal of Surgery 1037, 1039.

94 Fleck presented some of his own answers to the overall scepticism that democratic participation is realisable with his own experience (non-scientific observations) in conducting public consultations. Making use of Rawlsian ideas, Fleck sustains that agreements is possible (even when society seems divisive), because a common agreement may always be struck in some aspect of the discussion See. Leonard M Fleck, 'Just Solidarity: The Key to Fair Health Care Rationing' [2015] Diametros 44, 50–51.

to work towards difficult agreements. If for instance, there is more than one treatment that is "just enough" for a matter in discussion, people would need to agree on the "least reasonably rejectable" one.[95] Fair decisions would also demand people being sensitive to others' needs when adopting rules of distribution in a manner that does not normally occur. The most important question raised by Fleck is how people could be ethical towards a diverse minority of patients with very specific healthcare circumstances set against broad efficiency indicators.[96] Similarly, Daniels has advised that more studies are needed in order to better implement a deliberative process, paying attention to the adverse participation of interest groups (pharmacy companies or lobbyists) and the different personal aptitudes which win over debates.[97]

In addition to the problem that it cannot ensure that decisions are actually procedurally fair or rigorously implement the A4R tenets, the second issue is that procedural justice lacks the substantive content of an HRBA. A problem with Daniels' account of justice is that it accepts criteria chiefly based on "value for money", including aggregated cost-effectiveness, which are not necessarily bound to human rights principles.[98] The environment generated by HTA agencies is propitious for aggregative thinking (which may harm the consideration of minorities, in comparison to the major groups) and privileges certain type of evidence over other values more compatible with human rights (such as priority for the worse off). The model is also susceptible to vested interests of economic actors, and using value for money as one of the criteria may hide secondary commercial interests that do not substantively protect the centrality of human rights implementation as a goal throughout policy-making.

Moreover, A4R does not address extraprocedural values grounded in human rights, lacking mandatory substantive principles, such as non-discrimination, and substantive policies against structural problems that render circumstances unfair, such as inequalities in economic powers and high-cost medicines. For instance, in deciding a minimum healthcare basket by an agreed relevant criteria, it would be necessary to determine whether that could result in discrimination, the weight that should be placed on reducing inequities in the health system among patients or whether vulnerable groups

95 Ibid., 51.
96 Ibid., 52.
97 Norman Daniels, 'Some Remarks on Accountability for Reasonableness' (2018) 18 The American Journal of Bioethics 42, 43.
98 See chapter 5, 3.2 and 3.3 on value measurement and the right to health.

were prioritised.[99] In addition, the decision would need to justify whether policies could be put in place to avoid denial of healthcare in the first place or establish a plan to end this cause of inequalities (including scarcity) in the near future through progressive realisation. Those forms of addressing scarcity and substantive values will be further delineated in the following chapters, but suffice to say that none of the resource mobilisation principles that bind economic and social rights implementation need to be fulfilled under a procedural approach. Ideas such as resource maximisation or international cooperation to mitigate structural policy problems are not in the vocabulary of A4R. As we will see in the remainder of this book, those substantive elements are essential to an HRBA under the international right to health.

3 Conclusions

This chapter set out to justify why a procedural approach based on A4R *cannot* be the only determining factor of an HRBA. The reason is that procedural justice is insufficient to promote substantive fairness, in that it is more of an ideal (not fully implementable) and does not challenge the causes of scarcity in order to guarantee that decisions are made under circumstances compliant with human rights principles. However, this argument does not completely clarify the reasons why substantive principles of the international right to health *should* be used alongside procedural fairness in an HRBA, what they are and how they can help to improve HTA deliberations substantively. Considering Smith's critique of A4R (that procedures are fallible and often subject to a battle of political interests), we must know how far substance can take us before falling back on deliberative tools.[100]

The principal reason substantive rights principles should complement procedural approaches is because it is important to utilise the best possible efforts to realise rights without conceding to scarcity. What the international right to health offers as substantive standards will be examined in Chapters 4 to 7, with reference to the International Covenant on Economic, Social and Cultural Rights (ICESCR) under Article 2.1. Some of the usages of the right to health in resource allocation, in addition to the guarantee of a fair procedure, are: to regulate standards of the priority-setting criteria and prohibit discrim-

99 See, e.g. Smith's minimum health coverage case denying mental health services, which would be procedurally fair but substantively wrong. Smith, (n 12) 419.

100 William R Smith, 'Saving Environmental Justice From Proceduralism' (2018) 18 The American Journal of Bioethics 55, 56.

inatory decision-making (Chapter 5); to impose a duty to cooperate globally on methods and evidence-making (Chapter 6); and, most importantly, to adopt resource maximisation strategies with affordability policies to regulate the market to avoid scarcity (Chapter 4 and 7).

These principles will have particular influence on the practice and evidence employed, such as standards of economic evaluation methods, or prohibition of certain criteria considered discriminatory for medical evidence. In Chapter 5, on the principle of non-discrimination, the lines between procedure and substance in an HRBA will become less distinct and questions will be more deeply examined as to how procedure influences substance and vice-versa. For instance, as mentioned earlier, restrictive substantive criteria in HTA may cause problems of participation in a fair procedure.[101] Therefore, two interrelated categories of issues need to be addressed: a) policies to maximise resource and avoid scarcity during priority-setting, so rationing is not the primary practice; and b) substantive criteria complying with human rights in the decision-making.

In this case, HTA is regulated generally by various legal or authoritative sources that give effect to those substantive standards. Through law, international rights to health obligations are materialised within HTA. With this in mind, the following chapter will specify, in general terms, the scope of the law in HTA in order to support the argument that there are legal factors concerning the substantive aspects of an HRBA. It will help to explain how HTA, as a legal institution, can use laws to influence decisions substantively so as to improve the potential for accessing healthcare by following HRBA principles. From there, the other chapters will identify how this substantive HRBA is formed by legal obligations arising from the international right to health, which should be applied to HTA policies and regulations to inform the resource allocation procedure.

101 Smith, (n 12) 419.

CHAPTER 3

Mapping the Role of Law and Its Relation to the Right to Health within HTA

Having established that procedures should not be seen as the only feature of an HRBA to HTA, we should now explore the relationship of law with this process. To a certain degree, HTA constitutes a product of law and public health regulations. It may be heralded as a regulatory solution to the poor management of health services, allowing for (or even making compulsory) the systematic analysis of the funding options with well-informed reasoning.[1] Like any administrative system, HTA agencies may be organised differently, depending on the jurisdiction and procedures spelt out by a legal source, either by legislation or institutional rules.[2] This variable regulation of HTA agencies influences their structure, the binding effect of deliberations and the scope of the policy (internal insurance market, public health system or both).[3]

Thus, in developing an HRBA to HTA, the role of law within the organisations and procedures cannot be ignored. This chapter evaluates how law is

1 Thomas J Parisi, 'How Much Did You Pay for Your Heart: Is a Centralized Entity Performing Health Technology Assessment with Cost-Effectiveness Analysis the Answer to the Rising Costs of Health Care?' [2009] Jurimetrics 285, 304–312.

2 Steven Simoens, 'Health Technology Assessment and Economic Evaluation across Jurisdictions' (2010) 13 Value in Health 857, 857–858; Wija Oortwijn, Maarten Jansen and Rob Baltussen, *Evidence-Informed Deliberative Processes Version 2.0* (Radboud University Medical Center 2021) 21.

3 See, e.g.: Francesco Martelli and others, 'Health Technology Assessment Agencies: an International Overview of Organizational Aspects' (2007) 23 International Journal of Technology Assessment in Health Care 414; Ruth Schwarzer and Uwe Siebert, 'Methods, Procedures, and Contextual Characteristics of Health Technology Assessment and Health Policy Decision Making: Comparison of Health Technology Assessment Agencies in Germany, United Kingdom, France, and Sweden' (2009) 25 International Journal of Technology Assessment in Health Care 305; Akira Yuasa and others, 'Investigation of Factors Considered by Health Technology Assessment Agencies in Eight Countries' (2021) 5 PharmacoEconomics-open 57; Oortwijn, Jansen and Baltussen (chapter 1, n 67); Leticia García-Mochón and others, 'HTA and Decision-Making Processes in Central, Eastern and South Eastern Europe: Results from a Survey' (2019) 123 Health Policy 182; Hillegonda Maria Dutilh Novaes and Patrícia Coelho de Soárez, 'Health Technology Assessment (HTA) Organizations: Dimensions of the Institutional and Political Framework' (2016) 32 Cadernos de Saúde Pública 54–47.

 | HTTPS://DOI.ORG/10.1163/9789004730311-004

described in the literature and institutional practice to identify legal issues relevant to an HRBA. By understanding the role of law, we can trace the areas that can be regulated in line with human rights norms. The legal issues covered in this chapter will assist the analysis in the next chapters to progress from procedural-only approaches into complementary substantive issues as right to health obligations, including adequate legislation.

The central argument of this chapter is that HRBA should not be linked with law, solely through judicial decisions concerning procedures in HTA. There are alternative ways to understand the law substantively with respect to HTA criteria and HTA organisational structure that needs to be further explored. More importantly, scholarship has mostly neglected the standards derived from the international right to health and while there is an increasing recognition that law is an important element of HTA institutionalisation, the role of human rights is minimised compared to administrative law or jurisprudence.[4]

With this in mind, I claim that HTA may relate to the law in two categories, which can contribute to the implementation of an HRBA:

a) internally (how assessments address the law as a criterion to be weighed, the regulations of the procedure and the relevant criteria) and
b) externally (most commonly via what courts rule on cases involving HTA deliberations and how HTA influences the fulfilment of human rights obligations in health policies in practice).

This perspective takes the relation of HTA with the law as being a materialisation of the right to health, where HTA organisations are a "core social institution" in a health system ruled by human rights.[5] Factors that play an important function in an HRBA framework could be whether the regulations impose the observance of social values in the criteria or whether participation is facilitated by legal requirements such as publication of reports or open consultations. For instance, some jurisdictions, as Culyer and Bombard observe, may impose legal obligations to adopt equity considerations or non-discrimination in the criteria.[6] If the regulations or statutes that create HTA bodies or govern these organisations do not encourage compliance with human rights standards, it could be submitted that an "a priori" rights violation occurred internally in the assessment.

4 Clarke, Dhaene and Lisman (chapter 1, n 4) 20–21.

5 Freedman (chapter 1, n 11) 21.

6 Anthony J Culyer and Yvonne Bombard, 'An Equity Framework for Health Technology Assessments' (2012) 32 Medical Decision Making 428, 432.l.

In line with the foregoing, this chapter addresses both the internal and external relationship of HTA with the law. Section 1 compares the main internal components of HTA organisations and regulatory frameworks that may be determined by law. Section 2 will present two strands of literature relevant to the external relation of HTA and the law, first common law judicial review and then rights-based litigation. Section 3 will expose the reasons why one should be careful with an excessive reliance on procedural justice that has marked this body of research on health rationing and litigation. One conclusion is that research should shift focus to the internal relation with HTA and law and the right to health, not restricted to procedural regulations, but as one of the criteria in the decision-making on new health technologies.

1 Internal Relation with the Law

Legal provisions concerning HTA may be considered as a sub-field of public or health law governing this specific process.[7] For authors working in this area, several law disciplines bear upon resource allocation, from general public law to more specific fields of intellectual property, medical law, public procurement and human rights.[8] As a result, to make the case for an independent sub-branch in law means more than just connecting it with jurisprudence of lawsuits about treatments (external relation of HTA with Courts). Situating law in HTA goes further into the substantive sources that regulate cost-effectiveness and other evidence analysis according to each jurisdiction.

In order to shift the focus to the internal relation of law and HTA, this section outlines two ways in which law is commonly found in HTA reports and institutions, rather than simply declaring it as a subsidiary legal field. First, this section describes law as a theme in HTA reports (a specific area of study or subject in the assessment criteria and conclusions). Then, it engages

---

7 See e.g. Andre den Exter, 'Cost-Effectiveness: What's Law Got to Do with It?' [2014] Journal of the International Institute for Law and Medicine 285, 288–296; Robert Francke and Dieter Hart, 'HTA in den Entscheidungsprozessen des IQWiG und G-BA: Bestandsaufnahme und aktuelle Fragen der gesundheitsrechtlichen Regulierung' (2006) 49 Bundesgesundheitsblatt – Gesundheitsforschung – Gesundheitsschutz 241, 241; Daniel Widrig and Brigitte Tag, 'HTA and Its Legal Issues: a Framework for Identifying Legal Issues in Health Technology Assessments' (2014) 30 International Journal of Technology Assessment in Health Care 587; Robert Francke and Dieter Hart, 'Introduction to the Legal Aspects of HTAs' (2008) 102 Zeitschrift für Evidenz, Fortbildung und Qualität im Gesundheitswesen 63.

8 Ibid.

with the law as a matter of internal regulations of procedures and the criteria in general (the legal foundation of the activities in HTA bodies).

1.1 Law as Part of HTA Reports

As one of the criteria, in principle, law is often recognised as part of the checklist of knowledge areas to be examined in HTA methods. Its exact contribution, though, is not always well-defined in practice. Eddy outlines a set of criteria in HTA: "1) evidence-based medicine, 2) outcome analysis (what are the benefits and the risks involved), 3) economic appraisal (calculating costs); and lastly 4) ethical and legal considerations".[9] In fact, this structure could subtly represent the order of importance that areas of study receive in the reports. Not uncommonly, the legal-ethical step remains on the fringes: in the literature, the legal concerns are clustered together with everything other than medical evidence and cost-effectiveness, the so-called "ethical, legal and social issues" (ELSI).[10]

The "legal" in the ELSI of HTA has no universal meaning and the "ethical" and "legal" can have interdependent or confusing usages. Braunack-Mayer wrote a whole piece on the "ethical, legal and social" dimensions of appraisals but did not mention any more profound analysis of law.[11] The "legal" in ELSI can also be portrayed as giving shape to ethics and moral considerations, though it can only mandate or regulate it through "soft law".[12] Hopkins et al. collapse ethics, social values and law into the same category, without differentiating the appropriate procedures to analyse each item of this general non-medical/economic theme, as if they are all equivalent.[13] However, they observe that HTA is distinct from other evaluations, such as strict cost-effectiveness appraisals, precisely for having the opportunity to address non-economic matters.[14] On the other hand, merging these categories under

---

9 David Eddy, 'Health Technology Assessment and Evidence-Based Medicine: What Are We Talking About?' (2009) 12 Value in Health S6, 56.

10 Katherine Duthie and Kenneth Bond, 'Improving Ethics Analysis in Health Technology Assessment' (2011) 27 International Journal of Technology Assessment in Health Care 64, 65.

11 Annette Braunack-Mayer, 'Health Technology Assessment: Ethical, Legal and Social Issues' in Stella R Quah (ed), *International Encyclopedia of Public Health* (2nd edn., Academic Press 2017).

12 Louise Bernier and others, 'Legal Governance in HTA: Environment, Health and Safety Issues / Ethical, Legal and Social Issues (EHSI/ELSI), the Ongoing Debate' (2020) 3 Canadian Journal of Bioethics / Revue canadienne de bioéthique 88–89

13 Robert B Hopkins and Ron Goeree, *Health Technology Assessment: Using Biostatistics to Break the Barriers of Adopting New Medicines* (CRC Press 2015) 30.

14 Ibid., 18.

a single heading can undermine the quality of the assessment, as one of the areas can overshadow the others. This has been noted by Duthie and Bond when reviewing Canadian HTA reports that only referred to the law without examining ethical matters.[15] By contrast, for Hofmann et al. law and human rights can also be subsumed within questions raised in the ethical analysis.[16]

In this conflation between ethics, social values and legal norms, guidelines and policy papers offering the main steps to perform HTA lack proper recommendations on how to examine legal implications of new technologies. Even worse, when legal matters are considered, human rights still receive scant attention. For Lysdahl et al., in the legal analysis, despite international human rights standards exercising "influence on the development and use of health technologies", they are "very limited in comparison to national legislation".[17] In the HTA Core Model, a European Union-led project to promote a method for fully contextualised technology assessments, legal aspects are covered, but they remain mostly confined to "regulations and rules".[18] A much more limited focus on basic legislation regarding healthcare is outlined in questions that must be answered while conducting HTA.[19] In the example, the two questions most appropriate to legal concerns are: "What do laws/binding rules require with regard to appropriate processes or resources which would guarantee equal access to the technology?"; and "Does the implementation or use of the technology affect the realisation of basic human rights?" However, those questions do not directly examine the right to health and are indeterminate as to any human rights regime in question.[20]

15 Duthie and Bond (n 10) 65.

16 Bjørn Hofmann and others, 'Harmonization of Ethics in Health Technology Assessment: a Revision of the Socratic Approach' (2014) 30 International Journal of Technology Assessment in Health Care 3, 5–6.

17 Kristin Lysdahl and others, 'Guidance for Assessing Effectiveness, Economic Aspects, Ethical Aspects, Socio-Cultural Aspects and Legal Aspects in Complex Technologies' (Integrated Health Technology Assessment for Evaluating Complex Technologies (INTEGRATE-HTA) 2016) 102 <Available from: http://www.integrate-hta.eu/downloads/> accessed 21 August 2021.

18 EUnetHTA Joint Action 2, Work Package 8, 'HTA Core Model Version 3.0' 254–257 <www.htacoremodel.info/BrowseModel.aspx> accessed 11 February 2018.

19 Ibid.

20 Ibid., The assessment card, for the first question, simply states that HTA confers paramount importance to human rights, without explaining which human rights standards should be verified. The second question refers to EU legislation on equality of access, but does not indicate how to reconcile equal access before law with distributive decisions that may exclude some patients.

Policy guidance can be remarkably comprehensive as to the areas of law considered, yet standards under the right to health remain marginal (unless we accept bioethical / medical law issues as equivalent to human rights and public law). Guidelines such as Integrate-HTA list legal issues through general multilevel health policy standards (norms related to resource distribution and reimbursement); regulations related to the specific technology assessed, such as licences, intellectual property rights, marketing restrictions and safety rules; patients' rights in medical law, including autonomy, consent and privacy; professional regulation of healthcare workers; and legal requirements for experimental treatments.[21] The discussion will vary in terms of particular interventions. For example, for criminal purposes, if technologies are employed for abortion, it would be necessary to review the legal status of the foetus and in which circumstances, pregnancy termination is permissible (e.g. in a Down syndrome diagnosis).[22]

Further, among academics, few have explored a method to examine legal issues in HTA, and they have not paid in-depth attention to international human rights obligations, in general. Similar to policy guidelines, they tend to focus on medical law or private law. Widrig and Tag's model is based on two perspectives: the outside (at the macro level), looking at legal issues arising from the HTA process as a whole, and the inside (at the micro level), inquiring as to implications for patients, healthcare providers and professionals.[23] The outside perspective corresponds to the legal nature of the report commissioned (whether it is made by an external source on behalf of a government entity or a public organisation, etc.) and the legal status it acquires once produced (advisory or mandatory) to the institution that will adopt it.[24] The internal view addresses bioethical and professional ethics around health law. The authors do not cite explicitly specific international norms to address human rights but do raise concerns of dignity, citing the example of the reimbursement of weight-loss surgeries in Switzerland.[25] Lysdahl et al. offer a very similar framework in the Integrate-HTA project, an EU-funded initiative for the appraisal of complex technologies. Legal aspects are divided into Micro and Meso levels (legal issues in the doctor–patient relationship such as con-

21 Lysdahl and others (n 17).

22 Pedro Gallo, 'Integrating Ethical Enquiry and Health Technology Assessment: Limits and Opportunities for Efficiency and Equity' (2004) 2 Poiesis & Praxis 103, 107.

23 Widrig and Tag (n 7) 587–588.

24 Ibid., 588–589.

25 Ibid., 592.

sent and privacy) and Meso and Macro Levels (market authorisation, intellectual property and reimbursement rules).[26] Overall, Lysdahl et al. were mostly concerned with consent (with special regard to alternative forms of consent) and also on special medicine fields that may fall under specific legislation.

An exception to this trend of human rights neglect was made with a major WHO initiative to incorporate human rights in the criteria of evidence-based healthcare policy-making, the WHO-INTEGRATE framework.[27] Published in 2019, the authors systematically reviewed WHO principles and stakeholder contributions to build into the evidence-based decisions, a model conforming with UN and WHO norms and values (with an emphasis on the decisions of the CESCR and General Comment 14).[28] The framework is an encouraging sign towards HRBA, as it specifies that "all recommendations should be in accordance with universal human rights standards and principles" and interventions with higher equity effect should have better chances of approval.[29] Mainly, standards are drawn from the international human rights framework, but they do not remain fully consistent with socio-economic rights, in relation to resources and progressive realisation (though quality, acceptability and non-discrimination are included).

An important limitation is that human rights criteria in the WHO-INTEGRATE framework are assessed separately, and not as overarching principles in all aspects of evidence-making, including through economic and clinical research. For instance, if an intervention requires behaviour change, that would not generally be a human rights concern but a question of "feasibility and health system considerations".[30] The template also fails to make provisions for socio-economic rights aspects of producing evidence as a positive obligation to redress lack of data and exclusion of individual concerns, not deemed of research interest. It does not understand evidence-making in itself as a process which entails accountability and public participation. Patient

---

26 Lysdahl and others (n 17) 103–106.

27 Eva A Rehfuess and others, 'The WHO-INTEGRATE Evidence to Decision Framework Version 1.0: Integrating WHO Norms and Values and a Complexity Perspective' (2019) 4 BMJ Global Health e000844.

28 Jan M Stratil and others, 'Advancing the WHO-INTEGRATE Framework as a Tool for Evidence-Informed, Deliberative Decision-Making Processes: Exploring the Views of Developers and Users of WHO Guidelines' (2020) 11. International Journal of Health Policy and Management 629; JM Stratil and others, 'Development of the WHO-INTEGRATE Evidence-to-Decision Framework: an Overview of Systematic Reviews of Decision Criteria for Health Decision-Making' (2020) 18 Cost Effectiveness and Resource Allocation 8.

29 Rehfuess and others (n 27) 12.

30 Ibid., 8.

involvement in HTA is possible in the research prior to HTA and also through complementary qualitative studies about patient perspectives during the decision process.

Resources, or at least time, may be needed for new data collection or adjusted criteria adequate to patients. Consequently, evidence in an HRBA should be treated as a progressive realisation measure, integrated with resource allocation principles of the CESCR. Unfair conclusions might occur if based on lack of evidence, where a minority group with a legitimate interest would necessitate the acquisition of more knowledge in an under-researched area to substantiate their claims.[31] The authors acknowledge the limitation of the framework in attempting to determine substantive standards without addressing procedural criteria and legitimacy through deliberation (although reference was made to an informed-deliberative process).[32] The method is also based on a systematic literature review and a principles-based approach as "a normative foundation", but it is not clear how far any interpretation made by human rights-bodies and international law should have predominant authority.

Moreover, human rights standards in the criteria might be improved with a well-defined conceptualisation of the principles that are relevant to each health intervention. De Londras et al.'s human rights-evidence framework was developed in response to WHO-INTEGRATE, with a more comprehensive analysis to determine the relevant evidence required for the pertinent human rights standards (so every single health intervention has to reflect the human rights framework).[33] This approach does so in a way that is not comparable to an HRBA (i.e. there is no substantive duty to produce evidence and outline participatory procedures). Both this method and WHO-INTEGRATE appear to work more as a human rights impact assessment (measuring potential violations) than an HRBA to policies with procedural and substantive principles in evidence-making.

1.2 Law as Part of the Internal Procedures and Standards

Besides being one of the criteria in reports, the second relation of law with HTA is the regulation of procedures and standards serving as a determinant factor of the whole HTA structure. In this case, law is an element in more than

31 See chapter 5, section 1.1 on the human rights principles for evidence-making in HTA.
32 Rehfuess and others (n 27) 18.
33 Fiona de Londras and others, 'Integrating Rights and Evidence: A Technical Advance in Abortion Guideline Development' (2021) 6 BMJ Global Health e004141.

one of the areas of analysis in the recommendations and can in fact regulate the choice of criteria used in the assessment. In Germany, legislative reforms allowed for the introduction of the Institute for Quality and Efficiency in Health Care (IQWiG), which produces HTA reports for benefit coverage (§§139a – 139b of the German Social Security Book V), to ensure insurance coverage of treatments with greater patient benefits/outcomes.[34] The domestic legislation also imposes restrictions on the scope of studies in order to enforce a method of price control for new medicines. This is made through the determination of a "ceiling price" for the additional benefit, regarding a compared technology.[35] Until 2007, IQWiG was only examining clinical benefits, without a major role in the regulation of prices of new patented drugs, but by 2011, new legislation included cost-effectiveness analysis to support the enquiry about the maximum price acceptable for a given new technology launched in the market.[36] For new drugs, IQWiG cost-effectiveness studies are considered after additional benefit has been proved for patients or when no price negotiation has been successful between companies and the government.[37]

The legal requirement for coverage of therapies with additional benefits resulted in the development of a methodology peculiar to the German system, called "efficiency frontier", proposed by a group of experts commissioned to operationalise the German regulation.[38] Although the legislation refers to international standards, an international panel of experts formulated a cus-

34 Germany, Social Code (SGB) fifth book (V) – Statutory Health Insurance ((Article 1 of the law of December 20, 1988, Federal Law Gazette I p. 2477) § 35a Evaluation of the benefits of drugs with new active ingredients, authorisation to issue prescriptions).

35 Michael Drummond and Frans Rutten, 'New Guidelines for Economic Evaluation in Germany and the United Kingdom: Are We Any Closer to Developing International Standards?' [2008] OHE briefing 5–6; Victor Ivandic, 'Requirements for Benefit Assessment in Germany and England – Overview and Comparison' (2014) 4 Health Economics Review 12, 3–6.; Gesetz zur Stärkung des Wettbewerbs in der gesetzlichen Krankenversicherung (GKV-Wettbewerbsstärkungsgesetz–GKV-WSG).§31sec. 2a SGB V. Bundesgesetzblatt 2007 (Act to Strengthen Health Insurance Competition); Teil 1(11): 382.

36 Diana Ognyanova, Annette Zentner and Reinhard Busse, 'Pharmaceutical Reform 2010 in Germany' (2011) 17 Eurohealth 11, 12–13.

37 Corinna Klingler and others, 'Regulatory Space and the Contextual Mediation of Common Functional Pressures: Analyzing the Factors That Led to the German Efficiency Frontier Approach' (2013) 109 Health Policy 270, 273; Andreas Gerber-Grote and others, 'Decision Making in Germany: Is Health Economic Evaluation as a Supporting Tool a Sleeping Beauty?' (2014) 108 Zeitschrift für Evidenz, Fortbildung und Qualität im Gesundheitswesen 390, 393.

38 J Jaime Caro and others, 'The Efficiency Frontier Approach to Economic Evaluation of Health-care Interventions' (2010) 19 Health Economics 1117, 1117–1123.

tomised model to meet the German requirements of calculating additional benefits with economic principles they found compatible with the legal constraints, but this was criticised for departing from conventional health economics research.[39] Such comments were refuted by IQWiG on account of the German legal framework.[40] This approach differs from regulation based on utility-indicators (e.g. NICE in England and Wales), since Germany can employ these parameters occasionally only if relevant to compare technologies in the same area of treatment, with healthcare endpoints pertinent to the case (morbidity, quality of life, etc.).[41] Utility indicators may even be considered illegal in Germany, as noted by Kluger et al., for violating constitutional principles of dignity and the value of life.[42]

Thus, law can be responsible for major differences in the practice of HTA across jurisdictions, such as the IQWiG criteria. Comparative works on the regulatory frameworks from a legal perspective are limited and much of what is known is based on surveys that merely describe the main features in terms of the HTA procedure in each place, allowing the identification of some patterns in the HTA regulation or criteria.[43] Some categories of HTA institutional features, influenced by law, are as follows:

- The organisational model: HTA may be carried out by different actors in terms of their administration and public control. The structure may be centralised (UK, Brazil), subdivided in regional institutions producing information but integrated centrally (Sweden), in autonomous separate organs (Canada) or in multi-agency networks (France). As to the administrative regime of the organisations, Novaes et al. classify their constitution as governmental (Brazil, Mexico), quasi-governmental (Canada), independent

39 Werner BF Brouwer and Frans FH Rutten, 'The Efficiency Frontier Approach to Economic Evaluation: Will It Help German Policy Making?' (2010) 19 Health Economics 1128, 1128–1129.

40 IQWiG, 'Scientific Reply to Comments Regarding the "Methods for Assessment of the Relation of Benefits to Costs in the German Statutory Health Care System Version 1.0"' <https://www.iqwig.de/download/08-10-14_Scientific_Reply_to_Comments_v_1_0.pdf> accessed 3 December 2020.

41 Sara Mehmood Birchall Shah and others, 'A Regulatory Governance Perspective on Health Technology Assessment (HTA) in Sweden' (2014) 116 Health Policy 27, 273. See also German Social Security Code (AM-NutzenV) (chapter 3, n 34), section 2 para. 3.

42 S Kluger and others, 'Is QALY-Based Rationing Illegal in Countries with a Natural-Law-Constitution? A Multidisciplinary Systematic Review' (2020) 14 Ethics, Medicine and Public Health 100484.

43 See n 3.

public body (France), public–private (Colombia) or independent statutory authority (Australia).[44]

- The authority of the decisions (binding or non-binding): Agencies may issue different types of deliberations that can be taken as recommendations (Sweden) or enforceable judgments on policies (Brazil).[45] In Europe, legally binding decisions are found in England, France, Italy, Spain and Sweden, but not in Germany, Poland and the Netherlands.[46]
- Outputs: Guidelines, recommendations, reports or any document that may support a decision for health coverage or other policy-making.
- Mandatory criteria: Different HTA processes may take into account a range of parameters specific to their own regime (an illustrative inventory from different local practices includes clinical impact, economic impact, the burden of disease, the expected level of interest, existing evidence, the opportunity for revision, risks or controversial aspects of the technology or benefits from the assessment).[47]
- Transparency and public involvement: Engagement of external actors (patients, doctors or industry) may diverge amongst institutions from a more participatory approach to a closed one.[48] The existence of an appeal process, transparency in the decision and the methods of review are also not uniform.[49] HTA agency staff have pointed out that the organisational mandate and procedures are an important factor that may inhibit public involvement.[50] Depending on the organisation, participation can occur on an ad hoc or institutionalised basis, which will establish the methods that will select the participants (number of people recruited, individual characteristics, etc.) and the questions and tasks submitted to them (types of decisions or information they can provide).[51]

---

44 Novaes and Soárez (n 3) 8–9; Katherine Fierlbeck, William Gardner and Adrian Levy, 'New Public Governance in Health Care: Health Technology Assessment for Canadian Pharmaceuticals' (2018) 61 Canadian Public Administration 45.

45 Shah and others (n 41) 33.

46 Ronald L Akehurst and others, 'Variation in Health Technology Assessment and Reimbursement Processes in Europe' (2017) 20 Value in Health 67, 69.

47 Novaes and Soárez (n 3) 7–8.

48 Tania Stafinski and others, 'Health Technology Funding Decision-Making Processes Around the World: the Same, Yet Different' (2011) 29 PharmacoEconomics 475, 482–483.

49 Ibid.

50 Francois-Pierre Gauvin and others, '"It All Depends": Conceptualizing Public Involvement in the Context of Health Technology Assessment Agencies' (2010) 70 Social Science & Medicine 1518, 1519.

51 Abelson and others (chapter 2, n 87) 41–43.

Those regulatory provisions are embedded in the mandate or the statutory norms. This is in line with Thatcher's comparison with other independent regulatory agencies, whose powers are "usually set by law".[52] From a regulation perspective, the organisational and legal variations among different HTA producers lead to different organisational structures (which also limits the scope of stakeholder participation and influence over regulations, known as regulatory space).[53] On this view, there is a clear role for the law within the HTA models in each jurisdiction to transform and shape institutional practices. Authors have explored the regulatory space broadly in HTA in many ways, as to cultural inclination to different approaches of utility-measurement methods or, for instance, the viability of integrating market approval rules with HTA.[54] These types of variations by regulations and legal obligations are essential in determining the criteria and may play an important role into providing directions, priorities and values for the technologies to be reviewed.[55]

2 Law and HTA: External Relation with Courts and Right-to-Health Realisation

Beyond internal legal aspects, HTA also relates to the law externally and may either directly impact the realisation of the right to health or promote its violation. The positive association could be, for instance, the progressive realisation of the right to health, by virtue of achieving UHC and expanding services. Institutionalised HTA may be referred to as a means to bolster a health system in a well-planned manner in developing countries and to support

52 Mark Thatcher, 'Governance Structures and Health Technology Assessment Agencies: a Comparative Approach' (Department of Government, London School of Economics and Political Science 2010) 14 <http://eprints.lse.ac.uk/29471/> accessed 3 July 2021.

53 Leigh Hancher and Michael Moran, 'Organizing Regulatory Space' in Robert Baldwin, Colin Scott and Christopher Hood (eds), *A Reader on Regulation* (Oxford University Press 1998) 291–292; Colin Scott, 'Analysing Regulatory Space: Fragmented Resources and Institutional Design' [2001] Public law 283.

54 Klingler and others (n 37). Chris Henshall and others, 'Interactions between Health Technology Assessment, Coverage, and Regulatory Processes: Emerging Issues, Goals, and Opportunities' (2011) 27 International Journal of Technology Assessment in Health Care 253.

55 David Hailey and Alberta Heritage Foundation for Medical Research, *Elements of Effectiveness for Health Technology Assessment Programs* (Alberta Heritage Foundation for Medical Research 2003) 4, 23.

access to quality healthcare.[56] To ensure progressive realisation of the right health, HTA is part of the "processes to fairly establish and continually update guaranteed benefit plans, and to move beyond minimum thresholds".[57]

On the negative side, HTA may also restrict the real-world scope of the right to health when it improperly disinvests in or vetoes some treatments. When a health system adopts a health benefits package according to HTA reports, although it may positively build the coverage, it also delimits available services to those which gain approval. This could be a violation of the right to health in certain circumstances where right to health standards are not met, for instance, if the decision neglects human rights' substantive policies or does not respect a fair procedure. These decisions may be disputed by patients in courts or enforced by judges, modulating the implementation of the right to health.[58]

The aforementioned external relation of HTA has been central to the legal studies that will be examined in this section. A typical assumption is to correlate the right to health to A4R and then apply it to HTA via litigation. There are two problems with this. First, in practice, HTA in itself is complex and cannot be compared to A4R straightforwardly so that it is effortlessly enforced by courts.[59] Second, litigation studies have obscured the investigation of law within HTA organisations and made them merely procedural and passive entities, overseen by courts, not core social institutions governed by laws inspired by the right to health. The judicial approach does not inquire as to the organisational effects of the law on its own (general guidelines and internal regulations that constitute these bodies), as opposed to the procedures and decisions for a specific assessment. In what follows, two strands of litigation research that dominate the interpretation of the role of law in HTA will be described: "the judicial review" and "the rights-based" research schools. Both

56 Debjani Mueller, David Tivey and Davide Croce, 'Health-Technology Assessment: Its Role in Strengthening Health Systems in Developing Countries' (2017) 2 Southern African Journal of Public Health 6, 9–10. See also chapter 5, pp. 145–150.

57 Alicia Ely Yamin, 'Taking the Right to Health Seriously: Implications for Health Systems, Courts, and Achieving Universal Health Coverage' (2017) 39 Human Rights Quarterly 341, 354.

58 Amanda Glassman and others (eds), *What's in, What's out: Designing Benefits for Universal Health Coverage* (Center For Global Development 2017) 330.

59 By judicialisation, I refer to long-running litigation with claims in large numbers. This term is commonly used to refer to health litigation in Latin America. For a discussion on its meanings and political concepts, see: Rebecca Hamlin and Gemma Sala, *The Judicialization of Politics Disentangled* (Interactive Factory 2018).

were influential in the prevalent idea that law in HTA means litigation and adjudication of a fair procedure.

The first line of reasoning is formed by classic judicial review that focuses mostly on the procedural examination of rationing decisions. Hemminki et al. have expressed concern as to the potential threats of courts reviewing HTA decisions.[60] More recently, the focus of the WHO's guidance on HTA institutionalisation has been in classic judicial review.[61] Normally, rights-based studies tend to focus on the interaction of the jurisprudence with rationing in healthcare generally, rather than referring to HTA itself, but judicial review authors such as Syrett and Wang in the common-law system, pay attention directly to HTA (obviously, given the pioneering work of NICE in England).[62] But there is also limited research in other jurisdictions, such as Germany, New Zealand and other minor comparative jurisprudential rese-arch.[63] In Canada, even though the 1982 Canadian Charter of Rights and Freedoms allows for civil and political rights-based litigation, Sweatman and Woolard's analysis focuses more on classic procedural review.[64]

For lawyers in those jurisdictions, A4R was appealing because of its strong connection to the way public law is enforced through courts reviewing priority-setting policies. In the judicial review of HTA, this belief translates into the active participation of the courts by means of "deliberative agency" to hold to account the reasonableness of the steps and regular standards adopted by governments ensuring that they make a fully informed assessment considering all the necessary evidence available.[65]

60 Elina Hemminki, David Hailey and Meri Koivusalo, 'The Courts – a Challenge to Health Technology Assessment' (1999) 285 Science 203.

61 Clarke, Dhaene and Lisman (chapter 1, n 4) 14–16.

62 Keith Syrett, 'Health Technology Appraisal and the Courts: Accountability for Reasonableness and the Judicial Model of Procedural Justice' (2011) 6 Health Economics, Policy and Law 469, 479–476; Daniel Wang, 'From Wednesbury Unreasonableness to Accountability for Reasonableness' (2017) 76 The Cambridge Law Journal 642.

63 Timothy Stoltzfus Jost, 'The Role of the Courts in Health Care Rationing: the German Model' 18 Journal of Contemporary Health Law and Policy 7; Timothy Stoltzfus Jost, 'Health Care Rationing in the Courts: a Comparative Study' in Frances H Miller (ed), *Rights and Resources* (Routledge 2018); Rachael Baillie, 'Judicial Restraint When Reviewing Heath Care Rationing Decisions: a Healthy Approach' (2012) 18 Auckland UL Rev. 137.

64 Louise R Sweatman and Diane Woollard, 'Resource Allocation Decisions in Canada's Health Care System: Can These Decisions Be Challenged in a Court of Law' (2002) 62 Health Policy 275.

65 Keith Syrett, 'Revisiting the Judicial Role in the Allocation of Healthcare Resources: On Deference, Democratic Dialogue and Deliberation' (2005) 30 Journal for Juridical Science 1, 8–9.

By showing a certain degree of correlation of the jurisprudential evolution and institutional changes in a priority-setting organisation, scholars conversant with A4R have in fact showed that courts were connected to HTA by procedural justice. In the UK, HTA has been central to the rationing decisions with NICE, the organisation leading evidence-based policies of HTA in England and Wales.[66] Against this backdrop, Syrett (and more recently Wang) posited that, in fact, courts have not only applied procedural justice when using public law to review the legality of restricting health services but actually contributed to the consolidation of the conditions idealised by Daniels and Sabin to foster these principles within NICE.[67] This claim may need further investigation regarding a solid causation indication, as it depends on qualitative analysis to determine the real motivation of the policy developments in the National Health Service (NHS), but at least a certain degree of association by documentary research may be assumed, since those leading cases have been mentioned in the policy papers and similar texts.[68]

This research strand, however, has mostly targeted procedural aspects rather than inspecting the use of rights-approaches (which are not a feature of the English jurisdiction, for instance). The way this doctrine grounds itself in procedural checks reduces the appeal to present health rights within HTA in the belief that a fair model of distributive justice is being achieved.[69] The judicial review logic assumes an exercise of rights subordinate to very limited procedural aspects decided by judges. Newdick grounds the obligations of the British health system on public law norms controlled by constrained remedies that do not consider the substantive content of the obligation, but rather the fairness of the deliberation of the HTA process.[70] Syrett also appears to defend public law as a forum capable of delivering legitimacy to the allocation of scarce resources. His analysis hones in on the role of public law in general, not the application of human rights openly, considering that the English legal system provides less scope for rights-based decisions, at least on substantive grounds.[71] The author recognises that courts might be well equipped to exer-

66 Christopher Newdick, 'Health Care Rights and NHS Rationing: Turning Theory into Practice' (2014) 32 Revista Portuguesa de Saúde Pública 151.

67 Wang, (n 62) 668–669.

68 Ibid.

69 On the potential of human rights usage in HTA in the UK, which never proceeded, see: Charles Foster, 'Simple Rationality? The Law of Healthcare Resource Allocation in England' (2007) 33 Journal of Medical Ethics 404.

70 Newdick (n 66) 154–155.

71 Keith Syrett, 'Priority-Setting and Public Law: Potential Realised or Unfulfilled?' (2006) 7 Medical Law International 265, 276–277.

cise complementary responsibility in the use of public law rules in the process of deliberation of the healthcare package offered, even in very intricate HTA technical issues.[72]

To conclude, instead of attempting to identify legal rules or substantive principles that govern resource allocation, this strand of research inspects whether procedural aspects of the policy-making in rationing decisions match with the procedural justice imagined by courts. When litigation is concerned with human rights resulting in a substantive outcome, it usually falls under another cohort of research – the rights-based litigation.

2.1 Rights-Based Litigation

The second cohort of health litigation studies is composed of academics motivated by the enforceability of socio-economic rights, some of them under a cross-jurisdictional comparison across the Global South.[73] The widespread number of claims in some jurisdictions where socio-economic rights are justiciable encouraged an intense academic inquiry into the judicial effects on health policies beyond the judicial reserve of common law courts. It is worth mentioning that those scholars did not initially explore the linkage between litigation on rationing and HTA, which in many cases was not yet existent in those jurisdictions. Rather, they were interested in the priority-setting phenomenon more broadly by means of discussing the impact of litigating rights upon health policies under limited resources. Most of them follow the same analytical framework: to seek a profile of the lawsuit growth (who are the claimants and what are their goals); to identify what magistrates think; and to measure the level of implementation and actual social change (negative or positive) arising from this litigation.[74]

In these courts, plagued by uncontrolled rights-based litigation, this second stream of research discusses claims which are rather successful in the reallo-

72 Keith Syrett, 'Courts, Expertise and Resource Allocation: Is There a Judicial "Legitimacy Problem"?' (2014) 7 Public Health Ethics 112, 117–120.

73 Multi-comparative research on right to health litigation may be found in: Colleen M Flood and Aeyal Gross, *The Right to Health at the Public/Private Divide: a Global Comparative Study* (Cambridge University Press 2014); Brigit Toebes and others, *The Right to Health: a Multi-Country Study of Law, Policy and Practice* (TMC Asser Press 2014); Alicia E Yamin and Siri Gloppen (eds), *Litigating Health Rights: Can Courts Bring More Justice to Health?* (Harvard University Press 2011); Ebenezer Durojaye, *Litigating the Right to Health in Africa: Challenges and Prospects* (Taylor & Francis 2016).

74 Siri Gloppen, 'Litigation as a Strategy to Hold Governments Accountable for Implementing the Right to Health.' (2008) 10 Health and Human Rights 21, 25–31.

cation of resources.[75] Latin America has been the most common territory to witness this level of endemic litigation in healthcare, typically for drugs supply, where applicants have met with considerable success.[76] A number of Latin-American studies have focused on specific effects of health litigation in countries such as Brazil, Argentina, Costa Rica[77] and Colombia.[78] The upshot of mass human rights litigation has been reported as a financial burden from diversion from the overall budget to meet patient claims for treatments, whose efficacy is questioned for little clinical support.[79] Other countries, such as Germany and South Africa, have also experienced rights-based litigation. However, the relative number of claims is much smaller than in Latin America and the interpretation of rights more restrictive.

Although less explicitly than the judicial review studies, research on rights litigation has also made a direct and indirect reference to HTA. The indirect reference may be as subtle as a method of measuring the fairness of the impact of litigation (metrics of effectiveness may be taken from an HTA agency, as used in a survey in Costa Rica).[80] A methodology drawing on HTA information as a parameter to evaluate the impact of litigation on social outcomes has been developed by Norheim and Gloppen to classify the priority of drugs (as to the severity of the disease, the potential clinical benefit, the cost-effectiveness and the confidence of the scientific data on the treatment).[81] However, this approach does not allow us to make inferences about the

75 Leonardo Cubillos and others, 'Universal Health Coverage and Litigation in Latin America' (2012) 26 Journal of Health Organization and Management 390, 393–398.

76 Ibid., Ludovic Reveiz and others, 'Litigios por derecho a la salud en tres países de América Latina: revisión sistemática de la literatura' (2013) 33 Revista Panamericana de Salud Pública 213, 219.

77 Ole Norheim and Bruce lM Wilson, 'Health Rights Litigation and Access to Medicines: Priority Classification of Successful Cases from Costa Rica's Constitutional Chamber of the Supreme Court' (2014) 16 Health and Human Rights 47.

78 See: Alicia Ely Yamin and Oscar Parra-Vera, 'How Do Courts Set Health Policy? The Case of the Colombian Constitutional Court' (2009) 6 PLoS Medicine e1000032; Everaldo Lamprea, 'Colombia's Right-to-Health Litigation in a Context of Health Care Reform' in Colleen M Flood and Aeyal Gross (eds), *The Right to Health at the Public/Private Divide* (Cambridge University Press 2014) Benjamin Hawkins and Arturo Alvarez Rosete, 'Judicialization and Health Policy in Colombia: The Implications for Evidence-Informed Policymaking' (2019) 47 Policy Studies Journal 953.

79 Cubillos and others (n 75) 401–403.

80 Norheim and Wilson (n 77) 51–57.

81 Ole Norheim and Siri Gloppen, 'Litigating for Medicines. How Can We Assess Impact on Health Outcomes?' in Alicia Ely Yamin and Siri Gloppen (eds), *Litigating Health Rights: Can Courts Bring More Justice to Health?* (Harvard University Press) 304–332.

relation of HTA and the law, other than the use of technical documents to evaluate how properly the resources were administered following judicial interference.

Direct reference is made when HTA appears to be a government policy response to litigation. In this view, the deployment of priority-setting policies could be described as retaliation to judicial intervention. This approach was voiced in an inter-governmental commitment to control health litigation with HTA in the 28th Conference of the Pan-American Health Organization in 2012. The resolution stated that HTA "should help to safeguard the right to health" in the face of the growing judicialisation troubling the region.[82] Syrett has observed that the assimilation of HTA can ultimately result in a transformation in policy-making to establish a new health distribution culture.[83] More recently, rights-based litigation studies also have turned to HTA as the priority-setting instrument came into vogue as a solution for the lack of a "priority-setting culture" in the face of high litigation. The case of the establishment of an HTA agency in Brazil illustrates the possibility of rights-litigation inducing rationing policies as an unexpected long-term knock-on effect of judicialisation (a full account of this development will be given in the case study).[84] In Uruguay, HTA accession in 2013 represented a significant reduction of 10% in the litigation losses, but there was no drop in the total number of suits, as the programme was targeted at judges and lawyers to gain knowledge about the assessments.[85] According to Kershaw et al., after reviewing the extensive health litigation in Colombia, HTA should be made binding in order to address the burden of the right to health.[86]

---

82 Pan-American Sanitary Conference (PASC), "HTA and Incorporation into Health Systems, 28th Pan American Sanitarian Conference, Pan-American Health Organization", 19 September 2012 (CSP28.R9).

83 Keith Syrett, 'Evolving the Right to Health: Rethinking the Normative Response to Problems of Judicialization' (2018) 20 Health and Human Rights 121, 123.

84 Danielle da Costa Leite Borges, 'Individual Health Care Litigation in Brazil through a Different Lens: Strengthening Health Technology Assessment and New Models of Health Care Governance' (2018) 20 Health and Human Rights 147, 150–156. See chapter 7 for details of HTA and litigation evolution in Brazil.

85 Alicia Aleman and Ana Perez Galan, 'Impact of Health Technology Assessment in Litigation Concerning Access to High-Cost Drugs' (2017) 33 International Journal of Technology Assessment in Health Care 411, 412–413.

86 Angelica Leon Kershaw and Milena Izmirlieva, 'Rapid Increase of Health Litigation As A Means of Market Access For Innovative Medicines In Colombia And The Potential Role Of Health Technology Assessment' (2015) 18 Value in Health A810.

2.2 Limitation to Litigation Studies

Litigation provides only a partial understanding of how HTA and the law interconnect. In short, these two ecosystems of health litigation research have contemplated the following issues or operated under these common circumstances:

TABLE 3.1 Litigation research comparison (Source: Author's contribution).

	Judicial review	Rights-based litigation
Level of litigation	Individual/strategic	Mass litigation/individual/strategic
Resource allocation focus	Rationing	Expansion or restriction of rights obligations/investment without due process or criteria
Legal basis	Administrative law	Rights-based/Constitutional law
HTA	Present in the health system	Absent, in expansion or implemented to tackle judicialisation
Social outcome measured	Transparency of the health system, participation, procedural justice	Policy implementation, Inequity/equity, Health distribution, the realisation of the right to health

One point in common between both research cohorts is that they are preoccupied with the judge's view of law. This approach is not a good starting point for a discussion of how rights can be integrated into HTA through laws.[87]

A consequence of the litigation scholarship, in general, is that it might obscure the pitfalls of proceduralisation of health rationing, especially with the capacity of courts to verify the fairness of the procedures, and dramatically overstate the importance of courts. It cannot escape as well, as discussed in chapter 2, that much of this interpretation is grounded in a pure procedural view of justice, in line with the dominant HRBA to resource allocation today, which neglects substantive elements of resource mobilisation. And even if a procedural approach was the meaning of an HRBA to HTA, litigation studies

87 Colleen M Flood and Aeyal Gross, 'Litigating the Right to Health: What Can We Learn from a Comparative Law and Health Care Systems Approach' (2014) 16 Health and Human Rights 62, 66–67.

may spur overconfidence in the judicial application of procedural justice in HTA, as if courts could run a checklist for A4R with exactitude.

That being said, the exact scope of courts to maintain A4R seems unclear, even if proceduralisation could be the sole ideal of an HRBA. Commenting on the risks of the constitutionalisation of the right to health in Mexico, Daniels' preferential approach rests on judges showing "due deference to a fair deliberative process implemented by the health system".[88] This deference, however, is not to be confused with the complete absence of any scrutiny by courts over the reasonableness of decisions. Daniels appears to reject total deference, but does not explain what the precise grounds of review are when he says that courts should make sure that decisions "are consistently applied" and should "critically review the fairness of the process".[89] It is not evident whether the consistent application means that different deliberations should follow the same criteria or just that once an allocative decision is made, it should be enforced consistently (which limits, then, the court's power to revisit the criteria). The fairness of the process presumably concerns only the procedure and, as argued before in this chapter, there is in practice, little power for courts to review unfair criteria based only on the nature of the evidence or economic evaluation (as with utility indicators or cost-effectiveness). Daniels, however, does mention that courts should check whether there are efforts to create equity in the system and that would probably demand that judges review the criteria. Yet, it is still argued that all that courts can assess is whether there has been "a real attempt at integration to evaluate and show deference to" those rationing deliberations.[90] Thus, this approach does not explain what courts should do to balance equity and equality to enforce a right to a fair procedure.

Moreover, asserting a link between A4R and the interpretation of the law to provide fair rationing decisions, as some studies have done, is not the same as confirming that judges are well equipped to monitor this framework. Courts may depart slightly from the A4R conception when privileging one aspect more than another or giving a different construction to obtain the same result, as decisions about transparency and participation have illustrated.[91]

The most complicated aspect for judges to assess is the relevance condition, since they may have limited authority to modify it.[92] Syrett notes that courts

88 Daniels and others (chapter 2, n 1) 233.

89 Ibid.

90 Ibid.

91 Syrett, 'Health Technology Appraisal and the Courts' (n 61) 484–486.

92 Ibid., 480–481.

have been far more successful in examining questions of public participation, and relatedly matters of transparency.[93] Under the banner of classic judicial review, it is not their preeminent competence to establish what are the moral values to be employed as principles in HTA methods.[94] A prerequisite for the relevance condition is that only "fair-minded people" are engaged in the decision process, but this is problematic for courts to apply. The ability to attract the right people is also contested in A4R. Participants may not have the expertise to contribute to such debates.[95] The inevitable politicisation and capture of those HTA agencies by politicians and interest groups is a consequence very difficult to prevent.[96] People may naturally behave with different postures. Either voluntarily or by lack of control over deep-rooted bias, the required mindset may not be achieved, Ford observes, because of "the egocentric nature of the human state".[97] As technocrats have in their hands the power to set the level of evidence and design the studies, it is hardly imaginable that A4R could promote its vision of fairness at this level to secure some kind of degree of joint-decision to determine in every detail what will be the rules of assessment in the reports.

To definitively uphold A4R tenets, there are also very technical and untouchable internal regulations in HTA to which courts may not respond, even though they would be part of the relevance condition. For instance, institutions may have control over the thresholds of cost or the utility unit chosen for the studies (e.g. NICE has been criticised for the role of quality-adjusted life years [QALYs] and the caps on monetary values).[98] In accepting some technologies (above a cost-effectiveness threshold, such as £13,000 per QALY in NICE), institutions may issue decisions that take away resources which would be better applied to other patients.[99] These types of criteria could be part of a top-down decision, with patients holding no leverage over it. But judges are unlikely to be able to guarantee consistency within each treatment deliberation, as the same situations may lead to different deliberations according to

93 Ibid., 482.

94 Ibid.

95 Okuda (chapter 2, n 75).

96 Daniel Callahan, 'Reasonableness and Politics' in Akira Akabayashi (ed), *The Future of Bioethics: International Dialogues* (Oxford University Press 2014).

97 Ford (chapter 2, n 75) 219.

98 Michael Drummond and Corinna Sorenson, 'Nasty or Nice? A Perspective on the Use of Health Technology Assessment in the United Kingdom' (2009) 12 Value in Health S8, S10–S12.

99 Mike Paulden, 'Recent Amendments to NICE's Value-Based Assessment of Health Technologies: Implicitly Inequitable?' (2017) 17 Expert Review of Pharmacoeconomics & Outcomes Research 239, 240–241.

the members involved.[100] It totally leaves to the participants to figure out what criteria are pertinent to promote fairness each time, as A4R does not bind the criteria over time. Different compositions of stakeholders may determine what relevant principles will be adopted, hinging on very personal attributes of those in charge or in unfair comparisons between very distinct matters (such as measuring the effects of a heart surgery procedure against new low-burden colonoscopy equipment).[101] Moreover, courts may not be able to select criteria which are recognisably fair in terms of public acceptance. For instance, people may not want to justify health distribution in a maximisation approach (whereby people with less chance of survival would be disadvantaged) or aggregate individual results (since a small group's progress may be more important than small benefits for a large population).[102] Broadly, the public may decide for "giving people a fair (if not equal) chance at a benefit".[103]

Additionally, courts may have limited ability to interfere with the procedural rules governing the A4R incorporation (such as rules of appeal, the composition of assemblies and mechanisms of participation, which this theory does not address in detail). These might have a serious impact on A4R and participatory principles. Patient involvement in HTA does not normally satisfy what could be a full engagement, leaving stakeholders complaining of inaccessibility and lack of opportunities to be heard.[104] Moreover, the timeframe and the consultation may be severely impaired by an express HTA version (in contrast to the full systematic procedure), where off-the-shelf studies with less scrutiny are utilised as a means to speed up decision-making.[105] Thus, the deliberative process is not value-free, as Sabik and Lie note when addressing the pitfalls of the organisation of appeals in A4R that might undermine fairness for some parties.[106]

100 Ford (chapter 2, n 75) 219.
101 Mita Giacomini, 'One of These Things Is Not like the Others: The Idea of Precedence in Health Technology Assessment and Coverage Decisions' (2005) 83 The Milbank Quarterly 193, 215–217.
102 Daniels and Sabin, (chapter 2, n 36) 14–15.
103 Ibid., 14.
104 Lopes and others (chapter 2, n 92).
105 Amber Watt and others (chapter 2, n 93) 1039.
106 Sabik and Lie (chapter 2, n 75) 76–78.

3 Conclusions

In general, legal studies have explored the law and the right to health in HTA either through rights-based litigation or judicial review, and not as one of the relevant points of consideration by itself in regulations and decision criteria. This circumstance, also influenced by the limited instances where law has been explored systematically even by HTA bodies, seems unfortunate and does not allow deeper understanding of the legal issues in an HRBA. The focus on jurisprudence and court effects on A4R does not allow for reflection on what standards would govern HTA institutions if they were part of a deliberative democracy bound by human rights values.

To begin, the scope of law in HTA is much broader than just the external influence of courts. As this chapter has submitted, law should be understood as a factor to be gauged in internal decision-making either by becoming a topic in the technology study or in the frameworks that control the criteria and procedures in HTA. The right to health implementation is then the result of the interface of the two spheres of HTA and the law. In the internal relation, HTA plays host to all relevant legal factors affecting the deliberations, determining the legal standards, regulations and criteria. The application of the right to health, in turn, may be externally affected by courts, which may uphold or overrule HTA decisions. The same pattern may occur with the right to health, which may be broadened by the expansion of health services through HTA or restricted depending on how HTA is performed (as to the balance in equity, level of coverage or the fairness in the procedures).

An HRBA to HTA demands legal studies that consider HTA as a mechanism of public health regulation to strengthen a health system through laws supporting human rights (which are designed to facilitate resource realisation alongside distribution).[107] Relying on procedural justice managed by courts constrains any investigation away from the influence of the right to health within HTA bodies and may still be far from indicating fairness in priority-setting (noting all the criticism raised against overproceduralisation in the previous and current chapter).

Exactly because procedural justice is not foolproof, we must distinguish what an HRBA represents not only procedurally but also substantively for HTA, in particular by using the resource mobilisation principles provided by

107 World Health Organization, 'Advancing the Right to Health: The Vital Role of Law' (World Health Organization 2017) 11–12.

the right to health. Litigation research alone cannot reflect on what kind of principles would bind a deliberation if the criteria (or the relevance condition) were to reflect the current international human rights framework. It appears to be unlikely that in jurisdictions driven by utilitarian or other health-maximisation criteria, courts could review the decision to order a different or more appropriate method that follows rights-based substantive principles.

Doctrinal research must look at ways in which existing rights standards can be appropriated in HTA practice to enhance or impact internal decision-making on adoption of criteria, values and procedures compatible with human rights so that clear implementation behaviour can be promoted (and reviewed by courts, if needed). This is the precise reason for the current research, which could be beneficial even for litigation studies, delimiting substantive principles that can be used by courts in reviewing the lawfulness of HTA decisions. Legal scholarship should be able to answer what type of laws and regulations, within HTA, are in harmony with an HRBA substantively, including using evidence and criteria that reflect human rights principles.

In what follows, this book will further explain this argument of extending the scope of law and the right to health within HTA, delineating what an HRBA means substantively when engaging with scarcity. This doctrinal analysis will set out what the substantive policies around HTA should look like in terms of State conduct under the international human rights framework to guide concrete actions that should be taken by HTA bodies to realise the right to health. By contrast, procedural approaches do not help to deliver substantive policies to control scarcity and ensure that the best efforts are made to make a new technology available; instead, they accept economic pressures and costs as inflexible variables.

An HRBA should be regarded as a means to immediately embed human rights principles in this process to avoid discrimination and ensure that rights-holders enforce progressive realisation substantively, not constrained only by the notion of fair distribution. The following chapters move forward with an articulation of socio-economic principles most appropriate to resource allocation in order to include substantive values and standards to inform HTA decisions and criteria. Chapter 4 introduces the ground rules of socio-economic rights that integrate progressive realisation and maximum available resources throughout resource allocation. These standards will be further examined in Chapters 5, 6 and 7, considering principles of non-discrimination, international cooperation, and affordability applicable to an HRBA to HTA.

As the following chapter will show, the right to health can set out standards to verify whether the State is taking positive actions that prevent unnecessary rationing or make a coverage decision more possible. This could also change the way accountability is enforced through courts today (either by only examining the procedure or granting absolute rights) through a more extensive analysis of substantive policies that are integrated within HTA to promote access to new technologies.

PART 2

The Right to Health Framework

CHAPTER 4

The General Socio-economic Rights Framework for Resource Allocation and Scarcity in Healthcare

This chapter offers a broad fundamental framework to determine how the international right to health should guide priority-setting in the face of scarcity. This is an important step in laying the groundwork towards incorporating substantive principles into an HRBA to HTA – as proposed in this book – as the previous articulations of the right to health in resource allocation have neglected substantive aspects relative to resource mobilisation (see Chapter 2) charted in the remainder of this research. For many, the right to health is a path of little avail in discussions of healthcare policies and priorities. Given the competing claims that may be made under the right to health, Lie maintains that non-discrimination is the only legal principle that could apply to resource allocation because all human rights can provide is the obligation to do "something" about access to health, without designating what specifically.[1] As the right to health under international law does not ensure a clear orientation for decisions on competing health claims oscillating between individual needs, the whole community, and marginalised groups, defining priorities may seem to belong to health economics, medicine and the discretion of States.[2]

However, the main point defended in this chapter is that economic and social rights principles act simultaneously in resource distribution and mobilisation and, while this does not completely remove the competence of economists and clinicians to support priority-setting, it does create positive conditions for resource allocation beyond pre-determining the content of specific priorities or allowing a pure procedural approach. An example of how priorities are variable and difficult to pre-determine by applying the right to health is the COVID-19 pandemic. On the one hand, the need to control a contagious disease with the specific requirements of the novel coronavirus was not thoroughly defined by previous instruments and demanded coordination that had never been formulated on such a large scale, including the development of a

1 Reidar K Lie, 'Health, Human Rights and Mobilization of Resources for Health' (2004) 4 BMC International Health and Human Rights 4.

2 Laura Niada-Avshalom, 'Some Scepticism on the Right to Health: The Case of the Provision of Medicines' (2015) 19 The International Journal of Human Rights 527, 531–532, 540.

 | HTTPS://DOI.ORG/10.1163/9789004730311-005

vaccine and the supply of ventilators.[3] On the other hand, governments overcame unprecedented challenges by thinking creatively and seeking alternatives to maximise resources: swift set-up of low-cost pre-built or converted hospital rooms, accelerating the production of ventilators, or coordinating procurement strategies to secure enough vaccines.[4] This approach does not completely eliminate the need for priority-setting, but is a significant improvement in terms of progressive realisation rather than allowing preventable forms of scarcity to exist. The right to health standards, as advanced here, are less concerned with local priorities (which can vary among jurisdictions and specific realities over time) and more focused on how identified goals and healthcare needs will be achieved and genuine efforts to avoid scarcity.

Therefore, resource generation and distribution are two interdependent facets of scarcity in an HRBA and therein lies the main normative addition of socio-economic rights principles to orthodox procedural approaches to resource allocation and HTA. Instead of simply determining priorities in international law, this framework is designed to achieve an optimum level of resources in priority-setting in different local contexts. Thus, this chapter acknowledges that the right to health cannot pre-determine all resource priorities (as already outlined) and, instead, steers the decisions about solutions to the cause of the scarcity where possible. An economic and social rights framework can establish whether efforts are being taken to reverse scarcity, so lack of resources is not a blanket justification for all rationing decisions. Such a normative framework draws less on the content of the right to health and more on how general obligations common to all international socio-economic rights assist society to achieve priorities, remedying scarcity by appropriate means.

---

3 See e.g. Lisa Montel and others, 'The Right to Health in Times of Pandemic: What Can We Learn from the UK's Response to the COVID-19 Outbreak?' (2020) 22 Health and Human Rights 227. Dainius Pūras and others, 'The Right to Health Must Guide Responses to COVID-19' (2020) 395 The Lancet 1888; Kathleen Liddell and others, 'Who Gets the Ventilator? Important Legal Rights in a Pandemic' (2020) 46 Journal of Medical Ethics 421; Ezekiel J Emanuel and others, 'Fair Allocation of Scarce Medical Resources in the Time of Covid-19' (2020) 382 New England Journal of Medicine 2049.

4 See e.g. Frederick M Abbott and Jerome H Reichman, 'Facilitating Access to Cross-Border Supplies of Patented Pharmaceuticals: The Case of the COVID-19 Pandemic' (2020) 23 Journal of International Economic Law 535; Carlos López-Gómez and others, 'COVID-19 Critical Supplies: The Manufacturing Repurposing Challenge' (UNIDO, 2020) <https://www.unido.org/news/covid-19-critical-supplies-manufacturing-repurposing-challenge> accessed 1 September 2021; Simiao Chen and others, 'Fangcang Shelter Hospitals: A Novel Concept for Responding to Public Health Emergencies' (2020) 395 The Lancet 1305.

Drawing on international human rights law, this chapter considers three possible analytical approaches that can be adopted for interpreting State obligations in priority-setting decisions in general (and subsequently in HTA, the focus of this book). This doctrinal exercise asks which basic rules and principles we should look at to bind priority-setting decisions in healthcare under international economic and social rights. The first interpretation has the practical effect of a continuous commitment to finding resources where they become available and protecting against overstating the necessity of rationing, even though it cannot alone indicate priorities. The two other potential methods define areas of investment in healthcare, which may interact with each other and local decision-making in a less coherent way – a reason why the two latter approaches should not be recommended, despite indicating priorities.

- The first path is the *minimalist* approach derived only from regular treaty obligations. It considers what is provided under International Covenant on Economic, Social and Cultural Rights (ICESCR) provisions, which bring together the rules of maximum availability of resources and progressive realisation of rights, both assessed by the reasonableness doctrine. It serves to guarantee that the limitation of resources is not permanently used to legitimise automatic denial of socio-economic rights.
- A second alternative is an *intermediate* approach, from derived treaty obligations, which would use the Committee on Economic and Cultural Rights' (CESCR) recommendations to ascertain the core obligations under the right to health. From that point, the State would be liable to prioritise the essential levels of healthcare over other possible claims to the highest achievable standard of health. This interpretation would go beyond treaty obligations and conform to soft law created by the Committee on such matters as the most authoritative formulation of a hierarchy between the core and remaining obligations.
- The *expansive* approach would comprise all kinds of soft law issued by international organisations and would strive to accommodate those policy guidelines into local decisions from top-down governance, dictating what should be the local targets. This list of programmes and goals would be understood to represent the content of the right to health.

For each model, there is an underlying practical orientation to resource allocation. The first one would gear towards more than a fixed budget, pressuring for funds creation and cost reduction that would not take lack of economic means as an unchangeable reality. The second model would draw a baseline from which all priorities would converge, helping to judge what should be fulfilled immediately. The last variation, though extensive and complex, could list tan-

TABLE 4.1 Comparative summary of the main features of the different approaches under international human rights (Source: Author's own contribution)

Approach	Legal sources	Capacity to define specific resource destination	Legitimacy as to ICESCR parties and with reference to local priority-setting programmes	Definition of specific priorities	Application of socio-economic rights principles	Conflict with the content of the right to health
Minimalist (socio-economic approach)	Treaty-based	Low	High	Low	High	None
Core obligation	Treaty and general comments	Middle	Low	Middle	Low	Potential
Global Health Law	Global Health Law broadly (soft law)	High	Low	High	Low	High

gible targets that should be acted upon as a priority without a specific order, but with a more precise and delimited series of measures than the other two.

The attention here is directed at the management of resources solely with regard to the mobilisation process – the non-discrimination principle in distributing resources will be examined in Chapter 5 and the fair procedure aspects have been covered in Chapter 2 as normally developed by human rights. Each of the following sections will present one of the three different approaches to reading the international right to health in prioritisation, with its relevant sources and limitations in guiding policy-making.

1 The Minimalist Approach and the General Socio-economic Rights Stance on Scarcity

International socio-economic rights have a defiant stance towards scarcity, which is the spirit underpinning the minimalist approach. An HRBA to resource allocation in healthcare (and HTA) confronts the causes of scarcity.

In the face of scarcity in hospitals in Colombia, the CESCR recommended that the State "intensify its efforts to allocate sufficient resources", while also suggesting that the State should set forth appropriate tax reforms to reduce inequalities and increase "the resources available for the implementation of economic, social and cultural rights".[5] Other concluding observations of the Committee maintain the same rationale for recognising scarcity but also demand targeted actions and structural policy changes.[6] This is a fundamental stance, in contrast to the belief that human rights have entrenched neoliberalism and do no more than guarantee minimum levels of subsistence to support consumption.[7] Some would even say that, despite their potential to rebalance market power, historically human rights have achieved little in this regard.[8] Instead, they have nursed the same ideology as neoliberal thinking that forged the ascendency of capitalism and free markets.

This may be true to a certain degree; however, it may also be argued that socio-economic rights have a special character in times of recession and deprivation, which can benefit priority-setting in health. If there is anything the 2008–2009 economic crisis could teach us, it is that socio-economic rights can be promoted against austerity to generate solutions rather than surrendering to market forces.[9] This developing "new paradigm" of human rights

5 CESCR, "Concluding Observations on the Sixth Periodic Report of Colombia" 19 October 2017 (E/C.12/COL/CO/6), paras 19–20, 61–62.

6 See e.g. CESCR, "Concluding Observations on the Combined Second to Fourth Periodic Reports of Egypt"13 December 2013 (E/C.12/EGY/CO/2-4), para 21; "Concluding Observations on the Combined Third, Fourth and Fifth Periodic Reports of El Salvador", 19 June 2014 (E/C.12/SLV/CO/3-5) paras 21–23.

7 John Linarelli, Margot E Salomon and Muthucumaraswamy Sornarajah, *The Misery of International Law: Confrontations with Injustice in the Global Economy* (Oxford University Press 2018) 255–266.

8 See some of the accounts of the common origins of neoliberalism and human rights: Jessica Whyte, *The Morals of the Market: Human Rights and the Rise of Neoliberalism* (Verso Books 2019); Samuel Moyn, 'A Powerless Companion: Human Rights in the Age of Neoliberalism' (2014) 77 Law & Contemporary Problems. 147; Umut Ozsu, 'Neoliberalism and Human Rights: The Brandt Commission and the Struggle for a New World' (2018) 81 Law & Contemporary Problems 139; Joseph R Slaughter, 'Hijacking Human Rights: Neoliberalism, the New Historiography, and the End of the Third World' (2018) 40 Human Rights Quarterly 735, 765–769.

9 See e.g. David Bilchitz, 'Socio-Economic Rights, Economic Crisis, and Legal Doctrine' (2014) 12 International Journal of Constitutional Law 710; Aoife Nolan (ed), *Economic and Social Rights after the Global Financial Crisis* (Cambridge University Press 2014); Markus Krajewski, 'Human Rights and Austerity Programmes' in Christian Tietje, Rosa M Lastra and Thomas Cottier (eds), *The Rule of Law in Monetary Affairs: World Trade Forum* (Cambridge University Press 2014); Julia Dehm, 'Righting Inequality: Human Rights Responses to Economic Inequality in the United Nations' (2019) 10 Humanity: An International Journal of Human

calls for substantial State intervention, with rekindled interest in implementation and institutionalisation of HRBA in economic policies or for reducing inequality.[10] Among a variety of alternatives to scarcity, human rights scholars have appealed to taxation, monetary policies, market regulation and alternative instruments to support budgets or bankroll the public debt.[11]

Thus, socio-economic rights, while not always successful, may stand against neoliberal ideology in favour of the private market and support the welfare State and healthcare spending.[12] Since this reinvigorated attention to socio-economic rights, it has been possible to carve out some substantive principles for priority-setting decisions in HTA, as norms in international socio-economic rights practice have been unpacked over time to deal with resource constraints. International socio-economic rights have been associated with "constructive" or "expansive" visions to resources and scarcity, such as progressive realisation, maximum available resources, non-retrogressive measures and proportionality, as per Article 2.1 of the ICESCR.

The renewed impetus towards political economy to avoid scarcity has led to much clarification of State obligations and standard of review of rights implementation to demand, in times of crisis, policy alternatives that would prevent rights violations through provision of additional resources.[13] The growth-focused socio-economic rights standards were further developed in the 2010 response to successive global recessions.[14] In 2012, to warn States

Rights, Humanitarianism, and Development 443, 453–454. Radhika Balakrishnan, James Heintz and Diane Elson, *Rethinking Economic Policy for Social Justice: The Radical Potential of Human Rights* (Routledge 2016) 28–41.

10 Matthias Goldmann, 'Contesting Austerity: Genealogies of Human Rights Discourse' [2020] Max Planck Institute for Comparative Public Law & International Law (MPIL) Research Paper 35–44. Rodrigo Uprimny Yepes and Sergio Chaparro Hernández, 'Inequality, Human Rights, and Social Rights: Tensions and Complementarities' (2019) 10 Humanity: An International Journal of Human Rights, Humanitarianism, and Development 376, 387–389.

11 Magdalena Sepúlveda Carmona, 'Alternatives to Austerity: A Human Rights Framework for Economic Recovery' in Aoife Nolan (ed), *Economic and Social Rights after the Global Financial Crisis* (Cambridge University Press 2014) 25–30.

12 Audrey R Chapman, *Global Health, Human Rights and the Challenge of Neoliberal Policies* (Cambridge University Press 2016) 92–102.

13 David Birchall, 'Human Rights and Political Economy: Violations and Realization under Global Capitalism' [2021] SSRN Electronic Journal 11–15 <http://dx.doi.org/10.2139/ssrn.3780591> accessed 5 May 2021; Ann Blyberg and Helena Hofbauer, *Article 2 and Governments' Budgets* (International Budget Partnership 2014) 2 <https://www.internationalbudget.org/publications/escrarticle2/> accessed 21 February 2021.

14 Jernej Letnar Černič, 'The European Court of Human Rights, Rule of Law and Socio-Economic Rights in Times of Crises' (2016) 8 Hague Journal on the Rule of Law 227, 234–243.

of their obligations under the Covenant, the CESCR advised that restrictions should be:

1. A temporary measure, covering only the period of the crisis
2. Necessary and proportionate
3. Non-discriminatory and should mitigate inequalities that can grow in times of crisis (including through tax measures to support transfers to the most marginalised)
4. It [the State] should identify and protect the "minimum core content" or "social protection floor" (as defined by the ILO) of the rights and ensure the protection of this core content at all times.[15]

Despite not being able to undertake ambitious challenges to capitalism or against retrogressive measures, the CESCR turned its attention to inequality, unfair tax policies and the need to obtain resources through international cooperation to fulfil human rights duties.[16] More recently, human rights bodies (including the CESCR) have adopted a fairly nonconformist interpretation of the role of socio-economic rights against retrogressive measures and market liberalisation, especially during the COVID-19 pandemic to identify alternatives to the crisis.[17]

Another example of this trend of criticism towards inflexibility, in a similar context to HTA, is human rights budget-making.[18] As a form of HRBA to economic policies, human rights budget-making seeks to measure socio-economic rights compliance by tracking resource allocation with an approach more combative towards scarcity levels in order to seek resource mobilisa-

---

15 CESCR, "An Open Letter" 16 May 2012 (CESCR/48th/SP/MAB/SW).

16 Aoife Nolan, 'Not Fit for Purpose? Human Rights in Times of Financial and Economic Crisis' (2015)' 4 European Human Rights Law Review 358. See Warwick on the relaxation of the non-retrogressive doctrine and the avoidance to deal with non-retrogression obligations after the financial crisis: Ben TC Warwick, 'Socio-Economic Rights during Economic Crises: A Changed Approach to Non-Retrogression' (2016) 65 International & Comparative Law Quarterly 249; Ben TC Warwick, 'A Hierarchy of Comfort? The CESCR's Approach to the 2008 Economic Crisis' in Gillian MacNaughton and Diane F Frey (eds), *Economic and Social Rights in a Neoliberal World* (Cambridge University Press 2018) 143–146.

17 See e.g. CESCR, 'Statement on the Coronavirus Disease (COVID-19) Pandemic and Economic, Social and Cultural Rights', 6 April 2020 (E/C.12/2020/1) paras 13, 17, 19, 21; European Committee of Social Rights, 'Statement of Interpretation on the Right to Protection of Health in Times of Pandemic', statement (Strasbourg, 21 April 2020), pp. 3–6, https://rm.coe.int/statement-of-interpretation-on-the-right-to-protection-of-health-in-ti/16809e3640, accessed in 20 December 2020.

18 See e.g. UN OHCHR, *Realizing Human Rights through Government Budgets* (United Nations, 2017) <http://www.ohchr.org/Documents/Publications/RealizingHRThroughGovernmentBudgets.pdf>.

tion. HRBA to budget-making and HTA have at least a common principle of public participation and community involvement in the decisions that require changes in the design of public institutions.[19]

This is not to say that human rights budget-making is immune to criticism and, indeed, there are still problems with conceptual issues in the socio-economic rights framework, such as the already mentioned non-retrogression doctrine.[20] In rationing and procedural approaches for healthcare resource allocation, however, scarcity is taken as a fixed condition, while in human rights budget strategies this is not accepted. While health and human rights are viewed as questions of rationing and competition among scarce resources, human rights budgeting strategies envisage an opportunity for exercising economic policies and political control of available resources so as to encourage States to take seriously their obligations and also to debunk the notion that nothing else can be done.[21] The OHCHR has advised governments that budgets should be maximised through the State policy space with fiscal measures such as taxation (targeting additional sources of revenue without increasing social inequalities) and increasing the public deficit.[22]

The main conclusion is that at the very least socio-economic rights demonstrate some resistance and nonconformism to scarcity. In contrast, scholars writing on the right to health are reluctant to contest scarcity or even reject the supremacy of cost-effectiveness in the same way as other socio-economic rights have been advanced.[23] As a health budget decision-making entity, it will be shown that HTA can be governed by human rights principles similar to other budget-making institutions and can address the political economy issues that human rights have previously been deferential to in rationing health.[24] The socio-economic rights framework, in an HRBA to HTA developed throughout this book, lays out substantive principles to access to resources while making democratic deliberations, mindful that there is space to reduce scarcity within healthcare policy-making.

---

19 Jaakko Kuosmanen, 'Towards "Human Rights Compatible" Public Budgets – an Account of Institutional Virtues' (2016) 64 Political Studies 683.

20 On conceptual limitations of socio-economic rights in budget analysis, see Aoife Nolan, 'Putting ESR-Based Budget Analysis into Practice: Addressing the Conceptual Challenges' in Aoife Nolan (ed), *Human rights and public finance: Budgets and the promotion of economic and social rights* (2013).

21 Blyberg and Hofbauer (n 13) 13–24.

22 UN Office of the High Commissioner on Human Rights (n 18) 47–87.

23 See chapter 2, pp 31–33.

24 Amy Kapczynski, 'The Right to Medicines in an Age of Neoliberalism' (2019) 10 Humanity: An International Journal of Human Rights, Humanitarianism, and Development 79, 79–80.

1.1 Minimalistic Approach: Measuring State Conducts through the ICESCR

The progressive stance of socio-economic rights against scarcity is based on key principles set out in the ICESCR, Article 2.1. In this section, it is maintained that the international socio-economic rights framework provides principles to determine which substantive conducts are forms of implementation of the right to health in resource allocation. This approach combines the rules on maximum available resources, progressive realisation and the reasonableness standard to identify conducts to prevent scarcity where possible. Socio-economic rights have obligations of "conduct" (a State action towards a priority) or "result" (the priority itself). Result obligations should be measured by a definite outcome, while conduct obligations are complied with by determined acts or moves, not fundamentally dependent on achieving a result to be fulfilled.[25] Where States are unable to secure full implementation of a determined health priority, the alternative is to focus on resource generation conducts.

Thus, the key idea is that States are obliged to undertake specific conducts to seek the resources and measures that make progressive realisation of outcomes possible.[26] These conducts are policies that should take place simultaneously with resource allocation (e.g. to reduce taxation of medical imports to guarantee affordability) so that the results are possible.[27] Considering that priorities can only be set at a particular time and in a particular context, what is at stake is not deriving priorities from the right to health (results), but enforcing the conducts that are fundamental for progressing towards local priorities in health as ultimate results.

Yet, there is much ambiguity surrounding conducts and results as international obligations. The International Law Commission (ILC), in the context of State responsibility, has concluded that obligations of means were related to specific conducts or omissions, and results were to be valued by outcomes

25 The contentious point here is whether socio-economic rights oblige specific conducts or multiple course of actions. See Guy S Goodwin-Gill, 'Obligations of Conduct and Result' in Paul Alston and Katarina Tomasevski (eds), *The Right to Food* (Martinus Nijhoff 1984) 112–113.

26 Langford and King present an overview of the conduct/result dispute see: Malcolm Langford and Jeff A King, 'Committee on Economic, Social and Cultural Rights' in Malcolm Langford (ed), *Social Rights Jurisprudence* (Cambridge University Press 2009) 483–486

27 This argument is further explained in chapter 7, pp. 177–183.

only.[28] The effect was to leave wide "wriggle room" to States to decide on their course of action to meet the obligation of result, while obligations of conduct allow no other path than the specified conduct.[29]

Overall, a hybrid approach to conducts and results is more suitable to achieving socio-economic rights realisation through "taking steps" (conducts), but also to securing results, conditions permitting.[30] Despite the importance of conducts to mobilise resources, it is quite common to assume that socio-economic obligations always correspond to results, as this has been argued to be the practice of the CESCR, despite the typology not being uniformly referenced.[31] The Committee itself could not establish a sharp division between the two, since General Comment 14 accepts both forms of obligation, without declaring which of the Convention's obligations correspond to each category or both.[32] This ambiguity is fraught with an almost circular reasoning to isolate conducts from results, which would be a "more than futile, if complex, exercise", as Sepulveda warns.[33]

As a consequence, in resource allocation, it can be assumed that conduct obligations prevail when results cannot be immediately executed – States have an obligation of result when they have resources, if not, they must take steps (obligations of conduct). That is the understanding advocated by Alston and Quinn, whereby determining conducts (steps) is the only immediately realis-

28 See Roberto Ago, 'Document A/CN.4/302 and ADD.1–3 (Sixth Report on State Responsibility)' (1977) II Yearbook of the International Law Commission 3.

29 Ibid.

30 Eibe Riedel, Gilles Giacca and Christophe Golay, 'The Development of Economic, Social, and Cultural Rights in International Law' in Eibe Riedel, Gilles Giacca and Christophe Golay (eds), *Economic, Social, and Cultural Rights in International Law: Contemporary Issues and Challenges* (Oxford University Press 2014) 18. Compare also the example of the Convention on the Elimination of Racial Discrimination, joining the two obligations: Rudiger Wolfrum, 'Obligations of Result Versus Obligations of Conduct' in Mahnoush H Arsanjani and W Michael Reisman (eds) and *Looking to the Future: Essays on International Law in honor of W. Michael Reisman* (Martinus Nijhoff Publishers 2011) 380–381.

31 See e.g. David Beetham, 'What Future for Economic and Social Rights?' (1995) 43 Political Studies 41, 49.

32 CESCR, "General Comment No. 3: 'The Nature of States Parties' Obligations' (GC 3)" 14 December 1990 (E/1991/23), para. 1. Comments in Lisa Forman and others, 'Conceptualising Minimum Core Obligations under the Right to Health: How Should We Define and Implement the "Morality of the Depths" (2016) 20 The International Journal of Human Rights 531, 538.

33 Magdalena Sepúlveda Carmona, *The Nature of the Obligations under the International Covenant on Economic, Social and Cultural Rights* (Intersentia 2003) 195.

able obligation in socio-economic rights.[34] Fukuda-Parr et al. also uphold that outcomes are not sufficient to measure State compliance, and given the circumstances that are not under the control of a government, the focus should be on the conducts.[35] When a State fails to achieve results, it has at least to take obligatory and concrete "steps" proportionate to its capacity.[36] The main question rests upon how to discern what the corresponding conducts are so as to make more resources available when allocating them. Among the possibilities are, price regulation of healthcare products and services, taxation, price control, patent pooling, enforcement of competition regulation, public–private partnerships, international purchase cooperation, and resort to intellectual property flexibilities.[37]

Those measures are specific to local conditions and the nature of the health good to be attained, and no single set of conducts can be devised or anticipated without particular attention to the healthcare need concerned (this is different from normal obligations of conducts described by the ILC, as the conducts are not predetermined). If no measures are possible, then there is no immediate necessity of result. Attention to conducts departs considerably from a "violation approach" to socio-economic rights. Since what is measured are the efforts to realise human rights and mobilise resources, it is much more a question of violation by omission than by State action, as described in the typology proposed by Chapman and endorsed by the Limburg Principles (a statement made by an expert group in the Netherlands in 1980) and some decisions of the Committee.[38]

A violation approach requires the commission of acts "as policies or laws that create conditions inimical to the realization of recognized rights".[39] It is established by (1) violations resulting from actions and policies of govern-

34 Philip Alston and Gerard Quinn, 'The Nature and Scope of States Parties' Obligations under the International Covenant on Economic, Social and Cultural Rights' (1987) 9 Human Rights Quarterly 156, 165–166.

35 Sakiko Fukuda-Parr, Terra Lawson-Remer and Susan Randolph, *Fulfilling Social and Economic Rights* (Oxford University Press 2015) 22.

36 See e.g. how "steps" are viewed as results in General Comment No. 3: "The principal obligation of result reflected in article 2(l) is to take steps 'with a view to achieving progressively the full realisation of the rights recognised'", Manisuli Ssenyonjo, 'Reflections on State Obligations with Respect to Economic, Social and Cultural Rights in International Human Rights Law' (2011) 15 The International Journal of Human Rights 969, 977.

37 See chapter 7, 2, pp. 185–198.

38 Audrey R Chapman, 'A Violations Approach for Monitoring the International Covenant on Economic, Social and Cultural Rights' (1996) 18 Human Rights Quarterly 23, 43.

39 Ibid.

ments; (2) violations related to patterns of discrimination; and (3) violations related to a State's failure to fulfil the minimum core obligations of enumerated rights.[40] This classification refers to positive actions and omissions in such a way that conducts and progressive realisation would not actually occur in practice. To implement some health policies, States must undertake conducts of resource mobilisation to accomplish obligations of result. During progressive realisation, the primary obligations lie more on undertaking certain conducts, such as in market regulation, than to not interfering with rights (excluding healthcare for certain groups) or directly fulfilling an obligation of result (establishing a health service). Although there is no list of specific conducts to achieve obligations of result, some general principles that identify conducts States should undertake are set out in Article 2(1) ICESCR, which reads:

> Each State Party to the present Covenant undertakes to take steps, individually and through international assistance and co-operation, especially economic and technical, to the maximum of its available resources, with a view to achieving progressively the full realization of the rights recognized in the present Covenant by all appropriate means, including particularly the adoption of legislative measures.

This is a very intricate Article but two main concepts stand out: maximum availability of resources and progressive realisation.[41] Because not all priorities can be immediately achieved, progressive realisation and maximum availability of resources are two immediate conduct obligations in resource allocation (through policies connected with efforts to manage and expand resources through deliberations or by financing mechanisms, such as taxation, etc.). As the Article emphasises "adoption of legislative measures", conducts consisting only of legislative measures (as in market regulation) may likely be regarded as immediately realisable obligations for not being contingent on existing resources, yet being used to generate more resources.[42]

Further, such State conduct must be towards a legitimate obligation of result within the right to health in keeping with the general principles of the ICESCR and aforementioned Article 2.1. Just as the Covenant is silent on the

40 Chapman, (n 38) 43.
41 Matthew CR Craven, *The International Covenant on Economic, Social, and Cultural Rights: A Perspective on Its Development* (Clarendon Press 1998) 151; Ssenyonjo (n 36) 974.
42 Langford and King (n 26) 486–489.

list of appropriate conduct obligations in resource mobilisation, it is broad and vague on the possible health priorities that must be fulfilled by the State as obligations of result. The Covenant enumerates programmatic results that should be taken for the full realisation of the right to health, but with no hierarchy.[43] Every step should fall within this broader list, but the actual conduct of States in complying with these obligations is subject to the method of assessment of the implementation of socio-economic rights (progressive realisation/maximum available resources). Moreover, this interpretation does not engage with the principle of non-retrogression, which has been referred to by the Committee as the principle of continuity of enjoyment of rights achievements, a legal doctrine not explicitly included as a treaty obligation and still not fully elaborated.[44] The framework as provided by the Covenant, therefore, can be summarised in Figure 4.1:

The next three subsections will turn to the practical effects of each of the principles that determine the State obligations of conduct in resource alloca-

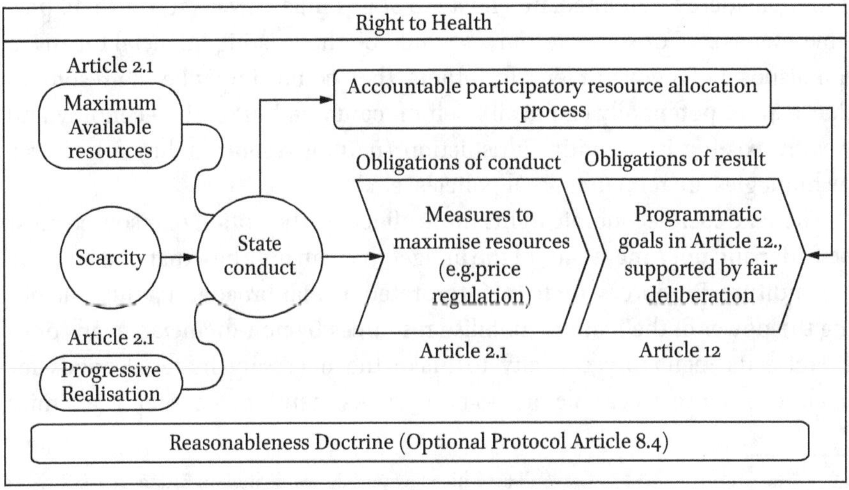

FIGURE 4.1 International right to health sources under the ICESCR associated with different State obligations and the State conduct to mitigate scarcity

43 ICESCR (chapter 1, n 31) Art. 12: It sets outs the following targets: "a) reduction of the stillbirth-rate and of infant mortality and for the healthy development of the child; b) improvement of all aspects of environmental and industrial hygiene, c) prevention, treatment, and control of epidemic, endemic and occupational diseases, d) conditions to assure all medical care for the sick".

44 Ben TC Warwick, 'Unwinding Retrogression: Examining the Practice of the Committee on Economic, Social and Cultural Rights' (2019) 19 Human Rights Law Review 467, 468–475.

tion for local health priorities. After exploring the two principles of Article 2(1) (maximum available resources and progressive realisation), the reasonableness standard will be integrated into this approach to help to define the substantive policies that must be in place in health priority-setting as a State conduct.

1.2 Maximum Available Resources

In resource allocation, the principle of maximum available resources aids in the determination of the extent to which governments must devote resources to realising socio-economic rights. In general, the Committee has understood this level of resources to be contextual with local capacities.[45] The idea of maximum available resources can be contradictory since "maximum" is the ideal while "available" is the reality, as Robertson reminds us.[46] However, no matter what the level of resources, the obligation to maximise their availability is considered of immediate effect (so States must always resort to all possible means).[47] For some, resources would be the existing financial means at the disposal of a government; for others, they could simply be the resources that a State potentially can avail itself of, contained in all the economy and wealth existing in an entire jurisdiction (natural resources, human capital, technologies, incremental fiscal policies, etc.)[48]

To make socio-economic rights more effective, the notion of resource must be wider and not a mere slice of the budget that can only be expanded by more expenditure. Resources are to be interpreted in a far broader manner, including the power of the State to mobilise resources by non-financial means or to exercise its regulatory capacity to make the necessary material goods for healthcare more accessible or less costly.[49] As mentioned earlier, academics

45 See Craven (n 41) 136. Craven bases his view on Badawi El Sheikh, E/C.12/1989/SR.7.

46 Robert E Robertson, 'Measuring State Compliance with the Obligation to Devote the Maximum Available Resources to Realizing Economic, Social, and Cultural Rights' (1994) 16 Human Rights Quarterly 693, 694.

47 Rodrigo Uprimny, Sergio Chaparro Hernández and Andrés Castro Araújo, 'Bridging the Gap: The Evolving Doctrine on ESCR and "Maximum Available Resources"' in Katharine G Young (ed), *The Future of Economic and Social Rights* (Cambridge University Press 2019) 629.

48 Radhika Balakrishnan and Douglass College, 'Maximum Available Resources & Human Rights: Analytical Report' (Center for Women's Global Leadership 2011) 2, CRC, Day of General Discussion on 'Resources for the Rights of the Child – Responsibility of States', 46th session, 21 September 2007 (CRC/C/46/CRP.1), para. 24.

49 Robertson (n 46) 704–713.

and treaty-body reports are increasingly conscious that resource capacity is not only ascertained through available funds.[50] The portfolio of measures proposed by treaty-bodies and experts revolves around traditional macroeconomic market interventions concerning fiscal, monetary and budget policies to mobilise potential resources.[51]

The more restrictive the notion of resources, the lower the onus of socio-economic rights on the State. If resources are just the current financial capacity of a State, it may be assumed that the State would be allowed to indefinitely allocate the same level of resources to comply with the right to health (at least at a given time). How resource availability is expanded can sometimes be construed strictly as a form of money transfer (either internationally through external State assistance, in an early opinion held by treaty-bodies, and now through taxation, as developed by experts and in the general comments after the 2008–2009 financial crisis).[52] Kendrick adopts this view when proposing a method of determining the level of resources that should be expected to be reserved to the right to health under a particular economic situation by taking into account only financial resources.[53] However, this approach cannot quantify how much a State can gain through efficiency in utilising its political resources that would reduce cost or increase the production of healthcare products and services. Socio-economic rights can justify economic policy decisions and regulation of private actors that would not be achieved if there was no State involvement.[54]

The Committee has so far only partially developed a doctrine to measure additional resources that can be availed by each country, concentrating on tax policies and lost revenue. Uprimny et al. propose some key points of analysis, which draw on some of the interpretations of the Committee (such as the presumption that resources were insufficiently employed where core obligations are violated or corruption as evidence of improper use of resources).[55] An emerging doctrine of maximum available resources, as described by Uprimny,

50 See e.g. chapter 1, pp. 15–17, and chapter 3, p. 65.

51 For instance, Balakrishnan et al. examine the creation of resources for human rights reviewing: "(1) government expenditure; (2) government revenue; (3) development assistance (both official development assistance and private resource flows); (4) debt and deficit financing; and (5) monetary policy and financial regulation": Balakrishnan and Douglass College (n 48) 5.

52 Ibid.

53 Abby Kendrick, 'Measuring Compliance: Social Rights and the Maximum Available Resources Dilemma' (2017) 39 Human Rights Quarterly 657, 669–678.

54 Wiktor Osiatynski, *Human Rights and Their Limits* (Cambridge University Press 2009) 136–137.

55 Uprimny, Chaparro Hernández and Araújo (n 47) 649–653.

is being delineated, though there are still difficulties to determine methods of measuring the failure to use all available resources.

1.3 Progressive Realisation

As resources are mobilised, progressive realisation comes into operation. This principle presupposes a continuous level of implementation over time – a feature that for too long has been unfairly associated only with socio-economic rights as a way of distinguishing them from immediately realisable civil and political rights.[56] A form of non-compliance with progressive realisation may be found where there has been no growth in expenditure with rights-related investments for a long period while the economy has grown.[57] Steps should be constantly implemented and the condition of progressivity should not be argued to unduly defer compliance.[58] Hence, under the Covenant, States are not only obliged to make efforts to their maximum ability but also to uninterruptedly seek to go further through progressive realisation. The Limburg Principles assume that it is not fundamental that more resources are employed, as long as there is expeditious expansion of the realisation of rights with a focused programme: "the obligation of progressive achievement exists independently of the increase in resources; it requires effective use of resources available".[59] Effective, in this sense, means actual application of all available resources (which do not necessarily need to be financial, as with "societal resources").[60] In that sense, non-economic resources may also be taken into account when developing policies that enhance the enjoyment of rights in a country, including regulatory State powers such as price controls.

As outlined above, the idea of progressive realisation is not just a deliberative procedure to rearrange a health system for cost-effectiveness but an obligation to forge ahead continuously finding solutions for financial constraints

---

56 Ssenyonjo (n 36) 977; For the usages beyond socio-economic rights, see: E Brems, 'Human Rights: Minimum and Maximum Perspectives' (2009) 9 Human Rights Law Review 349, 365.

57 See e.g. CESCR, "Concluding observations: Angola", 1 December 2008 (E/C.12/AGO/CO3) para. 20.

58 Shareen Hertel and Lanse Minkler, 'Economic Rights: The Terrain' in Shareen Hertel and Lanse Minkler (eds), *Economic Rights: Conceptual measurement and policy issues* (Cambridge University Press 2007) 17.

59 Cornelis Flinterman, '"Limburg Principles on the Implementation of the International Covenant on Economic, Social and Cultural Rights"(1987)' 9 Human Rights Quarterly 122.

60 Ibid., art. 24.

by effective usage of any other available resource.[61] This contrasts with the interpretation advanced by global health scholars, who claim that the minimum basket of health services offered to the majority of the population – known as Universal Health Coverage (UHC) – has its progressive realisation ensured by public accountability and setting priorities around the most cost-effective interventions.[62] This progressive realisation as a procedure presupposes identifying priorities without heeding efforts to expand the budget or intervening in structural policies that maximise available resources, rather than simply reallocating them. If a health system needs reorganisation and has sufficient funds, that could be enough to redistribute the coverage in a manner that would satisfy equity considerations and population needs. Conversely, if there are structural barriers related to insufficient funding or inadequate market regulation that depend on extra efforts, a procedure would generally not remedy unavailability or unaffordability of some healthcare services.

A problem with progressive realisation is that it does not define in itself what the State conducts are that should permanently be pursued. Because there is more than one single method to achieve a higher level of enjoyment of rights, this principle does not in itself indicate the right pathway of progress, which could vary according to the local reality or the order of obligations pursued.[63] Jacobs argues for a dialogical and cooperative interpretation of progressive realisation, taking into account all stakeholders – from NGOs, international bodies, governments and civil society – that build this notion according to the local constraints and priorities.[64]

Conversely, international law already provides a mechanism for interpretation of the Covenant obligations that can help us estimate what is permissible in a State's powers under the doctrine of reasonableness, as presented in the next subsection. Reasonableness serves to establish a range of conducts according to the State's circumstances, which should represent substantive policies in addressing resource mobilisation and progressive realisation along-

61 Rob Baltussen and others, 'Progressive Realisation of Universal Health Coverage: What Are the Required Processes and Evidence?' (2017) 2 BMJ Global Health e000342, 6. Compare with Lisa Forman, 'Decoding the Right to Health: What Could It Offer to Global Health?' (2015) 8 Bioethica Forum 7, 93.

62 Baltussen and others (n 61) 2–5.

63 On progressive realisation's lack of concreteness, see: Lesley A Jacobs, 'Adapting Locally to International Health and Human Rights Standards: An Alternative Theoretical Framework for Progressive Realisation' in MR Madsen and G Verschraegen (eds), *Making Human Rights Intelligible: Towards a Sociology of Human Rights* (Hart 2013).

64 Ibid.

side priority-setting. Since progressive realisation needs to be interpreted in conjunction with the requirement of maximum available resources, it is necessary to adopt a more "robust" interpretative approach to substantive policies towards rights realisation, rather than only accepting that a fair procedure is the only reasonable conduct.[65] This robust approach to reasonableness as regards local priorities asks what conducts can be feasibly undertaken if the State is truly committed to exhausting all possible forms of policies (maximum available resources) in a specific health goal without reducing other services and how it may interfere with the market to this effect.

1.4 Defining State Conduct: The Role of Strong Reasonableness

The reasonableness standard sets the boundaries of progressive realisation and maximum available resources against scarcity. As a legal doctrine, reasonableness has, per se, a degree of deference to the State and should provide a list of programmes that a particular government could adopt until an obligation is satisfied, while not determining a preferred course of action regarding health policies. As described by Arosemena, reasonableness is a means to provide an "adverbialisation" of conducts, meaning that it can qualify efforts that are appropriate to transcend scarcity.[66] The argument is that reasonableness places on the State the burden of confronting scarcity where it is avoidable and proves that economic deficiency is the final justification for non-compliance with the progressive realisation of rights. Under international socio-economic rights, reasonableness should not be confused with its narrow scope under other branches of international law or philosophy of law.[67] Both are related to providing justification or rationales (which would be deemed reasonable). Scarcity could be one of those arguments admitting rationing below maximum resources but it is argued here that the full potential of reasonableness is not simply to accept scarcity in a static and resigned manner.

As compared to other elements stipulated under the ICESCR, reasonableness has a less solid base, as it is not found in the original treaty, but in the Optional Protocol to the Covenant, which inaugurated an individual com-

65 Gustavo Arosemena, *Rights, Scarcity, and Justice: An Analytical Inquiry into the Adjudication of the Welfare Aspects of Human Rights* (Intersentia 2014) 109.

66 Ibid., 99–101.

67 For an overview of reasonableness under international law, see: Olivier Corten, 'Reasonableness in International Law', *Max Planck Encyclopedias of International Law* (Oxford University Press) <https://www.oxfordbibliographies.com/view/document/obo-9780199796953/obo-9780199796953-0127.xml> accessed 27 July 2019.

plaint mechanism to the monitoring system.[68] This standard resulted from long negotiations in the drafting of the protocol when some State-Parties were not sufficiently convinced that the oversight of the treaty obligation would not create undue interference in domestic affairs.[69] An alternative standard of review in the debates was the proposal of emphasising the margin of appreciation of States to determine the measures required to implement the Covenant, but that also instilled the fear that the new mechanism would be significantly restricted.[70]

Additionally, little has been published that attempts to define the real meaning of reasonableness so as to operationalise it in relation to what should be considered a resource and mobilise it for the right to health. Tobin observes that "international law accommodates the reality of the need for States to prioritise the allocation of scarce resources, provided a state is able to demonstrate that the process for allocating these resources can be shown to be reasonable".[71] However, Tobin examines reasonableness only as to rationing and cost-containment and does not touch upon what could be deemed reasonable as concomitant policies to scarcity or make the market more accessible to patients. Tobin's conceptual inventory enumerates only the observance of human rights principles (as set out by the CESCR, and in particular non-discrimination), evidence-based medicine and accountability conventions that are akin to Daniels' model described (in a form of a process) as being "consultative, participatory, transparent and evaluative".[72] Reasonableness, to Tobin, is an extended version of accountability for reasonableness (A4R) where the relevant criteria are determined both by medical expertise and human rights principles.

As to linking reasonableness with progressive realisation and resources in health, a most successful attempt would be from Perehudoff et al. who proffer a complete framework that addresses the value of reasonableness to counter scarcity.[73] The reason why Perehudoff et al. set out a more comprehensive view of reasonableness is that it directly harmonises the principles of max-

68 UN General Assembly, 'Optional Protocol to the International Covenant on Economic, Social and Cultural Rights' 10 December 2008 (A/RES/63/117).

69 Brian Griffey, 'The "Reasonableness" Test: Assessing Violations of State Obligations under the Optional Protocol to the International Covenant on Economic, Social and Cultural Rights' (2011) 11 Human Rights Law Review 275, 301.

70 Ibid.

71 John Tobin, *The Right to Health in International Law* (Oxford University Press 2011) 226.

72 Ibid., 237.

73 Katrina Perehudoff and Lisa Forman, 'What Constitutes "Reasonable" State Action on Core Obligations? Considering a Right to Health Framework to Provide Essential Medicines' (2019) 11 Journal of Human Rights Practice 1, 9–16.

imum availability of resources and progressive realisation with indicators of reasonable measures (such as duties to mobilise resources, seek low-cost alternatives and obtain external assistance, which include, for instance, price reduction and intellectual property mechanisms). This conceptualisation of reasonableness does not spring from resource allocation per se but primarily considers the implementation of the obligation of access to medicines. Their view is significant inasmuch as it is a deviation from the normal understanding that scarcity is a barrier for a reasonable expectation of government measures and that resource allocation under the right to health remains limited to procedural aspects without forcing the expansion of the current budget. Reasonableness, as outlined by the authors, questions the sufficiency of resources and the capacity of the State to marshal extra funds and execute other policies that positively address scarcity. For them, the focus on the distribution of resources, evading other measures:

> is akin to questioning whether the host has fairly divided the cake among expectant partygoers before asking if the cake was in fact made large enough to satisfy all celebrants. Not to explore the options to maximize resources and leverage efficiencies would be a disservice to the government's capacity to realize rights and to those who stand to benefit from more targeted and efficient use of resources.[74]

However, a concern that can be raised when invoking a reasonableness standard relates to the domestic courts that originally developed it and how deferential they proved to be. This is what can be denominated as the weak form of reasonableness. In a weak approach, a mere formal assessment of reasonableness would rest on considering procedural aspects of the decision, the governance of the policies and whether the rationale was appropriate to pursue a goal, without discussing the content of the right.[75] This would result in considering a priority-setting decision solely on the basis of how the decision-making took place in terms of participation and public justification.

In South Africa, reasonableness received criticism for being too deferential to the scarcity of resources, as courts were not always able to determine whether the State had failed to promote other feasible courses of action. Griffey points out how reasonableness has been inconsistently employed in different jurisdictions – in the case of the South African Constitutional Court, limitations are due also to the SA constitutional text, which, different from the

74 Ibid., 1, 2.

75 Arosemena (n 65) 105–108.

Covenant, requires only "access to" and not "adequate levels" of socio-economic rights.[76] It might be conceivable that the Court did not coordinate reasonableness with two other international norms (progressive realisation and maximum resources) – so that not much thought went into the feasible alternatives that should have been explored to discharge State obligation. The hurdles of adjudication in South Africa are related to judicial mechanisms entrenched in an administrative law model that could not give reasonableness wide-enough scope.[77] Moreover, the views of courts should be distinguished from the prescriptive nature of an HRBA, which is focused on formulating policies and incorporating international standards into practice.

Being an independent legal regime, international law can advance the reasonableness standard in a manner not constrained to the SA jurisprudence, which proved to be incapable of maintaining the criteria it set for itself in *Grootboom*.[78] As contended here, reasonableness is the linking element that can offer interpretative support to the obligations (conducts) that are already directly laid down under the Covenant and the Additional Protocol, which could be further interpreted by the CESCR. In this sense, reasonableness is a measure of sufficient effort of progressive realisation and maximum availability of resources as a standard of review recognised in international law.[79]

2 The Intermediate Approach and Core Obligations

A more robust variant of reasonableness engages with core obligations to establish clear cut-off points by which the denial of certain healthcare services is unjustifiable, therefore, such provisions are a central priority.[80] At present, this interpretation remains impractical without a broader consensus over the content of core obligations under international law that would strip from the States the final word on the essential level of healthcare (in their context). As Forman puts it, the absence of a conceptualisation of core obligations precludes the assessment of reasonable steps towards the most pressing health needs for priority-setting or the key issues that should be addressed at the

76 Griffey (n 69) 314.

77 Stuart Wilson and Jackie Dugard, 'Constitutional Jurisprudence' in Malcolm Langford and others (eds), *Socio-Economic Rights in South Africa* (Cambridge University Press 2013) 44.

78 Ibid., 59.

79 See e.g. Wilson and Dugard on the reasonableness test in SA: "all it can do is tell us whether the measures actually taken are sufficient", Ibid., 52.

80 Arosemena (n 65) 114–117.

earliest opportunity for the most vulnerable.[81] This section discusses what core obligations could bring to priority-setting if they were better delimited under the right to health and why; because they are formulated under international soft law, they are not currently a suitable parameter.

Academics are still trying to operationalise core obligations into State practice, but in the meantime a common understanding of the term is that core obligations aim to *"ensure the satisfaction of, at the very least, minimum essential levels of each of the rights are incumbent upon every State party"*, as per General Comment 3 of the CESCR.[82] This idea, as noted by Tassioulas, creates for human rights claims a benchmark for a minimum floor that is immediately realisable.[83] Another practical result of a core obligation is that it allows drawing attention to and prioritising more persuasive topics in human rights advocacy and practice. As Young notes, the minimum core "trades rights inflation for rights ambition", inasmuch as it reduces the burden of expansive rights interpretation to concentrate efforts and material resources on the most central items to guarantee at least a sufficient realisation for human existence (which, as a downside, may leave other obligations with no time limits for realisation).[84]

Such status of core obligations is unclear because of the speculative nature of this interpretation. As they are laid down under international law via non-binding instruments, this set of obligations is not well-delineated as a matter of customary law or via interpretation of the Covenant obligations.[85] With little academic consensus on the attributes of core obligations, as well their practical repercussions in resource allocation, the most common instrument that could signal the existence of a minimum right is the CESCR Comments. Among the rights that had their core set out by authoritative interpretation in

81 Lisa Forman, 'What Future for the Minimum Core? Contextualizing the Implications of South African Socioeconomic Rights Jurisprudence for the International Human Right to Health' in John Harrington and Maria Stuttaford (eds), *Global Health and Human Rights: Legal and Philosophical Perspectives* (Taylor & Francis 2010) 74.

82 CESCR, GC 3 (n 32), para 10.

83 John Tasioulas, *Minimum Core Obligations: Human Rights in the Here and Now* (World Bank 2017) 4–5. See also: UNGA, "Right of everyone to the enjoyment of the highest attainable standard of physical and mental health" 5 August 2016 (A/71/304) para. 28.

84 Katharine G Young, 'The Minimum Core of Economic and Social Rights: A Concept in Search of Content' (2008) 33 Yale International Law Journal 64.

85 Katharine G Young, 'Waiting for Rights: Progressive Realization and Lost Time' in Katharine G Young (ed), *The Future of Economic and Social Rights* (Cambridge University Press 2019) 665–666.

the General Comments of the CESCR are the right to health, food and education, with such provisions not found in the original treaty.[86]

In the CESCR, health core obligations may not be formulated well enough for specific substantive priorities.[87] As Forman et al. note, they are more of a structural set of standards sparing poor countries unreachable aims of substantive realisation of costly health services.[88] That soft and generic approach has been the most recent interpretation derived from General Comment 14, which States obligations that do not in themselves regulate the allocation of resources and establish objective priorities for a specific context:

> (a) to ensure the right of access to health facilities, goods and services on a non-discriminatory basis, especially for vulnerable or marginalised groups...
> (f) To adopt and implement a national public health strategy and plan of action, on the basis of epidemiological evidence, addressing the health concerns of the whole population; the strategy and plan of action shall be devised, and periodically reviewed, on the basis of a participatory and transparent process; they shall include methods, such as right to health indicators and benchmarks, by which progress can be closely monitored; the process by which the strategy and plan of action are devised, as well as their content, shall give particular attention to all vulnerable or marginalised groups

The right to health has a further complication because its classification creates an intermediate layer of obligations, as per General Comment 14, para 44: the obligations of comparable priority.[89] It could be arguable that after the realisation of core obligations, the next step would be implementing comparable obligations, instead of giving them the same priority.[90] Separating comparable

86 See e.g. CESCR, "General Comment No. 4: The Right to Adequate Housing" 13 December 1991 (E/1992/23), paras 8–10 and 13; "General Comment No. 12: The Right to Adequate Food (Art. 11 of the Covenant)" 12 May 1999 (E/C.12/1999/5), paras 8, 14 and 17; GC 14 (chapter 1, n 34) paras 43–44; General Comment No. 15: The Right to Water, 20 January 2003 (E/C.12/2002/11), para 37(a)-(i). These instruments are referred in John Tasioulas, 'The Minimum Core of the Human Right to Health' (World Bank 2017) 4.

87 Kirsteen Shields, 'The Minimum Core Obligations of Economic, Social and Cultural Rights: The Rights to Health and Education' (World Bank 2017) 23–24.

88 Forman and others (n 32) 537.

89 CESCR, GC 14 (chapter 1, n 34) para. 44.

90 Lisa Forman and others, 'What Do Core Obligations under the Right to Health Bring to Universal Health Coverage?' (2016) 18 Health and Human Rights 23, 28; Tasioulas, *Minimum Core Obligations* (n 83) 7.

and core obligations, though, is not a straightforward task, given that they are frequently referred to as having equal weight.[91]

Moreover, the classification of the right to health obligations is not an isolated case. Socio-economic rights obligations in themselves are already complex to establish, given the limited definition developed in local jurisdictions and the absence of a long-standing jurisprudence of socio-economic rights internationally.[92] The concept of the core obligations takes this difficulty to a further level, raising questions of what is the minimum necessary in a particular State according to domestic possibilities or as a minimum level that should be regarded as sufficient anywhere in the world.[93] Core obligations can easily be confused with the closely related concept of minimum thresholds, which is a form to operationalise a vital standard of living first proposed by Andreassen et al. in 1985.[94] They both reinforce each other, but it is important to note that they are not always equivalent, as some core obligations are made in the abstract and impose qualitative aspects of the enjoyment of rights (e.g. non-discrimination, participatory process, etc.) that are not a necessary part of a benchmark or a quantitative measurement.[95]

This leads us to a legitimacy problem with core obligations to healthcare, as they can be context-based and not mirror an internationally devised minimum threshold.[96] Core obligations may be an easy achievement for wealthy countries, but for the poorest States, it is more contentious to impose a set of minimum obligations when there is meagre State support, and even more arduous to designate what is the essential level in such a precarious back-

91 See e.g. George Jotham Kondowe, 'Implementing Economic and Social Rights in 'Domestic' Jurisdictions: Understanding the Minimum Core Obligations Approach' (2020) 46 Commonwealth Law Bulletin 314, 325; Stephen P Marks, 'Normative Expansion of the Right to Health and the Proliferation of Human Rights' (2016) 49 George Washington International Law Review. 97, 105.

92 Sepúlveda Carmona (n 33) 7.

93 Amrei Müller, 'The Minimum Core Approach to the Right to Health Progress and Remaining Challenges' in Sabine Klotz and others (eds), *Healthcare as a Human Rights Issue* (Verlag 2017) 62–63.

94 Bård-Anders Andreassen and others, 'Assessing Human Rights Performance in Developing Countries: The Case for a Minimal Threshold Approach to the Economic and Social Rights' (1987) 1997–1998 Yearbook of Human Rights in Developing Countries 333.

95 Kitty Arambulo, *Strengthening the Supervision of the International Covenant on Economic, Social and Cultural Rights: Theoretical and Procedural Aspects* (Intersentia 1999) 141–142.

96 Katharine G Young, *Constituting Economic and Social Rights* (Oxford University Press 2012) 69–70.

ground.[97] For Muller, internationally developed core obligations, "would not cover the vastly different health experiences of individuals around the world, and would thus be ineffective in changing the life to the better of human beings whose individual experiences do not resonate with".[98]

The uncertainty surrounding the development of core obligations at a universal level may hinder their priority-setting application locally. To become functional, a health prioritisation strategy derived from core obligations would necessitate three conditions: a) a list of core objectives must be delineated; b) those objects should be clearly separated from other health claims; and c) the focus of all subsequent actions should be directed towards those core objectives above all else.[99] Arosemena argues that these three elements are difficult to give effect to, because of a lack of boundaries between obligations.[100] It is not immediately obvious how the first obligation can be separated from the others and how to guarantee that all central obligations are realised for the entire population before the remaining issues are realised.

These conditions are not fulfilled by core obligations, especially if one relies only on the comments made by the Committee, whose authority to define the precise content of core obligations at a local level may be disputed.[101] The idea of core obligations is not regulated by the Covenant and is simply a separate creation of the Committee with respect to legitimacy and currency in local jurisdictions. Once the Committee commenced operation, it faced the problem of deciding which posture it would take: either by strictly following the text of the Covenant, or by helping to clarify the essential aspects of rights, the latter being rebuttable by the States for the Committee's lack of competence.[102] Though the mandate of the Committee is known to have interpretative power and auxiliary supervision of the implementation of the Covenant, such authority does not imply necessarily the creation of new categories of

97 Audrey R Chapman, 'Core Obligations Related to the Right to Health' in Sage Russell and Audrey R Chapman (eds), *Core Obligations: Building a Framework for Economic, Social and Cultural Rights* (Intersentia 2002) 195–196.

98 Müller (n 93) 75.

99 Arosemena (n 65) 127–132.

100 Ibid.

101 On the controversial normative role of the Committee, there is a divide between accepting only "norm-filling" capacity or a true "norm-creating" power. See Mátyás Bódig, 'Soft Law, Doctrinal Development, and the General Comments of the UN Committee on Economic, Social and Cultural Rights' in Stéphanie Lagoutte, Thomas Gammeltoft-Hansen and John Cerone (eds), *Tracing the Roles of Soft Law in Human Rights* (Oxford University Press 2016) 78–80.

102 Phillip Alston, 'Out of the Abyss: The Challenges Confronting the New U.N. Committee on Economic, Social and Cultural Rights' (1987) 9 Human Rights Quarterly 332, 352–353.

obligations.[103] The Committee has never addressed the issue of its competence to determine core obligations and never tried to respond to criticisms raised by scholars, such as lack of precision and the need for an indication of the rationale for selecting the minimum core of a right.[104]

After surveying the variety of academic arguments for and against core obligations, Forman et al. conclude that the core "requires going considerably beyond the status quo to develop each constituent component of entitlements, content and duties".[105] It can be argued that the core obligations are in fact fundamental for the good implementation of the treaty and, if not recognised, the satisfactory execution of the Covenant's rights would be hindered.[106] Tobin considers, nevertheless, that even if the core is seen as being essential for the realisation of the rights and direct State action, the problem of establishing what the core obligations are still lingers.[107]

To become a rigorous standard, core obligations would need a precise definition to meet the first condition (list of obligations). There is no clear indication of a rationale or special rule of recognition of the core obligations already enunciated through General Comments. The Committee has not yet built consensus, though key characteristics have been associated with core obligations (namely, non-derogability, meaning that States are compelled to respect it even when in a state of emergency; minimal level, which points to the lowest level from which all other obligations build; and a sense of urgency, prioritising the core over other needs up to full rights implementation).[108] The formulation of core obligations also depends on how they come into existence (e.g. whether by consensus of States in a common denominator; by interpretation of human principles or values; or through the interpretation of experts in the CESCR). Some scholars expect that the Committee may soon turn to this omission.[109]

---

103 Describing the nature of General Comments can be very nebulous, with their function associated with "guidance", "interpretation" and "understanding" of methods of implementation of rights by the State-Parties. See: Marco Odello and Francesco Seatzu, *The UN Committee on Economic, Social and Cultural Rights: The Law, Process and Practice* (Taylor & Francis 2013) 29.

104 Bódig (n 101) 77–78.

105 Forman and others (n 90) 119.

106 Tobin (chapter 1, n 32) 242–243.

107 Ibid.

108 Tasioulas, *Minimum Core Obligations* (n 83) 16–20.

109 Lisa Forman, 'Can Minimum Core Obligations Survive a Reasonableness Standard of Review under the Optional Protocol to the International Covenant on Economic, Social and Cultural Rights?' (2016) 47 Ottawa Law Review 557, 572.

Those shortcomings are interwoven with the question of the legitimacy of the Committee in declaring the status and the content of the core in relation to national governments. The vagueness over the content of core obligations is long familiar in the context of the reasonableness approach, which has been accused of not fully fleshing out the essential content of which rights should be first satisfied as a matter of urgency.[110] In the South African Constitutional Court, the absence of the clarification of the minimum core has been criticised for not helping the government to make policy choices and plan budgets.[111] This judicial posture has been rejected by some as a flawed mechanism, which fails to guarantee immediate relief for those in greater need and establish precise and coherent scrutiny in grave violations.[112]

There also remain problems with the separation and weight of each core and non-core obligation to create a hierarchy on health prioritisation. A possible interpretation is that progressive realisation prioritises core obligations as being a matter of immediate execution.[113] For instance, the World Bank published a report written by Tasioulas who confidently advances that core obligations are of immediate realisation for all States, independently of the resources available.[114] He notes that justiciability is desirable, in as much as the Committee admits that any right in the Covenant can be brought to court; thus there is no differentiation in terms of obligatory admissibility of such claims. This position concurs with the 1997 Maastricht Guidelines on Violations of Economic, Social and Cultural Rights, which proclaim that the core is of immediate effect irrespective of resource insufficiency.[115] However, several scholars have questioned such a posture.[116] For instance, Young objects to the distinction and sequencing of core and other obligations as low or higher

110 Marius Pieterse, 'Eating Socioeconomic Rights: The Usefulness of Rights Talk in Alleviating Social Hardship Revisited' (2007) 29 Human Rights Quarterly 796, 810–811.

111 Sandra Liebenberg, *Socio-Economic Rights: Adjudication under a Transformative Constitution* (Juta and Company Ltd 2010) 142.

112 Pieterse (n 110) 810–811.

113 Brems (n 56) 355.

114 Ibid.

115 International Commission of Jurists (ICJ), "*Maastricht Guidelines on Violations of Economic, Social and Cultural Rights*", 26 January 1997, available at: https://www.refworld.org/docid/48abd5730.html accessed 13 August 2021.

116 For a review of criticism of the prevalence of core obligations, see: Forman and others (n 32).

priority, similar to the political and economic rights division, claiming that rights should be engaged locally according to the needs of each place.[117]

The tension between a pre-determined core and the local reality grows more complex the further the right-to-health framework is expanded. The following section will analyse this in more detail, considering what can be described as the expansive approach to health priorities and human rights. It will be argued that these same core obligations may be diffused in different instruments in the multilayered realm of Global Health Law (GHL), which lends a sense of urgency to many health targets that stand on equal footing, without the specific hierarchy of core obligations but with problems in the correlation of the content of the right to health with other global health instruments.

3 Expansive Interpretation of Global Health Law

The third approach to prioritisation refers to GHL and its expansive number of concurrent sources. GHL, as proposed by academics, is constituted by a mixture of traditional hard law and soft law instruments that give rise to a purported original legal regime to promote higher standards of public health based on global justice.[118] It is not a completely settled branch of international law, as this attribute has been disputed by some authors.[119] Among other func-

117 Katharine G Young, 'The Immediacy of Economic and Social Rights' (*James g Stewart*, 23 May 2018) <http://jamesgstewart.com/the-immediacy-of-economic-and-social-rights/> accessed 15 June 2020.

118 This is drawn from Gostin's definition: "the study and practice of international law – both hard law (e.g. treaties that bind states) and soft instruments (e.g. codes of practice negotiated by states) – that shapes norms, processes and institutions to attain the highest attainable standard of physical and mental health for the world's population". Lawrence Gostin, *Global Health Law* (Harvard University Press 2014) 59.

119 For a challenge to GHL as international law branch, see Brigit Toebes, 'International Health Law: An Emerging Field of Public International Law' (2015) 55 Indian Journal of International Law 299, 301–302; Brigit Toebes, 'Global Health Law: Defining the Field' in Gian Luca Burci and Brigit Toebes (eds), *Research Handbook on Global Health Law* (Edward Elgar Publishing 2018) 2–3. For criticism of the coherence of GHL and foundational issues, such as non-enforceability and lack of a normative framework, see George P Smith, 'Aspirational, Paradoxical, or Oxymoronic?' in Belinda Bennett, Sarah Hawkes and Michael Freeman (eds), *Law and Global Health: Current Legal Issues* (Oxford University Press 2014).

tions such as disease control and health security, setting global health priorities is part of GHL.[120]

This section argues that, even though GHL aims to establish priorities and manage resources, the prioritisation is not fundamentally derived from human rights obligations and can lead to conflicts. There are three reasons for that: a) the different normative status of human rights and GHL instruments, b) the dispensable role of human rights to justify global health instruments, and c) competing priorities among human rights and GHL soft law.

On the legal status of different sources, GHL, as part of a defended academic interpretation, notably emerged from a law-making process ascribed to the WHO, mostly through soft law, which may be produced independently of HRBA.[121] Soft law instruments come into being as non-binding norms that can be flexibly adopted by States and, in global health governance, have been treated as a flexible means of addressing pressing health issues of international relevance by a more responsive but less formal method.[122] Human rights have gained growing recognition for their relevance to GHL, though the centrality of this connection in global health governance is still controversial.[123] The WHO has been either cautious or inconsistent in taking normative inspiration from human rights frameworks – decision-making at WHO has been criticised for its utilitarian and economic concerns.[124] There is, of course,

---

120 Gostin, *Global Health Law* (n 118) 77.

121 WHO Constitution (1948), Article 21. This article provides the law-making powers of the WHO in the health field related to health threats of international scale of legally binding nature. However, use of this prerogative has been limited. Gian Luca Burci, 'Global Health Law: Present and Future' in Gian Luca Burci and Brigit Toebes (eds), *Research Handbook on Global Health Law* (Edward Elgar Publishing 2018) 492–493.

122 Those soft law norms are recognised to be passed by intergovernmental organisations: Suerie Moon, 'Global Health Law and Governance: Concepts, Tools, Actors and Power' in Gian Luca Burci and Brigit Toebes (eds), *Research Handbook on Global Health Law* (Edward Elgar Publishing 2018) 34.

123 For confident views of a vital relationship between human rights and global health governance, see: Lance Gable, 'The Proliferation of Human Rights in Global Health Governance' (2007) 35 The Journal of Law, Medicine & Ethics 534, 13–16. As a counterpoint to this suggested interrelation, see Adrien M Viens, 'Interdependence, Human Rights and Global Health Law' (2015) 23 Health Care Analysis 401.

124 Smith, 'Aspirational, Paradoxical, or Oxymoronic?' (n 119) 459–460. Benjamin Mason Meier and Florian Kastler, 'Development of Human Rights through WHO' in Lawrence Gostin and Benjamin Mason Meier (eds), *Human Rights in Global Health*, vol 1 (Oxford University Press 2018) 126; Lawrence O Gostin and others, 'The next WHO Director-General's Highest Priority: A Global Treaty on the Human Right to Health' (2016) 4 The Lancet Global Health e890; BM Meier and W Onzivu, 'The Evolution of Human Rights in World Health Organization Policy and the Future of Human Rights through Global Health Governance' (2014) 128 Public Health 179, 182–84. For the period of neglect

a broad range of documents and soft law at the WHO that do refer to the right to health, but that does not automatically mean that the right to health has been taken into account in all international relations or has in practice been used to shape programmes and ground political decisions in all areas, including recommendations on resource allocation.[125]

Hence, GHL instruments may have foundations other than human rights. A case in point is the health policies in the Sustainable Development Goals (SDG), a soft law instrument, which may collide with the priority order in the international right to health and possibly local resource allocation decisions.[126]. As Tasioulas et al. contend, global health governance need not be solely grounded in human rights and the SDGs have shown that there are aims other than the right to health and principles that foster global health governance.[127] As one of its first architects, Gostin initially drew out the aspirations of GHL around instruments to secure health security and international health threats response, with human rights only exercising a secondary part. His own definition does not conceptualise GHL as explicitly connected to human rights law.[128] Gostin has come to accept the normative importance of the right to health to GHL, but noted the imperfect nature of socio-economic rights regarding enforceability and ambiguity of content for implementation.[129]

---

of human rights at the WHO, see: Benjamin Mason Meier, 'Organization, the Evolution of Human Rights, and the Failure to Achieve Health for All' in John Harrington and Maria Stuttaford (eds), *Global Health and Human Rights* (2010) 172–175.

125 For the history of the right to health and global governance, see: Lawrence Gostin and others, '70 Years of Human Rights in Global Health: Drawing on a Contentious Past to Secure a Hopeful Future' (2018) 392 The Lancet 2731.

126 GHL is, for some, also known as international health law, though the former holds more currency. See Toebes, 'International Health Law' (n 119).

127 Tasioulas et al. maintain that the global agenda should go beyond the right to health and uphold also other rights and principles. John Tasioulas and Effy Vayena, 'Getting Human Rights Right in Global Health Policy' (2015) 385 The Lancet e42.

128 Gostin defines GHL as: "the study and practice of international law – both hard law (e.g., treaties that bind states) and soft instruments (e.g., codes of practice negotiated by states) – that shapes norms, processes, and institutions to attain the highest attainable standard of physical and mental health for the world's population. Normatively, the field seeks innovative ways to mobilize resources, set priorities, coordinate activities, monitor progress, create incentives, and ensure accountability among a proliferation of global health actors". Gostin, *Global Health Law* (n 118) 59–60.

129 Lawrence Gostin and Allyn L Taylor, 'Global Health Law: A Definition and Grand Challenges' (2008) 1 Public Health Ethics 53, 59.

Without integration, some GHL instruments may compete with the set of obligations of the international right to health, since they are not bound by the same priorities. The issue is that if one were to accept GHL soft law, there would be no reason not to accept human rights soft law, such as General Comment 14 (which could arguably be a special kind of source, being the most authoritative form of the right to health interpretation). However, there is no hierarchy in the instruments of global health governance in the form of "human rights soft law" and "health-themed soft law" and no clear direction as to what should be a consolidated interpretation of the two types of priorities (if no rights are referenced), as States could presumably find themselves lost in various, similarly authoritative, recommendations[130]. Human rights obligations, under General Comments 3 and 14, could be interpreted as a strict set of priorities (core obligations), whereas the SDGs have a list of coexisting goals with no hierarchy among them. In contrast to core obligations, target 3 (health) of the SDGs has 13 agreed sub-goals, all with the same weight and not subject to individual opt out by States.

Additionally, the SDGs and human rights have two different systems of compliance and legal status. The SDGs result from a General Assembly resolution with a different international legal status from treaty-based human rights norms.[131] The High-Level Political Forum is the report mechanism for the SDGs on a voluntary basis, which has generated a certain distrust in its efficiency given the lack of rigorous accountability and involvement of stakeholders.[132] This contrasts with the notion of accountability under human rights monitoring bodies, which goes beyond mere voluntary reporting and is able to declare violations of human rights.

Despite these differences, SDGs and the right to health may look superficially similar, and it may misleadingly be suggested that achieving one health target on one side will fulfil the right to health obligation on the other. The target of UHC serves as an example. UHC does not entail principles and structural conditions that are expressly described only in the right to health by

130 For a discussion on the various possible sources of GHL, see Moon (n 122) 33–36.

131 UN General Assembly, *Transforming Our World: The 2030 Agenda for Sustainable Development* (UN, 2015).

132 Format and organisational aspects of the HLPF are set by the following documents: UNGA, "Format and organizational aspects of the high-level political forum on sustainable development" (Resolution 67/290) 23 August 2013 (A/RES/67/290), "Follow-up and review of the 2030 Agenda for Sustainable Development at the global level" (Resolution 70/299), 18 August 2016 (A/RES/70/299). See also: Åsa Persson, Nina Weitz and Måns Nilsson, "Follow-up and Review of the Sustainable Development Goals: Alignment vs. Internalization" (2016) 25 Review of European, Comparative & International Environmental Law 59, 61.

means of General Comment 14, such as citizen involvement in priority-setting or even the strict observance of a list of services defined as core obligations or obligations of comparable priority. As Puras observes, "not all paths to UHC are consistent with human rights requirements".[133] Authors have pointed out the lack of human rights principles in the SDGs, namely the need for participation in those deliberations that may exclude subgroups and in the possibility of achieving UHC by solely extending coverage and not reaching out to the most vulnerable or migrants.[134]

Furthermore, other health targets may compete with an equitable realisation of UHC. For instance, in a country marked by life-expectancy imbalances between rural and urban population, using more funds to comply with other SDGs focusing on subgroups without redressing this discrepancy will probably privilege groups like children, HIV patients or even drivers (through policies preventing road accidents) but will not promote the full realisation of the right to health with geographical equity. In the end, States need to exercise a level of discretion that only local priority-setting can achieve by using the general principles under socio-economic rights.

4 Conclusions

What international human rights law regulates in respect of resource allocation in health may be different depending upon whether a more restrictive or expansive posture is taken in asserting the content of international obligations. This chapter has compared three alternatives in the international sources and principles of resource allocation (taking the right to health as a socio-economic right) and defended the use of the basic principles of maximum available resources and progressive realisation.

133 Dainius Puras, 'Universal Health Coverage: A Return to Alma-Ata and Ottawa' (2016) 18 Health and Human Rights 7, 8. UNGA, "Right of Everyone to the Enjoyment of the Highest Attainable Standard of Physical and Mental Health", 5 August 2016 (A/71/304) para. 76.

134 Audrey R Chapman, 'Assessing the Universal Health Coverage Target in the Sustainable Development Goals from a Human Rights Perspective' (2016) 16 BMC International Health and Human Rights 20–22; Claire E Brolan and others, 'The Right to Health of Non-Nationals and Displaced Persons in the Sustainable Development Goals Era: Challenges for Equity in Universal Health Care' (2017) 16 International Journal for Equity in Health 14; Madhulika Sahoo and Jalandhar Pradhan, 'Sustainable Development Goals and Reproductive Healthcare Rights of Internally Displaced Persons in India' (2019) 12 International Journal of Human Rights in Healthcare 38.

All three alternatives have weaknesses and benefits, but as sources in international law are further created, the less it seems that there is a central component to unify global health in priority-setting decisions locally and worldwide. Core obligations are ill-defined but could potentially create a more rigid order between various health provisions. GHL has a great sense of political engagement and international cooperation, but, in its production of new soft law materials that can set different health priorities, it jars with the human rights frameworks and their methods of compliance. The minimalist approach is at least the most coherent formula, but cannot unequivocally indicate to governments what they should decide and define as the top priorities in health. Moreover, the fact that a minimalist method relies fundamentally on the treaty text does not weaken its force.

Socio-economic rights principles in the Covenant serve as a rather ambiguous, yet constructive, framework for HTA in an HRBA. The right to health under international law complements fair procedure and can mitigate the consequences of relying only on rationing procedures in HTA to address scarcity. HTA, as a core social institution, by its nature can exert political influence on the causes of scarcity and may be a coordination space for policies that mobilise resources while identifying priorities. Though still vague, the ICESCR provisions have more legitimacy than other norms formed under soft law and could aid in refuting the paradigm that scarcity is a justification for government inaction. This could be done by simple measures such as price negotiation or stronger regulation of pharmaceutical companies.

Thus, HTA stands at the intersection of priority-setting and resource mobilisation to bring to fruition progressive realisation and maximum available resources. While local priority-setting should continue, negating access to health should only be the ultimate option when there are other mechanisms that can help a State avoid unnecessary rationing. Chapter 7 will further develop this view with reference to the legal strategies available in market regulation and pharmaceutical access policies to make healthcare more affordable within an HRBA-to-HTA rooted in the international right to health.

The framework of Article 2.1 of the ICESCR, however, is not limited to domestic resource mobilisation in relation to internal State conducts. Other principles of international socio-economic rights can be useful in resource allocation decisions and can help the governance of HTA in the criteria and knowledge production. Chapters 5 and 6 will discuss, respectively, non-discrimination and international cooperation, two other attributes of Article 2.1 that can justify the interplay between HTA and the right to health in international law, both in mobilising and distributing resources.

CHAPTER 5

The Non-discrimination Principle: Value and Quality of Evidence-Making

As an evidence-informed practice, HTA is primarily organised around multidisciplinary research regarded as valid and reliable under scientific standards or economic models.[1] Much of the evidence in HTA concentrates on measurements of quality and value of new technologies through selected outcomes required in the criteria of each jurisdiction, such as utility indicators for cost-effectiveness and clinical efficacy.[2]

Two dimensions have already been considered in the previous chapters (fair procedure and progressive realisation/maximum resources to control scarcity). A third principle, that of non-discrimination, will be explained in this chapter. Together, they form what will be termed as the three core principles (3Ps) of evidence-making in health policy-making and in HTA criteria. The present chapter examines evidence and indicators for the HTA criteria and how they should be employed and developed in an HRBA to measure value and quality of healthcare. In Chapter 3, it was argued that the right to health could manifest itself as part of the substantive criteria (legal issues) or determining the relevant criteria (which evidence will be covered). We have also seen that only recently evidence has been discussed as a question of human rights standards in healthcare decision-making; however, that issue has never been handled as an application of socio-economic rights principles.[3] This chapter, therefore, identifies the socio-economic rights principles that may govern evidence-making and the criteria in HTA.

Evidence-making is to be understood as an evaluative process, not wholly objective or based on pre-existing definitive knowledge, but influenced by

1 The term "evidence-informed" differs from "evidence-based", as the latter denotes a strict high standard of evidence, while the former allows and reflects on several types of knowledges and experiences to interpret evidence: Isaac Nevo and Vered Slonim-Nevo, 'The Myth of Evidence-Based Practice: Towards Evidence-Informed Practice' (2011) 41 British Journal of Social Work 1176, 1193–1195. On the link between HTA and evidence, see e.g.: Banta (chapter 1, n 26).

2 Ingrid Zechmeister-Koss, Petra Schnell-Inderst and Günther Zauner, 'Appropriate Evidence Sources for Populating Decision Analytic Models within Health Technology Assessment (HTA): A Systematic Review of HTA Manuals and Health Economic Guidelines' (2013) 16 Value in Health A591, 289–293.

3 See chapter 3, 1.2.

 | HTTPS://DOI.ORG/10.1163/9789004730311-006

patient and social values in political decisions.[4] This stance in HTA is also described as an "evidence-informed deliberative process" (EIDP), demanding co-creation in interpretative gaps in evidence for HTA through participation in policy-making involving six steps: 1) situational analysis, 2) formation of stakeholder panels, 3) identification of relevant criteria, 4) collection of evidence on criteria, 5) deliberation, and 6) recommendation for implementation.[5] This framework unifies principles from A4R (discussed in Chapter 2) and multicriteria decision analysis (MCDA), a tool to support identifying the key factors and context necessary for deliberation-centred questions that measure quality and value for patients. To return to the main argument in this book, the purpose of the linkage of the 3Ps with an EIDP is to ensure that HTA promotes the establishment of a health system as core social institution, in a deliberative democracy bound by human rights principles. The emphasis of this chapter will be on the non-discrimination principle, as both fair procedure and progressive realisation can either remedy or, if not applied, result in discrimination. However, the whole 3P framework should be applied to the evidence of value and quality in the HTA criteria, as the principles are co-dependent.

Other interdependent terms in HTA and evidence-making are "value" and "quality" of healthcare, which can be used in circular definitions and variations depending on the context in play. A value-based healthcare may be related to optimal allocation of resources, while value-based quality medicine is measured by patient preferences in indicators of quality of life (QoL).[6] In health measurement, quality of health and value of one's health are interdependent, since the individual "amount of health", as Hausman claims, is

4 Michael P Kelly and Tessa A Moore, 'The Judgement Process in Evidence-Based Medicine and Health Technology Assessment' (2012) 10 Social Theory & Health 1; Michael P Kelly and others, 'The Importance of Values in Evidence-Based Medicine' (2015) 16 BMC Medical Ethics 1.

5 Baltussen and others (chapter 1, n 69) 615–616.

6 See e.g. Ivo P. Janecka, 'Quality vs. Value' (2009) 339 BMJ b4346; Fiona Godlee, 'Effective, Safe, and a Good Patient Experience' (2009) 339 BMJ b4346; Joseph R Betancourt, 'In Pursuit of High-Value Healthcare: The Case for Improving Quality and Achieving Equity in a Time of Healthcare Transformation' (2014) 30 Frontiers of health services management 16, 16–18; Muir Gray, 'Value Based Healthcare' (2017) 356 BMJ: British Medical Journal (Online); Jong-Myon Bae, 'Value-Based Medicine: Concepts and Application' (2015) 37 Epidemiology and Health 2. See also terminological criticism in: Joni Jabbal and Matthew Lewis, 'Approaches to Better Value in the NHS: Improving Quality and Cost: CEBM Report' (Centre for Evidence-Based Medicine 2018) 6–7 <https://www.cebm.net/2019/04/defining-value-based-healthcare-in-the-nhs> accessed 1 January 2021; Ali Mohammad Mosadeghrad, 'Healthcare Service Quality: Towards a Broad Definition' (2013) 26 International Journal of Health Care Quality Assurance 203, 204–205.

not objectively quantifiable and can only be measured indirectly by determining the value of each health status through a particular indicator.[7]

Because of terminological variation and ambiguity between the notions of value and quality in healthcare, this chapter separates those categories in terms of evidence used, namely, quality of healthcare (clinical indicators) and value of healthcare (economic indicators). Value may be associated with economic metrics, performance measures such as efficiency, or simply "value for money" – the selected effect per amount paid.[8] Quality frequently concerns achievement of health goals or outcomes, safety, or the effectiveness of a treatment established by clinical evidence.[9]

To bring such human rights principles into effect, we should treat them as progressive and programmatic standards that operate at policy level – the same way we already consider the formulation of EIDP for HTA decision, which has been advocated as a path of experimentation and continuous adjustment to finally incorporate broader societal views and more inclusive participatory tools in determining the appropriate evidence method.[10] Even the very idea of EIDP, which is a central platform for the procedural approach to HTA, is not to be seen as a "blueprint" or quick-start solution to be implemented, and is more described by Baltussen et al. as an "aspirational goal".[11] Thus, human rights principles in the context of evidence-making in HTA should not be mistaken for immediately enforceable legal obligations in all scenarios. Instead, we are engaging with a transformative and forward-looking approach to rights standards to policy-making – one that seeks to dismantle structural barriers in knowledge production and address inequalities in the evidence and methods used in HTA.

The critical problem in HTA is that by moving towards fair procedures and engaging the public regarding selecting the adopted criteria is insufficient to

---

7 Daniel M Hausman, 'Can Health Be Measured?' in Nir Eyal and others (eds), *Measuring the Global Burden of Disease: Philosophical Dimensions* (Oxford University Press 2020) 5–7.

8 Peter C Smith, 'Measuring Value for Money in Healthcare: Concepts and Tools' (Centre for Health Economics, University of York 2009) 6–7, 12–15 <https://www.health.org.uk/sites/default/files/MeasuringValueForMoneyInHealthcareConceptsAndTools.pdf> accessed 1 January 2021; Jabbal and Lewis (n 6) 6.

9 Grant E Steffen, 'Quality Medical Care: A Definition' (1988) 260 Journal of the American Medical Association 56, 58.

10 Michael J DiStefano and Carleigh B Krubiner, 'Beyond the Numbers: A Critique of Quantitative Multi-Criteria Decision Analysis' (2020) 36 International Journal of Technology Assessment in Health Care 292, 295.

11 Rob Baltussen and others, 'Value Assessment Frameworks for HTA Agencies: The Organization of Evidence-Informed Deliberative Processes' (2017) 20 Value in Health 256, 257.

redress the deep-rooted epistemic injustice embedded in evidence production itself. Simply reaching agreement on what counts as admissible evidence in HTA does not resolve the underlying epistemic constraints that systematically disadvantage certain patient groups for not having acceptable evidence of their values and views. Building on Fricker's epistemic injustice analysis, "testimonial injustice" arises when the knowledge of some individuals – most often, in HTA, patients' lived experiences and desired outcomes – are not "heard" or recognised as valid or authoritative sources, in comparison to expert communities such as health economists or medical professionals.[12] Epistemic injustice can be of hermeneutic (or interpretative) nature, identified more specifically when there is no correct "language" to express the experience of certain groups, that is, the existing evidence available for HTA decisions, designed and presented by such expert communities, does not capture or correctly engage with what is valued by different patient groups.[13] This is the case where the evidence created exclude or does not adequately involve categories of patients such as women, migrants and ethnic minorities.

Tackling the structural forms of epistemic injustice in knowledge production is a complex policy challenge that requires innovative action and far-reaching reform in how evidence is generated through concerted State efforts and progressive realisation. As Michales rightly notes, a transition of this scale "is likely to be slow and incomplete and outside the control of those who must make decisions".[14] Indeed, such reforms include, for example, diversifying research agendas to account for parameters that more closely reflect patients' needs and aspirations. Other measures, however, may be more readily implemented through State laws and policies – such as ensuring transparency in data and research design, regulating clinical trials, involving excluded communities in evidence creation, and introducing conditional approvals linked to ongoing data collection for new technologies.[15]

These evidence challenges are not amenable to quick fixes. Rather, they demand a sustained agenda of ongoing evolution and collective learning in order to realise substantive equality among populations that differ in their access to research, representation, and the focus of evidence production. At

12 Miranda Fricker, *Epistemic Injustice: Power and the Ethics of Knowing* (Oxford University Press 2007) 17.

13 Ibid. 147.

14 Jonathan Anthony Michaels, 'Potential for Epistemic Injustice in Evidence-Based Healthcare Policy and Guidance' (2021) 47 Journal of Medical Ethics 417, 421.

15 Ibid. 421.

times, this involves engaging with forms of expertise and technical methods that are still in development and solutions that emerge only through collaborative efforts across academia, society, and the HTA bodies. State policies play a crucial role in this process, helping to revise existing tools, reshape economic methodologies and redirect research agendas towards inclusion and meaningful knowledge to patient experience.

To discuss the application of the 3Ps in evidence of value and quality, this chapter proceeds as follows. Section 1 discusses the problematic nature of indicators in human rights and how the discussion over metrics in general gives insight on possible difficulties of the indexes in HTA criteria. Section 2 presents the 3Ps framework and the difficulty of applying human rights to indicators and data collection. Section 3 introduces the principle of non-discrimination in socio-economic rights and the guidance it provides for the HTA criteria. Section 4 will consider the usage of clinical evidence in HTA in light of fair procedure and non-discrimination. Section 5 analyses the shortcomings in utility indicators and other measures in health economics regarding non-discrimination and fair procedure. Section 6 will conclude with progressive realisation, where States are under an obligation to provide the best possible evidence in a fair and non-discriminatory procedure.

1 Indicators and Evidence-Making in Human Rights

Evidence-making issues are not unique to HTA. Before outlining the principles for evidence-making, one should note the similarity of concerns regarding indicators for human rights monitoring which resemble HTA evidence limitations. Overall, indicators can be described as "the systematic, comparative organization and presentation of information that allows for comparison among units or over time".[16] In HTA, evidence involves some form of indicators, such as quality-adjusted-life-years (QALYs), that can indirectly shape how the performance of a technology is appraised and what aspects are being considered in a decision. They function as the markers of a "high-value" system, in the "triple aim" of "improving the individual experience of care; improving the health of populations; and reducing the per capita costs of care for populations".[17] As a basic comparison, numerical values used as evi-

16 Sally Engle Merry, *The Seductions of Quantification: Measuring Human Rights, Gender Violence, and Sex Trafficking* (University of Chicago Press 2016) 12.

17 Donald M Berwick, Thomas W Nolan and John Whittington, 'The Triple Aim: Care, Health, and Cost' (2008) 27 Health Affairs 759, 760–762.

dence in the HTA criteria may function in the same way as the measurement process in relation to human rights – they may edit the reality or cherry-pick attributes in a manner that would not be consistent with the 3Ps, particularly in that they contribute to discrimination.

Similarly, with human rights, indicators pose many challenges in actually measuring meaningful information about the implementation of State obligations. In international law governance, indicators generate knowledge about the application of human rights obligations by States drawing on rights in principle (standards) and in practice (the application of those standards).[18] Indicators can be also framed in terms of conducts and outcomes derived from human rights obligations that are equivalent to the classification of State obligations under international law.[19] An ideal right-to-health indicator, then, would be able to verify State conducts (policies) and results (desired outcomes) in fulfilling human rights obligations, as proposed by Hunt et al.[20] An unintended consequence is that they may supplant the norms upon which they are based to become targets in themselves to achieve only those conducts and results implicitly recognised in the data.[21]

Additionally, these targets may encounter methodological difficulties to truly embodying human rights, despite being well received by some researchers and international bodies to determine State compliance.[22] As statis-

---

18 See e.g.: Todd Landman, 'The Scope of Human Rights: From Background Concepts to Indicators' (2006) 2 Revista Iberoamericana de Derechos Humanos 109, 123–134; Todd Landman, 'Measuring Human Rights: Principle, Practice, and Policy' (2004)' 26 Human Rights Quarterly 906, 911–926.

19 Gauthier de Beco, 'Human Rights Indicators for Assessing State Compliance with International Human Rights' (2008) 77 Nordic Journal of International Law 23, 24. See also: Office of the High Commissioner for Human Rights, 'Report on Indicators for Monitoring Compliance with International Human Rights Instruments' (2006) HRI/MC/2006/7 preprint 7 <http://digitallibrary.un.org/record/575952>; Landman, 'The Scope of Human Rights: From Background Concepts to Indicators' (n 18) 134–136.

20 Paul Hunt and Gillian MacNaughton, 'A Human Rights-Based Approach to Health Indicators' in Mashood Baderin and Robert McCorquodale (eds), *Economic, Social, and Cultural Rights in Action* (Oxford University Press 2007)

21 Malcolm Langford and Sakiko Fukuda-Parr, 'The Turn to Metrics' (2012) 30 Nordic Journal of Human Rights 222, 233–234.

22 The CESCR has progressively called for the production of indicators by States in order to monitor rights' implementation. See e.g. AnnJanette Rosga and Margaret L Satterthwaite, 'The Trust in Indicators: Measuring Human Rights' (2009) 27 Berkeley Journal of International Law 253, 275–279. For works advocating indicators as a monitoring tool of human rights implementation, see e.g. Inga T Winkler, Margaret L Satterthwaite and Catarina De Albuquerque, 'Treasuring What We Measure and Measuring What We Treasure: Post-2015 Monitoring for the Promotion of Equality in the Water, Sanitation, and Hygiene Sector' (2014) 32 Wisconsin International Law Journal 547; Young, 'TheMi-

tical data have gained importance in international governance, performance measuring has become a form of political power used by international institutions.[23] Thus, indicators bring into question the legitimacy of the institutions which design the measurements and entail targets that may not reflect the needs of the populations involved.[24] Methodologically, they may be an untrustworthy surrogate for human rights in that they might not fully grasp the content of human rights norms.[25] Using quantitative data (counting the number of tangible elements) seems a more accurate method, but there is still the issue of whether what is being measured reflects the qualitative content of rights.[26] Qualitative information is even more difficult because what matters is not only what is being counted, but also how subjective assessment of notions such as liberty or equality can be turned into an objective metric.[27] The measurement techniques may not always pay attention to the experience of the population harmed by State policies and can give a wrong sense of achievement due to the lack of disaggregated data about the most affected groups.[28]

With these constraints in mind, it is true that indicators in HTA criteria and human rights indicators are two different domains, but they have in common the risks of shifting from a concept to a metric (see summary in Table 5.1). As a consequence, an HRBA must ensure that the evidence produced corresponds to the expected information (value or quality of health), and whether it distorts the reality or prevents effective engagement with patients, which would cause both discrimination and an unfair procedure. Some procedural concerns about indicators can be also found in the HRBA to data argued by the OHCHR, endorsing the principles of participation, data disaggregation and

---

nimum Core of Economic and Social Rights: A Concept in Search of Content' (chapter 4, n 84), 164–167; AnnJanette Rosga and Margaret Satterthwaite, 'Measuring Human Rights: UN Indicators in Critical Perspective' in Kevin Davis and others (eds), *Governance by Indicators: Global Power through Classification and Rankings* (Oxford University Press 2012) 315–316.

23 For indicators as a form of governance, see: Sally Engle Merry, 'Measuring the World: Indicators, Human Rights, and Global Governance' (2011) 52 Current Anthropology S83.

24 Mathias Siems and David Nelken, 'Global Social Indicators and the Concept of Legitimacy' (2017) 13 International Journal of Law in Context 436, 443–446.

25 Hadi Strømmen Lile, 'Lost in Operationalisation: Developing Legally Relevant Indicators, Questions and Benchmarks' (2017) 21 The International Journal of Human Rights 1378, 1383–1384.

26 OHCHR, "Human Rights Indicators: A Guide to Measurement and Implementation", 2012 (HR/PUB/12/5) p. 21.

27 Lile (n 25) 1383–1386; Simon Walker, 'Challenges of Human Rights Measurement' in Bård Andreassen, Hans-Otto Sano and Siobhán McInerney-Lankford (eds), *Research Methods in Human Rights* (Edward Elgar Publishing 2017) 319.

28 Langford and Fukuda-Parr (n 21) 235.

TABLE 5.1 Comparative Table of Measurements Limitations in Indicators (Source: Author's own contribution)

	Limitations in indicators and health metrics		
	Human Rights indicators	**Health Status Indicators**	**Economic Indicators**
Evidence	Human Rights compliance	Evidence of clinical effect quality of life	Economic evidence (cost-effectiveness)
Methodological problems	Unable to measure the implementation of the human rights norms they refer to	Unable to reflect patient values and preferences	Unable to integrate patient values and human rights principles
Effects	Discrimination, low legitimacy and compliance	Discrimination and unfair procedure	Discrimination and unfair procedure

accountability.[29] This approach, however, does not take into account the whole 3P framework, complemented by non-discrimination and progressive realisation. I now move on to discuss this.

1.1 3Ps Framework in Evidence-Making in HTA

HTA evidence-making is just as complex as that of human rights indicators. Suitable HTA studies depend greatly on the correct handling of the data to minimise any uncertainty, as in, for example, the sample variation (whether it is representative or not), the precise extrapolation of information in long-term scenarios without inconsistencies and the degree of confidence in the data.[30] Any simplification may result in disregarding outcomes relevant to human rights values and in utilising methods that would be incompatible with human rights principles, such as transparency and public participation.[31]

29 UN OHCHR, "A Human Rights Based Approach to Data" (United Nations, 2018) p. 3–20.

30 Richard Edlin and others, *Cost Effectiveness Modelling for Health Technology Assessment: A Practical Course* (Springer International Publishing 2015) 59–75.

31 Ibid.

As measurements and evidence-making in economics and health are not infallible, the 3Ps, in their usage and interpretation, serve to drive knowledge production towards human rights principles. Economists and other specifically trained professionals hold significant sway in determining the rules and angles, which can negate positive outcomes in a human rights context (e.g. interventions that allow school attendance for children).[32] Culyer asserts that economists should pose pertinent questions to the public or act under guidelines that cover most traditional HTA aspects.[33] As Culyer notes, social matters (as human rights ideals) may appear too vague or broad to be delimited in a specific scope.[34] It might also be materially impossible to cover all technological dimensions to very particular or unpredictable circumstances, which may prove to be very costly to research.[35] Moreover, patients could be excluded because what is under discussion is not what reflects their interests.

Additionally, on a normative level, evidence in HTA is already influenced by implicit social values or beliefs (utilitarianism, consequentialism, etc.), even though as a concept it has been traditionally treated as a neutral institution separate from value judgements.[36] The 3Ps function precisely as normative values that should regulate and determine evidence-making and criteria according to an HRBA, in a deliberative democracy bound by substantive standards (as described in Chapter 1).[37] To meet the 3Ps' standards, this deliberative democracy is implemented through an evidence-informed deliberative process that must ensure a fair procedure and non-discrimination so that patients are not in practice excluded from decisions for lack of appropriate evidence.

If no adequate evidence-making is currently feasible, then the situation must be remedied progressively and to the fullest capacity of the State in order to promote the first two principles to the highest level. At every new technology launch, patients may face several barriers to scrutinising methods of research and quality of evidence. This exclusion by research design can happen, for instance, in economic models that cannot be examined publicly,

32 Anthony J Culyer, 'Four Issues in Cost-Effectiveness Analysis and Health Technology Assessment: A View from the Touch-Line' in Juan E del Llano-Señarís and Carlos Campillo-Artero (eds), *Health Technology Assessment and Health Policy Today: A Multifaceted View of their Unstable Crossroads* (Springer International Publishing 2015) 89.

33 Ibid., 90–92.

34 Ibid.

35 Ibid.

36 Bjørn Hofmann, Ken Bond and Lars Sandman, 'Evaluating Facts and Facting Evaluations: On the Fact-Value Relationship in HTA' (2018) 24 Journal of Evaluation in Clinical Practice 957, 958–960.

37 See chapter 1, pp. 7–8.

which constitutes an unfair procedure. Those studies depend greatly on the correct handling of the data to minimise uncertainty, as mentioned above to avoid simplification resulting in loss of human rights value and incompatibility with human rights principles.[38]

Hence, in the model proposed in this chapter, the 3Ps are mutually influential. Any unfair procedure of evidence in HTA can bring about the effect of the "fruits of the poisonous tree" – if no patient-valued data is used, the whole priority-setting and participation process is jeopardised by evidence introduced in a way that penalises certain individuals. According to Figure 5.1, evidence must aim to meet the highest standards of non-discrimination and fair procedure. The red quadrant (low non-discrimination and high fair procedure) equates to a straightforward incidence of right to health violation. Progressive realisation should be in place in the blue and grey quadrants, to correct failures in the other principles to achieve evidence compliant with an HRBA.

For instance, consider a group of patients that benefits from a medical device (e.g. a prosthesis) widely used by most of that specific patient population but with no ethically permissible trials to measure its efficiency or efficacy in the same way as randomised controlled trials (RCT) do. Its use would be deemed unethical as it is not feasible to compare, for example, a "fake pros-

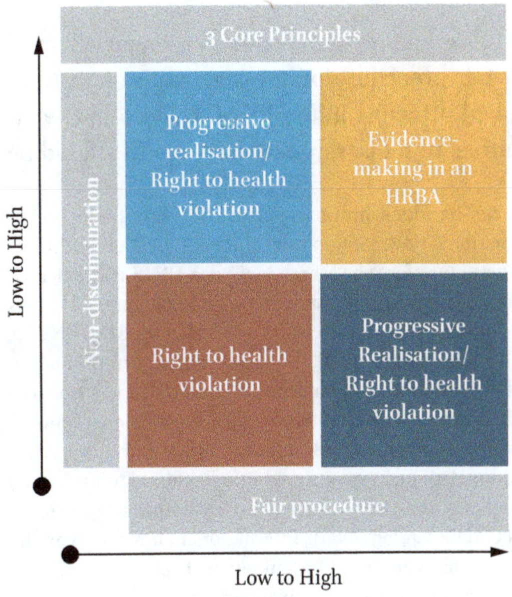

FIGURE 5.1 Interaction between non-discrimination and fair procedure principles in the progressive realisation or violation of the right to health (Source: Author's own contribution)

38 Edlin and others (n 30) 59–75.

thesis" or render completely blind the allocation of treatments to new patients. A government could, in theory, request clinical trials, even if patients already have a record of using such a treatment, since the lack of research itself would prevent a more rigorous clinical confirmation in an HTA. In this case, if the strict standards were used (by implicitly regarding only a specific type of research as valid), it would be challenging to meet the evidence requirements and therefore no positive decision could follow (resulting in discrimination). The evidence not collected about the clinical effects for some identifiable patient groups can create an unfair procedure by exclusion, which could occur, for example, for patients with a specific comorbidity, which is not part of a specific trial. The State would therefore be obligated to take immediate action to avoid evidence gaps (if an alternative exists) or recognise that further research should be undertaken as a matter of progressive realisation.

Therefore, it is clear that the 3Ps cannot be divorced from each other. As the relevant provisions of fair procedure and progressive realisation were examined in previous chapters, they will be referred to as applied in practice in evidence-making in the remainder of this chapter. Non-discrimination, however, will first be described in greater length in the next section.

2 Non-discrimination Principle

In the application of the 3Ps, discrimination stands out as a major effect of failure to meet the variables of fair procedure/progressive realisation. Non-discrimination is a well-established principle in the ICESCR and other treaties.[39] As asserted by the Committee, non-discrimination in health should be

39 Non-discrimination obligations can be found in a number of HR treaties and declarations. UDHR, art. 2 and 7; International Covenant on Civil and Political Rights (ICCPR) (adopted 16 December. 1966, entered into force 23 March 1976) 999 UNTS 171, Articles 2 and 7; ICESCR, Article 2. Also, see specific treaties: Convention on the Rights of Persons with Disabilities (adopted 13 December 2006, entered into force 3 May 2008) 49 UNTS 2; International Convention on the Elimination of All Forms of Racial Discrimination (adopted 21 December 1965, entered into force 4 January 1969) 660 UNTS 195; Convention on the Elimination of All Forms of Discrimination against Women (adopted 18 December 1979, entered into force 3 September 1981) 1249 UNTS 13; Convention relating to the Status of Refugees (adopted 28 July 1951, entered into force 22 April 1954) 189 UNTS 137; Convention on the Rights of the Child (adopted 20 November 1989, entered into force 2 September 1990) UN GAORes 44/25 (1989).; International Convention on the Protection of the Rights of All Migrant Workers and Members of Their Families; Convention on the Rights of Persons with Disabilities, Convention concerning Discrimination in Respect of Employment and Occupation (ILO Convention No. 111) (adopted 25 June 1958, entered into force 15 June 1960) 362 U.N.T.S. 31.

determined both by formal equality (equal consideration before law) and substantive equality (focusing on the worst-off) in areas such as reproductive rights.[40]

The interpretation of the right to health may fall roughly within one type, depending on whether non-discrimination is assumed to mean an equal right to health (formal equality, either on a one-to-one basis or between the averages among different groups) or to protect a group from their existing disadvantages (substantive equality) as a priority to the worse-off, defended by Fredman.[41] The approach suited to HTA and health priority-setting, however, is a middle-way: people cannot be absolutely barred or disadvantaged in healthcare solely because of a particular characteristic (formal equality), but may otherwise receive extra care or more prospects of a positive recommendation if they are in a vulnerable group (substantive equality). This section will examine these two sides of the principle of non-discrimination in healthcare resource allocation (formal and substantive), which will later be applied to evidence-making.

2.1 Non-discrimination and Formal Equality

Non-discrimination is primarily associated with formal equality, given that absolute equality or equality in outcomes in healthcare distribution are not the main purposes of non-discrimination.[42] Absolute equality, as proposed by Harris, would not permit any rationing weighting different cost-effectiveness levels, only neutral decisions (e.g. waiting lists, lotteries) could be adopted.[43] However, a stand-alone right to equality under socio-economic rights is far

---

40 See e.g. CESCR, "General Comment No. 22 on the Right to Sexual and Reproductive Health (Article 12 of the International Covenant on Economic, Social and Cultural Rights)"2 May 2016 (E/C.12/GC/22) paras. 22–24; "General Comment No. 20: Non-Discrimination in Economic, Social and Cultural Rights (Art. 2, Para. 2, of the International Covenant on Economic, Social and Cultural Rights)" 2 July 2009 (E/C.12/GC/20) para. 10.

41 In constitutional law, Fredman describes substantive equality as a duty to prioritise and reduce the burden of the most disadvantaged. She presents four dimensions that need to be addressed on substantive equality (disadvantage, stigma, voice and participation, and accommodation of difference and achieving structural change). See Sandra Fredman, 'Substantive Equality Revisited' (2016) 14 International Journal of Constitutional Law 712. Against this view, MacKinnon argues that hierarchy is the central issue to be addressed in substantive equality among groups. See: Catharine A MacKinnon, 'Substantive Equality Revisited: A Reply to Sandra Fredman' (2016) 14 International Journal of Constitutional Law 739.

42 Yamin and Norheim (chapter 2, n 1) 308.

43 John Harris, 'QALYfying the Value of Life.' (1987) 13 Journal of Medical Ethics 117.

from fully established, while the conclusion that non-discrimination amounts to absolute equality is also contested for collapsing two different ideas together.[44]

Additionally, non-discrimination in international law has been presumed to protect "negative equality", as opposed to absolute or positive equality (where being equal is the standard, except if there is a justification for not being so). Therefore, international law may allow any inequality unless it is forbidden.[45] The CESCR has never indicated that resources should be equally distributed to each patient; however, it does prohibit inequality based upon differential treatment according to one's status. For instance, health status, or "a person's physical or mental health" is one of the grounds of discrimination forbidden by the Committee.[46]

Thus, a more coherent interpretation for negative equality, alongside formal equality, is that no one can be disadvantaged or denied access to healthcare because of some attribute. However, the Committee does not distinguish clearly whether the exclusion from care is an absolute denial of access to services to a person (e.g. offering no coverage at all for people of certain groups or conditions) or whether absolute denial may consist of a specific exclusion from a treatment for only a particular illness or healthcare need due to a priority-setting policy.[47]

Other causes of discrimination provided by the Committee are variably related to health status under two categories: first, express grounds (race and colour, sex, language, religion, political opinion, national or social origin, property, birth) and second, other status (including disability, age, nationality, marital and family status, sexual orientation and gender identity, place of residence, economic and social situation and also health status).[48] Grounds of discrimination can also be based on one individual attribute associated with membership of a particular group and each type of patient can represent a different community.[49] The Committee also refers to multiple grounds of dis-

44 Some authors assume non-discrimination and equality as equivalent in treaty norms (see e.g. Daniel Moeckli, 'Equality and Non-Discrimination' in Daniel Moeckli and others (eds), *International Human Rights Law* (Oxford University Press 2010) 189. For counter-opinions, see: Gillian MacNaughton, 'Healthcare Systems and Equality Rights' (2011) 6 The Equal Rights Review 61, 68; Gillian MacNaughton, 'Untangling Equality and Non-Discrimination to Promote the Right to Health Care for All' (2009) 11 Health and Human Rights 47, 48.

45 MacNaughton, 'Healthcare Systems and Equality Rights' (n 44) 65–68.

46 CESCR, 'General Comment No. 20' (n 40) para. 33.

47 Ibid.

48 Ibid., paras 18–35.

49 Ibid., para. 16.

crimination that together can aggravate the situation for some individuals (by extension, this can cover patients with comorbidities).[50]

Those grounds of discrimination can affect individuals directly or indirectly in a policy, but in HTA it would normally occur through indirect mechanisms such as methods and indicators. The Committee understands that direct discrimination applies to an explicitly prohibited ground to disadvantage someone, while indirect discrimination refers to rules or policies that in practice will be detrimental to individuals based on prohibited grounds ingrained within the decision process.[51]

As a conclusion, with both formal and negative equality, the best view of non-discrimination, defended in this chapter, is that specific attributes cannot immediately exclude patients from the priority-setting process on prohibited grounds. At the same time, every patient formally has standing to be considered in the decision-making (but no equality of outcomes). However, such equal standing can be undermined if the policies have within them indicators or methods that in practice indirectly discriminate against groups of patients (this point will be demonstrated in the sections on clinical and economic evidence-making).

2.2 Non-discrimination and Substantive Equality

Alongside formal equality in non-discrimination, substantive equality comes as a complementary approach. Admittedly, substantive equality is a far-reaching term that could include wide forms of socio-economic exclusion (e.g. poverty) in broader policy areas than resource allocation for healthcare.[52] In the scope of priority-setting, the question should be: who are the persons to be recognised as of higher priority? The CESCR has granted priority to special groups by reference to terms such as "vulnerable", "disadvantaged" or "minorities".[53]

The prioritarian arm of non-discrimination has been developed by the CESCR's attention to the idea of vulnerability. Under international human rights law more broadly, what is most clear is that there is a primary concern for the vulnerable, supported in many international law instruments concern-

50 Ibid., 17.

51 Ibid., 10; CESCR, General Comment 22 (n 40) paras 26–28.

52 CESCR, General Comment No. 22 (n 40) paras. 22–24.

53 CESCR, 'General Comment No. 20 (n 40) paras 10, 16–35, Camila Teixeira, 'Priority, Agency and Cooperation: How International Human Rights Law Helps Fulfil the Economic and Social Rights of the Most Vulnerable' (2019) 24 The International Journal of Human Rights 1031, 1035–1039; Yamin and Norheim (chapter 2, n 1).

ing the protection of particularly disadvantaged populations.[54] The catalogue of persons that should be considered vulnerable or have recognised forms of vulnerability include, for instance, children, the elderly, ethnic minorities, racially segregated individuals, disabled persons and women.[55]

Identifying and determining the weight of vulnerable groups is complex, given that the right to health does not provide a grading system between them. In theory, vulnerability has been described as a condition shared by all humans as one of the foundations of human rights.[56] Hence, a State is under the obligation to equally protect everyone for their intrinsic vulnerabilities, yet it is also argued that higher priority should be given to the most disadvantaged.[57] The proportion of this special consideration towards the most vulnerable is not clearly established. Some would say that only improvement in the status of the worst-off is necessary, rather than reducing the gap between classes.[58]

Under this conceptual uncertainty, after reviewing formal and substantive equality in non-discrimination, all that can be concluded is that the criteria of HTA should protect formal equality in prohibiting direct or indirect discrimination (overt or implicit exclusions). Substantive equality should confer upon the vulnerable some form of extra consideration – although the effects and methods for this are not defined.

3 Applying the 3Ps in Clinical and Economic Evidence

Thus far, we have seen the dual nature of non-discrimination (formal and substantive equality) and described the broader context of indicators to measure human rights standards. After noting the constraints in human rights measurement, this section will consider what those issues mean to evidence-making in HTA so as to ensure non-discrimination in measuring quality and value of new health technologies. The present section will therefore turn to applying the 3Ps framework to complex measurement instruments in HTA and how those principles interact with each other in this process. As Table 5.2 shows, the principles are interrelated and interdependent: an unfair pro-

54 Ibid.

55 Alexander HE Morawa, 'Vulnerability as a Concept of International Human Rights Law' (2003) 6 Journal of International Relations and Development 139, 141–147.

56 Teixeira (n 53) 2–3.

57 Sarah S Willen and others, 'Syndemic Vulnerability and the Right to Health' (2017) 389 The Lancet 964, 965.

58 Yamin and Norheim (chapter 2, n 1) 307–309.

TABLE 5.2 Comparing the 3 core principles impact on equality in evidence-making (Source: Author's own contribution)

	3 Core Principles		
	Non-discrimination	**Fair procedure**	**Progressive realisation**
Formal Equality	– Does the evidence exclude a patient group explicitly or certain patient relevant outcomes? – Is there any indirect discrimination in the criteria?	– Is the evidence-making not participatory or the standards limiting public participation? – Is the evidence-making not accountable or transparent?	– Is the State taking steps to produce evidence relevant to patients or to improve their participation?
Substantive Equality	– Was the evidence obtained by any methodological adjustments to include minorities or vulnerable groups?	– Are minority groups affected consulted in the evidence-making? – Are there special provisions for minority groups to participate and provide qualitative contributions as evidence?	– Is the State taking steps to produce evidence relevant to minorities or vulnerable groups?

cedure causes discrimination and issues in evidence-making should be addressed through progressive realisation.

The first part of this section will address the 3Ps in evidence-based medicine (EBM) and QoL/health measurements. The second part will analyse value measurements, especially utility indicators. Each subsection will give a brief explanation of the methods involved in each type of measurement, but it is important to note that health measurements and QoL are interdependent and findings from clinical studies may be used for economic analysis. The third part will conclude with future actions and possible solutions that should be undertaken as a form of progressive realisation.

3.1 Clinical Evidence

There is a close connection between EBM and quality in human rights standards, but little guidance has been given about the limits and risks in associating clinical evidence with this category of evidence-making. The Committee has been explicitly inclined to take quality as reflected by EBM, particularly concerning reproductive rights.[59] Quality in the right to health is the Q of the AAAQ framework (availability, accessibility, acceptability and quality).[60] In EBM, doctors have to apply a strict scientific method in their recommendations to evaluate the quality of research used to measure the quality of treatments.[61] Though it can be defined as "the conscientious, explicit and judicious use of current best evidence in making decisions about the care of individual patients", EBM shapes policy decisions as a triad balanced between research evidence, clinical expertise and patient values.[62]

Despite policies and outcomes in an HRBA being "evidence-based", the requirements for evidence are normally entrusted to researchers and the scientific community.[63] Occasionally, non-observance of medical evidence in health policies is one of the issues raised in the CESCR and CRPD periodic reviews and plenary sessions, but how this interacts with patient values is

59 See e.g. CESCR, 'General Comment No. 22' (n 40) para. 21.

60 CESCR, GC 14 (chapter 1, n 34), para. 12.

61 Wendy Rogers, 'Does Evidence-Based Medicine Offer Fair Benefits for All?' (2004) 6 AMA Journal of Ethics 6.

62 David L Sackett and others, 'Evidence-Based Medicine: What It Is and What It Isn't' (1996) 312 British Medical Journal 71, 71; Evelyn Schlegl, Pierre Ducournau and Jörg Ruof, 'Different Weights of the Evidence-Based Medicine Triad in Regulatory, Health Technology Assessment, and Clinical Decision Making' (2017) 31 Pharmaceutical Medicine 213, 214–215.

63 See e.g. UNGA, "Report of the Special Rapporteur on the Right to Development" (30 July 2018) A/73/271, para. 11. e; HRC "Follow-up on the Application of the Technical Guidance on the Application of a Human Rights-Based Approach to the Implementation of Policies and Programmes to Reduce Preventable Maternal Mortality and Morbidity" (29 June 2018) A/HRC/39/26, paras. 43–44, HRC, "Report of the United Nations High Commissioner for Human Rights" (20 April 2018) A/HRC/38/37paras 30–31, HRC, "Guiding Principles on Human Rights Impact Assessments of Economic Reforms" (19 December 2018) paras 17.1–172.

not discussed and the requirements for evidence-based policies are more related to disaggregated data than the methods of research.[64]

For instance, the former Special Rapporteur, Dainius Pūras, attached great weight to EBM in the formulation of public policies concerning the right to health, but without much concern for the evidence-making process itself.[65] Pūras contends that there could be imbalances in evidence-based policies as to procedural fairness ("lack of transparency, accountability and political will to follow established principles and standards"), but this argument seems to refer just to how scientific evidence goes unheeded by governments.[66] An HRBA is compromised if decisions relating to public health depart from scientific evidence, particularly if this is a result of power imbalances between political groups and interests that tend to favour a more influential category of patients rather than comprehensive initiatives for the whole health system.[67]

This view says little about a duty to facilitate the creation of evidence itself in cases where patients lack research with appropriate EBM design or where criteria, which are indirectly discriminatory, need improvement. For instance, requiring rigorous controlled experiments can be unethical, either because there is evidence of efficacy by other means or because such studies would cause unnecessary deaths (as happened with a modified heart–lung machine for neonates).[68] In mental health, Pūras was even more critical of the role of evidence and how it should be integrated into practice and patient preferences, observing that "reliance on clinical trials (...) may skew treatment

64 See e.g. CESCR, "Concluding Observations on the Combined 5th and 6th Periodic Reports of the Philippines" 26 October 2016 (E/C.12/PHL/CO/5-6), paras 53–54. See also the calls for better statistical data in disability policies: CRPD "Concluding Observations on the Initial Report of Seychelles" (16 April 2018) CRPD/C/SYC/CO/1, paras 53–54; Conference of the State Parties of the CRPD "Improvement of Disability Data and Statistics: Objectives and Challenges" 1 April 2015 (CRPD/CSP/2015/3), paras. 4–12; United Nations and Department of Economic and Social Affairs, *Disability and Development Report: Realizing the Sustainable Development Goals by, for and with Persons with Disabilities : 2018* (2019) 275–283, Statistical Commission " Joint report of the Secretary-General, the Washington Group on Disability Statistics and international agencies" 20 December 2019 (E/CN.3/2020/34).

65 HRC, "Report of the Special Rapporteur on the right of everyone to the enjoyment of the highest attainable standard of physical and mental health, Dainius Pūras" 2 April 2015 (A/HRC/29/33), paras 49–51

66 Ibid, para. 51.

67 Ibid.

68 Marie-Caroline Schulte, *Evidence-Based Medicine – A Paradigm Ready To Be Challenged?: How Scientific Evidence Shapes Our Understanding And Use Of Medicine* (JB Metzler 2020) 53–55. Philip J Wolfson, 'The Development and Use of Extracorporeal Membrane Oxygenation in Neonates' (2003) 76 The Annals of thoracic surgery S2224, ss2226-27.

recommendations towards drugs", which are more often controlled by the pharmaceutical industry than by other stakeholders.[69] This comment recognises the need for local evidence production so as not to overrule traditional local practices with standardised guidelines not culturally and economically appropriate for a specific region.[70]

Moreover, what human rights bodies have not given much guidance on is whether the presumed superior level of clinical evidence purported by EBM is always justified or not. Some treatments may not be regarded by the patient as the best available options, but merely as the treatment with the best evidence in the hierarchy of research.[71] This section will now consider unfair procedure and discrimination on the grounds of lack of patient values and insights in two respects: research standards that set high thresholds of evidence compared to clinical evaluations, and instruments of health measurements that exclude patient experience or well-being benefits.

As for the first issue, EBM became the gold standard of scientific research to evaluate the effects of healthcare interventions after the seminal Cochrane publication in the 1970s defending a more rigorous form of evidence-making in medicine.[72] EBM can be distinguished from comparative effectiveness research (CER) in indicating whether, generally, a treatment can yield positive results (efficacy, or whether it can work). CER is more concerned with determining the real impact of an intervention in comparison to others (effectiveness or how well or better it works).[73] The findings of EBM are used in clinical guidelines and then defined as a standard of care for practitioners and, in some countries, with legally binding force.[74] In some cases, clinical efficacy

---

69 HRC, "Report of the Special Rapporteur on the Right of Everyone to the Enjoyment of the Highest Attainable Standard of Physical and Mental Health" 15 April 2020 (A/HRC/44/48), para. 19.

70 Ibid., paras. 18–20.

71 Rodolfo Gaeta and Nelida Gentile, 'Evidence, Discovery and Justification: The Case of Evidence-Based Medicine: Evidence, Discovery and Justification' (2016) 22 Journal of Evaluation in Clinical Practice 550, 551; Glenn W Jones and Stephen M Sagar, 'No Guidance Is Provided for Situations for Which Evidence Is Lacking' (1995) 311 BMJ 258; Simon Day, 'Evidence-Based Medicine and Rare Diseases' in Manuel Posada de la Paz, Domenica Taruscio and Stephen C Groft (eds), *Rare Diseases Epidemiology: Update and Overview* (Springer International Publishing 2017) 208–209.

72 Archibald Leman Cochrane, *Effectiveness and Efficiency: Random Reflections on Health Services*, vol 900574178 (Nuffield Provincial Hospitals Trust London 1972) Richard E Ashcroft, 'Current Epistemological Problems in Evidence-Based Medicine' (2004) 30 Journal of Medical Ethics 131, 132–133.

73 Luce and others (chapter 1, n 8) 262–264.

74 Brian Hurwitz, 'Clinical Guidelines: Legal and Political Considerations of Clinical Practice Guidelines' (1999) 318 BMJ 661, 661–662.

or comparative effectiveness is the major factor analysed and the history of HTA in some countries (e.g. the USA) developed first through clinical research, while cost-effectiveness was politically resisted.[75]

Most of what EBM does is to establish a hierarchy of evidence to support better decision-making in medical practice, whereby RCTs stand at the top and research conducted with fewer controls and individual reports are less well-regarded.[76] RCTs are conducted by comparing the results of two different groups, which are blindly given treatment or a placebo to minimise any confounding factors that may distort the effects.[77]

Despite the prominence of EBM, unquestioning adherence to RCT as the ultimate truth is disputed.[78] The EBM movement developed from the understanding that RCT reduces the bias in research statistically, but this can be contested – mathematically there will always be a certain feature randomly more salient among groups every time the experiment is performed.[79] It has been argued that only a large number of repetitions with different samples could solve this mathematical limitation, though some would argue that in most cases the effect observed is so significant that randomised trials are not even necessary.[80] Trials also measure the effects in a population sample – which cannot be generalisable in some circumstances or appropriate for a specific group (such as minorities) – confounding the exact gains (or even harms) to each class of patients.[81] Meta-analysis (reviewing several studies together) can also be contradictory or lead to an unreasonable conclusion for medical practice (as with the Cochrane study refuting HCV drug efficacy).[82]

---

75 Jennifer Wong, 'The History of Technology Assessment and Comparative Effectiveness Research for Drugs and Medical Devices and the Role of the Federal Government' (2014) 33 Biotechnology Law Report 221, 228.

76 Samuli L Saarni, 'Evidence-Based Medicine Guidelines: A Solution to Rationing or Politics Disguised as Science?' (2004) 30 Journal of Medical Ethics 171, 171–172.

77 Anthony K Akobeng, 'Understanding Randomised Controlled Trials' (2005) 90 Archives of disease in childhood 840, 840–841.

78 See e.g. Warren Pearce, Sujatha Raman and Andrew Turner, 'Randomised Trials in Context: Practical Problems and Social Aspects of Evidence-Based Medicine and Policy' (2015) 16 Trials 1.

79 Miriam Solomon, *Making Medical Knowledge* (Oxford University Press 2015) 135–141

80 Ibid., 137–140.

81 Pearce, Raman and Turner (n 78) 2; Dorothee Mielke and Veit Rohde, 'Randomized Controlled Trials – a Critical Re-Appraisal' [2020] Neurosurgical Review 3.

82 Stefan Z Wiktor and John D Scott, 'What Is the Impact of Treatment for Hepatitis C Virus Infection?' (2017) 390 The Lancet 107; John PA Ioannidis, 'The Mass Production of Redundant, Misleading, and Conflicted Systematic Reviews and Meta-analyses' (2016) 94 The Milbank Quarterly 485.

Because of limitations and persisting uncertainties in clinical studies, EBM should be taken in context and should not limit other forms of patient participation, at risk of promoting an unfair procedure. HTA, though, can place excessive weight on EBM to the detriment of patient preferences and real-world evidence.[83] This analysis may be so central to HTA that an assessment may also immediately conclude as soon as strong clinical evidence demonstrates that the candidate treatment is not safe, medically useful or is against clinical guidelines.[84] Yet, other forms of evidence can be just as important for defining the most appropriate treatment, especially to subpopulations that are not well represented in clinical trials. This includes real-world evidence (analysis of the data collected on clinical use of a technology) and mechanistic knowledge (understanding how a therapy works) to have a better understanding of the implications for patients.[85]

With the exclusion of some evidence, an unfair procedure may arise because an uneven playing field exists between experts and patients. This could particularly be the case in the drafting of clinical guidelines, which is dominated by doctors while patients have no power to describe their own experiences.[86] Clinical guidelines have always been a political decision (sometimes even as form of rationing policy) even before EBM, as recommendations usually required expert consensus, and similar internal dialogue still persists with little public scrutiny.[87] After reviewing the contrasts in guidelines in the Netherlands and the UK, the appraisal of evidence is not as much a result of scientific review, but rather that EBM is used as a discourse to legitimise normative and political decisions made by the medical community as a political regulation. Medical experience, though, does not generally prevail

---

83 Schlegl, Ducournau and Ruof (n 62) 214–215.

84 Luce and others (chapter 1, n 8) 258–259.

85 Wija Oortwijn, Laura Sampietro-Colom and Rebecca Trowman, 'How to Deal with the Inevitable: Generating Real-World Data and Using Real-World Evidence for HTA Purposes – From Theory to Action' (2019) 35 International Journal of Technology Assessment in Health Care 346, 1–2. Holly Andersen, 'Mechanisms: What Are They Evidence for in Evidence-Based Medicine?: Mechanisms Evidence for What?' (2012) 18 Journal of Evaluation in Clinical Practice 992.

86 See e.g. David James Hunter and others, 'Public Involvement in Health Priority Setting: Future Challenges for Policy, Research and Society' (2016) 30 Journal of Health Organization and Management 796, 801; Kathryn Oliver and Warren Pearce, 'Three Lessons from Evidence-Based Medicine and Policy: Increase Transparency, Balance Inputs and Understand Power' (2017) 3 Palgrave Communications 1, 4; Trisha Greenhalgh and others, 'Six "Biases" against Patients and Carers in Evidence-Based Medicine' (2015) 13 BMC Medicine 200.

87 Saarni (n 76) 173.

over EBM, as complementary knowledge from practical clinical judgement, real-world observations and patient experience are deemed a lower form of evidence.[88]

Lastly, bias and discrimination in EBM can occur by institutionalised exclusion of particular groups or research settings in comparison to others.[89] Biased research is likely to happen if designed to identify the "average patient" or interpreted as valid to any person, to the detriment of minorities and subgroups, including patients with comorbidities, who will respond less or have side effects to treatments.[90] Outcomes may also need different methods of measurement other than a survey of the general population, or even be calculated with a different weight. For example, aspects relevant to disabled persons in Alzheimer's research might not be identified using standard methods for the general population.[91]

Hence, research bias may cut across diverse patient groups who cannot be involved appropriately in the research prior to HTA. A common perception is that EBM can be gender-discriminatory for not involving significant clinical data of women, in disregard of their specific clinical results.[92] Studies conducted in developed countries may have no similarity to poor-resource settings where patients do not have a diagnosis or cannot take part in research, thus creating a "rich world bias".[93] Biased RCTs sponsored by the industry targeting outcomes not relevant to patients might also be assessed as good evidence, while at the same time open flexibilisation of research participation is less favoured (such as broadening access to experimental treatments in the AIDS crisis).[94]

---

88 Schulte (n 68) 90–97.

89 Rogers (n 61) 570.

90 Emma Tumilty, Simon Walker and Steve Tumilty, 'Tainting by Numbers – How the Disadvantaged Become Invisible within Evidence-Based Medicine' (2014) 19 Physical Therapy Reviews 367, 369; Richard L Kravitz, Naihua Duan and Joel Braslow, 'Evidence-Based Medicine, Heterogeneity of Treatment Effects, and the Trouble with Averages' (2004) 82 The Milbank Quarterly 661.

91 Rob Stewart, 'NICE Guidelines and the Treatment of Alzheimer's Disease: Evidence-Based Medicine May Be Discriminatory' (2001) 179 British Journal of Psychiatry 367.

92 Anita Holdcroft, 'Gender Bias in Research: How Does It Affect Evidence Based Medicine?' (2007) 100 Journal of the Royal Society of Medicine 2.

93 Helen Crowther, Wendy Lipworth and Ian Kerridge, 'Evidence-Based Medicine and Epistemological Imperialism: Narrowing the Divide between Evidence and Illness: EBM and Epistemological Imperialism' (2011) 17 Journal of Evaluation in Clinical Practice 868.

94 Pearce, Raman and Turner (n 78) 4–5; Mielke and Rohde (n 81) 3.

Thus, political participation of patients in the design of evidence and health measures is important in an HRBA. Rabeharisoa et al. have denominated "evidence-based activism": the initiative of patients to point to under-researched areas and contribute with their experiences.[95] Observing the NICE committees, Milewa and Barry found that there was supremacy of quantitative evidence compared to other forms of information submitted by stakeholders, concluding that the administration of relevant factors of clinical efficacy and cost-effectiveness "tended to take precedence over more subjective, experientially-based perspectives".[96]

Though administrators, of course, expect some reliable evidence, scientific research may not necessarily be able to substitute for the voice of patients. Large systematic reviews may not sufficiently capture questions of equity, especially in small social subgroups, or other divisions of gender, economic status or race. The rules of the health economics game have imperceptible nuances difficult for a patient to contradict in an open debate, from discount rates for costs and benefits to how exactly to quantify utility for a health outcome.[97] Difficult debates can also undermine participation, for example with trade-offs between two different health outcomes, which are problematic to compare or express personal preferences about, even after due consultation with patients.[98] Even when listening to patients, surveys may not be completely unbiased, as the criteria chosen to collect data also depend on some degree of subjectivism over what is the patient's view.[99]

As a result, insufficient availability of evidence requires progressive realisation of research policies to produce appropriate patient data through study designs tailored for the beneficiaries of the treatments or to accept qualitative submissions during patient participation in HTA. EBM may set high standards of research that might not be feasible in the short run for some treatments, but could allow, for instance, provisional approval until more evidence is pro-

95 Vololona Rabeharisoa, Tiago Moreira and Madeleine Akrich, 'Evidence-Based Activism: Patients', Users' and Activists' Groups in Knowledge Society.' (2014) 9 BioSocieties 111.

96 Timothy Milewa and Christine Barry, 'Health Policy and the Politics of Evidence' (2005) 39 Social Policy & Administration 498, 510.

97 John Hutton, "'Health Economics' and the Evolution of Economic Evaluation of Health Technologies: Evolution of Economic Evaluation of Health Technologies" (2012) 21 Health Economics 13, 14–15.

98 See chapter 2, 2 on obstacles to implementing participation in HTA.

99 Anthony J Culyer, 'Four Issues in Cost-Effectiveness Analysis and Health Technology Assessment: A View from the Touch-Line' in Juan E del Llano-Señarís and Carlos Campillo-Artero (eds), *Health Technology Assessment and Health Policy Today: A Multifaceted View of their Unstable Crossroads* (Springer International Publishing 2015) 78–81.

duced.[100] Additionally, follow-up studies require investments at the point of care to collect more suitable data from clinicians.[101] Moreover, some treatments may show different results in practice that can only be investigated in a clinical setting with real-world evidence, and CER also demands that new research be designed to monitor old and new technologies.

3.2 Quality of Life Measurement

This being said, the research design of EBM is not the only problem in clinical research. The second cause of inappropriate clinical evidence-making is how data on quality of life (QoL), as a clinical outcome, is determined without actually reflecting public values protected by human rights. This problem begins with QoL's subjectivity as a broad concept linked to abstract notions such as justice, well-being and patient autonomy.[102] As a subjective assessment, QoL has been defined by the WHO "as individuals' perceptions of their position in life in the context of the culture and value systems in which they live and in relation to their goals, expectations, standards and concerns".[103] A barrier to human rights and quality of health is that rights are interdependent, entailing assessment of all life dimensions, while standard instruments may be too strictly centred on health, reducing patient influence or ignoring their wider well-being.[104]

Calculating the "amount" of health of an individual or population (roughly denominated as health status) varies depending on the approach and factors considered.[105] For instance, QoL is commonly measured in the limited sense of health-related quality of life (HRQoL), with a focus only on health aspects of life. Measurement parameters have taken diverse forms (e.g. individual functioning, factors that affect health, health circumstances influencing the QoL, or the assigned value of a health state by the public).[106] For each different

100 Rachel A Lindor, 'Advancing Evidence-Based Medicine by Expanding Coverage with Evidence Development Comment' (2011) 52 Jurimetrics [i], 210.

101 Ibid., 210–211.

102 PPM Harteloh, 'Understanding the Quality Concept in Health Care' (2004) 9 Accreditation and Quality Assurance 92, 93–94.

103 Whoqol Group, 'Measuring Quality of Life' [1997] Geneva: The World Health Organization 1, 1.

104 John Edward Brazier and others, 'Future Directions in Valuing Benefits for Estimating QALYs: Is Time Up for the EQ-5D?' (2019) 22 Value in Health 62, 64–65.

105 See e.g. Marilyn Bergner and Margaret L Rothman, 'Health Status Measures: An Overview and Guide for Selection' (1987) 8 Annual Review of Public Health 191.

106 Milad Karimi and John Brazier, 'Health, Health-Related Quality of Life, and Quality of Life: What Is the Difference?' (2016) 34 PharmacoEconomics 645, 646–647.

perspective (e.g. patients or doctors), the focus may vary from technical clinical aspects to well-being and other values, so "quality is in the eye of the user".[107] Regardless of objective quantitative measurement of physical conditions and patient symptoms, health measurement is commonly a subjective evaluation of the perceived quality of health for each health state measured; therefore, there are indirect evaluations (or preferences) that will depend on who conducts or participates in the study.[108]

Indirect approaches are also called "preference-based measures" but, in reality, the answers do not correspond to free preferences, given that the possible answers are decided by a pre-defined questionnaire.[109] Hausman also criticises this evaluative process, which defines the quantity of health through a subjective health state (e.g. a sterilised woman may regard her state as positive or negative). In his view, health in itself is not measurable, only its value. Accordingly, traditional preference-based metrics should not be pursued because they are problematic in eliciting from the population answers to the questions being asked. In order to measure health, Hausman then proposes the adoption of public values based on feelings and activities that are important to the population (e.g. ability to work, or being involved in social life), which are easier for respondents to grasp than comparing two different health states over time (e.g. being in a wheelchair for a year and blind for a month).

From a human rights perspective, clinical assessments, which disregard patient objectives and life aspects would result in an unfair procedure – because of the limited power of patients to report the outcomes they consider important – and discrimination – because of decisions based on evidence that do not reflect people's needs and health status. Generic health measures may be discriminatory for not heeding some statistically relevant groups of patients through appropriate means.[110] Methods should then be appropriate to capture the relevant aspects for a particular group of patients. As different HRQoL methods may report varied dimensions of health, and the operations to derive those health states into utility value are also not uniform as to the weights

107 Elizabeth R Ransom (ed), *The Healthcare Quality Book: Vision, Strategy, and Tools* (2nd ed, Health Administration Press 2008) 30–32; PPM Harteloh, 'The Meaning of Quality in Health Care: A Conceptual Analysis' (2003) 11 Health Care Analysis 259, 262.

108 Daniel M Hausman, 'Valuing Health' (2006) 34 Philosophy & Public Affairs 246, 246–259.

109 Nancy Devlin, "'Preference-Based Measure' Is Misleading – Can We Agree on Something Better? – The Academic Health Economists' Blog" (*The Academic Health Economists' Blog*) <https://aheblog.com/2020/08/12/preference-based-measure-is-misleading-can-we-agree-on-something-better/> accessed 16 April 2021.

110 Trisha Greenhalgh and others, 'Evidence-Based Medicine: A Movement in Crisis?' (2014) 348 BMJ g3725, 2–3.

allocated to each attribute, they can reveal great inconsistency and unreliability between surveys.[111] It is generally believed, however, that those who have experienced a health state are better respondents than those who have only a description of such state, so specific methods for measuring health in a certain group ought to be preferred.

The next subsection will first consider the usages of health measurement for economic evaluation. Health measurements mentioned so far will be the source of data for comparison of treatment effectiveness in HTA as a step before economic analysis, but they can also be embedded into the units of measurement of cost-effectiveness or value for money.[112] From a distributive angle, health indicators and clinical evidence will feed into health economic analysis to determine the costs versus additional benefits, measured through quality of health or even direct outcomes (for example, weight loss or days in hospital).[113]

3.3 Economic Value and the 3Ps

This section will discuss how the centrality of measuring economic value in HTA may be in tension with human rights principles. It will do so by looking at how economic metrics are employed and two frequent approaches towards cost-effectiveness and cost–benefit analysis. The former is built on the measurement of health outcomes and the latter calculated through monetary values of the benefits of technologies.[114]

In pursuing economic evaluations and mathematical models, there is a risk that policymakers follow criteria that maximise health without considering other alternatives, which are not so cost-effective but rather are grounded in forms of social value relevant to human rights.[115] With cost-benefit analysis,

---

111 Duncan Mortimer and Leonie Segal, 'Comparing the Incomparable? A Systematic Review of Competing Techniques for Converting Descriptive Measures of Health Status into QALY-Weights' (2008) 28 Medical Decision-Making 66.

112 Melissa M Brown and others, 'Evidence-Based Medicine, Utilities, and Quality of Life': (1999) 10 Current Opinion in Ophthalmology 221, 222–223.

113 Rui Nunes, 'Evidence-Based Medicine: A New Tool for Resource Allocation?' (2003) 6 Medicine, Health Care and Philosophy 297, 299–300.

114 Directorate-General for Health and Food Safety (European Commission), 'Defining Value in Value-Based Healthcare: Report of the Expert Panel on Effective Ways of Investing in Health (EXPH)' 28–30 <https://op.europa.eu/en/publication-detail/-/publication/beaebce1-ac29-11e9-9d01-01aa75ed71a1> accessed 1 January 2021.

115 Alicia Ely Yamin, *Power, Suffering, and the Struggle for Dignity: Human Rights Frameworks for Health and Why They Matter* (University of Pennsylvania Press 2015) 119.

decisions are based on monetary footings that cannot reflect human rights values.

As part of the economic philosophy underscoring HTA, economic models commonly determine an institutional decision-making process that puts consequentialism and maximisation of resources before human rights principles such as non-discrimination or equal value of individuals.[116] A utilitarian approach may accept the loss of freedoms to maximise utilities or the exclusion of groups that do not yield great overall returns.[117] The health economists' overdominance in HTA allows observations such as that its "primary objective is to maximise population health", "no HTA report is complete without a section on cost-effectiveness" and the "HTA community currently adopts a 'Pontius Pilate' approach to health inequalities".[118]

Compared to cost-effectiveness, cost–benefit analysis employs a method particularly incongruent with human rights or dignity principles for using monetary units to compare the costs and benefits of a health intervention.[119] Estimating the value of a life or health state for its monetary value has been contested because of serious risks of discrimination (i.e. adopting different monetary values for lives based on age or disabilities), incompatibilities with a fair procedure due to lack of transparency and principally a general feeling of disrespect for human dignity by monetising life.[120] Cost–benefit analysis may be able to incorporate equity concerns and advances have been proposed to

---

116 See e.g. Kluger and others (chapter 3, n 42); Harris, 'QALYfying the Value of Life.' (n 43); Albert Weale, 'The Right to Health versus Good Medical Care?' (2012) 15 Critical Review of International Social and Political Philosophy 473, 485; Michael Freeman, 'The Right to Health' in Rhiannon Morgan and Bryan Turner (eds), *Interpreting Human Rights: Social Science Perspectives* (Routledge 2009) 50–51.

117 Allen E Buchanan, 'The Right to a Decent Minimum of Health Care' (1984) 13 Philosophy & Public Affairs 55, 60. Jennifer Prah Ruger, 'Toward a Theory of a Right to Health: Capability and Incompletely Theorized Agreements' (2006) 18 Yale Journal of Law & the Humanities 273, 280–281; Freeman (n 116) 50–52; Amartya Sen, 'Elements of a Theory of Human Rights' (2004) 32 Philosophy & Public Affairs 315, 321–330. On the problems of utilitarianism and individual rights, see e.g. Herbert LA Hart, 'Between Utility and Rights' (1979) 79 Columbia Law Review 828; Leslie A Mulholland, 'Rights, Utilitarianism, and the Conflation of Persons' (1986) 83 The Journal of Philosophy 323.

118 Alan H Williams and Richard A Cookson, 'Equity–Efficiency Trade-Offs in Health Technology Assessment' (2006) 22 International Journal of Technology Assessment in Health Care 1, 8.

119 Joanna Coast, 'Is Economic Evaluation in Touch with Society's Health Values?' (2004) 329 BMJ 1233, 1234.

120 On cost-benefit methods and critique see e.g. Richard O Zerbe Jr, 'The Legal Foundation of Cost-Benefit Analysis' (2007) 2 Charleston L. Rev. 93; Richard O Zerbe Jr, 'Cost–Benefit Analysis in Legal Decision-Making' in Francesco Parisi (ed), *Oxford Handbook of Law and Economics Methodology and Concepts* (Oxford University Press 2017) 357–361; Robert H

address the limitations of pure monetary evaluation, but that cannot overcome the fundamental moral barriers.[121] It may be argued that cost–benefit analysis is a less complicated alternative, in not using subjective health metrics to focus on the economic value of negative and positive aspects of technologies, but that is also deceptive. Cost–benefit analysis is difficult to scrutinise as it reduces the societal perspective to a monetary value and utilises problematic methods that cannot be publicly reviewed (e.g. the use of discount rates to bring all future benefits and costs into the present).[122]

Another feature which makes cost–benefit analysis fundamentally discriminatory and procedurally unfair is the adoption of methods such as willingness-to-pay (WTP) to determine the value of benefits. Basically, this technique inquires to what extent one would accept meeting the costs of an intervention oneself.[123] This would be logically contrary to the affordability criterion and represents a form of rationing through the ability to pay that is discriminatory and non-acceptable under an HRBA.[124] WTP surveys are prone to bias in some answers by the way questions are phrased as to the time given to the participants, the choice of treatments, the first reference cost and the order of possible responses.[125] This is at its most intense with the difference in income between participants, as those in higher classes are more willing to spend more.

On the other hand, cost-effectiveness or cost-utility does not require monetary values, but this alternative has its own set of criticisms (for procedural and discriminatory reasons). Whereas cost–benefit analysis quantifies life in monetary terms, cost–utility converts different health states of diverse patients and pathologies into utilities, mostly expressed as cost per

Frank, 'Why Is Cost-Benefit Analysis so Controversial?' (2000) 29 The Journal of Legal Studies 913.

121 See e.g. William J Aceves, 'Cost-Benefit Analysis and Human Rights' (2018) 92 St. John's Law Review 431, 446–450.

122 William J Aceves, 'Valuing Life: A Human Rights Perspective on the Calculus of Regulation' (2018) 36 Law and Inequality: A Journal of Theory and Practice 1, 7–13.

123 Mohan V Bala, Josephine A Mauskopf and Lisa L Wood, 'Willingness to Pay as a Measure of Health Benefits' (1999) 15 Pharmacoeconomics 9, 10–14.

124 See chapter 7, 1.2 on affordability criteria.

125 Richard Cookson, 'Willingness to Pay Methods in Health Care: A Sceptical View' (2003) 12 Health Economics 891; Dorte Gyrd-Hansen, 'Willingness to Pay for a QALY' (2003) 12 Health Economics 1049, 1056; Marlies Ahlert, Friedrich Breyer and Lars Schwettmann, 'How You Ask Is What You Get: Framing Effects in Willingness-to-Pay for a QALY' (2016) 150 Social Science & Medicine 40.

QALY.[126] For utility estimation, patient preferences are elicited for QoL matters. These evaluation techniques amount to a process itself with limited control and influence resting with patients and, as Dolan explains, measures of value set the rules of who will value, what they will value and through which approach.[127] Those utility scores directly influence what is being deliberated in HTA (fair procedure) and could lead to different conclusions on what is the most valuable option (discrimination). Next, these two main strands of criticism about cost-utility will be examined, in turn, with an emphasis on QALYs, for simplification of analysis.[128]

3.4 Cost-Utility Procedural Arbitrariness

This section refers to the procedural problems regarding utility scores used in HTA economic studies, in particular with cost-utility analysis. As economic utilities are based on HRQoL, they share much of the concerns already argued in relation to QoL measurement. Utilities, obtained as HRQoL, are numbers between 0 (dead) and 1 (perfect health) estimated by individuals whose preferences are asked according to their health state per year. This approach draws criticism for its different interpretation between patient groups and accuracy, since people's individual preferences of QoL may not be captured through different states of health and illness by the same questionnaire.[129]

Utility measurement feeds into economic indicators such as QALYs, a typical tool used in HTA to compare the outcomes of two different treatments, which pose a challenge in harmonising human rights standards with HTA criteria for several ethical, methodological and disease-specific reasons. The health economics catchphrase a "QALY is a QALY and a QALY is a QALY"

126 Richard Kirkdale and others, 'The Cost of a QALY' (2010) 103 QJM: An International Journal of Medicine 715, 717–718.

127 Paul Dolan, 'Developing Methods That Really Do Value the "Q" in the QALY' (2008) 3 Health Economics, Policy and Law 69, 70.

128 The WHO has recommended DALYs for global health cost-effectiveness studies, but QALYs are more associated with HTA. For an overview of utilities measurement in healthcare, see: Marthe R Gold, David Stevenson and Dennis G Fryback, 'HALYs and QALYs and DALYs, Oh My: Similarities and Differences in Summary Measures of Population Health' (2002) 23 Annual Review of Public Health 115.

129 For review on ethical limitations of utility-indicators, see e.g.: Andrew Edgar, *The Ethical QALY: Ethical Issues in Health Care Resource Allocations* (Euromed Communications Limited 1998); Pettitt Da and Raza S, 'The Limitations of QALY: A Literature Review' (2016) 06 Journal of Stem Cell Research & Therapy; Leah Z Rand and Aaron S Kesselheim, 'Controversy Over Using Quality-Adjusted Life-Years In Cost-Effectiveness Analyses: A Systematic Literature Review' (2021) 40 Health Affairs 1402.

summarises much of this ideology, ignoring individual differences for each patient by counting utilities.[130] For instance, Rawles says QALYs are "based on false premises, faulty reasoning and unjust principles" by assuming the life with suffering from distress or disabilities is worth less less than a life without it.[131] That would mean valuing less some individuals based on their physical characteristics, such as wheelchair users, who would be discriminated against lower utility returns.[132] Determining value with QALYs can also be controversial in an HRBA as it may not be conducive to affordability – higher QALYs may be used to justify a premium price for treatments.[133]

As to the procedural element, the "quality" of life employed by health economists in QALYs may seem too arbitrary as not all individuals can form an accurate opinion of a health state they have never endured. Utility-based indicators have been condemned for being a "pseudo-science" or an "imaginary world", in an aleatory process impossible to replicate.[134] This fictitious character of utility indicators could be better evaluated in HTA if there was enough transparency for public participation in the production of this data. However, the typical situation is that economic models are not shared and remain closed to scrutiny.[135]

To undertake utility measurements, there are indirect and direct approaches to survey population preferences.[136] Indirect measures are based on pre-designed questionnaires indicating health status, which are evaluated by the respondents. These are used with HRQoL (as seen on clinical evidence) and converted to cost-effectiveness studies.[137]

Equally, direct measurement of preferences can result in an unfair procedure. These examples are known to carry extreme subjectivity, are difficult to interpret and may vary depending on how they are framed. The most straight-

---

130 Milton C Weinstein, 'A QALY Is a QALY Is a QALY – Or Is It?' (1988) 7 Journal of Health Economics 289.

131 John Rawles, 'Castigating QALYs.' (1989) 15 Journal of Medical Ethics 143.

132 Martina Garau and others, 'Using QALYs in Cancer: A Review of the Methodological Limitations' (2011) 29 PharmacoEconomics 673, 670; Rawles (n 131).

133 See chapter 7, 1.2 on affordability criteria.

134 Paul C Langley, 'Great Expectations: Cost-Utility Models as Decision Criteria' (2016) 7 Innovations in Pharmacy 1, 4–5.

135 William CN Dunlop and others, 'Benefits, Challenges and Potential Strategies of Open Source Health Economic Models' (2017) 35 PharmacoEconomics 125.

136 Peter J Neumann, Sue J Goldie and Milton C Weinstein, 'Preference-Based Measures in Economic Evaluation in Health Care' (2000) 21 Annual Review of Public Health 587, 594–595; Sarah J Whitehead and Shehazad Ali, 'Health Outcomes in Economic Evaluation: The QALY and Utilities' (2010) 96 British Medical Bulletin 5, 8–14.

137 Ibid.

forward approach for preference elicitation is to have a scale from zero health to full health where respondents assign a number where their acceptability lies (but the reliability and ability of the respondent to accurately answer is low). In the time trade-off, what is valued is the preference of individuals who rank each scenario of the course of treatment in their judgement, in a scale from 0 (death) to 1 (full life). This judgement involves, for instance, interrogating people on how much they would accept a "lower health state" in place of another year of living or how much they would take a certain probability risk of death against a situation of assured poor health.[138] The most sophisticated and highly regarded technique is the standard gamble, whereby different scenarios are compared and the respondents rank their acceptable scenario.

In contrast to scientific experiments, the arbitrariness in the direct measurement of preferences is caused by the fact that the methodology resorts to public opinion that may differ every time a survey is applied, or depending on where the study is conducted (as explained with HRQoL).[139] For instance, for cultural reasons, the population in Japan may attach more importance to life expectancy of older people compared to other countries where younger people tend to be more valued.[140] QALYs are regarded as a homogeneous measure of health gain, but different people may attribute diverse weights to QALYs gained in some circumstances or for certain patients, such as in end-of-life treatments or life-saving ones.[141] This may create a scenario where different technologies are competing for resources but one appears to be more cost-effective simply because QALYs were estimated more favourably.

The distortion effect of biased evidence has discriminatory implications – if a category of patients is sidelined in the economic models, or misrepresented, it would not have standing in the same way as other groups. Moreover, health economics studies with utility measurement may not be sufficiently comprehensive to apply other meanings of value (in particular, patient-specific values, which would disenfranchise patients from participation and, hence, rule

138 Whitehead and Ali (n 136) 4–6.

139 In general, unsound methods of cost-utility analysis have been criticised as compromising the quality of economic assessment based on them. See Mark JC Nuijten and Dominique J Dubois, 'Cost-Utility Analysis: Current Methodological Issues and Future Perspectives' (2011) 2 Frontiers in pharmacology 29; Da and S (n 129) 1. A Simon Pickard, 'Is It Time to Update Societal Value Sets for Preference-Based Measures of Health?' (2015) 33 PharmacoEconomics 191.

140 Jörg Mahlich and others, 'Cultural Beliefs, Utility Values, and Health Technology Assessment' (2018) 16 Cost Effectiveness and Resource Allocation 1.

141 Emily Lancsar and others, 'The Relative Value of Different QALY Types' (2020) 70 Journal of Health Economics 102303.

out a fair procedure).[142] Patients with rare diseases may be disproportionately affected if QALYs are obtained by indirect measurement from specific reports that are not the standard for the algorithms to generate the utility score.[143] This suggested arbitrariness of utility measurements such as QALYs may be unable to ensure equal consideration of patients and human rights standards.

3.5 Discrimination in Utility Measurement

The second challenging question in economic analysis is the discriminatory impact of cost-effectiveness studies on certain groups through utility scores. Even though academics have been critical of utility measures, international human rights documents have not given specific consideration to this area. Broadly, it can be argued that the principle of non-discrimination in socio-economic rights should be premised on formal equality (same standing) and substantive equality (priority to the worst-off), as already discussed in Section 2. However, it is submitted in this section that this framework does not apply neatly to cost-effectiveness evidence within some groups. That is particularly the case among older and disabled persons, whose equal standing and status as worse-off is questionable in cost-effectiveness analysis. In Tomsons' view, despite the right to health having a precise scope that could be reduced to a bare minimum, "many procedural problems [exist] in the QALY approach" and "partly because of the injustices in which it eventuates [...] about the elderly or the disabled", utility measures are in conflict even with a very strict view of human rights.[144]

On the surface, QALYs treat all patients equally (formal equality), but the scores are higher among groups enjoying more years in full health (the younger and patients with no chronic diseases or disabilities).[145] Discrimination has been one of the reasons that QALYs are not well accepted in some jurisdictions, such as Germany and the United States, where they are restricted (not used in statutory decision-making or have not been accepted in government

142 Directorate-General for Health and Food Safety (European Commission) (n 114) 26.

143 Michela Meregaglia and others, '"Mapping" Health State Utility Values from Non-preference-Based Measures: A Systematic Literature Review in Rare Diseases' (2020) 38 PharmacoEconomics 557.

144 Kira Anita Tomsons, 'Denying Medical Treatment: The Right to Health Care and the "Quality-Adjusted Life-Year" (QALY)' (Queen's University: PhD Thesis 1998) 88.

145 Hanna I Hyry and others, 'Limits on Use of Health Economic Assessments for Rare Diseases' (2014) 107 241, 242; Greg Bognar, 'Impartiality and Disability Discrimination' (2011) 21 Kennedy Institute of Ethics Journal 1, 3–5.

policy evaluations).[146] Commentators have noted that QALYs are implicated in various forms of discrimination: indirect, in that they do not give equal opportunities for every person, with a bias to maximise health utility, or direct, if the treatment is only provided for those who have higher cost-effectiveness.[147]

Hence, age and disability are the most discriminatory grounds associated with QALYs in various contexts. Older patients score less for end-of-life treatments or palliative care.[148] Disabled patients are penalised for not expressing the same level of QALYs as average individuals or having disability-specific gains that are not covered by the scores. By producing evidence that better suits fully able patients, disabled persons are barred from expressing their own account of QoL. In that sense, QALYs have been accepted for taking into account "social preference or values", but it can be argued that only disabled patients can assess how they value the QoL in their particular health states.[149] Similarly, in some cases, patients with rare diseases are impacted by cost-effectiveness measures by surpassing thresholds normally allowed for higher treatment prices, coupled with utilities that do not count all benefits specific to their conditions.[150]

Despite this, the limitations of cost-effectiveness are only recognised sparsely in the human rights community, sometimes incidentally in broader discussions of the overdominance of economists or exemplifying forms of discrimination by distorted criteria.[151] Niada-Avshalom has stated that utility may jar with human rights for justifying decisions by looking at the aggregate value of an intervention without considering individual rights or by being disadvantageous to some particular groups such as the elderly.[152] In global

146 Kluger and others (chapter 3, n 42); Jim McKenna and William Smith, 'The Legality of QALY under the ADA' (Pioneer Institute 2020) <https://pioneerinstitute.org/download/the-legality-of-qaly-under-the-ada/> accessed 19 March 2021.

147 John Harris, 'It's Not NICE to Discriminate' (2005) 31 Journal of Medical Ethics 373, 374; Greg Bognar, 'Does Cost-Effectiveness Analysis Unfairly Discriminate against People with Disabilities?: Cost-Effectiveness Analysis and People with Disabilities' (2010) 27 Journal of Applied Philosophy 394, 396–397.

148 Anne B Wichmann and others, 'The Use of Quality-Adjusted Life Years in Cost-Effectiveness Analyses in Palliative Care: Mapping the Debate through an Integrative Review' (2017) 31 Palliative Medicine 306.

149 Laura M Cupples, 'Disability, Epistemic Harms, and the Quality-Adjusted Life Year' (2020) 13 IJFAB: International Journal of Feminist Approaches to Bioethics 45, 57–59.

150 Hyry and others (n 145) 242–243.

151 See e.g. Alicia Ely Yamin and Tara Boghosian, 'Democracy and Health: Situating Health Rights within a Republic of Reasons' (2020) 19 Yale Journal of Health Policy, Law, and Ethics 96, 123.

152 Niada-Avshalom (chapter 4, n 2) 535–536.

health, as described by Davis, cost-effectiveness has become central to the investment decisions of donors, pitting populations against each other and excluding comprehensive analysis of factors that are not incorporated into economic research, as an "epistemic silence" of matters valuable to specific populations.[153] In international human rights instruments, there is very scarce recommendation on the usage of cost-effectiveness and utility indicators concerning disability or age discrimination. More recently, though, the Special Rapporteur on the rights of persons with disabilities showed concern with utility metrics for being "controversial for the ethical implications of the disability weights and their impact on policymaking" but did not elaborate on how to prevent discrimination.[154]

In sum, these objections to economic methods as a form of discrimination are marginal among human rights academics. More commonly, the idea that resources are unavoidably limited and cost-effectiveness can assist in making a fair decision is supported by many human rights scholars and endorsed in some studies, albeit acknowledging problematic aspects.[155] Policy advice is also unclear on the role of human rights in economic decisions or the limitations of cost-effectiveness for fair priority-setting. The WHO Consultative Group on Equity and Universal Health Coverage notes that a deficient cost-effectiveness model is better than not having one at all, if aided by equity and worst-off considerations.[156] It does not address direct discrimination, so that any type of differential treatment would be discriminatory if not based on the comparative efficiency of alternative investments (e.g. excluding older people for reasons other than cost-effectiveness).[157] The report maintains that human rights prohibit discrimination on the basis of some attributes (race, ethnicity, religion, gender, political beliefs and sexual orientation), but remains silent on the common implicit categories of age and disability.[158]

Human rights standards do not explain how to reconcile economic methods that implicitly discriminate against older people. Kornfeld-Matte,

153 Sara LM Davis, *The Uncounted: Politics of Data in Global Health* (Cambridge University Press 2020) 115.

154 UNGA, 'Report of the Special Rapporteur on the Rights of Persons with Disabilities' 16 July 2018 (A/73/161) para. 32.

155 See e.g. Yamin, 'Democracy, Health Systems, and the Right to Health' (chapter 1, n 12) 200. See also chapter 3, pp 59–65, on the litigation studies and evaluation of resource allocation impact.

156 World Health Organization, 'Making Fair Choices on the Path to Universal Health Coverage: Final Report of the WHO Consultative Group on Equity and Universal Health Coverage' (World Health Organization 2014) 14.

157 Ibid., 40.

158 Ibid.

independent expert on the enjoyment of all human rights by older persons, stressed that there is no comprehensive legal instrument for the rights of older people, who are commonly "de-prioritised" in healthcare, lacking visibility in the human rights system and the support of a clear framework to guide the regulatory measures of States.[159] The Madrid International Plan of Action on Ageing (MIPAA), a political declaration made in 2002, calls for some priorities towards older persons (such as preventive and palliative care) but does not address the weight given to those policies or the way resource allocation decisions should be made to be non-discriminatory (despite determining that States should follow international obligations of non-discrimination).[160] More developed right-to-health guidance would have influence on priority-setting decisions and HTA practice as to the limits of life-extending technologies and weight of elderly care against other priorities.

In conclusion, as shown with the examples of age and disability, human rights practice may be oblivious as to indirect discrimination (in metrics) or even direct discrimination in policies for the aged population. Yet, substantive equality is visibly endorsed in socio-economic rights as priority to the worse-off (including aged and disabled persons). To devise an HRBA for cost-effectiveness criteria, the question is not whether cost-effectiveness is wrong per se (as there is no consolidated practice against it as a human rights issue), but in which circumstance it needs to be adapted, which methods are "off-limits" and how to favour the worse-off.[161] As many of the solutions do not exist or are not conventional practice in policy-making, the next section examines progressive realisation to find foolproof methods of addressing indirect discrimination where possible in order to promote substantive equality to the worst-off and to ensure a fair procedure with better measurement tools.

4 Progressive Realisation to Improve HTA Evidence

After reviewing major irreconcilable features of clinical and economic evidence in HTA, through QoL measurement and value analysis, we should investigate how human rights principles can be incorporated into the evidence-

159 HRC, 'Report of the Independent Expert on the Enjoyment of All Human Rights by Older Persons' 10 July 2018 (A/HRC/39/50) paras. 65, 88.

160 UN, "Report of the Second World Assembly on Ageing" 8–12 April 2002 (A/CONF.197/9) paras 74–76.

161 Pavel (chapter 1, n 1) 510.

making process to make the decision criteria acceptable. This section argues that States should have to take all appropriate steps to avoid unfair procedure or discrimination in the evidence employed by HTA bodies. In many instances, this could mean a complete overhaul of methods and approaches to economic analysis. The role of progressive realisation is to improve evidence-making in those epistemic gaps and develop the resources to collect the relevant clinical and economic information, especially where no appropriate methods exist or more policies for participation of affected populations are needed.[162] In certain cases, and for many countries, there will be very scarce, if any, relevant data for parts of the population or in a specific context, especially with regard to new technologies that have been recently approved.[163]

Knowledge production and research therefore needs to be a permanent policy around HTA to ensure a fair procedure. However, that is not to say that utility metrics or EBM cannot be used at all in HTA, only that their application should be in step with these principles. One example would be to use only cost-effectiveness metrics to compare treatments within a group of patients and not across distinct categories, such as between disabled and non-disabled persons. Valuations can be used as a reference but should not be the sole grounds for decisions so as to impair fair procedure and non-discrimination. For instance, QALYs provide a standard scale for comparison of technologies that are only marginally superior to others and can serve to measure additional benefits and negotiate prices.[164] A high QALY may be used to justify a more expensive treatment – an HRBA, however, should be mindful of the affordability of those treatments even when they are cost-effective.

In EBM, some policies should be introduced before deliberations (e.g. ensuring that patient voice is heard in evidence-making, and transparency in research), while others are conducted within the decision process (e.g. reducing the strict evidence hierarchy) or even after a recommendation is made (when further research must be conducted to better answer the question considered, including the impact on a vulnerable population).[165] Poor quality of

162 See e.g. HRC, "Human Rights of Older People: The Data Gap" 9 July 2020 (A/HRC/45/14) paras. 79–91.

163 See e.g.: Samantha A Hollingworth and others, 'What Do We Need to Know? Data Sources to Support Evidence-Based Decisions Using Health Technology Assessment in Ghana' (2020) 18 Health Research Policy and Systems 1, 9–12.

164 Steven D Pearson, 'Why the Coming Debate Over the QALY and Disability Will Be Different' (2019) 47 The Journal of Law, Medicine & Ethics 304, 305.

165 Oliver and Pearce (n 86) 1–3.

existing evidence is also a matter of progressive realisation (e.g. reducing industry bias, investing in transparent and publicly funded research, giving access to unpublished research or defining research priorities).[166] Another case of poor evidence is when RCTs are not available or desirable, such as for medical devices and surgery, which demand additional comparative research to track whether new treatments are superior to other alternatives.[167] Progressive realisation can also take the form of HTA positive coverage decisions being subject to further research to remedy RCT limitations or answer uncertainties raised.[168]

Progressive realisation may place a duty on States to improve current methods of producing utility indicators or to complement deliberations with other forms of knowledge and contextual information. Similar to EBM, practices in health economics may be revised to ensure fair procedure and non-discrimination, although the objectives of new economic methods are not so easily achieved. Because there are several methodological alternatives in discussion about economic evaluation, progressive realisation permits States to test and devise better tools of economic analysis in order to overcome QALYs discrimination.[169] Currently, human rights standards do not openly adhere to any method of evaluation to replace discriminatory measurements. Thus, States would have a certain margin of discretion in identifying non-discriminatory instruments.

For instance, to redress problems with utility indicators, efforts to insert "social values" into QALYs may be beneficial, but do not amount to engaging with human rights values or may still seem arbitrary. Some models attempt to give special weight to special groups, such as attaching an extra value at the end of life.[170] This strategy of giving special consideration to some groups may be formed in the economic evaluation through assigning preferences determined by the public, which are commonly aspects of age and severity of dis-

166 Susanna Every-Palmer and Jeremy Howick, 'How Evidence-based Medicine Is Failing Due to Biased Trials and Selective Publication' (2014) 20 Journal of Evaluation in Clinical Practice 908, 912.

167 Wendy Rogers, Christopher Degeling and Cynthia Townley, 'Equity under the Knife: Justice and Evidence in Surgery: Equity under the Knife: Justice and Evidence in Surgery' (2014) 28 Bioethics 119, 121–123.

168 Lindor (n 100) 220–226.

169 On alternative methods of cost–utility analysis, see: Josh J Carlson and others, 'Alternative Approaches to Quality-Adjusted Life-Year Estimation within Standard Cost-Effectiveness Models: Literature Review, Feasibility Assessment, and Impact Evaluation' (2020) 23 Value in Health 1523.

170 Jose-Luis Pinto-Prades and others, 'Valuing QALYs at the End of Life' (2014) 113 Social Science & Medicine 5.

ease.[171] They do not explain, however, which weights are prohibited or should be accepted by virtue of human rights. For compliance, human rights standards should prevail and the weights allocated in the utility measurement should follow suit, not contradict these.

The main confusion is that social preference (measured by a group of respondents that does not always involve the target patients) is assumed to be a social value (representing society and all opinions that need to be considered). In the last decade, equity considerations in QALYs have made considerable progress among scholars, who have proposed alternative methods to introduce "social values" in the distribution of resources.[172] This strand of research, also known as distributive cost-effectiveness analysis, seeks to establish how to balance effectiveness and equity or how much utility maximisation we may want to sacrifice to gain fairer distribution for some minorities. Despite economists' intentions, modified cost–utility evaluation with social values may be both difficult to realise and conflict with human rights values (if setting preferences that would disadvantage the worse-off). Klonschinski has fiercely opposed the idea that equity weight can rehabilitate cost–utility methods for the reason that this additional layer of re-distribution would not be enough to abandon the original motivation of giving priority to health maximisation.[173]

With equity weights, the essence of the health maximisation rationale and the basic issues of how to formulate the value of QALYs in the first place still remain. There is only a partial trade-off between equity and effectiveness, but the format of questions to which patients respond is influenced by a predominant utilitarian view.[174] Equally, equity weights would have to be defined through surveys to elicit social preferences through means that are just as procedurally arbitrary as calculating QALYs alone. One technique is the person trade-off, in which respondents have to compare their preferences in the distribution of resources between groups or diseases to determine what the

171 Yuanyuan Gu and others, 'Attributes and Weights in Health Care Priority Setting: A Systematic Review of What Counts and to What Extent' (2015) 146 Social Science & Medicine 41, 48–49.

172 Richard Cookson and others, 'Using Cost-Effectiveness Analysis to Address Health Equity Concerns' (2017) 20 Value in Health 206.

173 Andrea Klonschinski, *The Economics of Resource Allocation in Health Care: Cost-Utility, Social Value, and Fairness* (Routledge 2016) 99–110.

174 Andrea Klonschinski, "'Economic Imperialism' in Health Care Resource Allocation – How Can Equity Considerations Be Incorporated into Economic Evaluation?" (2014) 21 Journal of Economic Methodology 158, 167–170.

weight of some outcomes compared to others is.[175] Generally, though, they stem from an activity undertaken at a moment in time, according to the methods of elicitation, and are problematic in particular if the respondents adopt their own internal views instead of thinking what is best for the society.[176]

QALYs' constraints could be addressed, for instance, by recognising that QoL can have different meanings for different health conditions and to eliminate discriminatory elements within QALYs (such as by calibrating the scores by removing utility loss with disability or age).[177] For instance, QALYs can be replaced by patient-specific utility indexes to measure factors relevant to their conditions, not through generic HRQoL methods, but with customised surveys. A proposal was offered in the United States to generate utility measures that value life as a constant for all persons (which could be presented alongside the already established indicators of cost-effectiveness).[178]

Additionally, the capability approach provides another pathway to HRQoL that has been increasingly regarded as a viable option for an HRBA to public policies and human development.[179] With the capability approach, HRQoL is measured by dimensions referring to what people may aspire to do and be with their lives (functioning). A capability measurement is then the level of positive freedom of individual possible realisation of different functionings.[180] A promising candidate to replace utility-based scoring alongside the capability approach is the multidimensional first-order dominance approach (FOD), which does not require introducing subjective weights or preference-based utilities and aggregates different human rights values equally, preserving their interdependence.[181] The only assumption is that more welfare is bet-

175 Erik Nord, 'The Person-Trade-off Approach to Valuing Health Care Programs' (1995) 15 Medical Decision Making 201.

176 Peter J Neumann and Joshua T Cohen, 'QALYs in 2018 – Advantages and Concerns' (2018) 319 JAMA 2473, 2473.

177 Donald Franklin, 'Calibrating QALYs to Respect Equality of Persons' (2017) 29 Utilitas 65; Lancsar and others (n 141); John Browne and Donna Cryer, 'Is the QALY Fit for Purpose?' (2021) 9 The American Journal of Accountable Care 8, 10.

178 Pearson (n 164) 306.

179 See e.g. Richard Cookson, 'QALYs and the Capability Approach' (2005) 14 Health economics 817; Hareth Al-Janabi and others, 'An Investigation of the Construct Validity of the ICECAP-A Capability Measure' (2013) 22 Quality of Life Research 1831.

180 Cookson (n 179) 817–820; Joanna Coast, Richard D Smith and Paula Lorgelly, 'Welfarism, Extra-Welfarism and Capability: The Spread of Ideas in Health Economics' (2008) 67 Social Science & Medicine 1190, 1190–1193.

181 Channing Arndt and others, 'A Human Rights-Consistent Approach to Multidimensional Welfare Measurement Applied to Sub-Saharan Africa' (2018) 108 World Development 181, 181–182.

ter.[182] FOD eliminates the discrimination for age or disabilities and correlates various aspects of life measured independently of bias and without maximisation and ranks health gains in one single score (utilities).

Policymakers may also address the evidence constraints in HTA by performing additional studies "beyond safety, efficacy, and cost-effectiveness, since an assessment limited to these features must of necessity be insufficient to yield a decision".[183] A possibility is trying to develop methodological tools for engagement with multiple objectives in health policy (with MCDA).[184] There are also suggestions to hire ethicists or to create participatory methods to engage with society in selecting the measurements.[185] Even those who believe there is no conflict between ethical considerations and cost-effectiveness studies (since both might co-exist simultaneously and implicitly in the process) concede that a thorough ethical appraisal ought to be mandatory in some cases.[186] However, the controversy about covering ethical implications in HTA poses the question of whether these reflections should be presented as an extra external step or internally, within the cost-effectiveness part of the process.[187] But even with extra inputs relating to social values and the population voice, no guarantee could be given that those contributions will weigh as much as cost-effectiveness. Indeed, policymakers may prefer to rest their decisions primarily upon

182 See e.g. Alessandra Cenci and M Azhar Hussain, 'Epistemic and Non-Epistemic Values in Economic Evaluations of Public Health' (2020) 27 Journal of Economic Methodology 66.

183 Norman Daniels, Thalia Porteny and Julian Urritia, 'Expanded HTA: Enhancing Fairness and Legitimacy' (2015) 5 International Journal of Health Policy and Management 1, 1.

184 See e.g. Mira Johri and Ole Norheim, 'Can Cost-Effectiveness Analysis Integrate Concerns for Equity?' (2012) 28 International Journal of Technology Assessment in Health Care 125.

185 Mita Giacomini, Shawn Winsor and Julia Abelson, 'Ethics in Health Technology Assessment: Understanding Health Technologies as Policies' (2013) 26 Healthcare Management Forum 72, 74. Some consider that an intrinsic insertion of social values into the normal quantitative review of health economics is valid, and we should not worry about exposing the choices made by economists in interpreting what are the social values most legitimate. However, it cannot be safe to say that such deliberation would conform to the accountability principles if those values are adopted without public scrutiny. See: Erik Schokkaert, 'How to Introduce More (Or Better) Ethical Arguments in HTA?' (2015) 31 International Journal of Technology Assessment in Health Care 111, 111–112.

186 Anthony J Culyer, "HTA – Algorithm or Process?: Comment on 'Expanded HTA: Enhancing Fairness and Legitimacy'" (2016) 5 International Journal of Health Policy and Management 501, 502–503.

187 Payam Abrishami, Wija Oortwijn and Bjørn Hofmann, 'Ethics in HTA: Examining the "Need for Expansion"' (2017) 6 International Journal of Health Policy and Management 551, 551.

clinical and economic data, despite the inclusion of additional information from other areas.[188]

5 Conclusions

While the current guidance produced around clinical and economic indicators in an HRBA is not openly debated by scholars, there are still sufficient reasons to develop the application of Article 2.1 to HTA as a standard in evidence-making. Therefore, this interpretation adds to the substantive components of an HRBA as referred to in the original research question and indicates a practical usage of international right to health principles in the HTA criteria. By devising those standards, these obligations are part of necessary interpretative work on the compatibility of evidence-making. It allows us to monitor the continuous commitment to non-discriminatory evidence in an HRBA-to-HTA as a substantive element of a fair allocation process. This will depend on further analysis by scholars and practitioners to adapt those international general standards into HTA values and methods, including other specific human rights obligations not in the scope of this book (education, work, individual freedoms, etc.).

This chapter has thrown some light on the prospective application of the international right to health as a standard for the construction and employment of evidence in the HTA criteria. This evidence is currently characteristically represented by indicators of cost-effectiveness and clinical efficacy. Both have some similarities and are interdependent in many ways. For instance, through clinical guidelines, in contrast to clinical research, EBM may integrate economic impacts to serve as a rationing tool. A few studies have described EBM, under a political economic analysis, as the managerial and neoliberal control of clinical practice (yet Mykhalovskiy et al. warn that this interpretation might be too narrow).[189]

---

188 Ricard Meneu, 'The Wisdom Tooth of Health Technology Assessment' in Juan E Llano-Señarís and Carlos Campillo-Artero (eds), *Health Technology Assessment and Health Policy Today: A Multifaceted View of their Unstable Crossroads* (Springer International Publishing 2015) 40–41.

189 Ole Norheim, 'Healthcare Rationing – Are Additional Criteria Needed for Assessing Evidence-Based Clinical Practice Guidelines?' (1999) 319 BMJ 1426, 1426–1427; Saarni (n 76) 173; Eric Mykhalovskiy and Lorna Weir, 'The Problem of Evidence-Based Medicine: Directions for Social Science' (2004) 59 Social Science & Medicine 1059, 1060–1062; Nunes (n 113).

Procedural fairness, non-discrimination and progressive realisation are the three pillars common to these two strands of evidence-making. They operate in conjunction, either to expand the factors considered by those metrics, or to make allowances for the reality of vulnerable groups. Because health improvement may be variable in terms of time and quality of life, those parameters have to be procedurally adjusted to reflect the living conditions of each patient category and to demand a participatory process in its formulation. However, what may be a cause of unfairness in one study, may be the reason for arbitrariness in other evidence processes: for a fair procedure, EBM should have direct patient consultation, while, in economic analysis, patient surveys may give only a veneer of validity to utilities that cannot be compared between different groups.

The 3Ps, as proposed in this chapter, are far from a magic bullet and have some constraints, especially in distinguishing priority for the worse-off and determining in which ways to establish equality among different patients. The most appropriate understanding of equality is to have a decision criterion fostering equal consideration in access to health according to particular circumstances and not as if all humans have the same relation between quality of life and full physical aptitude. This entails some equality of opportunity (appropriately considered in an HTA as a relevant group) and substantive opportunity (offering some extra consideration for the worse-off). How to balance these two factors is still not well defined. Methodological adjustments in the way those metrics are produced should reflect the values of the subgroups to avoid discrimination (but preference elicitation appears arbitrary with current methods).

Overall, there are significant limitations because the guidance set by international law is generic and does not specify HTA particularities. Hence, the contribution of the right to health is much looser, with space for State discretion and few "red lines". One prohibited ground is explicit discrimination, but indirect discrimination is much more subtle. There is no advice on whether the bias from certain metrics would be compensated for by other means (extra criteria or equity weights) under a participatory procedure, which could elicit those values that are not covered by current evidence. International law does not define specific rules that would make certain cost-effectiveness criteria absolutely inadmissible, but broadly requires non-discrimination and procedural fairness and most likely could not accept cost–benefit analysis or even cost-effectiveness without other criteria. It also remains rather vague in indicating what special attention to the most vulnerable should entail, in particular how rationing criteria would meet this requirement.

Moreover, the level of particularisation and segmentation of the metrics cannot be attained successfully everywhere as there is neither sufficient data nor research available to customise metrics for every group or region. Progressive realisation must be at work when there is not enough data or research to individualise the verification of health states and adapt methods to specific patient realities.

In some jurisdictions, progressive realisation for new evidence is the only alternative to allow for participation and priority to vulnerable groups in HTA. Courts and human rights monitoring systems can require that States improve evidence-making, where there are means to do so. Although utility metrics are now a long-standing tradition in health economics, States do not necessarily have to adopt them rigidly and should, instead, choose to lay down regulations following human rights standards until better tools for assessing value of healthcare are developed.

However, comparatively, other obligations from Article 2.1 are much more explicit and straightforward for incorporation in HTA than are the 3Ps. The next chapter will turn to obligations of international cooperation and how these international norms fit squarely into the HTA international environment.

CHAPTER 6

Global Health and the Duty of International Cooperation in HTA

HTA has established itself as an international endeavour. In different jurisdictions, international cooperation is a fundamental factor in the uptake of HTA.[1] Networks assist local decision-makers to install new HTA bodies and even the evolving definition of HTA as a policy area has been mostly spearheaded by a global expert community.[2]

Given this intimate dialogue across jurisdictions, this chapter focuses on the duty of international cooperation in HTA as part of socio-economic rights obligations. The argument is that the right to health may form the basis of a duty of international cooperation, rooted in Article 2.1 of the ICESCR, which states that socio-economic rights may be realised through "international assistance and cooperation".[3] Assistance may be understood as financial contributions, while cooperation is normally employed as technical support or know-how transfer, with no significant funding connotation.[4]

Nevertheless, international cooperation in HTA appears to disregard the international right to health. In international development, there is both a lack of awareness of international cooperation as a State duty and an overemphasis on Universal Health Coverage (UHC) as a foundation of HTA. As this chapter seeks to show, this duty is one of the components of an HRBA, as proposed in this book, alongside other standards for socio-economic rights realisation (see Chapter 3) within the international legal framework examined so far. Under these principles, the right to health realisation is not only subject to internal resources, but also to the external resources (financial or non-financial) obtained through other countries. This creates a certain paradox for rights realisation and HTA – while the procedure purports to allocate

1 Recent examples are India, Thailand, Ghana, Indonesia, Vietnam and Philippines. See, e.g. Sripen Tantivess and others, 'Health Technology Assessment Capacity Development in Low- and Middle-Income Countries: Experiences from the International Units of HITAP and NICE' (2017) 6 F1000Research 2119.

2 O'Rourke and others (chapter 1, n 7) 2.

3 ICESCR (chapter 1, n 31) Article 2(1).

4 Margot E Salomon, 'Deprivation, Causation and the Law of International Cooperation' in Malcolm Langford and others (eds), *Global Justice, State Duties* (Cambridge University Press 2012) 261.

 | HTTPS://DOI.ORG/10.1163/9789004730311-007

internal resources, HTA is also a mechanism of international assistance or cooperation, which can guarantee external resources. This chapter will show that this external side should be better acknowledged in the HTA international community to establish State obligations that UHC alone cannot provide.

This chapter continues reviewing Article 2.1 as a form of substantive standard in an HRBA to HTA, employing the international right to health, as indicated in the previous two chapters. In this sense, the international cooperation obligation dictates appropriate measures to mobilise resources and progressive realisation of access to healthcare beyond a jurisdiction. Thus, international cooperation is complementary to a fair procedure and consolidates the substantive principles discussed in this book. The global practice of HTA also explains why the international right to health, defended here, is not simply a moral or domestic right to health: there is an international element to HTA institutionalisation that is apt for international law regulation. Therefore, international cooperation in HTA makes the case of normative guidance under the international right to health much stronger.

The first section (Section 1) will summarise the international ethos of HTA, mainstreamed by various influential networks. Section 2 shows how, within this internationalised context, UHC established itself as a form of normative discourse for HTA without regard for the right to health. In contrast, Section 3 introduces the frameworks that support the duty of international cooperation in general in international human rights law, and how that could be applied to HTA. Section 4 considers the discriminatory aspects of international cooperation with HTA networks, with different levels of partnership between countries, in which developed States build closer relationships to each other. This chapter concludes that the duty of international cooperation in HTA is valid in international law, but its content is not self-evident and needs further engagement of international networks to secure enforcement and clarity.

1 The International Nature of HTA

What makes HTA eminently globalised is that the establishment of this field was in part a result of the extensive cooperation of national agencies and international associations. HTA networks may be seen as a form of transgovernmentalism, a contemporary process of regulatory convergence among public authorities without involving the legislature or executive in diplomatic relations.[5] As a process of policy convergence, international networks may be an important factor in the adoption of international law norms, negotiation of agreements and compliance with existing treaties.[6]

The process of HTA diffusion has been typically preceded by a "learning period" where foreign experts and institutions acquaint local authorities with the first steps into the field. This has been the natural progression in countries such as Lithuania, Brazil, Austria and Spain.[7] Even countries with a long-held tradition of health technology studies, such as Sweden, may at some point start working closely with other jurisdictions to strengthen the process.[8] Thailand's celebrated HTA programme came into existence thanks to crucial players who studied abroad and made close connections with foreign institutions to instil best practices domestically.[9]

In many of those cases, HTA networks were directly involved in providing a venue for rich knowledge exchange over the years.[10] Back in their own jurisdictions, delegates of HTA bodies in international meetings were able to advance the regulatory and organisational changes to follow international standards. Inexperienced countries still in the early stages of HTA, such as those in Africa, are taking advantage of international networks, agencies and funders to build their own "critical mass" for research and evidence-making.[11]

Across these networks, a dynamic flow of data through HTA reports and research cooperation integrates many public and private organisations in an ecosystem chartered by Cinarogly and Baser.[12] Within this ecosystem, govern-

5 Kal Raustiala, 'The Architecture of International Cooperation: Transgovernmental Networks and the Future of International Law' (2002) 43 Virginia Journal of International Law 1.

6 Ibid., 70–83.

7 Jankauskiene Danguole, 'Development of Health Technology Assessment in Lithuania' (2009) 25 International Journal of Technology Assessment in Health Care 140, 140–141; Claudia Wild, 'Austria: History of Health Technology Assessment during the Past 20 Years' (2009) 25 International Journal of Technology Assessment in Health Care 74, 78.

8 Egon Jonsson, 'History of Health Technology Assessment in Sweden' (2009) 25 International Journal of Technology Assessment in Health Care 42, 44.

9 Anthony J Culyer, Chai Podhisita and Benjarin Santatiwongchai, *A Start in the East – A Short History of HITAP* (Health Intervention and Technology Assessment Program (HITAP 2016) 69–76.

10 David Hailey, 'Development of the International Network of Agencies for Health Technology Assessment' (2009) 25 International Journal of Technology Assessment in Health Care 24, 26.

11 Jane E Doherty and others, 'Strengthening Expertise for Health Technology Assessment and Priority-Setting in Africa' (2017) 10 Global Health Action 1370194, 4.

12 Songul Cinaroglu and Onur Baser, 'Network among HTA Ecosystem' (2019) 9 Health and Technology 153, 160–161.

mental institutions are the main actors in this information traffic, leaving private entities at the margins of data circulation.[13] The networks supporting international cooperation in HTA are diverse organisations, with varied goals, memberships and geographical area, as described on Table 6.1.

Success stories in national HTA have been attributed to international cooperation. In Europe, international cooperation in HTA is known to improve local priority-setting and to involve States at different stages of institutionalisation of procedures and expertise capacity.[14] Avoiding duplication, saving resources, accelerating recommendations, improving transparency and disseminating HTA techniques are only a few of the examples provided by the literature.[15] The highest level of technical cooperation is found in joint assessments, where a number of agencies work together in collecting and analysing relevant data (though smaller types of collaboration for sharing just a single item or specific information in a report can also be concluded).[16]

Benefits obtained by HTA collaborations are highly recommended as a means to achieve UHC worldwide. For instance, reports can be shared with other countries where the production of research is less common, thus minimising the costs of decision-making.[17] The following section explains how UHC has become a common narrative for HTA expansion. However, as will be shown, conversely, human rights have largely been overlooked as a fundamental tenet of cooperation and assistance among States.

13 Ibid.

14 Mirjana Huić and others, 'Collaboration In Health Technology Assessment (EUnetHTA Joint-Action, 2010–2012): Four Case Studies' (2013) 29 International Journal of Technology Assessment in Health Care 323, 323.

15 See e.g. Devidas Menon and Deborah Marshall, 'The Internationalization of Health Technology Assessment' (1996) 12 International Journal of Technology Assessment in Health Care 45, 49; Valerie Moran and Armin H Fidler, 'Health Technology Assessment in Europe: Communicating and Applying Lessons Learned from High-Income Countries to Middle-Income Countries' (2010) 3 Journal of Management & Marketing in Healthcare 141, 143.

16 Huić and others (n 14) 328.

17 Francesco Paolucci and others, 'Decision Making and Priority Setting: The Evolving Path Towards Universal Health Coverage' (2017) 15 Applied Health Economics and Health Policy 697, 704.

TABLE 6.1 International HTA network profiles

HTAi	Health Technology Assessment International, successor to the International Society of Technology Assessment in Health Care (ISTAHC). Launched in 2003, HTAi has the same goals as the previous organisation created by the first experts in the early days of HTA to advance knowledge in the field.[a] It is responsible for a leading journal with the same name.
HTAsiaLink	With an Asian membership, HTAsiaLink was founded in 2011 to coordinate capacity-building and knowledge exchange in the region.[b]
RedETSA	In one of the meetings of HTAi in 2011, the network was inaugurated with the support of the Pan American Health Organization. It includes local governments, research centres and regulatory authorities.[c] RedETSA seeks to consolidate HTA throughout the continent through collaborations on capacity-building, knowledge dissemination and standard-setting.
INAHTA	Originating after a meeting held in 1992 by the Canadian Coordinating Office for Health Technology Assessment (CCOHTA), the International Network of Agencies for Health Technology Assessment first began as a knowledge-sharing tool.[d] The partnership holds regular meetings, gathers reports distributed in its own collective database and has been involved in collaborative projects for joint assessments, research and guidelines.

a David Banta, Egon Jonsson and Paul Childs, 'History of the International Societies in Health Technology Assessment: International Society for Technology Assessment in Health Care and Health Technology Assessment International' (2009) 25 International Journal of Technology Assessment in Health Care 19, 22.

b Yot Teerawattananon and others, 'Historical Development of The HTAsiaLink Network And Its Key Determinants Of Success' (2018) 34 International Journal of Technology Assessment in Health Care 260, 260–261.

c RedETSA, 'What Is RedETSA?' (*RedETSA*) <http://redetsa.org/wp/?page_id=3952> accessed 5 May 2020.

d Hailey (n 10) 25.

TABLE 6.1 International HTA network profiles (*cont*)

EUnetHTA	The European Network for HTA was instituted under the auspices of the European Commission in 2006, building on smaller experiences from the 1980s when HTA began to develop.[e] It has been the principal point of convergence in HTA policies among European Union States and has produced robust guidelines to promote reuse of HTA studies, with a terminological glossary and the HTA Core Model, which, after 10 years, has successfully established technical standards to make findings more interoperable across jurisdictions.[f] A current proposal to deepen European cooperation under a common HTA process, exclusively for clinical effects, is on the agenda.[g]

e Livio Garattini and Anna Padula, 'HTA for Pharmaceuticals in Europe: Will the Mountain Deliver a Mouse?' (2020) 21 The European Journal of Health Economics 1, 1–2.

f Finn Børlum Kristensen and others, 'The HTA Core Model ® – 10 Years of Developing an International Framework to Share Multidimensional Value Assessment' (2017) 20 Value in Health 244, 249.

g European Commission, "Proposal for Regulation of the European Parliament and The Council on HTA and amending Directive 201/24/ EU" COM(2018) 51 final, Regulation (EU) 2021/2282 of the European Parliament and of the Council of 15 December 2021 on health technology assessment and amending Directive 2011/24/EU.

2 UHC: Normative Foundation of HTA Cooperation in International Practice

While international cooperation in HTA can benefit health systems and promote the right to health, technical expertise and cost-saving policies have been the basic premise anchoring HTA in UHC. The right to health may overlap with UHC when some conditions, such as public participation and transparency, are met, but they are not identical. UHC does not entail all the principles for resource mobilisation and any duty of international cooperation, which can instead be found through the right to health in international law. As a concept, UHC is about what type of healthcare a government should provide as a model of health system organisation to meet population needs.

In foreign aid, UHC has become a much stronger guiding principle to HTA and priority-setting programmes than human rights. The Center for Global Development has supported countries to achieve UHC, promoting the vision of "enhancing the value for money of global health investment".[18] The International Decision Support Initiative (iDSI) recognises that "everyone should have fair access to health, receiving the right treatment and the right medicines at the right time".[19] The Center has been tasked by the Bill and Melinda Gates Foundation, a global funder engaged with priority-setting projects in many countries, to create a reference framework to support informed local decisions.[20] The principles designed under this general template for local priority-setting seem to be more engaged with the quality of health economic analysis than with other values fundamental to the right to health, like accountability, progressive realisation and maximum availability of resources.[21] No specific right to health-underpinning is provided, except indirectly by the principles of transparency and equity in considering the implications of an economic evaluation.

Therefore, in contrast to the right to health, the usage of UHC appears to be more pragmatic and utilitarian, indicating that cost-effectiveness and HTA-informed decisions are unavoidable or "a key move" to the attainment of UHC.[22] HTA is regarded as a central methodological resource for conducting deliberations using economic evidence. Developing countries, within this view, necessarily depend on learning high-quality HTA cost-effectiveness analysis from external experts, as implemented by governments in the Global North.[23] International calls and public events with policy-makers attempt to consolidate the relationship between better HTA methods and UHC.[24] For instance, in Ghana and Tanzania, the HTA establishment, heavily influenced by external actors, has been associated with promoting UHC and propagating

18 See, e.g. Amanda Glassman, Victoria Fan and Mead Over, 'More Health for the Money: Putting Incentives to Work for the Global Fund and Its Partners' (Center for Global Development 2013).

19 International Decision Support Initiative (iDSI), 'About Us' (*iDSI*, 2020) <https://www.idsihealth.org/who-we-are/about-us/> accessed 22 August 2021.

20 Thomas Wilkinson and others, 'The International Decision Support Initiative Reference Case for Economic Evaluation: An Aid to Thought' (2016) 19 Value in Health 921, 923.

21 Ibid., 924.

22 Chalkidou and others (chapter 1, n 18) 235; Kalipso Chalkidou and others, 'Health Technology Assessment in Universal Health Coverage' (2013) 382 The Lancet e48, e48.

23 Thomas Wilkinson and Kalipso Chalkidou, 'Improving the Quality of Economic Evaluation in Health in Low- and Middle-Income Countries: Where Are We Now?' (2019) 8 Journal of Comparative Effectiveness Research 1041; Chalkidou and others (n 22).

24 Yot Teerawattananon and Alia Luz, 'Health Technology Assessment as a Priority-Setting Tool for Universal Health Coverage: The Call for Global Action at the Prince Mahidol Award Conference 2016' (2016) 34 PharmacoEconomics 1.

key technological expertise to implement a new decision-making system.[25] Similarly, the High-Level Expert Group on UHC in India has organised the creation of an HTA body in that country, a process that was accompanied by assistance from foreign experts and workshops arranged by international organisations.[26]

As a consequence, it is not surprising that some international experts, in promoting HTA, advise local authorities about necessary legislative changes, but omit the right to health.[27] Laws, or the legal mandate, are part of the guidance developed by international cooperation projects to assist countries to pursue their own national programmes.[28] The legal mandate has been much more concerned with procedural approaches to justice in health, and ultimately aspires to ward off decisions from judicial review, to ensure that deliberations are legally binding or to enhance HTA authority.[29] This can be seen in the training documents of the Decide network, a collaborative platform for health financial decisions hosted by the WHO and supported by major global investors in foreign aid in health, such as the Gates Foundation.[30]

Decide provides an illustration of how oblivious HTA networking can be to the potential of the right to health. A working group of this network focused on legal issues in HTA refers to "effective legal frameworks (…) to bolster a secured multi-stage process".[31] When the right to health is mentioned, it is referred to as a "trick", since "there is no right to health, as this would be

25 Hollingworth and others (chapter 5, n 163) 9–10; Gavin Surgey and others, 'Introducing Health Technology Assessment in Tanzania' [2019] International Journal of Technology Assessment in Health Care 1, 1.

26 Saudamini Vishwanath Dabak and others, 'Budgeting for a Billion: Applying Health Technology Assessment (HTA) for Universal Health Coverage in India' (2018) 16 Health Research Policy and Systems 115, 2.

27 Deinzel Uezono and others, 'Review of Philippine Health Laws and Its Implication to HTA Institutionalization' (2020) 30 European Journal of Public Health v748.

28 See e.g. EUnetHTA, 'EUnetHTA Handbook on Health Technology Assessment Capacity Building' 41 <http://eunethta.eu/eunethta-handbook-on-hta-capacity-building/> accessed 5 May 2020; World Health Organization, 'What Are the Legal Considerations: Reviewing or Establishing the Legal Framework', *Guidance for institutionalising HTA mechanisms for reimbursement* <https://decidehealth.world/en/node/7066> accessed 5 May 2020.

29 Ibid.

30 Decide – Health Decision, 'Welcome to Decide' (*Decide Health Decision Hub*) <https://decidehealth.world/en/where> accessed 10 September 2021; Melanie Bertram, Gwenaël Dhaene and Tessa Tan-Torres Edejer (eds), *Institutionalizing Health Technology Assessments: A How to Guide* (World Health Organization 2021) 8.

31 Decide, 'All You Need Is Law' (*Decide Health Decision Hub*) <https://decidehealth.world/en/law> accessed 5 May 2020.

impossible to fulfil", going on to suggest that it should rather be denoted as "the access of a reasonable set of public services".[32] The document concludes that resource allocation is inherent to a health system, so there is no conflict between HTA and the right to health.

Instead of focusing on human rights, the approach has been to resort to public law (regulation of State powers and procedures) to evaluate the most appropriate legislation for HTA authority and legitimacy.[33] Public laws are a component of the so-called "7 Cs of HTA clarity: clarity of process and selection criteria, clarity of principles and values, clarity of mandate, clarity of responsibilities, clarity of laws and regulations in the field of HTA, clarity as regards the interaction between stakeholders, clarification of financial consequences of decisions".[34] The clarity of values is not presented as a human rights-grounded principle, but as a means to "avoid administrative decisions being squashed by judicial review or requalified because of the open angle left by imprecise legal drafting".[35]

The lack of interest in the right to health prevails in the UN system as well. Alongside the Pan-American Health Organization Assembly (PAHO), which watered down human rights considerations in a preparatory report on HTA to emphasise the need to contain judicialisation, the WHO has so far taken a pragmatic approach, preferring to call attention to UHC rather than the right to health in HTA.[36] World Health Assembly (WHA) resolutions, experts and members of HTA agencies, and Ministries of Health have also elaborated a joint comment that underlines this interdependence of HTA and UHC: "connecting existing national processes and sharing HTA knowledge through global health diplomacy will not only broaden adoption of HTA as an evidence-based instrument but also strengthen countries' commitment and ability to progress towards UHC".[37]

Nevertheless, UHC differs from the right to health in that it does not bind States as an international norm to provide resources and assistance to develop

---

32 World Health Organization, (n 28).

33 Clarke, Dhaene and Lisman (chapter 1, n 4) 11–15.

34 World Health Organization, (n 28).

35 Ibid.

36 Pan-American Sanitary Conference (PASC), "Health Technology Assessment and Incorporation into Health System", 16 July 2012 (CSP28/11); CSP28.R9 (chapter 3, n 82), World Health Assembly, Health Intervention and Technology Assessment in Support of Universal Health Coverage, 24 May 2014 (WHA67.23), article 1 (4), (5). See examples of HTA projects anchored in UHC: Surgey and others (n 25) 1; Tantivess and others (n 1) 4; Doherty and others (n 11).

37 Chalkidou and others (n 22) e49.

HTA in other countries. Other than applying a public health framing to increase healthcare, human rights bind States to set up a health system and mobilise maximum resources as a socio-economic rights obligation (see Chapter 4). The duty of international cooperation is simply one of those socio-economic rights obligations that are not provided by UHC. Above all, the duty to international cooperation offers a better path to binding obligations to help other countries in HTA than UHC. The next section will detail this argument by presenting the framework of international cooperation for socio-economic rights and identifying how this principle should be read in the context of HTA.

3 Duty of International Cooperation in HTA under International Law

The duty of international cooperation is recognised by international law in different sources, including the United Nations Charter (Articles 55 and 56), human rights instruments and, more specifically, in Article 2.1 of the ICESCR, in relation to the right to health and other socio-economic rights.[38] Article 22 of the Universal Declaration of Human Rights contains an analogous formulation referring to the realisation of socio-economic rights "through national effort and international cooperation".[39] Formal recognition by normative texts does not, however, signify the consensual understanding of the implications of these obligations nor does wide reference to it in advocacy and compliance mechanisms.[40]

The nature of the obligations of international cooperation is questionable on several grounds: who are the duty-bearers, what are the type of collaborations involved, and can they be enforced among States as a mandatory duty?[41]

38 See also e.g. United Nations, *Charter of the United Nations*, 24 October 1945 1 UNTS XVI, art. 1(3), 55 and 56; Universal Declaration of Human Rights (adopted 10 December 1948) UNGA res 217 A(III) (UDHR), art. 22 and 28, ICESCR (chapter 1, n 31) art. 11(1), 11(2), 15(4), 22 and 23.

39 Universal Declaration (Ibid.) art 22.

40 Sigrun Skogly, *Beyond National Borders: States' Human Rights Obligations in International Cooperation* (Intersentia 2006) 17–18; Judith Bueno de Mesquita, Paul Hunt and Rajat Khosla, 'The Human Rights Responsibility of International Assistance and Cooperation in Health', *Universal human rights and extraterritorial obligations* (University of Pennsylvania Press 2012) 109–116.

41 For a discussion of these questions, see e.g. de Mesquita, Hunt and Khosla (n 40) 109–116; Emily A Mok, 'International Assistance and Cooperation for Access to Essential Medicines' (2010) 12 Health and Human Rights 73, 75–76; Magdalena Sepúlveda, 'Obligations of 'International Assistance and Cooperation'in an Optional Protocol to the Inter-

This section will not address in greater detail the general discussions about the status of international cooperation in human rights law, but will analyse, among the existing alternative interpretations of such status, what obligations of international cooperation can offer to an HRBA to HTA and examine the most persuasive one in the HTA context. There are three possible interpretations, and it is argued that the third one is the most acceptable. The first two forms of extraterritorial obligation of international human rights (weak or strong, depending on their obligation) are difficult to determine or implement. The third alternative, which seems more plausible, is a narrow duty to provide international cooperation across the world. This narrow duty is not the most impactful obligation (as seeking cooperation is not the same as enforcing results), but does not have to deal with the problems of the other interpretations.

3.1 Weak and Strong Extraterritorial Obligations in HTA

The first two interpretations equate HTA cooperation with realisation of the right to health by assuming that the State might implement, beyond national territory, socio-economic rights obligations under the ICESCR. International cooperation and assistance in this regard are not understood as self-standing obligations, but just one of the many ways to realise socio-economic rights in the assisted State.[42] In this case, international cooperation merely serves as a supplementary aid to the implementation of human rights in the territory in question (the domestic State is still the principal duty-bearer). The right to health would therefore be the main obligation, with international assistance and cooperation a secondary measure, indicating where resources can be found to implement socio-economic rights.[43]

The weak route to the duty of international cooperation interprets obligations, from the assisting State, as voluntary, non-binding and contingent upon richer States being willing to commit resources or non-financial support to the Global South (and presumably only when requested by the latter). Many States shared this position during the draft of the ICESCR: this was Sweden's defence during a visit of the Special Rapporteur regarding the right to health,

national Covenant on Economic, Social and Cultural Rights' (2006) 24 Netherlands Quarterly of Human Rights 271, 274–292.

42 Takhmina Karimova, 'The Nature and Meaning of "International Assistance and Cooperation" under the International Covenant on Economic, Social and Cultural Rights' in Eibe Riedel, Gilles Giacca and Christophe Golay (eds), *Economic, Social, and Cultural Rights in International Law* (Oxford University Press 2014) 170–171.

43 Ibid., 171.

and was equally the view of other countries during the drafting of the Optional Protocol to the Covenant.[44]

The stronger reading is the doctrine of extraterritorial obligations (ETOs), as presented by the Maastricht Principles on ETO, a non-binding expert opinion issued by 40 academics and today, a most respected interpretative reference. Such obligations result from State action or inaction within the scope of the jurisdiction of the State to protect, respect and fulfil socio-economic rights.[45] This is plausible because the Covenant, unlike other human rights treaties, has never restricted the territorial jurisdiction of the obligations.[46] However, this stronger view is based on an ETO triggered by some State activity or omission that generates a link with the territory of another State (Maastricht Principle 8a).[47] This contraposes the idea of obligations created by a norm of global character, which dispenses with any territorial link to the assisted State.[48]

The former Special Rapporteur on the right to health, Paul Hunt, has highlighted the binding nature of such obligations, rejecting that this undertaking would merely constitute "charity", although developed States still hold this stance. The Committee on Economic, Social and Cultural Rights (CESCR)

---

44 HRC, "Report of the Special Rapporteur on the right of everyone to the enjoyment of the highest attainable standard of physical and mental health", 5 March 2008 (A/HRC/7/11/Add.2), paras. 131–133; "Report of the Open-ended Working Group to Consider Options Regarding the Elaboration of an Optional Protocol to the International Covenant on Economic, Social and Cultural Rights on its Second Session", 23 May 2008 (E/CN.4/2005/52), para. 76, Takhmina Karimova, 'The Nature and Meaning of "International Assistance and Cooperation" under the International Covenant on Economic, Social and Cultural Rights' in Eibe Riedel, Gilles Giacca and Christophe Golay (eds), *Economic, Social, and Cultural Rights in International Law* (Oxford University Press 2014) 166.

45 'Maastricht Principles on Extraterritorial Obligations of States in the Area of Economic, Social and Cultural Rights' (2011) 29 Netherlands Quarterly of Human Rights 578, Principle 8.

46 Malcolm Langford, Fons Coomans and Felipe Gómez Isa, 'Extraterritorial Duties in International Law' in Malcolm Langford and others (eds), *Global Justice, State Duties* (Cambridge University Press 2012) 57–62.

47 Ralph Wilde, 'Dilemmas in Promoting Global Economic Justice through Human Rights Law' in Nehal Bhuta (ed), *The Frontiers of Human Rights* (Oxford University Press 2016) 156.

48 Some authors adopt the tripartite obligation to protect, respect and fulfil without requiring a territorial connection, see e.g. Magdalssena Sepúlveda Carmona, 'The Obligations of "International Assistance and Cooperation" under the International Covenant on Economic, Social and Cultural Rights. A Possible Entry Point to a Human Rights Based Approach to Millennium Development Goal 8' (2009) 13 The International Journal of Human Rights 86, 90–94.

has been unequivocal that it is "incumbent" on States to provide assistance to countries in need.[49] Similarly, on the right to health, ETO, several authors have incisively referred to international cooperation not as a question of beneficence, but as a truly recognised obligation.[50]

The triad "protect, respect and fulfil" would apply in the same way as the obligation to nationals, but also in international relations where those territorial linkages with another State's action or inaction arise.[51] "Respect" requires that the State avoids adopting measures that interfere with rights realisation elsewhere (such as imposing an embargo on exporting supplies). "Protect" refers to preventing non-State actors from taking actions that might hinder rights realisation. The category of "fulfilment" obligations is less straightforward and assumes that the State should provide for rights realisation with the resources it has at its disposal (without stipulating openly a minimum level for that) or promote proportionate conditions favourable to rights realisation. In conclusion, these tripartite obligations of the right to health translate to steering clear of any negative intervention to access to health in other countries, preventing private entities from breaching human rights abroad and supporting international collaborations to improve health among States by the promotion of human rights or through direct financial support.

The stronger view has been dominant in commentaries of the Committee, yet some obscurity in relation to the content of these obligations persists.[52] The major question is: who should be responsible for international cooperation in HTA? In the Committee pronouncements, the principle of incumbency on States to provide international assistance or cooperation is moderated by the clause of "economic capacity", which stipulates that States with available resources are "particularly incumbent" to support less-favoured States (though this distinction does not clarify what practical difference this brings as to the discharge of obligations).[53] The usual reading is that this obli-

---

49 CESCR, GC 14 (chapter 1, n 34) para. 39.

50 Benjamin Mason Meier and Ashley M Fox, 'International Obligations through Collective Rights: Moving from Foreign Health Assistance to Global Health Governance' (2010) 12 Health and Human Rights 61, 69; Gorik Ooms, Ines Keygnaert and Rachel Hammonds, 'The Right to Health: From Citizen's Right to Human Right (and Back)' (2019) 172 Public Health 99, 101.

51 Elena Pribytkova, 'What Global Human Rights Obligations Do We Have?' (2019) 20 Chicago Journal of International Law 384, 428–429; Meier and Fox (n 50) 67.

52 CESCR, GC 3 (chapter 4, n 32) para. 2.

53 See e.g. CESCR, GC 3 (chapter 4, n 32), para 14; "General Comment No. 15" (chapter 4, n 86) para. 34; "General Comment No. 19: The Right to Social Security" 4 February 2008 (E/C.12/GC/19); Ashfaq Khalfan, 'Division of Responsibility amongst States' in Malcolm Langford and others (eds), *Global Justice, State Duties: The Extraterritorial Scope of Eco-*

gation is not identically distributed among States and varies according to the capacity to assist or the need to be assisted. It is more widely agreed that the basic obligation to fulfil human rights rests firstly on the national State, and foreign States only have a subsidiary responsibility.[54] Even after acknowledging the existence of aided and donor States, it is not clearly determined what are the metes and bounds of need (to secure a minimum level so the State does not collapse, targeting core obligations, or to aim for a higher degree of development) nor the amount of resources that a State should be expected to transfer.[55]

Another problematic issue in the context of HTA is to determine how exactly State action or inaction in policies linked to priority-setting gives rise to obligations beyond national jurisdictions. ETO are complex to be determined, and there is no effective oversight mechanism to enforce State noncompliance.[56] Some may argue that only the principle of non-interference has a status of customary law (thus forcing States to respect human rights when acting abroad).[57] Conventionally, in the doctrine, the scope of external jurisdiction is established by two broad situations – namely, jurisdictional control or violation of socio-economic rights abroad by omission or action. The first case arises when a State exercises control over foreign territory or over a person in another State.[58] The second is a form of State responsibility for indirect or direct influence over the enjoyment of rights in another State, by action or omission, which has a foreseeable effect on socio-economic rights abroad.[59]

---

nomic, Social, and Cultural Rights in International Law (Cambridge University Press 2012) 324–329.

54 'Maastricht Principles on Extraterritorial Obligations of States in the Area of Economic, Social and Cultural Rights' (2011) 29 Netherlands Quarterly of Human Rights 578, principle 9;.

55 Ooms, Keygnaert and Hammonds (n 50) 101; Khalfan (n 53) 321–323.

56 Margot E Salomon and Ian Seiderman, 'Human Rights Norms for a Globalized World: The Maastricht Principles on Extraterritorial Obligations of States in the Area of Economic, Social and Cultural Rights: The Maastricht Principles on Extraterritorial Obligations' (2012) 3 Global Policy 458, 460.

57 Janelle M Diller, 'Economic, Social and Cultural Human Rights: The Journey towards Peremptory Norms in International Law' (2018) 36 Nordic Journal of Human Rights 19, 23.

58 Maarten Den Heijer and Rick Lawson, 'Extraterritorial Human Rights and the Concept of' jurisdiction" [2013] Global Justice, State Duties: the Extraterritorial Scope of Economic, Social, and Cultural Rights in International Law 153, 165–185.

59 See e.g. Martin Scheinin, 'Just Another Word?: Jurisdiction in the Roadmaps of State Responsibility and Human Rights' in Malcolm Langford and others (eds), *Global justice, state duties : the extraterritorial scope of economic, social, and cultural rights in international law* (Cambridge University Press 2013).

That principle would require some demonstration that States are interfering negatively with HTA abroad. Negative effects on HTA could be, for instance, trade agreements that offer unfavourable pricing schemes. Other areas, though, are less obvious, for example in cases such as local businesses domiciled in one country violating human rights abroad. General Comment 24, on socio-economic rights and business, restricts ETO to State activity directly connected to private enterprises (meaning that companies are acting on behalf of a State, such as under legislation, authorised representation or later acknowledgement of their actions).[60] A stringent standard like this, which adopts the same model as the Maastricht Principles, would definitely make it difficult to elicit ETO in HTA related to the actions of non-State actors.[61] Hence, the effects of private actors on HTA internationally would rarely be treated as an ETO obligation in cases involving irregular practices or abuse of economic power and political influence of companies abroad, including corruption.

Additionally, another doctrinal formulation of ETO relates to what the Maastricht Principles call "obligations of global character", which can be implemented individually or through international cooperation.[62] This interpretation does not require a linkage with another territory, but, beyond that, attempting to determine its content is problematic.[63] Furthermore, some authors adopt a normative approach based on the moral duties of global justice.[64] However, this could be beleaguered by disputes over enforceability and obligatory character, and even the Maastricht Principles acknowledge that there is no absolute certainty of this possibility in the legal doctrine.

In conclusion, ETO are difficult to implement in relation to HTA (in both weak and strong forms). The safest way to proceed would be to abstain from interpreting cooperation obligations as hinging on asserting jurisdiction abroad or as a global burden without restrictions, both of which would demand some specific circumstances of State foreign collaboration. The

60 CESCR, "General comment No. 24 (2017) on State obligations under the International Covenant on Economic, Social and Cultural Rights in the context of business activities" 10 August 2017 (E/C.12/GC/24) paras 25–37.

61 'Maastricht Principles (n 54) Principle 12.

62 Ibid., Principle 8-b.

63 Ralph Wilde, 'Socioeconomic Rights, Extraterritorially' in Eyal Benvenisti and George Nolte (eds), *Community Interests Across International Law* (Oxford University Press 2018) 391; Olivier De Schutter and others, 'Commentary to the Maastricht Principles on Extraterritorial Obligations of States in the Area of Economic, Social and Cultural Rights' (2012) 34 Human Rights Quarterly 1084, 1094.

64 Askin Elif, 'Economic and Social Rights, Extraterritorial Application' in Askin Elif, *Max Planck Encyclopedia of Public International Law* (Oxford University Press 2019) 24.

third approach is a better option since it allows for an obligation of international cooperation, independent of those considerations about extraterritoriality and resources. In this scenario, instead of States being legally required to act in relation to socio-economic rights fulfilment outside their jurisdictions, they have a less-ambitious obligation "to provide international cooperation" as a means to support rights realisation.[65] The next section will now address how this third interpretation arises in international law.

3.2 Intermediate Approach: International Cooperation *Stricto Sensu*

A pure duty of international cooperation is rather an attenuated and narrow obligation, but still fits well within international HTA networks. For the HTA international community, an obligation to provide international cooperation includes initiatives to create multiple networks and agreements among States. Compared to general ETO, such a duty constitutes an obligation of conduct and not of result – States would have to formulate HTA cooperation with a view to realise rights, but with no mandatory fulfilment because the focus is to coordinate, promote and enable the environment towards implementation.[66] Arguably, this duty falls on all States (as a peremptory norm, according to Diller) enshrined in the United Nations Charter and in line with the international practice of combining efforts and developing common institutions.[67]

The possible interpretation, then, would be that the only immediate obligations of global character for international cooperation consist of very basic conduct for an "enabling environment" not requiring resources. Specifically in the context of HTA, the constraint is less of a problem as part of the international collaboration is confined only to technical and political assistance, without resource implications. HTA networks and technical cooperation are the minimum form of cooperation a State should meet, regardless of resource capacity. Hence, with regard to the right to health, States should actively support each other technically and share knowledge internationally – this means providing every kind of immediately available cooperation to enhance access policies to healthcare across the world without discrimination. In this sense, while it is not currently a feature of HTA networks, cooperation could take the form of an international organisation (even also including non-governmental members) that substantively promotes policies bound by international law and human rights standards (e.g. facilitating healthcare coverage across juris-

65 Wilde (n 63) 390–391.
66 Pribytkova (n 51) 434.
67 Diller (n 57) 24.

dictions through technical assistance or regulating international markets for affordability).[68]

Under the Maastricht Principles, an obligation to provide international cooperation still entails that different States have varied degrees of capacity to help other States, but clearly, States must at least be open to working together. Two minimum conducts are most likely to be proportionate: striving for a mechanism of distribution of responsibilities internationally; and establishing an enabling international environment favourable to socio-economic rights (Principles 28, 29 and 30).[69]

However, even within those minimalistic duties more clarity is needed. For instance, a developed State could either promote cooperation in HTA to support less-developed States or simply promote a better international environment. Nor is it clear whether the duty of international assistance and cooperation can be read as a duty of the developing State to request the support to fulfil the socio-economic right at the discretion or not of developed States. International guidance in this regard is limited. In General Comment 25, on the right of everyone to enjoy the benefits of scientific progress and its applications (Article 15(1)(b)), the Committee affirms the duty "to promote an enabling global environment for the advancement of science and the enjoyment of the benefits of its applications", from which it cannot be assumed that this environment is primarily to give access to less-developed nations.[70]

All that can be said, then is that States have obligations of international cooperation with no precise preference, order and focus. At times, it seems that cooperation is subject to a request for support. In alluding to the international disparities in technological advances, the Committee articulates the developed States' obligations, which are conditional on the needs of other States and their requests: "If it is necessary, owing to financial or technological constraints, developing States should resort to international assistance and cooperation, with a view to complying with their obligations under the Covenant."[71] On the other hand, developed States "should contribute" by "adopting measures to achieve this", and while "developing aid and funding" and "a collaboration between scientific communities" are among the potential forms of support, there is no appropriate guidance on whether this obligation takes

---

68 Ibid., 34–36.

69 Wilde (n 63) 392; 'Maastricht Principles' (n 54) Principles 28–30.

70 CESCR, "General Comment No. 25: Science and Economic, Social and Cultural Rights (article 15 (1) (b), (2), (3) and (4) of the International Covenant on Economic, Social and Cultural Rights)", 30 April 2020 (E/C.12/GC/25) para. 77.

71 Ibid., para. 79.

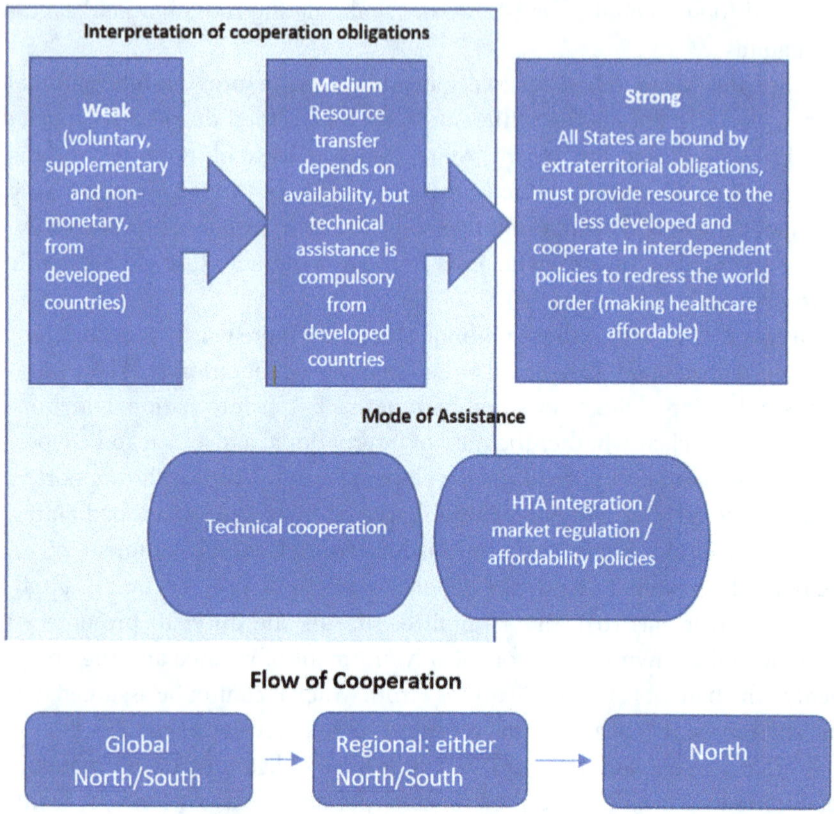

FIGURE 6.1 Comparative chart of the three forms of cooperation in HTA according to their legal strength and scope (Source: Own contribution)

place only once a State requests assistance or whether it is a permanent duty to achieve rights everywhere.[72]

4 International HTA Alliances: Non-discrimination and Pluralism in HRBA

Until now, the argument in this chapter has been that international HTA networks and agreements may materialise the duty of international cooperation. Yet, not all HTA partnerships and exchanges between States are equal, and to implement the right to health, States must also follow human rights standards. This section will now refer to potential problems that may arise when inter-

72 Ibid.

national networks do not follow HRBA in two particular circumstances. The first constraint is that HTA networks might not promote participation and recognise local circumstances within countries when providing assistance. The second point concerns whether existing HTA networks are equitably distributed or whether they sustain inequalities by discriminating between developed and developing States.

The first question to address in HTA cooperation is whether the reuse and sharing of studies across jurisdictions is valid from an HRBA standpoint in respect of the risk of disregarding the specificity of national populations. The evidence produced abroad could be taken up by countries which do not possess sufficient capacity to conduct such studies, but at the same time, research findings might persuade them to adopt models that are not derived from their own reality (see Chapter 5, on HTA evidence-making).[73]

An important cross-jurisdictional area of work in HTA is the standardisation of outputs and reports for interoperable exchange among agencies. International cooperation of the EUnetHTA has developed the HTA Core Model, which aims to improve interagency collaboration, reduce duplication of HTA procedures and make the evidence easily exchangeable between agencies and applicable to other locations.[74] This integration impetus should be conscious of local realities and the impact on local needs.

A second issue is whether HTA cooperation can be discriminatory when it sidelines agencies in certain geographic regions or from less-advanced economies. HTA cooperation does not necessarily have to follow the model of poor States aided by their richer counterparts and, in practice, developed countries often pursue a different direction, cooperating among themselves more intimately than with less-developed regions. For example, founded in 2016, the Beneluxa Initiative (joining Belgium, Netherlands, Luxemburg and Austria and, from 2018, also Ireland) is a coalition of States that joined forces to address affordability of drugs by coordinating sustainable pharmaceutical policies.[75] In this joint programme, HTA is only one of the key themes, alongside market regulation, horizon-scanning and price negotiation. By use of memorandums of understanding, governments secure more profound cooperation on an ongoing basis and with more clarity (though arguably more informally

73 Simoens (chapter 3, n 2) 858.

74 Kristensen and others (Table 6.1 n f) 245.

75 Beneluxa, 'The Beneluxa Initiative on Pharmaceutical Policy – Terms of Reference' <https://beneluxa.org/sites/beneluxa.org/files/2018-10/180622%20Terms%20of%20Reference%20Beneluxa%20Initiative.pdf> accessed 5 May 2020.

and not binding, as with a normal treaty).[76] Similarly, in the European Union, member-States are migrating to a more integrated regulation, introducing a mechanism of joint-assessment, limited to the evaluation of clinical evidence, that must be conducted before any submission to local HTA authorities.[77] EU clinical evaluation would then bind the clinical aspects of HTA recommendations locally, as member-States will not be able to re-examine information already reviewed.

This selectivity does not operate in the same way as individual discrimination and is more akin to preferential treatments in trade law (which states that favourable conditions should be open to all countries). Agreeing at least that resource dependency is what defines whether human rights obligations are immediately realisable or not, it follows that States ought not to refuse entering into cooperation with specific countries for reasons apart from limited resources. Yet, partnerships for information-sharing or public procurement pools that maintain low prices tend to be in place exclusively among countries of similar economic status.[78]

These agreements can initially start as a channel for a joint assessment process, which can progress to common recommendations and ultimately lead to a single procurement and price negotiation mechanism as Beneluxa has achieved.[79] The Nordics (Norway, Sweden, Denmark) instituted FINOSE, an interagency network, to share information and produce joint assessments with a view to gaining lower pharmaceutical prices.[80] Other agreements paving the way for joint assessments and pharmaceutical policy have been established between European countries, such as the Valletta Declaration and the Fair and Affordable Price (FAAP) group.[81]

The reality of power relations in HTA, in fact, is not well distributed. Generally, forerunner institutions in the developed world are viewed as "the global

---

76 On the "informal" status of memorandum of understanding in international law, see e.g. Anthony Aust, 'The Theory and Practice of Informal International Instruments' (1986) 35 International & Comparative Law Quarterly 787, 794–796.

77 Regulation (EU) 2021/2282.

78 On forms of affordability policies, see chapter 7, 2.

79 Emma Eatwell and Anna Swierczyna, 'Emerging Voluntary Cooperation between European Healthcare Systems: Are We Facing a New Future?' (2019) 3 Medicine Access @ Point of Care 239920261985231, 4.

80 FINOSE, 'Memorandum of Understanding' <https://www.fimea.fi/documents/160140/1454518/yhteisymm%C3%A4rrysp%C3%B6yt%C3%A4kirja.pdf/b5134913-8064-c224-270d-d23cd2c68e37> accessed 8 April 2020.

81 European Commission, 'HTA Sharing Experiences from the Regional Cooperations' <https://ec.europa.eu/health/sites/health/files/technology_assessment/docs/2018_regional_hta_reportsum_en.pdf> accessed 5 May 2020.

standard" of HTA, from which unversed countries should learn and follow suit. The image that transpires of capacity-building in HTA is of developed countries bestowing their knowledge upon low- and middle-income economies (LMICs) lacking expertise – HTA exporters come to the rescue of inefficient and inexperienced governments.[82] Even ex-importers such as Thailand can emerge as international technical advocates with a whole division (HITAP International Unit) for this mission.[83] International cooperation drives the process of institutionalisation of HTA in poor countries, arousing the interest of local leaderships, promoting a national agenda on priority-setting and establishing a culture of generating data and research to meet technical standards.[84]

However, a difference in treatment between developing and developed countries is problematic for the right to health. If developed States can support each other in more profound collaboration, pursuing market regulation to achieve affordability, would that mean that disadvantaged States should expect similar attention? By accepting an obligation of international cooperation under the international right to health, any country capable of offering technical assistance must take steps towards all countries where it is apt to assist (in line with resource availability and progressive realisation). Despite this, it cannot be disregarded that a closer relationship in HTA, though auspicious for affordability, faces its own challenges of sovereignty, guidelines congruence and effective management of a single negotiation strategy (e.g. there are some concerns with the Beneluxa states).[85] For instance, data on price negotiation, price transparency and reference pricing are fairly dependent upon the availability of information on external markets and coordinated operations. Agreements of that nature could reasonably be said to be restricted only to States with the same economic capacity or at the same stage of development. Considering the potential level of cooperation in HTA in some cases in the Global North and the focus on affordability and substantive policies that could shape the right to health realisation in other countries, the problem of differential treatment seems pertinent. Thus, it must be considered whether the said cooperation: a) is non-burdensome to the assisting State in the original agreement and b) can be feasibly extended to any other countries without any added economic onus.

82 Tantivess and others (n 1) 3.

83 Ibid.

84 Ibid., 8.

85 James F O'Mahony, 'Beneluxa: What Are the Prospects for Collective Bargaining on Pharmaceutical Prices Given Diverse Health Technology Assessment Processes?' (2019) 37 PharmacoEconomics 627, 627–629.

5 Conclusion: Making a Conscious Choice for HTA International Cooperation and the Right to Health

Against this background, three main options lie before think-tanks, HTA agencies and other groups involved in the promotion of priority-setting tools. First, we could dismiss a linkage of human rights and HTA and remain under the banner of UHC. This would miss the opportunity to give a more compelling ground to establish HTA international efforts and bring to bear more accountability and political pressure to ensure that States contribute in this realm collectively. The second way would maintain a restrained attitude but accept that at least there is a duty of international cooperation, so States ought to engage with networks and technical assistance. The last option would be to assert a full-fledged connection between HTA and the right to health in international relations, with all the consequences that brings for other policies involving market powers indirectly influencing the results of resource allocation decisions.

The simple fact that international cooperation is not always regarded as binding may seem to jeopardise any possibility of giving a legally authoritative alternative to the ideal of UHC. However, just as a choice has been made to adopt UHC as a compass for international cooperation in HTA, the right to health could equally be embraced as a deliberate decision. Hammonds et al. show that international actors (such as the Global Fund) can develop an understanding of the right to health in bringing it into action and sensitising States towards their duties in global health.[86] It is also important to note that advocacy of HTA implementation has largely been a product of Global North expertise, but an HRBA could drastically alter this vision of distribution of responsibilities, calling into action any State capable of playing a part in this process.[87]

An HRBA to international cooperation would also hinge on the importance given to those obligations – namely, whether cooperation were accorded only an intermediate weight (centred on pure technical development) or whether a complete right to health fulfilment was deemed to be the objective (which would force States to coordinate other policies with HTA at a higher international level to eliminate barriers on affordable healthcare in LMIC). Many questions would still follow in an HRBA. Are partnerships only reproducing

86 Rachel Hammonds, Gorik Ooms and Wouter Vandenhole, 'Under the (Legal) Radar Screen: Global Health Initiatives and International Human Rights Obligations' (2012) 12 BMC International Health and Human Rights 31, 12–14.

87 Wilde (n 47) 147–148.

data originated in the North, while not responding to the causes of scarcity in the South (for instance, by addressing pharmaceutical policies)? Can the Global South participate in other complementary forms of cooperation that could directly benefit access schemes in procurement and price negotiation integrated into HTA? Drawing on the experiences of these agreements in the North, a strong view of a duty to international cooperation (accepting ETO in every respect) would demand that States act towards the Global South in a non-discriminatory manner, as they would be capable of offering the same broader mutual collaboration without using extra resources.

Mere technical assistance in HTA would be the easiest offering for many countries, but the crucial aid for the development of a health system with resource allocation problems must not be limited to managerial tools. HTA support must not be a know-how package for transferring a model of resource allocation from a developed country as a form of alleviating its duty of intervention for rights realisation, that is, teaching how to spend without making substantive changes in power relations and economic development, both of which currently represent unsurmountable barriers to access to health technologies.

The challenge remains that the technical emphasis of HTA international cooperation does not meet the needs of the most comprehensive version of an HRBA. Thus, a strong view of human rights in HTA can only be grounded in obligations of international cooperation, if aimed at maximising resources and progressively realising the right to health. International HTA promotion may disregard the fact that for human rights, adopting well-grounded cost-effectiveness tools is insufficient to determine the progressive realisation of the right to health. While appropriate decisions on scarce resources are part of the measures regarded as one of the means to unleash maximum availability of resources, that is just one of the dimensions in resource mobilisation. An HTA sits also within substantive policies relating to unaffordability and adequate financing of a health system. Redistributing resources in a low-income setting to make the best use of a budget does not preclude infrastructure improvement and market regulation, to avoid rationing being the first port of call for any kind of supply shortage or underfunding.

Traditional international cooperation in HTA centres on the ability of the assisted states to take full advantage of a state of affairs (restrained by inequalities in market control), but that stance is not necessarily compliant with human rights, and limits the responsibility of developing countries to what seems possible in the current situation, without changing underlying unfair circumstances. Moreover, non-financial assistance should not mean that there are no substantive policies that can be put into effect to promote

more decisions to fund technologies in HTA. Market regulation, preferential trading terms and policies to combat excessive prices can guarantee that health technologies are more affordable for the aided States, without requiring financial disbursement from other States.[88] These development issues are not merely about a poor economy or insufficient foreign donation for budget deficits. Those barriers could be removed if cooperation focused, for instance, on the excessive profits of pharmaceutical companies, the issue of unbalanced trade agreements, and the lack of international sustainable models to steer the flow of goods and knowledge internationally. The Beneluxa partnership is a good example of how this association could be improved globally.

Therefore, HTA should be at the heart of the wealthy States' duties to fulfil human rights through international assistance and cooperation – but it also needs to be part of a broader range of interconnected policies to represent a real step towards the right to health. This is not to say that technical assistance is not an impactful part of HTA cooperation. Even on a voluntary basis, international donations can be guided by HTA and could actually be dependent on the endorsement of a local procedure so that those resources would represent an implementation of the right to health as a legitimate and informed decision. Since HTA is a tool to determine local priorities and to align investment to national health needs, external assistance not in consonance with HTA would lack the requirement of consent of the assisted State.

In addition, local policies in higher-income countries to monitor and regulate private actors – particularly when they impact on prices and affordability in other jurisdictions – could be deemed by international HTA leaderships as within the scope of the duty to protect other States. The scope of technical assistance could also be broader by not being restricted to HTA functioning, expertise or evidence, but by being available to aid in the development of systems to design new procurement mechanisms or marketing regulations that would ensure affordability.

An HRBA to international cooperation in HTA is still a new frontier for political transformation. In a certain way, HTA cooperation, in its current form, has already offered a counterexample to the normal paradigm of distribution of responsibilities among States centred on the North to South orthodox relation. Some forms of collaboration emerging between the Global South and others are more deeply integrated within the North. The ample diffusion of HTA among different international alliances demonstrates that economic capacity cannot be a waiver of duties of international cooperation, as many States can form unions to develop knowledge and mutual support even in

88 Meier and Fox (n 50) 67.

more fragile health systems. As HTA agencies and advocacy organisations have never fully seized the binding duty of cooperation, it is impossible to predict entirely its impact on policies, though we should at least gradually achieve more political pressure on non-collaborating States through HTA agreements.

One area in which international cooperation could be particularly useful in HTA is market regulation, to enable affordability of new technologies. There are signs, with the Beneluxa cooperation, that international agreements can further foment this duty of introducing appropriate laws to tackle healthcare needs. As the next chapter will argue, the substantive standards laid down by Article 2.1 of the ICESCR can be read as creating a duty to enact adequate legislation – including market regulation – so that resources are not compromised by excessive prices or insufficient production.

CHAPTER 7

The Right to Health, Affordability and Legal Determinants of Scarcity

Supporters of a more procedural approach to resource allocation, and HTA by extension, may overlook the opportunities open to policymakers to control prices, stimulate domestic production and facilitate access to healthcare while still undertaking distributive choices. At the international level, experts propose legally binding instruments for international cooperation to solve transnational problems of affordability and access to healthcare.[1] Known as "access policies", these measures to reduce the occurrence of scarcity through market exploitation are intimately linked to the law within HTA and simultaneously to resource allocation, as a substantive dimension of HRBA.[2]

This chapter further examines the "resource-generating" nature of socio-economic rights in international law and offers a way of maximising resources in HTA by law. Affordability legislation, it is submitted, comprises obligations of immediate effect, which require State regulation over scarcity. These obligations are inferred by reading in conjunction the rules of maximum available resources and progressive realisation of the right to health, as per Article 2(1) of the ICESCR, examined in the general framework of Chapter 4. Since HTA is a core social institution, where political decisions about resource distribution and generation can happen at the same time, some of those access policies and affordability measures may arise within or alongside priority-setting.

The interpretation of State obligations submitted in this chapter will be argued via two interrelated ideas. The first point is that socio-economic rights impose obligations of immediate effect, whereby States must take measures to maximise their resources by all means available, including legis-

1 Examples include a WHO Convention on International Tiered Pricing and Compulsory Licensing . See: Gorik Ooms and others, 'Could International Compulsory Licensing Reconcile Tiered Pricing of Pharmaceuticals with the Right to Health?' (2014) 14 BMC International Health and Human Rights 37.

2 Sabine Vogler, 'Access to High-Cost Medicines in Europe' in Zaheer-Ud-Din Babar (ed), *Equitable Access to High-Cost Pharmaceuticals* (Academic Press 2018) 148. Verena Stühlinger, 'Health Technology Assessment (HTA) and Access Policies' (2020) 27 European Journal of Health Law 274, 278–283; Sabine Vogler and others, 'How Can Pricing and Reimbursement Policies Improve Affordable Access to Medicines? Lessons Learned from European Countries' (2017) 15 Applied Health Economics and Health Policy 307, 309–313.

 | HTTPS://DOI.ORG/10.1163/9789004730311-008

lation to ensure healthcare affordability. This is a global interpretation of the provisions contained in the framework of Article 2.1 of the ICESCR (resource mobilisation plus duty to enact legislation, discussed in Chapter 4). The legal structure in a jurisdiction is then a determinant (or not) of scarcity, according to its effect on the price and availability of healthcare. The second idea, of empirical significance, is that prices and costs may be influenced by law, as an alternative to simply rationing healthcare to reduce volume of use.[3] The fundamental challenge is to identify the laws that can assist in reducing the costs and increasing the availability of healthcare products, being conscious of the local context and risks of negative effects on the market, such as suppliers leaving a jurisdiction. HTA, however, may play a fundamental role in this regard as it is a process apt to determine the specific causes of unaffordability.

The final part of this chapter summarises different legal instruments employed for tackling scarcity in health through affordability strategies, which are not generally used in an HRBA: namely, direct price control, negotiation and procurement strategies, competition law and public–private partnerships (PPPs). Those are policies that should be integrated into HTA to guarantee that each deliberation on healthcare coverage is carried out under conditions of lowest cost or most competitive prices. It concludes that the affordability criteria in an HRBA presuppose legal frameworks to maximise resources in the negotiation, production and regulation of prices of healthcare interventions – a group of policies closely associated with HTA as a core social institution, but unjustifiably not coordinated in a single process.

1 Legal Determinants of Scarcity

This section begins by defining the scope of the "legal determinants of scarcity" mentioned above and how they may be construed within a socio-economic rights framework. By the term "legal determinants of scarcity" we mean laws that influence positively or negatively a policy for resource availability (e.g. taxation), or serve as a precondition for a policy that can minimise scarcity (e.g. a competitive procurement system that is not prescribed by law).[4] This

3 Toon van der Gronde, Carin A Uyl-de Groot and Toine Pieters, 'Addressing the Challenge of High-Priced Prescription Drugs in the Era of Precision Medicine: A Systematic Review of Drug Life Cycles, Therapeutic Drug Markets and Regulatory Frameworks' (2017) 12 PLOS ONE e0182613, 3.

4 Sabine Vogler, Valérie Paris and Dimitra Panteli, 'Ensuring Access to Medicines: How to Redesign Pricing, Reimbursement and Procurement?' (European Observatory on Health

is an analogy with the academic move towards "legal determinants of health", aimed at public health outcomes through laws, but not as much at causes of scarcity in healthcare.[5]

Gostin et al.'s ideal of legal determinants of health consists of any legal instruments that can be used against "underlying social and economic causes of injury and disease", but the economic reasons for low levels of access to healthcare and health technologies, including market failures and poor price control, do not have a dominant place in this agenda.[6] Although the Lancet Commission's main report on the topic does briefly mention PPPs and intellectual property issues, the reference is made within the context of law and governance and not in the context of their effectiveness as a leverage tool to avoid rationing.[7] In general, authors have not fully addressed the options available to increase affordability, other than patents, even though affordability is mentioned as one objective of the legal determinants.[8]

Moreover, legal determinants of scarcity overlap with some forms of economic or health policy to reduce healthcare prices. The examples mentioned here are discussed in the 2020 "WHO Guideline on Pharmaceutical Price Policies" and, as the title suggests, were treated as policies (the report also makes reference to HTA and value-based pricing).[9] In general, those policies imply some legal basis and do not operate outside the scope of law, administrative authorisations and competences to control excessive prices beyond the intellectual property (IP) regime.[10]

Some of these legal determinants of scarcity arise in the price environment and not at the research & development (R&D) and patents level, where human rights scholarship is traditionally focused.[11] The range of measures is

---

Systems and Policies, 2018) 20. David Clarke, 'Law, Regulation and Strategizing for Health' in Gerard Schmets and others (eds), *Strategizing national health in the 21st century: a handbook* (World Health Organization 2016) 1–3.

5 Lawrence O Gostin and others, 'The Legal Determinants of Health: Harnessing the Power of Law for Global Health and Sustainable Development' (2019) 393 The Lancet 1857.

6 Ibid 1857.

7 Ibid 1865–1867.

8 Ibid 1900.

9 World Health Organization, *WHO Guideline on Country Pharmaceutical Pricing Policies* (2nd ed, World Health Organization 2020) <https://apps.who.int/iris/handle/10665/335692> access 20 September 2021.

10 André den Exter, 'Fighting Excessive Pharmaceutical Prices: Evaluating the Options' (2020) 28 European Journal of Health Law 68, 70–80.

11 For a distinction between these environments, see Nora Franzen and others, 'Evidence Underlying Policy Proposals for Sustainable Anticancer Drug Prices: A Systematic Review' (2020) 6 JAMA Oncology 909, E3–5.

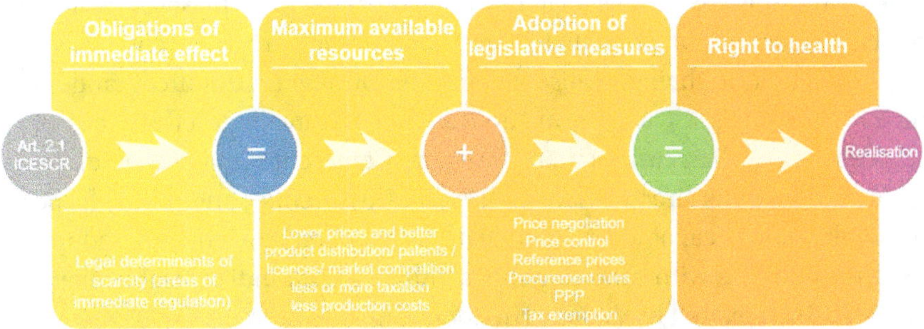

FIGURE 7.1 Summary of the framework (Source: Author's own contribution)

structurally different as to the stage of production of the healthcare good at hand: for instance, the price of drugs can be checked as early as the R&D stage, but other policies can also be enforced later in the drug life-cycle (e.g. through procurement and reimbursement regulations).[12] Even if R&D policies account for a large proportion of the final price, the right to health is examined under current technologies, in the later stages of a product life-cycle, excluding resources applied to research and approval of future technologies.[13]

Finally, regarding the legal basis for this legislation under the international right to health, this chapter proposes reading in conjunction the principles of Article 2.1 of the ICESCR: maximum available resources, obligation to enact legislative measures and the affordability standard. Jointly, the provisions contribute to the progressive realisation of the right to health via affordability of healthcare (this relationship is outlined in Figure 7.1, which also lists the resources obtained and the form of regulations associated). The rule of maximum available resources was described in the previous chapter as a comprehensive duty to seek alternatives to reduce scarcity. Now, two additional components to address legal scarcity are respectively presented in the next subsections: a) legislative measures and obligations of immediate effect and b) the affordability standard.

1.1 Legislation and Obligations of Immediate Effect

The State duty to enact laws for affordability argued in this chapter consists of an obligation of immediate effect. Normally, the key criterion of obligations of

12 Vogler, Paris and Panteli (n 4) 2.

13 Gronde, Uyl-de Groot and Pieters (n 3) 7.

immediate effect is the lack of resource-dependency.[14] In socio-economic rights, obligations of immediate effect differ from progressively realisable ones – the latter being realisable only according to resources and over time.[15] In the ICESCR the term "obligations of immediate effect" has only gained more explicit currency since General Comment 13 was adopted, drawing on conclusions already made in General Comments 3 and 9, which specified obligations "capable of immediate application".[16] Generally, adopting legislation in line with human rights standards is an indispensable element of an HRBA, as stated by various HR bodies.[17]

On the other hand, the whole range of right to health obligations of immediate effect remains "a work-in-progress".[18] The question of immediacy versus resources still remains controversial. For example, courts in India and South Africa have interpreted the right to health through either core obligations or obligations of an urgent nature as obligations of immediate effect – even if they have resource implications.[19] As core obligations remain disputed, equating them with immediate realisation regardless of resources is also contentious.[20]

Despite any conceptual limitation about resource-dependency, the passing of legislation should be regarded as an obligation of immediate effect with more certainty. Such a consideration is less relevant to the obligations to adopt laws, as passing adequate legislation would not normally require further resources.[21] If the measure is dependent only on a legislative act, that could be

---

14 See e.g. Dinah Shelton and Ariel Gould, 'Positive and Negative Obligations' in Dinah Shelton (ed), *The Oxford Handbook of International Human Rights Law* (OUP 2013); Keir Starmer, 'Positive Obligations under the ECHR in the Area of Medical Negligence' in Jeffrey Lowell and Jonathan Cooper (eds), *Understanding Human Rights Principles* (Hart Publishing) 146–147.

15 Bruce Porter, 'Rethinking Progressive Realization: How Should It Be Implemented in Canada?' 2 <http://www.socialrights.ca/documents/publications/Porter%20Progressive%20Implementation.pdf> accessed 21 November 2019.

16 CESCR, GC 3 (chapter 4, n 32) para. 5, "General Comment No. 9, The Domestic Application of the Covenant ", 3 December 1998 (E/C.12/1998/24), para. 10, "General Comment No. 13: The Right to Education (Art. 13)" 8 December 1999 (E/C.12/1999/10), paras 31, 43 and 51–52.

17 See e.g. UNHCR "Good Practices and Challenges to Respecting, Protecting and Fulfilling All Human Rights in the Elimination of Preventable Maternal Mortality and Morbidity" 13 July 2020 (A/HRC/45/19), B;.

18 Paul Hunt and others, 'The Right to the Highest Attainable Standard of Health' in Roger Detels and others (eds), *Oxford Textbook of Public Health* (2009) 339.

19 Alicia Ely Yamin and Fiona Lander, 'Implementing a Circle of Accountability: A Proposed Framework for Judiciaries and Other Actors in Enforcing Health-Related Rights' (2015) 14 Journal of Human Rights 312, 321–322.

20 See chapter 4, 2.

21 Langford and King (chapter 4, n 26) 487.

considered as a non-resource dependent measure – say, by establishing price limits, resources are made available and costs reduced. In some cases, though, legislative measures involving resource mobilisation may be resource dependent (e.g. by increasing taxation), and therefore it could be said that there would be no obligation of immediate effect.

1.2 Affordability Standard (versus Fair and Value-Based Pricing in HTA)

After obligations of immediate effect to pass legislation, the second component is the State duty to ensure affordable healthcare. To adopt affordability as a necessary end of State's immediate obligation to enact laws, Article 2.1 of the ICESCR requires a comprehensive interpretation of the duty to maximise resources by all appropriate means (including legislation).[22] While it cannot be said that international law requires that those relevant norms be articulated as human rights, legal frameworks must be designed so as to maximise resources. Flynn and Guzman suggest that duties to respect human rights are directly associated with applying laws harmonised with human rights regimes (and one of the obligations is to regulate excessive prices).[23] As they explain, the issue may be more about the inaction of local authorities than the consequences of international law rules.

In an HRBA, affordability distinguishes itself from misleadingly interconnected terms such as fair-pricing and value-based pricing, widely used in global health. This subsection will examine affordability as an HRBA standard and contrast it with these two other influential and concurrent models of healthcare pricing in global health governance.

In socio-economic rights, affordability is part of the AAAQ framework, which stands for availability, accessibility, acceptability and quality, the key criteria of implementation in human rights practice as already covered in Chapter 5.[24] The centrality of affordability in an HRBA is subsumed under the accessibility criteria as "economic accessibility".[25] General Comment 14 elaborates on economic accessibility by stating that "health facilities, goods

---

22 See e.g. CESCR, "An Evaluation of the Obligation to Take Steps to the 'Maximum Available Resources' under an Optional Protocol to the Covenant" 10 May 2007 ((E/C.12/2007/1), para. 8.

23 Sean Flynn and Luisa Guzman, Program on Information Justice and Intellectual Property, American University Washington College of Law, http://www.unsgaccessmeds.org/inbox/2016/2/28/sean-flynn-and-luisa-guzman, access 03 December 2019.

24 CESCR, GC14 (chapter 1, n 34), para 12 a–d.

25 IBID, para 12.b.

and services must be affordable for all".[26] First advocated in the access policies described by the Special Rapporteur on the right to education, Katarina Tomasevski, affordability as a human rights standard was carried over more extensively to General Comment 14 in the right to health.[27] The Committee has reiterated the significance of AAAQ to assess human rights implementation in a number of General Comments, but Hesselman et al. note that the criteria have been less scrutinised in the general literature, except through some specific research attempts to operationalise them into health policies.[28]

Further, a caveat that should be placed is that the HRBA notion of affordability does not imply that healthcare is objectively affordable – meaning objectively low in cost. Affordability should be read as costs proportionate to the capacity to pay for each population (or equitably determined by the economic conditions of each group).[29] It must be noted that this idea of affordability in healthcare access policies pre-dates Tomasevski's report and the subsequent adoption in General Comment 14, but there is no indication that policy guidance (which exists for other public services as well) has directly influenced affordability as a matter of human rights.[30] In the 2000s, healthcare management studies had already come to regard affordability as the capacity to pay before General Comment 14. For instance, the WHO and Management Sciences for Health (MSH) have defined affordability as "the relationship between the price of health goods and services and a user's disposable income".[31]

---

26 Ibid.

27 Ibid, Commission on Human Rights, Preliminary report of the Special Rapporteur on the right to education, Ms. Katarina Tomasevski, submitted in accordance with Commission on Human Rights resolution 1998/33, 13 January 1990 (E/CN.4/1999/49), paras 42–74.

28 Brigit Toebes, Marlies Hesselman and Antenor Hallo de Wolf, 'International Guideposts for Essential Public Services Provisions and Socio-Economic Rights' in Marlies Hesselman, Antenor Hallo de Wolf and Brigit Toebes (eds), *Socio-Economic Human Rights in Essential Public Services Provision* (Taylor & Francis 2016) 300–3001.

29 CESCR, (chapter 1, n 34).

30 Prior to affordability recognition as a human rights standard, public policy and healthcare research has already discussed and defined this term. See the definition of access of by Pechansky and Thomas and also Choi et. al. for a comparison on pre-human rights frameworks on access / affordability: Yoonjoung Choi, Madeleine Short Fabic and Jacob Adetunji, 'Measuring Access to Family Planning: Conceptual Frameworks and DHS Data' (2016) 47 Studies in Family Planning 145, 146–148; Roy Penchansky and J William Thomas, 'The Concept of Access: Definition and Relationship to Consumer Satisfaction' [1981] Medical care 127.

31 Center for Pharmaceutical Management, Defining and Measuring Access to Essential Drugs, Vaccines, and Health Commodities: Report of the WHO-MSH Consultative Meet-

Under this interpretation, an HRBA does not need to address the real value of healthcare or the fairest compensation for suppliers. Compared to affordability, the parallel notion of value or fair prices has gained more weight in HTA practice. For instance, the WHO renamed the HTA section in its guideline for pharmaceutical pricing as "value-based pricing".[32] However, the WHO report on value-based healthcare fell short of presenting affordability as a main pillar of access to healthcare and focused more on the quality, cost-effectiveness and equitable distribution of a set of patient-oriented health benefits package.[33]

This policy is problematic for human rights for being premised on measuring health outcomes to determine healthcare price by its "value" (raising the question as to how value is measured and by which outcomes, as seen in Chapter 5, in relation to non-discrimination and HTA criteria).[34] Thus, estimating value can be far too subjective, prolonging the decision-making process and, eventually, upholding higher prices when patents expire (because the evaluation of outcomes that support higher expenditure will not change).[35] With value-based systems, HTA may determine the additional value of each intervention for different indications or it can decide how much more should be paid for a superior treatment in comparison to the value of previous ones.[36] Sovaldi, a drug which has been deemed cost-effective but unaffordable in most health systems, would presumably be regarded as proportionately priced under a value-based system.[37] A value-based pricing system can prove to be expensive for many countries or for certain patients (e.g. those receiving novel cancer treatments) and determining the price only by a value-based approach

ing, Ferney-Voltaire, France, December 11–13, 2000 (Management Sciences for Health, 2003), p. 8.

32 World Health Organization, (n 9) 4.

33 World Health Organization. Regional Office for Europe and others, *Building on Value-Based Health Care: Towards a Health System Perspective* (World Health Organization Regional Office for Europe 2020) <https://apps.who.int/iris/handle/10665/336134>.

34 Panos Kanavos and others, 'Short-and Long-Term Effects of Value-Based Pricing vs. External Price Referencing' [2010] Eminet. LSE 30.

35 Barbara Arzymanow and Julia Manning, 'Value-Based Pricing: The Wrong Medicine for the Nation?' (20/20health 2014) 3–4 <https://2020health.org/publication/value-based-pricing-the-wrong-medicine-for-the-nation/> accessed 21 January 2020.

36 Patricia M Danzon, 'Affordability Challenges to Value-Based Pricing: Mass Diseases, Orphan Diseases, and Cures' (2018) 21 Value in Health 252, 252–253.

37 Theresa C Mahfood, 'Sovaldi: The High Price for a Cure' (2018) 27 Annals of Health Law 37, 22–27.

has been vehemently criticised by global health practitioners at the WHO as detrimental to poor countries.[38]

Therefore, a value-based approach faces various methodological hurdles in respect of affordability. In principle, different indications of the same technology may have different thresholds of cost-effectiveness which can be used to authorise reimbursement for lower prices between different uses of the same drugs, where they do not perform so well.[39] However, there are serious concerns as to how to operationalise this value-based pricing system, such as how to differentiate prices between indications, without discriminating between patients as well.[40]

In the UK, NICE has refused to adopt a value-based pricing system on the basis of patient complaints of discriminatory effects, but still assigns different thresholds for funding treatments according to the overall value for patients.[41] Those thresholds can sometimes reduce costs, but are not what the affordability criteria seeks in many circumstances because they are a rationing tool and technologies will end up being unfunded for being too expensive.[42] Value-based approaches with explicit limits can also be detrimental to affordability, as the cost-effectiveness threshold can serve as a standard that companies will pursue when setting their prices.[43]

Likewise, affordability is arguably also at variance with the fair-pricing system. Originally, there were various forms of words to describe unfair prices: for example, an excessive profit on a patented product, prices way beyond the costs of R&D, prices of generics surpassing the branded version, or simply prices at a level above what is offered in other countries – all these without

---

38 Mattias Neyt, 'Value-Based Pricing: Do Not Throw Away the Baby with the Bath Water' (2018) 36 PharmacoEconomics 1, 1; World Health Organization, *WHO Guideline on Country Pharmaceutical Pricing Policies* (n 9) 15.

39 *OECD Health Policy Studies Value for Money in Health Spending* (OECD Publishing 2010) 10.

40 Jorge Mestre-Ferrandiz and others, 'Multi-Indication Pricing: Nice in Theory But Can It Work in Practice?' (2018) 36 PharmacoEconomics 1407, 1408–1414; J Raftery, 'Value Based Pricing: Can It Work?' (2013) 347 BMJ f5941, 3–4; Carlos Campillo-Artero and others, 'Price Models for Multi-Indication Drugs: A Systematic Review' (2020) 18 Applied Health Economics and Health Policy 47, 52–54.

41 NICE Board Meeting, 'Value Based Assessment. Item 4' (Nice 2014) <http://www.pruceconsulting.co.uk/ITEM%2004%20-%20Value%20Based%20Assessment%20of%20Health%20Technologies.pdf?attredirects=0> accessed 15 January 2020.

42 Sarah Garner, Andrew Rintoul and Suzanne R Hill, 'Value-Based Pricing: L'Enfant Terrible?' (2018) 36 PharmacoEconomics 5, 5–6.

43 *OECD Health Policy Studies Value for Money in Health Spending* (n 39) 94.

any reference to affordability.[44] Today, though, affordability has gained more attention. Moon et al.'s definition of fair pricing appears to commit to the affordability component fundamental to an HRBA. They present fair pricing as "affordable to the buyer while covering the seller's costs and providing a reasonable profit margin" and use a formula that places the fair price in a spectrum where affordability is a function of the economic capacity of each country.[45]

More progress needs to be made in establishing a fair price model and its exact adherence to affordability. Participants in the Fair Pricing Forum at the WHO have expressed difficulty in finding a denominator for this pricing model, without defining affordability as the principal attribute for fairness.[46] At the Forum, the WHO has referred to fair pricing as a balance between affordability (low costs) and the conditions to ensure sufficient investments in production and R&D.[47] The WHO underlines that the concept of affordability is independent of fair pricing and includes patented medicines by making sure that low-cost non-patented therapies can still be produced even when they are no longer economically attractive.[48]

Ultimately, affordability should take precedence in an HRBA, both for value-based and fair-pricing models. At least, if a fair or value-based model is to be implemented in HTA, significant provision for affordability would need to be included to meet different capacities to pay. An unfair price for insufficient margins of profit would be perfectly compatible with the right to health if lying within the affordability band of a country. This is more significant as levels of affordability can be better tracked than profits, given the lack of pharmaceutical companies' transparency.[49]

2 Identifying the Legal Determinants of Scarcity

As explained above, an HRBA presupposes the existence of laws to increase affordability in healthcare, with immediate effect on HTA, by reducing the

44 Steven G Morgan, Hannah S Bathula and Suerie Moon, 'Pricing of Pharmaceuticals Is Becoming a Major Challenge for Health Systems' [2020] BMJ l4627, 2.

45 Suerie Moon and others, 'Defining the Concept of Fair Pricing for Medicines' [2020] BMJ l4726, 3.

46 'Global Forum on Fair Drug Pricing and Access to Medicines' (2019) 826 PharmacoEconomics & Outcomes News 1, 1.

47 Fair Pricing Forum, Fair pricing forum Q&A, https://www.who.int/medicines/access/fair_pricing/q_a-fair_pricing_meds/en/, access 03 December 2019.

48 Ibid.

49 Moon and others (n 45) 4.

prices of new technologies simultaneously with any recommendation. Having established this, a second step is to determine the most appropriate material laws to achieve this aspiration. Traditionally, what has been advocated by a number of human rights scholars is the reform of domestic IP laws.[50] This section will demonstrate that this approach is not enough, and that policy-makers and patients should explore other routes such as those listed in the WHO pharmaceutical policy guidance, including price control and procurements laws. This section argues that legal determinants of scarcity are indirect or circumstantial to health affordability. Therefore, they are not a guarantee of affordability of healthcare, but instead they have to be carefully customised among many options to minimise potential downsides.

There are two parts to this section. First, the disproportionate importance given to IP in HRBA regarding access to healthcare will be described, with examples of the limitations of this single approach. Second, the potential alternative regulatory frameworks in the scope of legal determinants of scarcity will be explored, considering current WHO guidance. However, widening the scope of the law to ensure affordability as a precondition to resource allocation, is complex and not without risks of reducing availability of new technologies. Section 3 will deal with these caveats separately.

To begin, in contrast to other legal areas, IP as a human rights issue has been widely discussed. The discontent with IP laws among human rights practitioners has been more evident since the 2000s with General Comment 14 and the UN Sub-Commission on the Promotion and Protection of Human Rights' subsequent resolution on Intellectual Property Rights and Human Rights (Resolution 2000/7), followed by a continuous cycle of other similar texts issued at UN level reiterating the need to flexibilise IP laws in the face of health needs.[51] A similar discussion followed in respect of Article 15(1)(b) ICESCR (access to science) which, it can be argued, prevails over patent holders' rights to property.[52]

A common approach takes the form of political pressure to have the right to health considered within IP laws, where health should prevail over property

50 Duncan Matthews, 'Right to Health and Patents' in Christophe Geiger (ed), *Research Handbook on Human Rights and Intellectual Property* (Edward Elgar Publishing 2015) 500–502.

51 UN Sub-Commission on the Promotion and Protection of Human Rights, "Intellectual Property Rights and Human Rights", 23 November 2000 (E/CN.4/2001/2), Laurence R Helfer, 'Pharmaceutical Patents and the Human Right to Health' in Terence C Halliday and Gregory Shaffer (eds), *Transnational Legal Orders* (Cambridge University Press 2015) 327–328.

52 See e.g. Aurora Plomer, 'The Human Rights Paradox: Intellectual Property Rights and Rights of Access to Science' (2013) 35 Human Rights Quarterly 143.

rights. Authors such as Dreyfuss have argued that IP rights do not amount to a subset of human rights or are enforceable by them.[53] Others have described this context as a paradoxical relationship and claim that the irregular protection of patents could signal a right to health violation.[54] In an HRBA to legislation for access to medicines, the primary concern remains with the implementation of exceptions to patents or non-exclusively affordable approaches, such as fair prices (e.g. proportionate compensation to the patent-holders, with no link to development costs).[55]

Accordingly, overdominance of IP as a human rights barrier is equally salient in international political dialogues on drugs affordability. During the UN Secretary-General's High-Level Panel on Access to Medicines, most of the external submissions revolved around IP policies. Exceptions were some allusions to competition laws, negotiation power, and local product development.[56] France complained about the IP focus of the reports affirming that "by reducing the scope (...) the panel significantly limits its methods and conveys a limited interpretation of issues affecting access to medicines".[57] In the final report, the text also gives strong emphasis to IP, as if all costly drugs were the result of the failures in IP regimes. Alternative policies are only seen in terms of permissible measures to the patent system (for instance, raising competition issues as a subfield of the regulation of non-patented drugs).[58]

53 Rochelle Cooper Dreyfuss, 'Patents and Human Rights: Where Is the Paradox' in Willem Grosheide (ed), *Intellectual property and human rights: a paradox* (Edward Elgar 2010).

54 Ibid. Lisa Forman, 'Trade Rules, Intellectual Property, and the Right to Health' (2007) 21 Ethics & International Affairs 337.

55 See e.g. HRC, Resolution 41/10 19 July 2019 (A/HRC/RES/41/10), paras 3–9, Resolution 32/15 1 July 2016 (A/HRC/RES/32/15) paras 3–10, "Report of the Special Rapporteur on E/CN.4/Sub.2/2001/13 on the Right of Everyone to the Enjoyment of the Highest Attainable Standard of Physical and Mental Health, Anand Grover" 31 March 2009 (A/HRC/11/12); "The Impact of the Agreement on Trade-related Aspects of Intellectual Property Rights on Human Rights, Report of the High Commissioner" 27 June 2001 (E/CN.4/Sub.2/2001/13).

56 See e.g. contributions from Regional Health Service, Madrid; Germany; Sean Flynn and Luisa Guzman, http://www.unsgaccessmeds.org/list-of-contribution, accessed 20 January 2020.

57 Catherine Dauphin-Llorens, Ministry of Foreign Affairs, France, http://www.unsgaccessmeds.org/inbox/2016/3/8/da4dfoue2b1m98b9txoq3m1fd1s1wf, accessed 3 December 2019.

58 UN Secretary-General and Co-Chairs of the High-Level Panel, The United Nations Secretary-General's High-Level Panel on Access to Medicines Report: Promoting Innovation and Access to Health Technologies.
http://www.unsgaccessmeds.org/final-report/, p. 18, accessed 3 December 2019.

Few have linked other policies to laws that promote affordability. In a major exception to the IP focus in human rights, in 2013 the Special Rapporteur on the Right to Health, Anand Grover, produced one of the most comprehensive reviews of the alternative policies open to States to ensure affordability of medicines, mentioning direct interventions in the market such as price control and competition laws.[59] The report to the General Assembly expanded the boundaries of IP barriers and noted the significance of measures such as price control, taxation and competition laws. Although this represented considerable progress in the scope of State obligation, the report fell short of indicating that legislation or regulatory frameworks should be reformed to avoid a right to health violation with the same emphasis that IP laws have received. Grover leaves the possible measures to State judgement, with rules on price control, abusive prices or anti-competitive behaviour not specified as an obligation of immediate effect to promote adequate legislation in an HRBA.

Human rights practice, in the following years, has not taken up this call in more detail and the linkage of human rights with other policies is still rarely emphasised beyond IP laws. For instance, in the aftermath of the COVID-19 pandemic, calls from human rights bodies were mainly focused on relaxing IP rules to promote access to new vaccines and drugs.[60] This dogmatic vision within human rights scholarship does not recognise that, in many cases, those policies will not succeed and there are other legal tools that should be exercised.

2.1 Limits of HRBA to IP Policies

Empirically, resorting to IP flexibilities – exceptions to IP provisions for public health reasons, as with compulsory licences (CL) of patented pharmaceuticals or parallel imports of generic versions – is not a predictable and infallible tool.[61] These two policies have curiously dominated HRBA to access to medicine, masking their own limitations in terms of human rights advocacy and policy guidance.

---

59 HRC, "Report of the Special Rapporteur on the Right of Everyone to the Enjoyment of the Highest Attainable Standard of Physical and Mental Health, Anand Grover, on Access to Medicines", 1 May 2013 (A/HRC/23/42), paras 11–39.

60 See e.g. CESCR, "Statement on the Coronavirus Disease (COVID-19) Pandemic and Economic, Social and Cultural Rights"(6 April 2020) E/C.12/2020/1, para 21.

61 Ellen FM Hoen and others, 'Medicine Procurement and the Use of Flexibilities in the Agreement on Trade-Related Aspects of Intellectual Property Rights, 2001–2016' (2018) 96 Bulletin of the World Health Organization 185, 188–189.

In the case of CL limitations, such a measure has only succeeded in a few cases, predominantly for HIV treatments (and without comparing what could be achieved by a combination of other policies).[62] As CL might not always be crucial to or effective for affordability, this is a noteworthy example where human rights advocacy around IP flexibilities could be better served by other policies.[63] To make matters worse, CL may result in negative impacts on affordability, despite frequent support from academics.[64] Ideally, just signalling the possibility of a CL can persuade a producer to cut prices, particularly where countries already benefit from local industrial power, or external generic makers may be accessed.[65] In practice, research has shown that the potential discounts were not as great as when there was a combination of other policies (as experienced by countries with the highest savings, particularly when producing locally is more expensive than procurement abroad).[66]

These hurdles are even more challenging for developing countries, where human rights advocacy has persistently urged legislative changes in IP laws. In fact, most States, including some African countries, often do not fully exploit IP flexibilities, which has raised concerns from the Global Commission on HIV and the Law about the low employment of CL or parallel imports and encouraged their diffusion.[67] However, for the poorest countries, economic models can predict that instruments such as CL may not be successful because a CL threat, which is not considered "credible" will not change the monopoly status of the branded drug to influence prices. Pharmaceutical companies and exporting States can exercise political pressure for IP implementation or, in the case of suppliers, by blackmailing a country with market withdrawal or exclusion from new research.[68] Examples that in fact generate price reduction

62 Ibid 186–187.

63 Samira Guennif, 'Is Compulsory Licensing Bad for Public Health? Some Critical Comments on Drug Accessibility in Developing Countries' (2017) 15 Applied Health Economics and Health Policy 557.

64 Gorik Ooms and Johanna Hanefeld, 'Threat of Compulsory Licences Could Increase Access to Essential Medicines' [2019] BMJ l2098.

65 Shyama V Ramani and Eduardo Urias, 'Access to Critical Medicines: When Are Compulsory Licenses Effective in Price Negotiations?' (2015) 135 Social Science & Medicine 75, 76.

66 Reed F Beall, Randall Kuhn and Amir Attaran, 'Compulsory Licensing Often Did Not Produce Lower Prices For Antiretrovirals Compared To International Procurement' (2015) 34 Health Affairs 493, 499.

67 United Nations Development Programme, Regional issues brief: Intellectual Property Rights and Access to Medicines, 2011, p. 10 https://hivlawcommission.org/wp-content/uploads/2017/06/Africa-RIB-IP.pdf, accessed in 6 December 2019.

68 Ramani and Urias (n 65) 76.

are generally from countries, which are able to threaten the patent-owners with alternatives to importation or with local production.[69] The situation is even worse for countries without access to products manufactured in the Global South, making it necessary to effectively apply the Doha Declaration to permit imports from high-income producing countries (with Rwanda being so far reportedly the only case of that).[70] Even so, a State with good industrial capacity will not always opt for the most cost-effective option, as local production may be more expensive with a CL.

However, as previously mentioned, the problem with regulating IP is also that it cannot work in isolation from other policies. For instance, unaffordability of patented and non-patented products requires intervention in the pricing environment (the moment at which technology producers set their prices or profits).[71] Some of these regulations are the so-called "semantic flexibilities", measures allowed in the IP regime under domestic laws or not specifically prohibited by the TRIPS (Agreement on Trade-Related Aspects of Intellectual Property Rights) (e.g. price controls or a doctrine prohibiting excessive prices).[72]

Furthermore, there are common challenges that do not require improvements in IP regulations in relation to many non-patented drugs. The existence of generic drugs does not always lead to lower prices, since the competitors may increase prices indiscriminately just like branded products.[73] Normally, manufacturers have free rein to bring prices of generics higher because of low levels of competition, a reduced number of patients or no alternative treatments, being in practice a monopoly.[74] Low-income countries may also face great variation among non-branded and branded generics without any policy

69 Eduardo Urias and Shyama V Ramani, 'Access to Medicines after TRIPS: Is Compulsory Licensing an Effective Mechanism to Lower Drug Prices? A Review of the Existing Evidence' (2020) 3 Journal of International Business Policy 367, 375.

70 Ooms and Hanefeld (n 64) 2.

71 Franzen and others (n 11) E2–5.

72 Frederick M Abbott, 'Excessive Pharmaceutical Prices and Competition Law: Doctrinal Development to Protect Public Health' 6 UC Irvine Law Review 281, 283–285; Daniel J Gervais, 'Patentability Criteria as TRIPS Flexibilities: The Examples of China and India', *Patent Law in Global Perspective,* (Oxford University Press 2014) 542–547; UNCTAD, *Tool Box for Policy Coherence in Access to Medicines and Local Pharmaceutical Production* (UNCTAD 2018) 47–48.

73 Philip FitzGerald, 'State Regulation of Generic Drug Price Gouging' (2019) 2 Belmont Health Law Journal 100, 102–108.

74 Rajiv Kumar and Jagjit Singh, 'Biosimilar Drugs: Current Status' (2014) 4 International Journal of Applied & Basic Medical Research 63, 66.

of price control that will affect access to medicines by patients and public services.[75]

Another affordability barrier to access to medicines is caused by the registration of biological products and non-patented versions called biosimilars. Because these drugs are much more complex, biosimilars are not identical compounds to a reference drug, as are generic drugs, and must undergo more rigorous safety and efficacy tests to prove their equivalence, since minimal variations in their production may produce different reactions.[76] The real obstacle for lower-costs with a biosimilar is not so much patent protection, but the costs of re-examining the bioproduct properties and ensuring the same results in the reference medicine.

For these cases, flexibilisation of IP laws can be just the first step in ensuring affordability, because there are other legal determinants obstructing low-cost products deeper in technical regulations, not apparently related to patents.[77] For human rights advocacy to embrace other policies, though, we must consider the full spectrum of alternatives available to obtain affordability to regulate the market and access to new health technologies beyond IP law, as will be considered in the following subsection. The main complementary policies that can be explored in an HRBA are listed in the WHO guidelines for access policies: namely, direct price regulation or control, price negotiation and contractual mechanisms, competition laws and PPPs. All those are alternative legal determinants of scarcity rarely advocated on the basis of the right to health and the duty to seek laws promoting affordability.

2.2 Direct Price Control

A very intuitive tool that can be incorporated by human rights advocacy is to call for laws and regulations to directly control pharmaceutical prices. Even in the USA, a predominantly free-market model, laws to protect the uninsured from overcharges in hospitals can be found.[78] Many countries have introduced price regulation through different legal formulae and institutions: some have national agencies mandated to dictate the prices of patented

75 Ramesh Sharma Poudel, Shakti Shrestha and Arjun Poudel, 'Immense Price Variation of Branded Generic Medicines in Low-Income Countries: The Need for an Inclusive Price Control Policy' (2020) 16 Research in Social & Administrative Pharmacy: RSAP 1326.

76 Kumar and Singh (n 74) 66.

77 Alessandra Ferrario and others, 'Strategies to Achieve Fairer Prices for Generic and Biosimilar Medicines' [2020] BMJ l5444.

78 See: Frank Griffin, 'Fighting Overcharged Bills from Predatory Hospitals' (2019) 51 Arizona State Law Journal 1003.

drugs (Brazil, Canada), but can also have arrangements at regional level (e.g. Canada, with a coordinated generic price control).[79]

The two most common forms of price control are price mark-ups (or price caps) and reference pricing (RP), which imposes values of reimbursement for different categories of drugs to stimulate lower spending from the prescribers or to induce the industry to mark down its products.[80] RP is mainly found in health systems based on insurance reimbursement of private dispensation of the drugs to patients, such as Germany, which pioneered this approach in Europe.[81] External reference pricing (ERP) is used to benchmark the cost of the product in other selected jurisdictions and set limits within the average or other evaluation of the prices practised in those markets. For example, ERP can have a direct relation to negotiations prior to or after their start and can also be a parameter for better healthcare contracts. On the other hand, price caps can be introduced to contain the costs of pharmaceutical products by imposing limits on the prices in the market, but mark-up limits can also be applied to the prices of any item in the supply chain until the final product.[82] Mark-up has been the preferred form of regulation in many Asian jurisdictions for its simple administration. Another model used in countries such as Japan and Australia is called cost-plus, where a profit rate is set against all product costs (including R&D), but this is not generally recommended given lack of studies and replicable methods.[83]

2.3 Negotiation and Procurement Laws

While laws may impose direct control over prices, they can also create conditions whereby governments can obtain discounts on retail prices for public

79 'Generic Drugs | pCPA' <https://www.pcpacanada.ca/generic-drug-framework> accessed 9 March 2021.

80 Angela Acosta and others, 'Pharmaceutical Policies: Effects of Reference Pricing, Other Pricing, and Purchasing Policies' [2014] Cochrane Database of Systematic Reviews 10–11.

81 Kurt R Brekke, Ingrid Königbauer and Odd Rune Straume, 'Reference Pricing of Pharmaceuticals' (2007) 26 Journal of Health Economics 613, 614.

82 Kurt R Brekke, Astrid L Grasdal and Tor Helge Holmås, 'Regulation and Pricing of Pharmaceuticals: Reference Pricing or Price Cap Regulation?' (2009) 53 European Economic Review 170, 171; World Health Organization, (n 9) 18.

83 Hiroaki Mamiya, 'Update of Drug Pricing System in Japan' (Ministry of Health, Welfare, Japan 2018). Australian Government Department of Health, 'Pharmaceutical Benefits Scheme (PBS) | Fact Sheet – Setting an Approved Ex-Manufacturer Price for New or Extended Listings' <https://www.pbs.gov.au/info/industry/pricing/pbs-items/fact-sheet-setting-an-approved-ex-manufacturer-price> accessed 9 March 2021.

procurement. These regulatory areas that can foster affordability subject to appropriate legislation are: 1) negotiation, 2) transparency and 3) procurement.[84] These are dealt with in turn below.

First, there is great scope for advancing negotiating powers of governments in healthcare, as not all countries operate a policy of price negotiation with suppliers.[85] However, in the United States this option was made illegal by the federal government.[86] The continuous pharmaceutical crises in the country had led to support for a legislative change in this regard and debates as to what such laws can bring about.[87] In 2017, New York became the first US State to pass legislation mandating cost limits established by value assessment and negotiation in certain conditions for medical coverage of drugs regarded as high cost.[88] In other countries, such as France, government regulations allow greater negotiation powers than in the USA, particularly if new medications do not provide significant additional benefits.[89]

Similarly, developing countries have sustained access to medicines by continuous negotiation, such as the HIV programme in Brazil (though this policy may be less effective in countries lacking institutional capacity or bargaining power).[90] Negotiation may be complementary or strengthened by other policies, such as CL, which can be a leverage to bargain lower prices.[91] In addition, procurement laws and regulatory provisions can make negotiation mandatory and more effective in some jurisdictions, which is now the practice in China, with significant price reductions in consequence.[92]

84 World Health Organization, (n 9) 25.

85 Ramani and Urias (n 65) 75.

86 *See* 42 U.S.C. § 1395w-111(i) (2012).

87 Richard G Frank and Len M Nichols, 'Medicare Drug-Price Negotiation – Why Now ... and How' (2019) 381 New England Journal of Medicine 1404, 1404–1405. Lee B Staley, 'A Drug's Worth: Why Federal Makes It Hard to Pay for Pharmaceutical Performance' (2018) 98 Boston University Law Review 303, 308.

88 Senate Bill S2007B, New York State Senate, amending Public Health (PBH) (NYS), Chapter 45, article 2-A, Title 2, Section 280.

89 Véronique C Raimond and others, 'Why France Spends Less Than the United States on Drugs: A Comparative Study of Drug Pricing and Pricing Regulation' (2021) 99 The Milbank Quarterly 240, 258–259.

90 Eduardo Muniz Pereira Urias, *Improving Access to HIV/AIDS Treatment in Brazil: When Are Compulsory Licenses Effective in Price Negotiations?* (Datawyse/Universitaire Pers Maastricht 2015) 81–104.

91 Adam Fundytus, Richard Sullivan and Christopher M Booth, 'Toward Affordable Cancer Drugs: Do We Need Firmer Price Negotiation, Me-Too Drugs, or a Biosimilar Silver Bullet?' (2020) 47 Seminars in Oncology 353.

92 Greenberg Traurig, LLP, 'Lessons from China's Negotiation of Drug Prices in 2020' (*The National Law Review*) <https://www.natlawreview.com/article/china-move-lesson-

Second, the negotiation environment can be enhanced by price transparency laws to make the market more competitive. "Gag" laws have been repealed in a number of American States to authorise pharmacists to inform patients of the difference between a direct purchase or the costs of co-payment by insurance reimbursement.[93] The American States' legislative initiatives on transparency vary – some of them are focused just on the overall costs of R&D and production, but they can be much more detailed and require information on costs of the advertising or licensing contracts.[94]

Transparency laws can be used in a justificatory manner so that manufacturers are obliged not only to disclose cost but to indicate reasons for it. The requirement can be imposed in many forms: for example, by a prior notification of a planned increase or a report about new drugs approved in a market.[95] Transparency is also related to access to information on how the price is fixed in other markets. Where prices in other countries are public, States can benchmark between markets (through ERP policies, as explained above).[96]

Third, with the power to enter into agreements with pharmaceutical companies, governments may set schemes or arrangements to obtain lower prices. In the UK, the Pharmaceutical Price Regulation Scheme is an informal agreement between the government and industry to contain prices of branded drugs more generally. Moreover, procurement laws have also been associated with lower costs in healthcare in specific negotiations, with some positive evidence in both high- and low-income countries.[97] Comparative analyses of procurement policies in different countries suggest that a combination of factors, such as centralised purchasing, results in better deals.[98] Conversely, a

china-s-national-negotiation-drug-prices-2020> accessed 11 April 2021; Ying Liu and Jian Yang, 'A Study of Legal Framework of National Drug Price Negotiations in China' (2017) 10 Chinese Journal of Health Policy 20.

93 William V Padula, 'State and Federal Policy Solutions to Rising Prescriptions Drug Prices in the U.S. Symposium' (2019) 22 Journal of Health Care Law and Policy 15, 17–18.

94 Seth Whitelaw, Nicodemo Fiorentino and Jennifer O'Leary, 'Drug Pricing-The Next Compliance Waterloo' (2018) 44 Mitchell Hamline Law Review 1165, 1184.

95 Ibid 1184–1185.

96 Sabine Vogler and Kenneth R Paterson, 'Can Price Transparency Contribute to More Affordable Patient Access to Medicines?' (2017) 1 PharmacoEconomics – Open 145, 145.

97 Nikolaos Maniadakis and others, 'Shaping Pharmaceutical Tenders for Effectiveness and Sustainability in Countries with Expanding Healthcare Coverage' (2018) 16 Applied Health Economics and Health Policy 591, 593–594.

98 See e.g. Simona Baldi and Davide Vannoni, 'The Impact of Centralization on Pharmaceutical Procurement Prices: The Role of Institutional Quality and Corruption' (2017) 51 Regional Studies 426; Kerry A Millington and Minakshi Bhardwaj, 'Evidence and Experience of Procurement in Health Sector Decentralisation' (Institute of Development Studies 2017).

badly designed procurement process can result in gains in one tender being annulled by losses in another contract for similar drugs, as experienced in Belgium.[99]

An HRBA may be facilitated with special procurement clauses that have affordability in mind. Conditional contracts for adoption of new technologies are denominated Managed Entry Agreements (MEA), setting out the expected delivery, budget or clinical outcomes in order to clarify uncertainties and guarantee lower costs. Clauses in MEA are variable and may offer different avenues to balance access to technology with reduced costs, while sharing the risks between government and manufacturers for specific goals: for example, budget control; safety monitoring, clinical efficacy and cost-effectiveness; or usage and distribution of a technology.[100] When specific targets are attached, such agreements can be described as performance-based ones, structured with some key features for conditional reimbursement, namely: a) a process to collect data, b) an observation period, c) a list of outcomes and d) existing uncertainties over a technology that need to be mitigated.[101]

2.4 Competition Laws

Current competition law, designed to regulate market abuse and distortions of prices, may sometimes be applied against the pharmaceutical industry in a way that can facilitate access to new technologies.[102] However, there may occur some inability or reluctance to enforce a more competitive market due to circumstances such as methodological barriers to determine excessive prices and lack of transparency and access to data relating to items making up

---

99 F Arickx and others, 'Public Tendering for off Patent Medicines in Belgium – the Simvastatin Case' (National Institute for Health and Disability Insurance 2009).

100 Marianne Klemp, Katrine B Frønsdal and Karen Facey, 'What Principles Should Govern the Use of Managed Entry Agreements?' (2011) 27 International Journal of Technology Assessment in Health Care 77, 78.

101 Louis P Garrison and others, 'Performance-Based Risk-Sharing Arrangements – Good Practices for Design, Implementation, and Evaluation: Report of the ISPOR Good Practices for Performance-Based Risk-Sharing Arrangements Task Force' (2013) 16 Value in Health 703, 75.

102 The application of competition laws in the pharmaceutical industry can be patchy, yet it has been successful in some cases, e.g. Hazel Tau et al. v. GlaxoSmithKline, Boehringer Ingelheim, et al. & Aids Healthcare Foundation et al v. GlaxoSmithKline, Boehringer Ingelheim, et al. Case Numbers: 2002sep226 & 2002jan357 (South African Competition Comission). In India, see e.g. Natco Pharma Limited v Bayer Corporation, comments by Naval Satarawala Chopra and Dinoo Muthappa, 'The Curious Case of Compulsory Licensing in India' (2012) 8 Competition Law International 34.

the costs of healthcare products.[103] Even though there are some positive cases, they may still be articulated without human rights language. The 1998 South African Competition Act, for example, has a poorly designed regulation that limits "excessive price" by defining it as a disproportion between the price charged and the "economic value", a notion which requires further clarification to produce results.[104]

In developing countries, competition laws in general have only recently taken effect, and, despite some good progress, many still have little practice in the field and face difficulties in investigating, identifying and prosecuting any misconduct.[105] For smaller economies, an HRBA to competition laws for HTA would also mean the structuring of institutions to increase enforceability of competition laws in the healthcare sector and interpreting them in a way that favours affordability and considers public health goals to obtain the best costs for the new technology evaluated.[106] The European Commission has concluded that reduced competitiveness in the pharmaceutical market regionally is due to the common use of delay agreements with generic producers, some of which have been found to be in breach of EU competition law.[107]

While HRBA in health privileges affordability over value and fairness, these factors are not the most common justifications for enforcement under com-

103 Abbott (n 72) 305–315.

104 Section 2(a) and (c) of the Competition Act, 89 of 1998. Cases submitted to the SA authorities end up without substantive references to human rights frameworks. For instance, given the lack of precedents internationally, the regulation made it more challenging for South African advocates to build their complaint against the unjustifiable conduct of GlaxoSmithKline and Boehringer Ingelheim in price policies for ARV drugs.

105 See e.g. Umut Aydin, 'Competition Law & Policy in Developing Countries: Explaining Variations in Outcomes; Exploring Possibilities and Limits' (2016) 79 Law and Contemporary Problems 1; Jonathan Berger, 'Advancing Public Health by Other Means: Using Competition Policy' in P Roffe and DV Eugui (eds), *Negotiating Health: Intellectual Property and Access to Medicines* (Taylor & Francis 2012); Natasha Nyak, 'Advancing Competition Frameworks in the Low – and Middle-Income Country Context' in Frederick M Abbott and others (eds), *Using Competition Laws to Promote Access to Medicines: A Guidebook for Low – and Middle – Income Countries* (United Nations Development Programme 2014) 128–132; Mor Bakhoum, 'The Interface between Intellectual Property Rights and Competition Law: Implications for Public Health in Sub-Saharan Africa' in Deborah Healey, Michael Jacobs and Rhonda L. Smith (eds), *Research Handbook on Methods and Models of Competition Law* (Edward Elgar Publishing 2020).

106 Vitor Henrique Pinto Ido, 'Designing Pro-Health Competition Policies in Developing Countries' (South Center 2020) 125 27–30.

107 See e.g. European Commission, 'Competition Enforcement in the Pharmaceutical Sector (2009–2017)' (European Union 2019) 19–20 <https://op.europa.eu/en/publication-detail/-/publication/9cb466c8-7b71-11e9-9f05-01aa75ed71a1> accessed 1 October 2020.

petition laws, even among richer countries. In the European market, EU law does not rely exclusively on unaffordability as a sign of unfair pricing and has been timid in considering substantive human rights in competition laws.[108] In EU case-law, definitions of value and fairness have been rather muddled in examining excessive pricing (this concept also being ambiguous), and competition authorities have made little difference.[109] In those cases, even though competition laws could be objectively associated with rights violations, a human rights framework is yet to be established more comprehensively in the literature, which could be one way of enhancing the role of HTA in signalling where prices are not competitive. Yoo has only recently advocated a connection between the right to health and competition laws, considering the context of the pharmaceutical market of the United States and alluding to issues of market abuse by intermediaries and collusion between brand-owners by purchasing the right to delay the production of generic suppliers.[110] However, such views are centred on business and human rights guidelines to regulate business actors, thus lacking enforceable character.[111] For an HRBA to resource allocation, the environment for competition laws must be considered if a State is to provide the best conditions for low costs in healthcare before rationing is indeed justifiable in HTA.

2.5 Public–Private Partnerships

More recently, PPPs have been encouraged to facilitate investment in R&D for neglected diseases and other areas, which private investment would not consider economically interesting. This approach deals with one type of scarcity concerning the lack of scientific projects, local technology development and private investment – that could eventually lead to lower prices if the drugs discovered are publicly produced. The main benefits for price control are when PPPs are used not to develop new health technologies, but to facilitate local production of treatments that otherwise would have to be imported at much higher cost.

108 Amber Darr, 'Competition Law and Human Rights: A Complex Relationship' [2021] Wirtschaft und Wettbewerb 388, 389–392.

109 Claudio Calcagno, Antoine Chapsal and Joshua White, 'Economics of Excessive Pricing: An Application to the Pharmaceutical Industry' (2019) 10 Journal of European Competition Law & Practice 166, 166–167.

110 Kwanghyuk Yoo, 'Interaction of Human Rights Law and Competition Law: The Right to Access to Medicine and Consumer Welfare in The U.S. Pharmaceutical Sector' (2018) 43 Vermont Law Review 30, 136–149.

111 Ibid 131–134.

The success of PPPs may require specific supporting laws that will authorise and govern the delegation of public services, or provide more safeguards for the parties involved.[112] Countries without specific legislation on PPPs may not perform as well as others with adequate legal provisions, though initially this has not been the rule as PPP laws have been adopted more widely by developing countries without institutional capacity or appropriate regulation.[113] Currently, specific PPP laws appear attractive to encourage investment in countries where other procurement laws and institutional capacity do not offer certainty and flexibility to attract private financing.[114] The underlying legal framework is not of necessity strictly dedicated to PPPs – the UK, for example, has implemented an agreement under existing commercial laws.[115] The types of laws relevant to PPPs hinge on the nature of the service at hand, but in most cases should comprise rules related to concessions and governance of the projects.[116]

In healthcare, the limitations to PPPs are not well defined, and practitioners are still debating the ethical aspects of privatising healthcare and accepting this model as a means to obtain more resources – including ulterior motives of companies, corruption and conflict of interests among parties.[117] However, in the drug market, PPPs are now being promoted as a viable response to private market deficiencies (in this case, this policy allows the involvement of govern-

---

112 For an overview of legal aspects governing PPPs, see: Cesar Queiroz and Alejandro Lopez Martinez, 'Legal Frameworks for Successful Public–Private Partnerships' in Piet De Vries and Yehoue Etienne B. (eds), *The Routledge Companion to Public-Private Partnerships* (Routledge 2010).

113 EBDR, '2017–18 Public-Private Partnership Assessment' (EBDR 2018) 18 <https://www.ebrd.com/cs/Satellite?c=Content&cid=1395278802473&d=&pagename=EBRD%2FContent%2FDownloadDocument> accessed 20 November 2020.

114 Dmitri Vinogradov, Elena Shadrina and Larissa Kokareva, 'Public Procurement Mechanisms for Public–Private Partnerships' (2014) 14 Journal of Public Procurement 538, 540–542, 558–561.

115 See e.g. Jonathan H Marks, 'Toward a Systemic Ethics of Public–Private Partnerships Related to Food and Health' (2014) 24 Kennedy Institute of Ethics Journal 267; Imrana Qadeer and Sunita Reddy, 'Medical Care in the Shadow of Public Private Partnership' (2006) 34 Social Scientist 4, 15–18; L Kostyak and others, 'A Means of Improving Public Health in Low- and Middle-Income Countries? Benefits and Challenges of International Public–Private Partnerships' (2017) 149 Public Health 120, 125–126.

116 Queiroz and Martinez (n 112) 78–79.

117 Michael R Reich and others, 'Workshop on Public Health Law and Ethics I & II: The Challenge of Public/Private Partnerships (PPPs)' (2003) 31 Journal of Law, Medicine & Ethics 90.

ment in a sector dominated by private agents),[118] and the effectiveness of PPPs in this arena has been attributed to sound regulatory frameworks.[119]

One field where PPPs have shown great potential is in respect of biosimilars. While biosimilars generate expenses with R&D regarding the reference drugs, the biotechnology used to make these compounds is far too complex to be employed in some countries (particularly because of safety issues or lack of clinical data).[120] To find a way through this, PPPs can favour cooperation to build domestic capacity around technologies that will reduce the cost of production of biosimilars.

3 Unintended Consequences and Lack of Human Rights Practice

This section will discuss some of the limitations of the proposed framework as an alternative to a human rights practice centred on simply intellectual property advocacy. The main caveat in linking human rights to affordability policies is that no specific pathway can be indiscriminately prescribed for all healthcare technologies and jurisdictions. This places a great burden on HTA information gathering to detect the causes of unaffordability for a particular technology and which types of alternative policies can be recommended. The WHO recommends monitoring the effects of reference pricing on affordability and access to medicines and, after a systematic review, has concluded that there is poor data in developing countries, despite this intervention appearing effective to reduce prices.[121] In addition to inconsistent evidence, some policies may be more or less successful depending on how they are implemented (e.g. price caps may be less effective than mark-ups in the supply chain).[122] These policies need to be evaluated individually. For instance, supporting

118 Kostyak and others (n 115) 122–123.

119 Mariateresa Torchia, Andrea Calabrò and Michèle Morner, 'Public–Private Partnerships in the Health Care Sector: A Systematic Review of the Literature' (2015) 17 Public Management Review 236, 248.

120 See: Bryan A Liang and Timothy Mackey, 'Public–Private Partnerships to Promote Biosimilar Access, Affordability, and Patient Safety in Emerging Markets' (2014) 7 Stanford Journal of Law, Science and Policy 1, 9.

121 World Health Organization, (n 9) 9.

122 World Health Organization, 'Web Annex A. Systematic Reviews for the Update of the WHO Guideline on Country Pharmaceutical Pricing Policies. in *WHO guideline on country pharmaceutical pricing policies* (2nd edn, 2020) 157 <https://apps.who.int/iris/rest/bitstreams/1309693/retrieve> accessed 3 March 2021.

measures for negotiation (such as ERP or CLs) can enhance price negotiation, but equally carry some risk (e.g. retribution from other States).[123]

Therefore, provided that sufficient evidence or plausibility of affordability improvement is demonstrated, these policies could be promoted through socio-economic rights advocacy in HTA. To rein in prices, governments may need to resort to a mix of policies, specific to the nature of the technology or domestic context.[124] As a minimum, the benefits should outweigh the eventual losses, which can be reduced by combining with other policies, such as price negotiation.[125] Thus, identifying legal determinants of scarcity in an HRBA depends on understanding the effects of legislation on healthcare affordability, which is not a straightforward analysis, because there is no obvious link between those laws and HRBA (so human rights practice is oblivious and does not refer to them in monitoring procedures and statements) or the risks are poorly understood.

This complex scenario is compounded by limitations in making non-State actors accountable under international law and how responsibility of controlling prices is divided between private actors and public institutions. States remain the foremost duty-bearers of human rights to protect citizens from private actors, and other forms of obligations on private parties are yet to be clarified.[126] On the one hand, tackling the issue of exorbitant costs by using State regulatory power avoids having to deal with disputes over the binding character of international norms on private actors, such as pharmaceutical companies.[127] On the other, instruments that declare the responsibility of non-State actors, such as the Ruggie Principles and the Hunt Principles, are non-binding declarations secondary to the main obligations upon States.[128]

123 Klemp, Frønsdal and Facey (n 100) 79.

124 Sabine Vogler, Peter Schneider and Nina Zimmermann, 'Evolution of Average European Medicine Prices: Implications for the Methodology of External Price Referencing' (2019) 3 PharmacoEconomics – Open 303, 307.

125 Peter Schneider and Sabine Vogler, 'Practice of External Price Referencing', *Medicine Price Surveys, Analyses and Comparisons* (Elsevier 2019) 347.

126 Lisa Forman and Jillian Clare Kohler, *Access to Medicines as a Human Right: Implications for Pharmaceutical Industry Responsibility* (University of Toronto Press 2012) 5–6.

127 On the arguable shared responsibility of pharmaceutical companies, see "Human Rights Guidelines for Pharmaceutical Companies in Relation to Access to Medicine" in UNGA, "Report of the Special Rapporteur on the right of everyone to the enjoyment of the highest attainable standard of physical and mental health" 11 August 2008 (A/63/263) Annex.

128 Ibid, UNGA, "Report of the Special Representative of the Secretary-General on the Issue of Human Rights and Transnational Corporations and Other Business Enterprises, John Ruggie"(21 March 2011) A/HRC/17/31, Suerie Moon, 'Respecting the Right to Access to

Hence, it behoves governments to employ the full power of laws to ensure lower prices, but the availability and prices of healthcare are not just the result of adjusting those prices but also depend on the reaction of the economic actors to regulation. The impacts of those laws are still under research and there have been reports or suggestions of "unintended consequences" on affordability and product availability because of how private actors make decisions internationally in that companies may decide simply to leave the market or increase prices of some lower-cost products within or across jurisdictions.[129] Parallel imports to arbitrate lower prices from less expensive producer countries can have their savings cancelled out by traders who use local price regulation to gain any difference in price as profit.[130]

To complicate matters further, in measuring the impact of those policies on affordability, there are significant methodological pitfalls.[131] Gathering information on price levels can be difficult for comparisons because of factors such as different drug concentration, costs in distribution or types of treatments included. Studies on price regulation of pharmaceuticals have mostly reported and described the existence of mechanisms to control prices in higher- and medium-income countries, whereas these schemes can sometimes be totally

---

Medicines: Implications of the UN Guiding Principles on Business and Human Rights for the Pharmaceutical Industry' (2013) 15 Health and Human Rights 13.

129 See e.g. World Health Organization, *Technical Report: Pricing of Cancer Medicines and Its Impacts: A Comprehensive Technical Report for the World Health Assembly Resolution 70.12: Operative Paragraph 2.9 on Pricing Approaches and Their Impacts on Availability and Affordability of Medicines for the Prevention and Treatment of Cancer* (World Health Organization 2018) 95–101 <https://apps.who.int/iris/handle/10665/277190?show=full> accessed 5 January 2021. William B Rouse, 'Impacts of Healthcare Price Controls: Potential Unintended Consequences of Firms' Responses to Price Policies' (2010) 4 IEEE Systems Journal 34; Sara Parker-Lue, Michael Santoro and Greg Koski, 'The Ethics and Economics of Pharmaceutical Pricing' (2015) 55 Annual Review of Pharmacology and Toxicology 191, 193–95; Nada Abdel Rida and Mohamed Izham Mohamed Ibrahim, 'Medicines Pricing Policy and Strategies in Developing Countries: A Review' in Mohamed Izham Mohamed Ibrahim, Zaheer-Ud-Din Babar and Albert I Weirtheimer (eds), *Social and Administrative Aspects of Pharmacy in Low-and Middle-Income Countries* (Elsevier 2018) 121–22; Gronde, Uyl-de Groot and Pieters (n 3) 15–16. Brekke, Grasdal and Holmås (n 82) 183.

130 Benoît Durand, 'Competition Law and Pharma: An Economic Perspective' in Pablo Figueroa and Alejandro Guerrero, *EU Law of Competition and Trade in the Pharmaceutical Sector* (Edward Elgar Publishing 2019) 1.14.

131 See e.g.: Patricia M Danzon and Jeong D Kim, 'International Price Comparisons for Pharmaceuticals: Measurement and Policy Issues' (1998) 14 PharmacoEconomics 115.

unrepresented among low-income countries, with no cases of price negotiation and very few of other affordability measures.[132]

In terms of risks, application of the legal determinant of scarcity has to be carefully planned in order to be implemented alongside HTA to effectively ensure affordability. Price controls can have negative effects in low-income countries (e.g. when increasing prices by high-income countries as a reference). They can also cause price spikes by driving up lower prices and impeding access to new technologies that do not enter the market by delaying product launches.[133] Moreover, transparency can in fact create a common denominator for the prices of wealthy countries to be applied in the rest of the world and many advisers urge governments to be careful when assuming that transparency will bring lower costs.[134] Another concern would be some countries being influenced by reference prices published by others, which have more generous pricing policies because of smaller populations, or for ethical reasons.[135] Procurement strategies with MEA are also of limited benefit on certain occasions.[136] The special clauses of MEA cannot always be enforced or, if they are, can result in high costs. Given that such agreements are commonly confidential, the level of discount achieved through this means cannot be fully ascertained.[137] Many provisions in MEA could facilitate affordability, but the results may lean towards a value-based price (and not always a more economical one).

---

132 Nikos Maniadakis and others, 'Comprehensive Taxonomy and Worldwide Trends in Pharmaceutical Policies in Relation to Country Income Status' (2017) 17 BMC Health Services Research 371, 4.

133 Rida and Ibrahim (n 129) 121–122. Rena M Conti, Kevin H Nguyen and Meredith B Rosenthal, 'Generic Prescription Drug Price Increases: Which Products Will Be Affected by Proposed Anti-Gouging Legislation?' (2018) 11 Journal of Pharmaceutical Policy and Practice 29, 6–7. Sarang Deo and others, 'Did India's Price Control Policy for Coronary Stents Create Unintended Consequences?' (2020) 246 Social Science & Medicine 112737Kenneth C Shadlen, Bhaven N Sampat and Amy Kapczynski, 'Patents, Trade and Medicines: Past, Present and Future' (2019) 27 Review of International Political Economy 1, 4.

134 Vogler and Paterson (n 96) 145–146.

135 Afschin Gandjour, 'Reference Pricing and Price Negotiations for Innovative New Drugs: Viable Policies in the Long Term?' (2013) 31 PharmacoEconomics 11, 12–13.

136 Klemp, Frønsdal and Facey (n 100) 79; Alessandra Ferrario and Panos Kanavos, 'Dealing with Uncertainty and High Prices of New Medicines: A Comparative Analysis of the Use of Managed Entry Agreements in Belgium, England, the Netherlands and Sweden' (2015) 124 Social Science & Medicine 39, 40.

137 See e.g. Vogler, Paris and Panteli (n 4) 14. Thomas Morel and others, 'Reconciling Uncertainty of Costs and Outcomes with the Need for Access to Orphan Medicinal Products: A Comparative Study of Managed Entry Agreements across Seven European Countries' (2013) 8 Orphanet Journal of Rare Diseases 198, 12.

4 Conclusions: Application of Legal Determinants of Scarcity to HTA in an HRBA

The central contention in this chapter is that States have the duty to apply legislation where price formation is optimised so as to privilege the AAAQ framework by reasons of resource maximisation and progressive realisation of the right to health. However, the level of uncertainty in the effect of laws and the diversity of market dynamics involving medical products require a sound knowledge of the regulatory consequences of each measure. HTA, as an evidence-based tool, needs to support regulators to identify the bottlenecks impeding affordable prices.

In many jurisdictions, rather than focusing on a breach of the right to health, alternative policies that could enhance affordability are thought to be obstructed by "legal barriers" or lack of "legal input" or necessary regulation (for instance when a State does not recognise some forms of procurement).[138] Differing from IP law, such measures may simply be regarded as a flaw in the market regulation or as a technical issue. Several US states have adopted laws to mitigate excessive pricing without needing to endorse a general right to health, most significantly in Maryland, New York and Massachusetts, which were followed by similar bills in other states (not always passed).[139]

Equally, the procurement and negotiation environment to reduce prices is rarely framed as an HRBA when it comes to pharmaceutical products. This is not to say that State transactions with business and contractual relations in public services have never been considered in relation to human rights in general, but studies do not view those instruments as being related to a duty to regulate prices but tend to engage with human rights more broadly.[140] Transparency has attracted more concerns as a violation of the right to health,

138 See e.g. Vogler, Paris and Panteli (n 4) 20; Marianne Klemp, Katrine B Frønsdal and Karen Facey, 'What Principles Should Govern the Use of Managed Entry Agreements?' (2011) 27 International Journal of Technology Assessment in Health Care 77, 80; Managing Drug Supply, 'Managing Access to Medicines and Health Technologies' [2012] Management Sciences for Health. 6.6–67 available at https://msh.org/resources/mds-3-managing-access-to-medicines-and-health-technologies/ accessed 20 January 2020.

139 Padula (n 93) 18–19. For an overview of legislative action in the US, see The National Academy for State Health Policy: "State Legislative Action to Lower Pharmaceutical Costs" https://nashp.org/rx-legislative-tracker-2019/, accessed 1 January 2020.

140 See e.g. Olga Martin-Ortega and Claire Methven O'Brien, 'Public Procurement and Human Rights: Interrogating the Role of the State as Buyer' in Olga Martin-Ortega and Claire Methven O'Brien (eds), *Public Procurement and Human Rights* (Edward Elgar Publishing 2019) 8–16.

through corruption and misspending, than for its ineffective negotiating power to craft clauses with the lowest costs and maximum benefits.[141]

Thus, there is great scope to advocate alternatives not currently being undertaken because of lack of capacity and insufficient human rights pressure in developing countries, which could be achieved through human rights monitoring systems or enforcement in domestic courts. For instance, direct price control, such as price regulation, is more widely employed among developing countries (due to its uncomplicated adoption), whereas developed countries have more sophisticated schemes of indirect price control with negotiation and purchase agreements.[142] Each of these policies (divided into the above-mentioned categories) has been described, including the potential risks, so that their application in an HRBA can be done on a case-by-case analysis.

This review of these bottlenecks (legal determinants of scarcity) has mostly used examples from the pharmaceutical industry, which has a vast literature on possible routes to affordability untapped by socio-economic rights scholarship and advocacy. Such laws constitute a considerable number of policies, which cannot provide a "one-size-fits-all" response to specific questions related to local development and market behaviour. Policymakers and human rights experts share a common tendency to look at affordability problems as a matter of IP laws, and that has limited the range of rights-based approaches to legislative shifts against scarcity. It is important to establish with targeted research alongside health economists and pharmaceutical policy analysts what the specific measures are that are more likely to create the right mix of regulation for each healthcare intervention or product. This will also contribute to satisfying the reasonableness test as to the meaningful steps towards implementation of the right to health by indicating that the State has at least aimed to improve the legal environment.

The existence of legal determinants of scarcity is pivotal to understanding how substantive policies connect with procedures in HTA. In an HRBA, where HTA facilitates the establishment of a health system as core social institution, information gathered in resource allocation may reveal specific unaffordability problems that can be followed up with State measures. HTA can be present as a requirement in countries where the price is negotiated, alongside price

141 See e.g. Sharifah Sekalala, Haleema Masud and Rebekah Thomas Bosco, 'Human Rights Mechanisms for Anti-Corruption, Transparency and Accountability: Enabling the Right to Health' (2020) 13 Global Health Action 1699343, 8.

142 Maniadakis and others (n 97) 3–10.

control tools, centralised procurement, etc.[143] As explained earlier, the legal sections of their reports are mostly neglected and overlook the option of recommending actions to manage the legal determinants of scarcity.[144]

As an integral part of a core social institution, HTA does not need to accept market prices, and, indeed, the literature has demonstrated the growing role of HTA in influencing price negotiation and providing decision-makers with technical information beyond mere cost-containment. The components of a rights-based approach to affordability should make HTA consider two questions: a) which laws can promote affordability for health technology in a given jurisdiction and b) what are the potential negative effects of those laws on other pillars of HRBA conditions (accessibility, availability and quality)? HTA can be both a site of diagnosis of the laws required to create affordability or instrumental in defining the best policies to pursue. In competition law, HTA is able to evaluate excessive prices.[145] Recently, procurement flexibilities in MEA have come into use associated with HTA, particularly in Europe, where medical uncertainty and higher prices have also been addressed for orphan drugs.[146]

The policies presented here serve to demonstrate that the boundary between resource distribution and price fixation is blurred and that an HRBA demands that HTA committees react accordingly.[147] As Garattini and Padula note, "prices can hardly (if ever) be really right in a 'market failure' context".[148] Consequently, the HTA body needs to remain vigilant to the threats to affordability by actively applying rules that would render excessive prices much less likely.

With the foregoing conclusion in mind, the next chapter will illustrate unequivocally that a State can directly influence legal determinants of scarcity during HTA recommendation. The human rights obligations and standards discussed throughout the book will be confirmed in a case study, corroborat-

143 Ibid 4; Michael Drummond and others, 'Reimbursement of Pharmaceuticals: Reference Pricing versus Health Technology Assessment' (2011) 12 The European Journal of Health Economics 263, 270.

144 See chapter 3, 1.1.

145 Calcagno, Chapsal and White (n 109) 169.

146 See e.g. Morel and others (n 137).

147 Sabine Vogler, 'Fair Prices for Medicines? Exploring Competent Authorities' and Public Payers' Preferences on Pharmaceutical Policies' (2019) 46 Empirica 443, 445.

148 Livio Garattini and Anna Padula, 'Pharmaceutical Pricing Conundrum: Time to Get Rid of It?' (2018) 19 The European Journal of Health Economics 1035, 1036.

ing the relevance of the proposed obligations for human rights advocacy in public health. The case study will not only demonstrate that HRBA with substantive policies is theoretically viable in HTA as an argument, but also reflect tested and common strategies, which can be replicated as human rights obligations.

PART 3

Applying the Right to Health in HTA

CHAPTER 8

Tracing International Socio-economic Rights Principles in HTA Decisions: Lessons from Brazil

Thus far, this work has considered the relationship between HTA and the law and the ways in which principles of international socio-economic rights apply to this practice. In short, the standards under the international right to health are expected to lead to concrete and focused conducts in order to progressively realise a full level of access to healthcare. This refers not only to spending on healthcare but also to making healthcare affordable. To achieve such goals, HTA should be part of a series of policies that are associated with resource allocation and minimising the impact of scarcity. Laws and policies should then be harmonised into or around HTA to maximise resources through appropriate regulations alongside a deliberative process.

This chapter presents a practical and easily observable example of the principles laid out in the previous chapters by exploring a case study of HTA in Brazil. This country has been chosen for two main reasons: it has long-established litigation enforcing the right to health, and HTA came into existence as a result of such litigation (specifically, the external relationship with the law, as proposed in Chapter 3). This case study is significant not only because it demonstrates law taking effect within HTA reports, but also how law and government regulation can in fact contain scarcity in a manner that renders resource allocation more than a procedural mechanism guided by A4R. What Daniels prescribes, as we will show, is not the reality in HTA, because policy-makers do not live in a world of immutable scarcity in which there is only one question (namely, how to share the same fixed amount of resources). Overall, HTA reports allow us to map out substantive policies that can be regarded as reasonable steps towards the right to health where sharing resources is also a moment of imagining or mobilising new resources, including through government regulation. The data also provide a valuable opportunity to track the existence or not of rights-based approaches and the substantive influence of laws and policies in the assessments, rather than procedures as part of administrative law.

By screening HTA official records in Brazil, this chapter confirms many of the arguments made in this book. In a quest for evidence of substantive measures as to the progressive realisation of the right to health, this chapter corroborates the relevance of socio-economic rights principles to maximise resources

HTTPS://DOI.ORG/10.1163/9789004730311-009

(as shown in Chapter 4). HTA is influenced by many of the legal determinants of scarcity examined in Chapter 7 (price control, procurement tools, PPPs and so on) suggesting a more ill-defined division between procedural and substantive approaches. Brazil is particularly noteworthy in this regard, as access policies (which ensure affordability) have been adopted in the country and can be implemented alongside HTA.[1]

This chapter comprises three main sections. First, Section 1 will give an institutional overview of HTA in Brazil. In describing HTA in Brazil, this study takes the form of a portrayal of the two-tier relationship (external and internal) of HTA and the law in practice, as seen in Chapter 3. It will explain the legal status and the composition of the HTA entity in the Brazilian national health system (internal relation) and then the role of litigation in HTA in Brazil (external relation). Section 2 describes the structure of Brazilian HTA reporting outputs, which will be part of the dataset. Next, Section 3 will present the methodology of the case study using content analysis focused on the internal relation of HTA with the law. Section 4 then goes on to report the findings of the content analysis considering two main types of documented issues concerning human rights: a) nominal allusion to the law and human rights; and b) substantive policies that confirm socio-economic rights principles (discussed in Chapters 4 to 7). The first categorisation shows the usages of law and the weight given to human rights and litigation by the HTA body. The second range of screened data relates to conducts amounting to steps to realise socio-economic rights, such as price controls. With this in mind, this case study provides a picture of real-world application of socio-economic rights standards in HTA, which are substantively related to maximising resources.

1 The Legal Profile of HTA in Brazil

The implementation of HTA in Brazil has great legal significance. For more than 30 years, HTA has been gradually assimilated within the Brazilian government decisions, at first just in price regulation studies; but over the years, domestic legislation has been fundamental for its current authority and legitimacy.[2] Before any specific laws, HTA-assisted decision-making was not an

1 The right to health is guaranteed by Article 196 of the Brazilian Constitution, which provides that "health is the right of all and a duty of the State and shall be guaranteed by universal access to all activities and services for its promotion, protection, and recovery". Constitution of the Federal Republic of Brazil of 1988, art. 196.

2 Ramiro E Gilardino and others, 'Implementing Health Technology Assessments in Latin America: Looking at the Past, Mirroring the Future. A Perspective from the ISPOR Health

accountable process, lacked scientific knowledge adequate to the reality and only became more publicly accessible in the 2000s, with its uptake as a resource allocation method.[3] One of the precursors of an official HTA body in Brazil was CITEC, a very limited unit operating under administrative ministerial regulations from 2006 to 2011.[4] This body had less well-defined procedures, without timescales, evidence standards, publicity or public participation.[5] After CITEC, a watershed moment was the passage of Federal Act 12.401/2011 creating basic HTA procedural rules in Brazil and founding an official HTA body by federal law, the Conitec (National Committee for Incorporation of Health Technologies), under the Ministry of Health (Ministério da Saúde, MS).[6]

The establishment of Conitec by law laid the foundations of the current HTA procedural rules in Brazil. Decisions are to be made within 180 days from the date of an application, extendable for a further 90 days, where appropriate.[7] The Committee comprises 13 members (or their deputies), as compared to five in the previous body, representing different government departments and agencies engaged with health policies.[8] In contrast to NICE in the UK, Conitec is not technically organised as an independent agency, and still functions as a committee subordinated to the MS.

Conitec acts alongside the Department of Management and Incorporation of Health Technologies (DGITS), which provides the main technical assistance for recommendations to the MS.[9] The DGITS staff are responsible for preparing the reports and submitting them to the members of the Committee. The assessments judged by the members of Conitec may recommend an inclusion,

---

Technology Assessment Roundtable in Latin America' (2020) 23 Value in Health Regional Issues 6, 8.

3 Alex Gertner, 'Health Technology Assessment and Incorporation in Brazil: Critical Reflections on an Emerging Public-Private Field' (2009) 2 Jornal Brasileiro de Economia da Saúde. 57, 58–59; Flávia Tavares Silva Elias and Denizar Vianna Araújo, 'How Health Economic Evaluation (HEE) Contributes to Decision-Making in Public Health Care: The Case of Brazil' (2014) 108 Zeitschrift für Evidenz, Fortbildung und Qualität im Gesundheitswesen 405, 406. David Banta and Rosimary T Almeida, 'The Development of Health Technology Assessment in Brazil' (2009) 25 International Journal of Technology Assessment in Health Care 255, 258.

4 Brazil, Ministry of Health, Portaria n.º 152/GM, 19 January 2006; Portaria n º 3.323, 27 December 2006 .

5 Conitec, Changes from Citec to Conitec, http://conitec.gov.br/index.php/en/changes-from-citec-to-conitec, accessed 12 March 2020.

6 Brazil, Federal Law Nº 12.401, 26 April 2011.

7 Brazil, Ministry of Health, Decreto Nº 7.646, 21 December 2011, art. 15.

8 Ibid.

9 Brazil, Ministry of Health, Portaria GM/MS nº 2.009/2012, art.11-12 (Anexo XVI da Portaria de Consolidação GM/MS nº 1/2017).

exclusion or alteration of health technologies in the national healthcare services, or approve clinical protocols and therapeutic guidelines (CPTG). The recommendations are then passed forward to the MS's Secretariat of Science, Technology, and Strategic Inputs (SCTIE), which gives binding effect on the government.[10] An SCTIE approval has to be implemented within 180 days for all public healthcare, which was not mandatory before the 2011 statute.[11] Patients may be involved during a consultation process or public hearings and can request assessment of specific technologies and appeal decisions, though citizen representation is made formally by consultative bodies such as the National Health Council, which advises the MS and has seats on Conitec.[12]

More than a product of law, Conitec came into existence as a reaction to the law as applied by courts. The bill establishing Conitec was tabled to make resource allocation more open and just against the indirect influence of judicial orders on priority-setting.[13] Early opinions expressed in public hearings held by the Brazilian Constitutional Court (Supremo Tribunal Federal or STF) to discuss the limits of health judicialisation vented the idea of setting up a better official mechanism of HTA as early as 2009.[14] The final Conitec bill, in 2011, "sought to contain the exponential growth of litigation (...), which is disarticulating the process of planning, budgeting, and management of health departments".[15] As Borges holds, this legislative change reflects a concrete transformation brought about by litigation in Brazil, beyond single claims, as an institutional response to mass claims.[16]

Despite optimistic predictions surrounding the creation of an HTA agency, the number of cases in courts has not subsided and judges still do not seem to

10 Ibid, art. 20.

11 Ibid, art. 25.

12 Anke-Peggy Holtorf and others, 'Pilot Approach to Analyzing Patient and Citizen Involvement in Health Technology Assessment in Four Diverse Low-and Middle-Income Countries' (2021) 37 International Journal of Technology Assessment in Health Care 6.

13 Wang, 'Right to Health Litigation in Brazil' (chapter 2, n 1) 639.

14 Isabela Scarabelot Castro Alves, 'Judicialização do direito à Saúde ou Saudicialização do Judiciário: uma análise da audiência pública n 4 do STF' (Sociedade Brasileira de Direito Público) 95. Borges (chapter 3, n 84) 150–151.

15 Brazil, Texto inicial – PLS 338/2007.

16 Danielle da Costa Leite Borges, 'Individual Inputs and Collective Outputs: Understanding the Structural Benefits of Individual Litigation on Healthcare in Brazil' in Marlies Hesselman, Antenor Hallo de Wolf and Brigit Toebes (eds), *Socio-Economic Human Rights in Essential Public Services Provision* (Routledge 2016) 253–267.

be persuaded by Conitec technical recommendations.[17] Between 2012 and 2016, the Committee deliberated on 485 applications for review of health interventions, of which 372 were concluded with a favourable recommendation.[18] During that time, the number of new judicial claims was steadily growing. In the State of Sao Paulo alone, in 2015, there were 18405 lawsuits, almost twice as many as 2010.[19] The soaring litigation went on despite the body undertaking to disseminate among judges and government officials informative reports about drug efficacy and uses. From 2011 to 2015, 800 consultations were opened by the Committee, and briefings with key facts about requested drugs were made available online, for speedy reference during lawsuits.[20]

The difficulties encountered by HTA in containing the expansion of health litigation in Brazil have deep jurisprudential roots.[21] The ever-growing num-

17 Daniel Wang and others, 'Health Technology Assessment and Judicial Deference to Priority-Setting Decisions in Healthcare: Quasi-Experimental Analysis of Right-to-Health Litigation in Brazil' (2020) 265 Social Science & Medicine 113401.

18 Rosângela Caetano and others, 'Incorporação de Novos Medicamentos Pela Comissão Nacional de Incorporação de Tecnologias Do SUS, 2012 a Junho de 2016' (2017) 22 Ciência & Saúde Coletiva 2513, 2516.

19 Robert Domingues and others, 'Strategies to Deal with Drug Lawsuits in the State of São Paulo' (2017) 6 Cadernos Ibero-Americanos de Direito Sanitário 35, 43.

20 Eliete Maia Gonçalves Simabuku and others, 'Comissão Nacional de Incorporação de Tecnologias No SUS e a Judicialização Do Acesso à Saúde' (2015) 6 Revista Eletronica Gestão & Saúde 3024, 3034.

21 On the unrestricted application of the right to health by courts in Brazil, see e.g.: Florian F Hoffmann and Fernando RNM Bentes, 'Accountability for Social and Economic Rights in Brazil' in Varun Gauri and Daniel M Brinks (eds), *Courting Social Justice* (Cambridge University Press 2008); Octávio Luiz Motta Ferraz (ed), 'The Judicialisation of the Right to Health', *Health as a Human Right: The Politics and Judicialisation of Health in Brazil* (Cambridge University Press 2020); Lenir Santos, 'Judicialization of Health: The Theses of the STF' (2021) 45 Saúde em Debate 807; Daniel Wang, 'Courts and Health Care Rationing: The Case of the Brazilian Federal Supreme Court' (2013) 8 Health Economics, Policy and Law 75.

STF has delivered several decisions on the right to health, contradictory among themselves and incapable of deterring unrestrained litigation. In 2010, STF imposed constraints to patient claims: a) the treatment has to be covered by the government under clinical guidelines, b) clinical safety has to be evaluated by the Brazilian national sanitary authority (Anvisa) and c) no experimental treatments without clinical consensus can be awarded. However, this jurisprudence was not followed to the letter in the subsequent years. A more recent appeal (RE 566471) awaits a final pronouncement from STF since 2020. The Court held that high-cost drugs, not part of the reimbursement list, should not be provided in principle, but the exceptional circumstances in which that could be authorised were adjourned. See: STF, ADPF 45, STA 175, STA 175, STA 211, STA 278, SS 3724, SS 2944, SS 2361, SS 3345, SS 3355, SL 47, RE 657718 and RE 566461.

ber of lawsuits in Brazil is partly in association with persistent government judicial defeats and boundless interpretation by judges of the right to health. Rights-based litigation in Brazil corresponds to a different form of perception of public law.[22] Courts have followed a position atypical from a classic judicial review of administrative acts, not turning to whether the administrative procedure, resulting in the rationing decision, complied with the standards prescribed by law, but investigating whether there was any violation of a substantive right.[23] Quantitative works have shown judges as being in favour of litigants, at a level as high as 89% of rulings.[24]

2 HTA Reporting Patterns

This section concerns the source material for the documentary analysis of HTA in Brazil. It describes the format of reports in Brazil and how they relate to the internal relation of HTA to the law. Discussing legal issues or frameworks, or even ethical and social implications, is not explicitly a mandatory part of the reports. Conitec's rules of procedures include only three minimum categories of evidence:

> I – scientific evidence on effectiveness and safety of product or procedure, by the market registration authority, II – economic evaluation of costs and benefits against technologies already in use, including as to homecare, outpatient or inpatient care, III – the impact of incorporation of the technology in the health system.[25]

Reports are examined and voted on by Conitec members during plenary sessions, which are not publicly held, and a negative or positive recommendation is referred to SCTIE (which in practice always assents to the report). The drafting of a report can either be initiated by an internal request by the MS or by a filing by an external party (either a public entity such as State governments, the judiciary or private parties, such as civil groups, medical societies or

22 See chapter 3, 2.1.

23 Ricardo Perlingeiro, 'Procedural and Substantive Judicial Review of the Right to Health in Brazil' [2014] SSRN Electronic Journal 23–24.

24 João Biehl and others, 'Between the Court and the Clinic: Lawsuits for Medicines and the Right to Health in Brazil' (2012) 14 Health and Human Rights 36, 46.

25 Decreto Nº 7.646 (n 7), Art. 18; l, Federal Law 8.080, 19 September 1990, Art. 19-Q § 2º, I–II.

pharmaceutical companies).[26] Once a request is underway for the incorporation, exclusion or alteration of a technology, the decision-making process follows a standard workflow: documents review, first report reading by the Committee Plenary; public consultation; the final decision of the secretary of SCTIE (who may order another public hearing); and the final administrative resolution published in the official gazette.[27]

HTA reports in Brazil can be inconsistent and seem not to follow a uniform procedure. Frequently, Conitec's outputs fail to comply with internal rules (omitting the above cited mandatory items) because Health Economics Evaluation (HEE) is not correctly considered in the reports. Youba et al., reporting in 2012 to 2017, found that HEE is not consistently applied in 87.1% of favourable decisions, issued without thorough economic assessment of cost-effectiveness thresholds.[28] Brazilian reports were divided into categories of full-HTA (all economic and efficacy considerations examined, with remaining factor optional), mini-HTA (same as full, without cost-effectiveness analysis) and rapid-HTA (no cost-effectiveness analysis and no budget impact). In 199 reports, only 79 fall into the category considered as a "full HTA report" with all required content, and 82 were described as not coinciding with any particular model.[29]

This lack of compliance with the Committee's own regulatory standards is related to the fact that the authorities involved have expressed more concern with clinical data and health outcomes than economic analysis.[30] Utility measures, such as QALYs, are rarely used, as local indicators are not commonly available, given the lack of national studies, and cost-utility thresholds are not officially employed.[31]

26 Decreto Nº 7.646 (n 7) Art.15.

27 Portaria GM/MS nº 2.009/2012 (n 9) Arts. 29-45, Federal Law 8.080 (n 25) Art. 19-R. For a simplified process outline in Brazil, see: Sofía Charvel and others, 'Challenges in Priority Setting from a Legal Perspective in Brazil, Costa Rica, Chile, and Mexico' (2018) 20 Health and Human Rights 173.

28 Tania Yuka Yuba, Hillegonda Maria Dutilh Novaes and Patrícia Coelho de Soárez, 'Challenges to Decision-Making Processes in the National HTA Agency in Brazil: Operational Procedures, Evidence Use and Recommendations' (2018) 16 Health Research Policy and Systems 1, 6.

29 Ibid 5.

30 Kleize Araújo de Oliveira Souza and Luis Eugênio Portela Fernandes de Souza, 'Incorporação de Tecnologias No Sistema Único de Saúde: As Racionalidades Do Processo de Decisão Da Comissão Nacional de Incorporação de Tecnologias No Sistema Único de Saúde' (2018) 42 Saúde em Debate 48, 56.

31 Elias and Araújo (n 3) 409.

Because the range of HEE evidence is not uniform, HTA-published decisions can also vary significantly in length as a result.[32] Some less-important filings with no budget impact, made at the initiative of the government, are succinctly reported in very few pages. Other documents may analyse far more than the internal regulation prescribes, such as a comparison with foreign countries' HTA agencies, or more detailed comments on public participation. The existence or not of public consultation generally contributes to the extent of the report, since new input may require re-estimation of economic impact or quality of clinical results.

From the Committee's standpoint, the classification of reports is not made as per breadth of evidence, but by procedural steps (with or without public consultation). Hence, only the existence of a public consultation explicitly impacts content length in this formal classification.[33] Into this category, generally fall evaluations to exclude a technology, at the request of the government, when an outdated product or procedure is eliminated. Such reports will mostly have a shorter HTA without public consultation and, subsequently, more concise evidence.

3 Methods

This chapter will now turn to the contents of the Conitec reports. The analysis has two purposes: to describe how law and human rights matters are depicted in those documents and to explore whether the State measures reflect the progressive realisation of socio-economic rights under international law.

This linkage with international law, however, differs from other studies, which are focused on textual and linguistic references to human rights. For instance, the publication of the Sustainable Development Goals (SDGs) received such analysis and Brolan et al. inquired whether the right to health was implicitly or explicitly recognised within the UN General Assembly reso-

32 Tracy Merlin and others, 'What's in a Name? Developing Definitions for Common Health Technology Assessment Product Types of the International Network of Agencies for Health Technology Assessment (INAHTA)' (2014) 30 International Journal of Technology Assessment in Health Care 430, 430–437.

33 As an example of a simplified report, see: Conitec, 'Cipionato de Hidrocortisona, Comprimidos de 10 Mg e 20 Mg, Para Tratamento de Hiperplasia Adrenal Congênita de Recém-Nascidos Diagnosticados No Programa Nacional de Triagem Neonatal – PNTN' (Conitec 2015) 146.

lution that lays down targets for access to health.[34] Thus, empirical studies may tend to view legal verbatim references as "human rights language" (HRL) derived from international law sources. The rights-language tracking studies, as I describe this strand of research, engage with both international and domestic legal systems, but international law is the main reference. The result moves away from the political and divisive sense of human rights and remains centred on the legal aspects and mainstreaming of the right to health. In this sense, HRL in health consists purely of a reproduction of treaty and international soft law in domestic law.[35] This approach has been applied to identify the incorporation of human rights in health system frameworks around the world by examining whether rights language appears in constitutions for access to medicines in terms of its explicit recognition of international frameworks of obligations to protect, respect and fulfil the right to health.[36]

In contrast, the standpoint taken in this case study is whether what is written constitutes, in essence, a positive step, as provided by international human rights law (regardless of explicit links to human rights). As seen in Chapter 4, resource allocation needs to be assessed in relation to State conducts and substantive policies.[37] The reason for this perspective is the State-centred reality of international human rights law, which is independent of the usage of rights language by local actors.[38] From the perspective of a State, political discourses around human rights and the language in which they realise their policies are immaterial if one wants to assess the level of compliance with these norms – the execution of an obligation is an objective circumstance.

34 Claire E Brolan, Peter S Hill and Gorik Ooms, '"Everywhere but Not Specifically Somewhere": A Qualitative Study on Why the Right to Health Is Not Explicit in the Post-2015 Negotiations' (2015) 15 BMC International Health and Human Rights.

35 See e.g. Katrina Perehudoff, Brigit Toebes and Hans Hogerzeil, 'Essential Medicines in National Constitutions: Progress Since 2008' (2016) 18 Health and Human Rights 141; Sofia Gruskin and others, 'Human Rights in Health Systems Frameworks: What Is There, What Is Missing and Why Does It Matter?' (2012) 7 Global Public Health 337.

36 See e.g. Katrina Perehudoff, 'Health, Human Rights & National Constitutions' [2008] WHO (July 31, 2008); Paul Hunt, Sonia Bhalotra and Carmel Williams, 'The Role and Impact of the Right to Health: Evidence from Brazil's Family Health Program' (2022) 44 Human Rights Quarterly 111.

37 See chapter 4, 1.1.

38 Frédéric Mégret, 'Nature of Obligations' in Sangeeta Shah and others (eds), *International Human Rights Law* (3rd edn, Oxford University Press 2017) 88–92.

3.1 Content Analysis and Coding Scheme

To systematically analyse HTA reports in Brazil, this study employs content analysis, which is defined as a technique to make methodical, valid and replicable inferences from literal texts.[39] Here, content analysis is both quantitative (identifying the number of references to themes) and interpretative (determining contextual and implied meaning and intentions).[40] In law, content analysis has been used to methodically examine a large set of data consisting of judicial decisions in a way that can be reproduced reliably by other researchers to trace statistical patterns of jurisprudential attributes (subject matter, outcomes, context) and to describe the methods of judges (reasoning and language usage).[41] Unlike traditional content analysis in law, this study considers only non-legal technical documents issued by an HTA agency.

Keywords were derived from theory and inductively from the reports. The codes applied to the data reflect the frequency and presence of law and human rights across the reports and which conducts and policies qualify as reasonable steps to social rights implementation, particularly with reference to resource allocation. In light of this, the coding scheme is determined by the following rules, "a" to "d" being deductive codes and "e", partly inductive codes:

a) terms related to legal references (cases or statutes);
b) terms related to constitutional human rights;
c) concepts associated with a) and b), such as justice, fairness, litigation or rights, but not expressly a legal provision;
d) conducts or policies related to progressive realisation (maximising resources and reasonable steps to allocate resources, Chapter 4) such as price negotiation, special programmes or other alternatives, including tax exceptions or price limits (legal determinants of scarcity, Chapter 7); and
e) any other content deemed pertinent to the progressive realisation of the right to health under international law.

Additionally, reports were classified according to the following attributes: year, outcome, the existence of resource mobilisation (PPP, price negotiation/reduction, price cap), original applicant, treatment type and whether it was a simplified procedure (no public consultation).

---

39 James W Drisko and Tina Maschi, *Content Analysis* (Oxford University Press 2015) 2.

40 Ibid 4–5.

41 Mark A Hall and Ronald F Wright, 'Systematic Content Analysis of Judicial Opinions' (2008) 96 California Law Review 63, 90–93.

All files in .pdf format containing the reports from Conitec were gathered directly from the official homepage of the MS.[42] A list of the available documents was downloaded for the period from 2011 to 2017, comprising 285 files. Documents for patient/public communication and other non-HTA records have been excluded, reducing the first eligible sample to 246 cases for strict legal analysis (codes a to c). A second sample was refined with HTA reports of drugs, medical devices and clinical procedures selected for a full coding beyond legal analysis (230 files, for codes a to e). Files were saved in a project folder on Nvivo (an automated software tool for content analysis), which ran the searches for the coding and sorted the files by individual attributes. The coding was conducted both automatically (by querying key terms related to law and resource mobilisation in Portuguese) and manually when the terminology differed or another language was used for the themes of interest.

3.2 Limitations to This Research

HTA reports were screened, as formulated by the Committee. They provide the observations and opinions of the Committee or reference to studies in so far as the drafters decided to register formally any view and findings to the public. Oral debates and non-documented discussions made when the Committee convenes cannot be probed because there are no minutes or transcriptions of all individual comments and extra-report consensus. Frequently, concluding remarks will not indicate any reason for a decision. It is impossible to know, unless clearly stated, for example, which was the main reason for a specific determination. Reports are linear and have no weighted criteria.

Further, a legal or qualitative analysis of the nature of this study does not permit a specific informed review of the quality and adequacy of medical and economic comments beyond tracking what are the legal aspects that may be at stake. This being a legal study, it is beyond the narrow aim of this research to scrutinise the Committee's capacity to gather the most suitable evidence, nor is it capable of reassessing the validity of the Committee's technical conclusions.

42 Conitec, Recomendações da Conitec, http://conitec.gov.br/decisoes-sobre-incorporacoes, accessed 10 August 2019.

4 Findings: How Law Is Described

The first conclusion that can be made from the HTA reports is that these documents are very legally motivated or infused with a "legal discourse". Some of them contain over 18% of content coded as being legal, up to 22.98% (normal birth clinical guidelines) in a single assessment. On average, the level of textual reference to laws was of 4.51%, including all the files.[43]

In this vein, legal content in the reports is mostly explanatory and descriptive of government authority in making a decision, or the legal circumstances that apply to a particular technology. Variation in the legal text is minor, the routine legal introduction and the final resolution being typical structures. Exceptions are some clusters of technologies, such as for people with disabilities or access to HIV treatment, put in the context of pertinent legislation and programmes that may favour additional funds or the importance of the particular health need (see Section 4.2 for examples).[44] Legal contextualisation also occurred for public health and pharmaceutical regulation of individual technologies or drugs.[45]

One reason for the frequent occurrence of legal comments in the reports is the use of an introductory standard explanation for the HTA functioning and legal standing in the country. This preamble gives a summary of the HTA process and the powers and deadlines for Conitec. At the end of the document comes a resolution, with the decision ratified by the MS, and published in the federal gazette as an administrative act. This denotes the very legalistic nature of the HTA recommendation as the result of a formal administrative process.

This persistence in providing a legal context and the reproduction of an entire official decree in closing the reports can be viewed as an intention to convey a more legally authoritative status to the documents. As exposed by empirical litigation studies, HTA in Brazil is part of a broader conversation between authorities, patients and the judiciary over the extent to which administrative decisions can be disputed under the law, so reports are not justifying allocation choices as a piece of research, but creating a legally authoritative decision.[46] In one case, the procedure for an antibiotic was

43 See Annex 1.

44 Conitec, 'Cadeira de Rodas Para Banho Em Concha Infantil, Cadeira de Rodas Para Banho Com Encosto Reclinável e Cadeira de Rodas Para Banho Com Aro de Propulsão Na Tabela de Órteses, Próteses e Materiais Especiais Não Relacionados Ao Ato Cirúrgico Do SUS' (Conitec 2013) 53.

45 See e.g. Conitec, 'Talidomida Para Tratamento Da Síndrome Mielodisplásica' (Conitec 2014) 134.

46 See chapter 3, 1.1.

referred to the Committee after a request from a Federal Court out of a class action.[47]

4.1 Human Rights and Litigation

Another less common form of manifestation of law is the reference to the high level of litigation for access to medicines, denominated as "judicialisation". In total, 19 cases were found with allusions to litigation, with an average of 0.36% text coverage. Those sections are equally made of reports or extracts of patient comments after consultations, or in the main text, as part of the explanation of the health technology in question and the associated level of judicialisation.

In comparison, although the reports contain legal terms, the quality and the diversity of those statements are low in terms of examining relevant standards of the right to health to HTA. The human rights of patients are raised in 20 reports and some would mention the right to health as a moral argument, as opposed to the constitutional right to health and its meaning for the particular deliberation. In some cases, human rights are referred to as patient legal frameworks, as the legal basis for a group of patients (see examples in Section 4.4 below on budgets defined by laws). The drafters mentioned, for instance, reproductive rights, according to legislation, when assessing technologies that could benefit women's and adolescents' family planning, and not as human rights standards.[48]

Moreover, those remarks are always attributed to a vulnerable group such as by stating that "the aim of ensuring the right to life and health to every child is still to be attained".[49] In contrast, allusions to patient rights made by the public are even less specific and imbued with a sense of social justice or moral obligation: "access to new medicines is a right" or "it is just that everyone has access to something that is a matter of right".[50] The submissions from the patients are broad, without specifying the constitutional provisions that would be enforced before a Brazilian court.

Effectively, this posture makes judicialisation the closest reference in the analysis of human rights as a legally binding obligation to provide healthcare.

---

47 Conitec, 'Antibiótico Inalatório (Tobramicina) Para Colonização Das Vias Aéreas Em Pacientes Com Fibrose Cística' (Conitec 2016) 217 4.

48 Conitec, 'Implante Subdérmico Liberador de Etonogestrel 68 Mg Para Anticoncepção Em Mulheres de 15 a 19 Anos de Idade.' (Conitec 2016) 208 8.

49 Conitec, 'Teste Do Coraçãozinho (Oximetria de Pulso) Na Triagem NeoNatal' (Conitec 2014) 115 1.

50 Conitec, 'Ambrisentana e Bosentana Para o Tratamento Da Hipertensão Arterial Pulmonar' (Conitec 2013) 90 21.

Reports may provide statistics on the scale of litigation by the number of lawsuits for a technology.[51] Aside from that, the Committee shows no recognition that a right to health is enforceable or any following obligation that might affect HTA decision-making, procedure or the substantive policies of the government in connection with access to health technologies. The threat of judicialisation is sometimes raised at public consultations. Since reports do not provide the full contributions of the consultations, some of them being only excerpts or summaries, it is impossible to measure fully the frequency that litigation is brought up in discussions. Patients submit that judicialisation is the only effective instrument to secure access to healthcare.[52] Additionally, local governments may provide information about the repercussions of judicialisation on their administration of technologies under review.[53]

For instance, the producer of Pertuzumab for HER2-positive breast cancer maintained that budget impact should consider the savings resulting from a lower level of judicialisation after the technology is approved.[54] The Committee rejected this idea, stating that not all lawsuits are related to non-authorised treatments and their purview is to gauge only cost-effectiveness and eligibility for the health system.[55]

Among the 19 cases where litigation has been brought to the fore, it should be noted that the judicialisation factor seems to give a small advantage for positive outcomes. With this theme mentioned, 12 reports had a positive decision against 7 negative, whereas in the general sample, 129 were approved against 85 rejections. The odds ratio for a negative outcome in the cases citing judicialisation was 0.87, showing some decrease in the probability of negative outcome.

4.2 Legal Determinants of Scarcity and Progressive Realisation

Up to this point, it has been described how the law is expressly laid out in HTA reports, which do not seem to engage with the legal aspects of the right to

---

51 Conitec, 'Inibidores de Protease (Boceprevir e Telaprevir) Para o Tratamento Da Hepatite Crônica C' (Conitec 2012) 01 56.

52 Conitec, 'Clozapina, Lamotrigina, Olanzapina, Quetiapina e Risperidona Para o Tratamento Do Transtorno Afetivo Bipolar' (Conitec 2015) 140 36.

53 Conitec, 'Apixabana, Rivoraxabana e Dabigratana Em Pacientes Com Fibrilação Atrial Não Valvar' (Conitec 2016) 195 25.

54 Conitec, 'Pertuzumabe Para o Tratamento Do Câncer de Mama HER2-Positivo Metastático Em Primeira Linha de Tratamento Associado Ao Trastuzumabe e Docetaxel' (Conitec 2017) 319 46.

55 Ibid 47.

health under Brazilian constitutional law, let alone international socio-economic rights. Nevertheless, even invoking rights does not seem to be sufficient to clarify the obligations of the right to health to mobilise resources progressively and to the highest level. For instance, searching only for legal references cannot instantly reveal which possible measure should be enacted for a health technology to be priced at an affordable level, even though that is the ultimate purpose of international rules. Therefore, this section will list practical actions or State conducts found in the reports that have relevance to socio-economic rights implementation concerning resource maximisation and the control of scarcity via affordability policies, some of them premised on adequate laws or legal effects (legal determinants of scarcity).

For these reasons, the second strand of coding was called "resource mobilisation", referring to topics d and e in the coding scheme. In the reports, this cluster is less common than legal coding. Resource generation mechanisms were present as special funds (financial resources secured prior to the assessment); that is, price negotiation, price offer (a company setting a different price for procurement) and price caps (when the State conditions the inclusion of a price reduction or the cost of a similar intervention); PPP (an agreement to allow sustainable and more affordable local production); cost-reduction (acknowledgment of wider indirect cost reduction after the technology is available); and tax (fiscal exemptions to reduce the technology cost). In general, reports mentioning resource mobilisation topics appear to have an equivalent success rate to those without this theme.

4.3 Price Negotiations and Price Caps

As examined in Chapter 7, one of the legal determinants of scarcity is to regulate or facilitate negotiation of prices so as to expand resources through healthcare affordability. HTA, then, can become a place of price adjustments right from the beginning of the decision-making process, either voluntarily or compulsorily. For instance, a drug that initially was not considered cost-effective may have its value for money re-calculated as a consequence of a company submitting a lower asking price.[56] This type of conduct has been described as price negotiation, but Conitec can also determine a price limit following a negotiation or just by mandatory negotiation (requiring only a

56 Conitec, 'Fumarato de Dimetila No Tratamento Da Esclerose Múltipla Remitente-Recorrente Após Falha Com Betainterferona Ou Glatirâmer' (Conitec 2017) 286 43–44; Conitec, 'Abatacepte Para o Tratamento Da Artrite Reumatoide Moderada a Grave' (Conitec 2015) 133 20.

price reduction). HTA recommendations can therefore have the effect of a regulatory act, if they impose a mandatory condition in the final text. This can also be done less strictly, as with requiring price negotiation without mentioning any target price.[57]

During the HTA process, voluntary negotiations can take many forms and have different outcomes. The fact that the producer initially set a more attractive price does not mean that the government cannot demand a further decrease. The report for new anti-HCV drugs conditioned that there would be no minimum volume for purchase and set appropriate renegotiation, depending on therapeutic success.[58] A counter-offer can be made during the public participation stage as well.[59] Price negotiation may be incidentally posited during the discussions, but any requirement may be omitted in the final administrative act converted into legal ordinance, which makes the decision official.[60] The budget impact may also observe discounts obtained by procurement strategies or price offers before or during the HTA.[61] Furthermore, even before any discount is obtained or required, the economic evaluation can be based on potential scenarios where a reduction is projected.[62]

Companies can even pre-emptively bid a more cost-effective rate when submitting a consultation in the middle or beginning of the process.[63] Roche offered the drug Trastuzumab at R$ 3,446.89, while the sales price in Brazil at the time was R$ 9,317.81, 97% higher than the international average.[64] A seller may offer a higher price in one assessment and, after being unsuccessful, file another evaluation with a lower price. In 2015, ABBVIE presented a report

57 Conitec, 'Medicamentos Biológicos (Infliximabe, Etanercepte, Adalimumabe, Rituximabe, Abatacepte, Tocilizumabe, Golimumabe e Certolizumabe Pegol) Para o Tratamento Da Artrite Reumatóide' (Conitec 2012) 12 14.

58 Conitec, 'Simeprevir, Sofosbuvir e Daclatasvir No Tratamento Da Hepatite Crônica Tipo C e Coinfecções' (Conitec 2015) 164 69.

59 Conitec, 'Teriflunomida Para Primeira Linha de Tratamento Da Esclerose Múltipla Remitente Recorrente' (Conitec 2017) 259 40.

60 Conitec, 'Fingolimode Para o Tratamento Da Esclerose Múltipla' (Conitec 2014) 113 54; Conitec, 'Trastuzumabe Para Tratamento Do Câncer de Mama Avançado' (Conitec 2012) 08 55.

61 Conitec, 'Ambrisentana e Bosentana Para o Tratamento Da Hipertensão Arterial Pulmonar' (n 50) 20; Conitec, 'Everolimo Para Imunossupressão Em Transplante Hepático Em Adultos' (Conitec 2015) 174 30.

62 Conitec, 'Inibidores de Protease (Boceprevir e Telaprevir) Para o Tratamento Da Hepatite Crônica C' (n 51) 63.

63 Conitec, 'Simeprevir, Sofosbuvir e Daclatasvir No Tratamento Da Hepatite Crônica Tipo C e Coinfecções' (n 58) 48.

64 Conitec, 'Trastuzumabe Para Tratamento Do Câncer de Mama Avançado' (n 60) 27–28.

using a list price of US$ 3,166.67 for one month of a combination of oral antiviral agents for Hepatitis C and, after a negative decision, re-submitted in 2017, an economic evaluation using an asking price of US$ 1,483.33.[65]

Mandatory conditions, including compulsory price negotiation, are also very diverse. Though it may seem reasonable that such an aim is sought in any price negotiation, a recommendation can define clauses phrased as simply "subject to price reduction" without stating a discount to be achieved or reference to prior negotiation.[66] Another similar form of control of costs is the use of price caps, which are not structured consistently and are very intertwined with price negotiation. A requirement of price reduction (which assumes negotiation) may stipulate a price below a similar healthcare treatment, setting out an actual price cap.[67] Price caps can be imposed, having as the maximum value the conventional or preceding treatment or the less expensive method of administration of a drug.[68] Price caps and voluntary price negotiations can be directly inter-related when the price cap established by the Committee corresponds to a negotiated price in the course of the report elaboration. In the Abatacept recommendation, the price set as a maximum for the subcutaneous version of the drug was the same paid for the intravenous one, after the drug-maker offered to use the intravenous price.[69]

The clauses discussed may not always be effective and this study could not estimate how often price negotiation led to the actual implementation of

65 Conitec, 'Veruprevir, Ritonavir, Ombitasvir e Dasabuvir Para o Tratamento de Hepatite C Crônica Causada Por Infecção Pelo Genótipo 1 Do HCV' (Conitec 2015) 197 18; Conitec, 'Veruprevir, Ritonavir, Ombitasvir e Dasabuvir Para o Tratamento de Hepatite C Crônica Causada Por Infecção Pelo Genótipo 1 Do HCV' (Conitec 2016) 233.

66 Conitec, 'Inibidores de Protease (Boceprevir e Telaprevir) Para o Tratamento Da Hepatite Crônica C' (n 51) 84; Conitec, 'Cinacalcete e Paricalcitol Para o Tratamento de Pacientes Com Hiperparatireoidismo Secundário à Doença Renal (HPTS), Em Diálise e Refratários à Terapia Convenciona' (Conitec 2015) 176 65; Conitec, 'Trastuzumabe Para Tratamento Do Câncer de Mama Avançado' (n 60) 29.

67 Conitec, 'Tofacitinibe Para o Tratamento de Pacientes Adultos Com Artrite Reumatoide Ativa Moderada a Grave Com Resposta Inadequada a Um Ou Mais Medicamentos Modificadores Do Curso Da Doença' (Conitec 2016) 241 65; Conitec, 'Fingolimode Para o Tratamento Da Esclerose Múltipla' (n 60) 54.

68 Conitec, 'Abatacepte Para o Tratamento Da Artrite Reumatoide Moderada a Grave' (n 56) 21. Conitec, 'Erlotinibe Para Câncer de Pulmão de Células Não Pequenas' (Conitec 2013) 63 29; Conitec, 'Gefitinibe Para Câncer de Pulmão de Células Não Pequenas Em Primeira Linha' (Conitec 2013) 62 32. Conitec, 'Maraviroque Para Pacientes Em Terapia Antirretroviral' (Conitec 2012) 14 29. Conitec, 'Stent Farmacológico Para o Tratamento Da Doença Arterial Coronariana (DAC)' (Conitec 2014) 111 51.

69 Conitec, 'Abatacepte Para o Tratamento Da Artrite Reumatoide Moderada a Grave' (n 68) 20.

negotiations leading to lower prices and inclusion of new technologies. Price negotiation, for one indication, may not encompass other prescriptions for the same drug (an issue complained about by patient organisations and noted in the report of Everolimus for breast cancer, which had lower defined prices for transplants).[70] In the report of Ambrisentan and Botensan for pulmonary hypertension, in 2013, Conitec acknowledges that the provision for price reduction set out in a previous assessment in 2011 of Botesan was never met and only a price negotiation during the latest process enabled the treatment to be added.[71]

4.4 Budget Priorities Made by Law

Extra funding may be also designated by law (as a special fund reserve or priority area prior to the budget-making or technology assessment), which produces relatively propitious conditions for approval in HTA. In these cases, the level of attention to medical evidence in the reports may be lower and the concerns with the financial sustainability of the incorporation are less decisive, in contrast to the appeal to patient quality of life and equitable treatment.[72] This demonstrates that law can drive HTA by enforcing deliberations about funds and priority areas made by political deliberations in other institutions, such as Congress. For instance, legal entitlements, compensation measurements, and equity goals can be stressed in pursuing new interventions that are already part of a programme, which is legally established and publicly subsidised. For the acquisition of wheelchair-appropriate postural support accessories and the small base tetrapod for people with mobility limitations, the undertone used to describe the potential outlay for this expenditure was more benevolent and socially conscious: "it is undeniable the need to incorporate the supporting technologies above described to set right this historical

70 Conitec, 'Everolimo Para Tratamento Do Câncer de Mama Avançado Na Pós-Menopausa' (Conitec 2013) 91 31.

71 Conitec, 'Ambrisentana e Bosentana Para o Tratamento Da Hipertensão Arterial Pulmonar' (n 50) 19.

72 See similar observations in: Conitec, 'Procedimento Bengala de 4 Pontas Na Tabela de Órteses, Proteses e Materiais Especiais Nao Relacionados Ao Ato Cirurgico Do SUS' (Conitec 2013) 83.

debt that the unified health system (SUS) has in the rehabilitation field and with disabled persons".[73] Remarkably, this statement was made under the heading "means of financial coverage".[74]

A similar attitude was seen in 2014 with auditory implant procedures, which had a budget impact analysis interwoven with an emphasis on subgroup equity, the existence of authorised funding and "new regulations" to reorganise and improve access to assistive technologies for people with hearing disabilities.[75] As a form of legal context, technologies for disabled patients are discussed with reference to the National Plan for the Rights of Persons with Disabilities (Decree no. 7.612, 17 November 2011), adopted to expand access to implants and mobility aids, a priority originally financed through the Strategic Action and Compensation Fund.[76]

4.5 Public–Private Partnerships

PPP can serve as an important catalyst to the inclusion of an intervention. These agreements are formed before or during the HTA request from the government, suggesting plans to adopt the intervention in the health system.[77] Without these agreements, positive recommendations would be generally less feasible. For instance, projections in the reports already bear in mind future savings when the technology is transferred by lower costs of purchases not

73 See similar observations in: Conitec, 'Cadeira de Rodas Para Banho Em Concha Infantil, Cadeira de Rodas Para Banho Com Encosto Reclinável e Cadeira de Rodas Para Banho Com Aro de Propulsão Na Tabela de Órteses, Próteses e Materiais Especiais Não Relacionados Ao Ato Cirúrgico Do SUS' (n 44).

74 Ibid. See also: Conitec, 'Cadeira de Rodas Tipo Monobloco e Cadeira de Rodas (Acima de 90 Kg) Na Tabela de Órteses, Proteses e Materiais Especiais Nao Relacionados Ao Ato Cirurgico Do SUS' (Conitec 2013) 52; Conitec, 'Adaptação Postural Em Cadeira de Rodas Na Tabela de Órteses, Próteses e Materiais Especiais Do SUS' (Conitec 2013) 51; Conitec, 'Cadeira de Rodas Para Banho Em Concha Infantil, Cadeira de Rodas Para Banho Com Encosto Reclinável e Cadeira de Rodas Para Banho Com Aro de Propulsão Na Tabela de Órteses, Próteses e Materiais Especiais Não Relacionados Ao Ato Cirúrgico Do SUS' (n 44). Conitec, 'Cadeira de Rodas Motorizada Na Tabela de Órteses, Proteses e Materiais Especiais Nao Relacionados Ao Ato Cirurgico Do SUS' (Conitec 2013) 50.

75 Conitec, 'Procedimenots Relativos à Assistência à Saúde Auditiva Hospitalar Na Tabela Do SUS' (Conitec 2014) 99 11–12,17.

76 Conitec, 'Procedimento Bengala de 4 Pontas Na Tabela de Órteses, Proteses e Materiais Especiais Nao Relacionados Ao Ato Cirurgico Do SUS' (n 72).

77 Conitec, 'Alfataliglicerase Para o Tratamento Da Doença de Gaucher' (Conitec 2014) 124 7.

subject to dollar fluctuation or external market shortages.[78] However, it is not clear from every assessment, exactly how influential is the pre-existence of a PPP upon a positive recommendation or the actual price reduction achieved by introducing this process.[79]

Despite this, PPP clearly exemplifies the slim boundary between resource allocation decision-making and substantive steps to create healthcare access. HTA results may be used to inform further negotiation and suggest to the government that it is worth pursuing extra policies to contain prices and make an intervention cost-effective. This took place with the HPV vaccine, which after clinical evidence and economic analysis of the HTA procedures, motivated the government to establish a partnership to secure sustainable local production at more attractive prices.[80]

Local development promoting self-sufficient production or the domestic supply of healthcare goods is a key aspect of the access to those treatments. In agreeing to furnish recombinant factor VIII concentrates for haemophiliac patients, the Committee observed that "there is the risk of compromising the supply, given that the large amounts demanded and the limits of production of pharmaceutical companies, besides other further restriction from shortages of raw materials in the international market".[81] The Committee also goes on to explain that the PPP was aimed at the technology transfer as a priority and the initial acquisition of the products with the supplier of 50% of stocks until full self-sufficiency was attained.[82]

However, the existence of a partnership for the same drug for other treatments does not seem to persuade decision-makers that the price can be negotiated for a lower amount or be referred to as a reason for a successful outcome. In the Everolimus assessment for breast cancer, the fact that there was already a partnership for Everolimus was dismissed, as the contract with the government covered only a molecule in a different concentration supplied exclusively for transplant patients. Consultees argued that the partnership should be relied on to set a less onerous cost, but that was not agreed by the

78 Ibid 16; Conitec, 'Fator VIII de Origem Recombinante Para Profilaxia Primária e Tratamento de Pacientes Com Hemofilia A' (Conitec 2012) 48.

79 Conitec, 'Vacina Tetraviral (Sarampo, Caxumba, Rubéola e Varicela)' (Conitec 2013) 21 120. Conitec, 'Clozapina, Lamotrigina, Olanzapina, Quetiapina e Risperidona Para o Tratamento Do Transtorno Afetivo Bipolar' (n 52) 29.

80 Conitec, 'Vacina Contra HPV Na Prevenção de Câncer de Colo Do Útero' (Conitec 2013) 83 25–26.

81 Conitec, 'Fator VIII de Origem Recombinante Para Profilaxia Primária e Tratamento de Pacientes Com Hemofilia A' (n 78).

82 Ibid.

Committee.[83] In 2015, even though a partnership for transplantations had been already in place, there was no express mention of that in the report that approved Everolimus for liver transplants (although the quotes in the economic considerations noted that prices would decrease in the following years).[84]

4.6 State Inaction in HTA Reports (Progressive Realisation and Resource Mobilisation)

Some of the State obligations argued in this book are in place to induce continuous access to healthcare by ensuring affordability as an alternative to raising expenditures from market pressure (as examined with the legal determinants of scarcity). Normally, progressive realisation can be seen as a principle used for mobilising more resources to meet growing costs, but we have seen that States can force down prices to obtain healthcare products within the existing budget. A question that can be raised is at which moment one can distinguish non-implementation, owing to an insurmountable form of scarcity from instances in which scarcity is perfectly remediable.

As demonstrated by the reports, Conitec may remain silent on possible solutions to make a technology available without intensive resource expenditure. Of all 9 recommendations with a prior assessment, only 3 had a negative conclusion. As previously mentioned, in 2011, the preceding agency (CITEC) decided in favour of Ambrisentan and Bosentan, but the price conditions were not satisfied until 2013, giving inadequate attention towards follow-up actions.[85] In theory, there can be cases where an intervention presents reasons to be incorporated immediately, but Conitec decides against it (for lack of evidence or costs) until a new reassessment finds more advantageous conditions without government interference. This situation effectively marks a dividing line between an excusable scarcity situation to justify non-implementation and non-implementation as a rights violation for not mobilising alternative resources (which were only found in the second process of assessment after a negative decision).

This suggested inaction may take the form of a lack of interest in producing further data on a new technology to subsidise reports by not addressing poor

83 Conitec, 'Everolimo Para Tratamento Do Câncer de Mama Avançado Na Pós-Menopausa' (n 70) 32.

84 Conitec, 'Everolimo Para Imunossupressão Em Transplante Hepático Em Adultos' (n 61) 30.

85 Conitec, (n 50).

evidence with future research. This can be seen as a problem of discrimination and lack of a fair procedure, as analysed with the 3Ps framework in Chapter 5. At the very minimum, the State should designate what its policy is for future research or specify what evidence is to be collected to support safety and efficacy evaluation.[86] In the report for endobronchial valve implants, Conitec concluded that there was insufficient evidence but, unlike NICE, did not issue a recommendation for further action specifying appropriate studies required for a reassessment.[87] It might also happen that a technology is already thoroughly researched and available to a subgroup of patients, but is still not well monitored enough among different subgroups or treatment indications necessary for a more restrictive approval.[88]

4.7 Obligations of International Cooperation

In Chapter 6, it was submitted that international cooperation is one obligation under the right to health that complements well the flourishing HTA networks across jurisdictions.[89] Research, standards and organisations in HTA are international in nature and, accordingly, Conitec reports illustrate the fact that agencies may allude to recommendations abroad to justify appraisals. The Brazilian reports do not give objective examples of active promotion of international cooperation from a developing-country position at the receiving-end of resources transfer (e.g. actively joining cooperation agreements or using co-produced research with other countries). On the other hand, it is clear that international agencies and foreign HTA bodies bring to bear certain influence on Conitec decisions just by their knowledge diffusion or being cited as a source of comparative information. This confirms the role of foreign collaboration or knowledge-sharing passively, even if only as a consequence of making available domestic HTA recommendations to other governments.

Such subtle influence may arise through international organisation standards as well. In the assessment for a tetra vaccine (measles, mumps, rubella and chickenpox), Conitec identified that, depending on the criteria adopted

86 See, for instance, cases where Conitec did not expressed interest in further research in areas of low or conflict evidence: Conitec, 'Brometo de Tiotrópio Para Tratamento Da Doença Pulmonar Obstrutiva Crônica' (Conitec 2013) 68 16–21.

87 Conitec, 'Implante de Válvulas Endobronquiais Unidirecionais Para Tratamento Do Enfisema Pulmonar Heterogêneo' (Conitec 2014) 122 26.

88 Conitec, 'Medicamentos Biológicos (Infliximabe, Etanercepte, Adalimumabe Eustequinumabe) Para o Tratamento Da Psoríase Moderada a Grave Em Adultos' (Conitec 2012) 13 21–23.

89 See chapter 6, 1.

for the maximum international threshold of cost-effectiveness for an intervention, the economic model would have a different outcome.[90] The World Bank encourages a cost of only 1 times the Gross National Product (GNP) per capita, only one-third of what is recommended by the WHO. Conitec observed that the vaccine would only be cost-effective, in line with International Bank for Reconstruction and Development guidelines, if the prices were reduced, but decided to use the WHO guidance to recommend the programme with a cost lower than three times the GNP per capita.

Comparing evidence review in alternative jurisdictions may be made directly by reference to HTA reports of other agencies, but that is not always an accurate representation of the evidence assessment abroad. In 2013, Canakinumab was rejected by Conitec in a report citing that NICE could not make any conclusion about the evidence on the new drug (which was not submitted by the company).[91] In reality, the treatment has been commissioned by NHS England since 2013, after an evidence review validating the efficacy studies.[92] In contrast, Conitec called into question the quality of the existing studies (despite admitting that an orphan drug would not have comparators other than placebos). The evidence criteria were distinct between agencies, and adequate international comparison in future would help a more robust analysis of whether, for equity reasons, patients of orphan drugs should be subject to rigid research requirements or trigger a duty of progressive realisation to promote further research.

International comparison offers indications of inequalities among countries as to negotiated prices, suggesting a link with substantive State obligations to regulate markets. In a case involving women's reproductive rights, Conitec found that for menorrhagia, having a non-surgical therapy with a Levonorgestrel-releasing Intrauterine System (LNG-IUS) is less cost-effective than hysterectomy. Patients and other participants of the public consultation inquired why the drug was available in other countries, and Conitec responded that because in Brazil, the company had imposed a less competitive price than other markets, hysterectomy stood as the most cost-effective policy (though the question of reproductive rights was not discussed).[93]

90 Conitec, 'Vacina Tetraviral (Sarampo, Caxumba, Rubéola e Varicela)' (n 79) 28.

91 Conitec, 'Canaquinumabe – Síndromes Periódicas Associadas à Criopirina(CAPS)' (Conitec 2013) 76 24.

92 NHS England, '013/14 NHS Standard Contract For Cryopyrin Associated Periodic Syndrome (All Ages)' <https://www.england.nhs.uk/wp-content/uploads/2013/06/e13-cryopyrin-ass-periodic-syn.pdf>. Accessed 20 July 2020.

93 Conitec, 'Sistema Intrauterino Liberador de Levonorgestrel Para o Tratamento Da Menorragia Idiopática' (Conitec 2013) 60 28–30.

5 Conclusion: Lessons of Progressive Realisation of the Right to Health in HTA Reports in Brazil

In practice, the findings show how HTA may break the wall between the deliberative process and substantive policies in resource allocation. This case study reinforces the argument that philosophical idealisation of an accountable process for procedural fairness, where resource allocation stands segregated from other political choices, is not the entire role of an HRBA to resource allocation and HTA. The reports show that policy-makers in Brazil went beyond A4R to explore avenues to reduce the impact of scarcity in healthcare. The inquiry through an HRBA opens a new horizon – if a technology exists but cannot be paid for, what is wrong with a market that requires that this problem be addressed, and how should that be done? To determine whether an HTA body is compliant with the right to health in international law, one must analyse if positive steps are being taken so that HTA becomes a constituent part of a health system conceived as a core social institution, in which all policies that can influence access to healthcare are taken into account (and not only cost-effectiveness and prices as immutable realities).

As shown in this case study, HTA agencies are not static bodies, merely functioning as price-takers subject to the market and completely passive to scarcity. At the moment, the empirical findings from this study in Brazil are an important aspect of resource deliberations that has been largely overlooked in the procedural fairness theory, as proposed so far in the literature. However, when those policies and substantive measures are taken into consideration, the HRBA delineated in this book seems a much more appropriate form of addressing scarcity and complying with the right to health than the logic of "a right to a fair procedure".

The arsenal of measures outlined in Brazil may not be exhaustive, but it provides a completely different language of growth. The resource mobilisation orientation of economic and social rights is a much more promising approach to achieving access to healthcare than a narrow vision focused on taking negative market economic forces as an absolute fact. Many of the access policies raised in the reports reflect the framework in Chapter 7: progressive realisation and maximum available resources, corresponding to the legal determinants of scarcity (price negotiation, price caps, PPP). Further case studies need to create a full inventory of possible interventions. As an evidence-based process, HTA can help policy-makers by producing research and investigating what are the barriers for affordability, as to regulation and policies, so that technology receives a favourable recommendation. In addition, HTA processes must trace points of disadvantages ("what if" scenarios such as lower prices or taxation) where regulation and government action can create pathways for cost-effectiveness or clinical evidence.

The international HTA community would do well to foreground its practice standards in an HRBA to spell out the reasonable steps which States should take (instead of narrowly focusing on UHC, as described in Chapter 6). For instance, progressive realisation requires sustained measures over a reasonable time and HTA may lay bare the omission of States in maximising resources by applying alternative approaches to reduce health costs. One problem is how to determine whether there has been a delay in implementing affordability policies. A plausible allowed period between an assessment and the effective implementation of a decision (lowering or negotiating a price) may prove contentious. Closer examination of the conditions of access to a new technology should determine the exact amount of time for each decision, while future studies should also provide average timeframes for access policies.

Although HTA reports are a good source of inspiration for the right to health implementation, they have never been directly rooted in international human rights standards. The Brazilian jurisdiction has no similar range of principles for economic and social rights, beyond constitutional provisions, setting out a general duty to supply healthcare. Paradoxically, HTA has been used as a negative response to constrain litigation in Brazil, but the process is not capable of providing legal justification and justice principles that are respected by patients. This makes a stronger case to apply ICESCR standards and impose duties on the State to regulate the market to prevent the need for a technology exclusion or to deliver some response towards resource mobilisation as genuine efforts. Such a framework could ground other forms of applying the right to health by courts through the enforcement of access policies and control over scarcity within HTA. Despite requiring further clarification, key principles of socio-economic rights under international law offer a more constructive and sustainable outlook to reform HTA practices than employing the narrow constitutional obligations in Brazil, which demand resources with no pathways of change.

CHAPTER 9

Conclusion: The Right to Health as a Theory of Change for HTA

As highlighted from the outset of this book, one of the main challenges in defining the added value of the international right to health in public health is the indeterminacy and complexity of an HRBA.[1] This book has asked how this right could serve as a normative basis for HTA policies and laid down a coherent method of analysis to this effect. In sum, what this book achieves is the unpacking of long-held principles in international human rights law, which recognises the difficulties of scarcity, and systematically applying them to the HTA context, without resorting to procedural fairness as the default rule. Article 2.1 of the ICESCR, which directly engages with resource allocation, has unfortunately received no attention in the context of HTA. By grounding the analysis in this Article, this book allows the right to health to reclaim its underlying nature as an economic and social right which should shape priority-setting in HTA, in comparison to a restricted "right to a fair share".

By contrast, the prevalent model in global health and health and human rights scholarship, pursuing UHC and the conditions of Daniels' A4R, falls short of disrupting the status quo and economic barriers that are the very reason rationing is needed. Scarcity is primarily to be indiscriminately endured by public institutions, while not being consciously redressed through development policies and political decisions. This traditional approach revolves around accepting scarcity as a rigid reality and not a socially constructed and politically influenced burden that can be overcome through political engagement in resource allocation. A4R, as the underlying framework, wastes the opportunity of political debates to focus on a much too narrow question – namely, "How can we share the existing resources under an expected scarcity?" – instead of conceiving solutions for the causes of preventable scarcity, such as pharmaceutical price gouging or inefficient procurement strategies. This requires a wider understanding of resources determined by State powers to regulate market forces through law.

For countries without sufficient resources, a dangerous discourse gains force with procedural approaches to respond to economic deprivation. This view does not blame scarcity on global inequalities, reckless policy-making

1 Chapter 2, pp. 29–33.

 | HTTPS://DOI.ORG/10.1163/9789004730311-010

and market failures, but unwise spending and lack of priority-setting based on cost-effectiveness to attain the most basic package of services (as with UHC). The same may be said of developing countries that have some pharmaceutical infrastructure and economic power (such as in the case study of Brazil), which can actually make their way past these hurdles by standing up against the market. The orthodox proceduralisation is, ultimately, a very short-sighted method of dealing with scarcity by civic participation, indifferent to the possibilities of adopting principles derived from the ICESCR, which are outlined in this book, such as progressive realisation, maximum available resources, obligations of international cooperation and even non-discrimination for evidence-making.

Moreover, this book makes more than a normative contribution because it empirically demonstrates that, with the correct substantive intervention, a State can foster conditions that define affordability (and, indirectly, cost-effectiveness) to enable an environment conducive to positive HTA recommendations. In the case study, by virtue of laws and access policies, Brazil has created a political space to discuss substantive policies to control prices or reduce the effects of market-motivated scarcity. As an original contribution to the literature, the reports analysed in this book offer examples of the real-world application of the economic and social rights framework to HTA, with conducts amounting to positive steps towards the right to health beyond resource distribution. Resource mobilisation, as demonstrated, may be employed within HTA by virtue of public–private partnerships, price negotiation, fixation of prices and tax discounts to make new technologies more affordable.

What the right to health has to offer to HTA, in this sense, is an effective and empirically grounded theory of change. In development programmes, a theory of change is made up of a set of assumptions to justify programme decisions and strategies towards an ultimate goal for social transformation.[2] The notion of theory of change, in the literature, has been associated with rights-based approaches in steering development policies at the UN level and international

2 Dana H Taplin and Helene Clark, 'Theory of Change Basics: A Primer on Theory of Change' [2012] New York NY: ActKnowledge; Danielle Stein and Craig Valters, 'Understanding Theory of Change in International Development' (Justice and Security Research Programme, International Development Department, LSE 2012) JSRP Paper 1; STAP, 'Theory of Change: A Short Literature Review and Annotated Bibliography' (Scientific and Technical Advisory Panel (STAP), United Nations Global Environment Facility (GEF)) GEF/STAP/C.57/Inf.05 <https://www.thegef.org/council-meeting-documents/theory-change-short-literature-review-and-annotated-bibliography> accessed 3 April 2022.

cooperation.[3] HRBA are, therefore, forms of a theory of change resting on the assumption that fulfilling (attaining rights goals) and respecting rights in the policy process will engender positive social transformation. With this in mind, the international right to health constitutes a productive theory of change for HTA in which every State must limit the preventable weight of scarcity and maximise resources while conscious of any prioritisation needs, at least in the short term. An HTA, grounded in only UHC, on the other hand, seems to lack this programmatic vision and critical approach to political economy, development problems and the root causes of unaffordability.

1 Debunking the Scarcity Assumption of A4R with the Right to Health

This book has called into question the procedural approach to the right to health in resource allocation and, as an alternative, has argued for the entrenchment of substantive obligations within HTA. The overemphasis on procedural approaches in the scholarship and the persistent influence of A4R on priority-setting and the right to health was discussed in Chapter 2. This has led to a flawed understanding, in the literature, of the application of legal frameworks substantively within HTA, in that the right to health was conceived as replicating A4R conditions when it comes to priority-setting. In Chapter 3, we noted that HTA is in fact a product of laws, internally and externally, via internal rules and judicial control, but that it does not need to be limited to procedural approaches to resource allocation and court rulings. The internal and substantive role of law in HTA demonstrates the potential of creating conditions of resource allocation beyond the strict notion of a fair procedure.

Unlike the premises of A4R (which are indifferent to the causes of unfairness in the healthcare market), the theory of change provided by the right to health is, then, a dramatic turn to progressive policies and State intervention. These substantive usages of laws and human rights standards were derived from Article 2.1 of the ICESCR, dictating how States should engage with questions of resources when implementing their resource-related obligations: progressive realisation, maximum available resources, international cooperation, non-discrimination and, implicitly as a subsidiary standard, affordability.

3 See e.g. Vandenhole and Gready (n 3) 292; Paul Gready and Wouter Vandenhole, *Human Rights and Development in the New Millennium: Towards a Theory of Change* (Routledge 2013).

Thus, HTA should be seen as a core social institution, catalysing development and increasing access to healthcare through all available political means.

On this view, Chapter 4 laid down the essential framework set out by the ICESCR, with a focus on resource generation to propose solutions to scarcity before making rationing the conventional instrument. This set of rules was further delineated from Chapters 5 to 7 as guiding tenets that must be embedded throughout HTA. First, international cooperation may at least determine an environment supportive of capacity-building that, if interpreted more rigorously, could also impose a more profound model of assistance towards common regulations and access policies between richer and poorer States. Second, the right to health entails non-discrimination and positive steps to produce evidence where knowledge is scarce, allowing patients to prove personal benefits and specific outcomes not covered by standard research and economic analysis. Non-discrimination is then intertwined with a fair procedure and progressive realisation, as they both guarantee the development of new forms of evidence to promote meaningful engagement of different populations. Third, States should, at the very least, employ their regulatory power to promote conditions that facilitate affordability with immediate effect, in what are termed "legal determinants of scarcity".

Moreover, a procedure-only model is constructed under theoretical conditions or as a method not based on HTA real-life application of priority-setting. As seen in the case study from Brazil, in reality, A4R is not the approach of policymakers who have the willingness and power to control the conditions of scarcity. With the Brazilian model, we have learned that the questions proposed by A4R are insufficient to devise a theory of change necessary to achieve access to resources in Brazil. A fair procedure cannot alone be a theory of change because even if a State applies all Daniels' theory conditions there would be no resulting significant change that would eliminate the causes that make a new technology unaffordable. Despite the wide usage of fair procedure as a normative framework in global health, it is only when States take measures equivalent to the ICESCR principles that implementation occurs despite apparent scarcity. Turning exclusively to A4R in HRBA might be problematic as it could implicitly endorse a system designed for exclusion and inequality among patients, such as pharmaceutical monopolies or poor supply management. In this sense, A4R is based on ideal circumstances of fair-minded decision-makers while discounting the unfair reality of market abuses and deficiencies, which creates the very reasons for rationing.

Therefore, Daniels' theory should not be directly fused with the right to health in international law. An HRBA has procedural elements, but it also opens a new deliberative space where individuals can act constructively to devise strategies to bring scarcity under control. With Daniels' fair procedure, scarcity is a given and the focus should be on making fair choices to attain legitimacy through public deliberation. In an HRBA, the principle is that States shall act in a way that maximises resources and rationing deliberations can only take place when all possible steps have been taken to promote the correct policy environment to ensure access to healthcare. This is not the same as to deny scarcity or be indifferent to resource limitations, but rather a comparatively more flexible attitude that explores alternatives to remediable scarcity during an accountable procedure. HTA, in an HRBA, seizes the opportunity of a fair procedure to influence the market, with in-depth analysis of why a technology is not affordable so as to advance possible solutions.

2 Possible Usages of Economic and Social Rights Principles in HTA and Beyond

The practical implementation of the right to health framework in the HTA environment means more than merely distribution criteria and participatory rules. Though the health and human rights literature has already covered the need for transparency and public participation in deliberations by assimilating A4R, the advocated principles expand State obligations in multiple areas, such as international cooperation, evidence-making, and access policies.

For international cooperation, the right to health could take the centre stage of international standards by requiring States to facilitate knowledge exchange and foster common regulations for affordable prices. Some countries boast a higher level of HTA integration, in particular across Europe, but networks moving towards joint assessments still need to recognise the scope of the right to health in their activities to bring cooperation to the fore of political debates and create conceptual frameworks to reduce world inequalities.[4] This also allows for advocating a broader regime of HTA cooperation, focused on supporting the Global South, as opposed to preferential treatments for wealthy countries capable of generating rapid policy research responses.[5]

4 See, for instance, the conceptualisation of the EUnetHTA with no regard to the right to health: Zoe Garrett, Iñaki Imaz-Iglesia and Anne Willemsen, 'Building a Model of Health Technology Assessment Cooperation: Lessons Learned from EUnetHTA Joint Action 3' (2022) 38 International Journal of Technology Assessment in Health Care 7.

5 For instance, note the emphasis of private organisations, such as the Access Project, to pursue collaboration only with the Global North. 'The ASSESS Project FAQ' (*The ASSESS Project*) <https://assessproject.org/faq> accessed 29 March 2022.

The mainstreaming of the right to health in the process of creation and selection of evidence could be essential to States' acceptance of responsibility over pervasive epistemic injustice towards minorities, vulnerable groups and extra-economic values not covered by current appraisals. Evidence-making should shift towards specific, locally sourced data and patient-centred outcomes, addressing methodological failures and measuring values beyond cost-effectiveness.[6] However, responding to these issues would require significant research investments and new forms of scientific studies. Those efforts should be recognised as routine public policy and State obligation (and not merely the result of gradual, unsupervised or haphazard academic research). Real-world data and coverage along with evidence development are commonly discussed routes to approving technologies with lower levels of research, which could be further promoted apropos the right to health, progressive realisation and non-discrimination.[7] The "three core principles" (3Ps) approach is a robust form of analysis of the implementation of non-discriminatory policies in evidence-making, which should be used as a benchmark for an HRBA to HTA across jurisdictions.[8]

Further, having economic and social rights principles as a legal foundation in HTA would impose the affordability criterion as a vital element of resource allocation. The whole framework of maximum available resources and progressive realisation being coupled to HTA could better signal the State's course of action. Currently, international guidance on possible measures to contain cost and obtain better prices for patients is voluntary in nature, a form of recommendation at best, produced by health economists without the authority and binding force of international law. The framework suggested here would prove to be a much more coherent regime, which introduces

---

6 See e.g. Sophie Staniszewska and Sophie Werkö, 'Patient-Based Evidence in HTA', *Patient Involvement in Health Technology Assessment* (Springer 2017); Sophie Staniszewska and Sophie Söderholm Werkö, 'Mind the Evidence Gap: The Use of Patient-Based Evidence to Create "Complete HTA" in the Twenty-First Century' (2021) 37 International Journal of Technology Assessment in Health Care.

7 See e.g. Augusto Afonso Guerra-Júnior and others, 'Health Technology Performance Assessment: Real-World Evidence for Public Healthcare Sustainability' (2017) 33 International Journal of Technology Assessment in Health Care 279; Hannah Sievers, Angelika Joos and Mickaël Hiligsmann, 'Real-World Evidence: Perspectives on Challenges, Value, and Alignment of Regulatory and National Health Technology Assessment Data Collection Requirements' (2021) 37 International Journal of Technology Assessment in Health Care; Nirosha Mahendraratnam and others, 'Understanding Use of Real-world Data and Real-World Evidence to Support Regulatory Decisions on Medical Product Effectiveness' (2022) 111 Clinical Pharmacology & Therapeutics 150.

8 See chapter 5, 1.1.

access policies as a duty by which States must enforce better market conditions, even if the industry is not interested in promoting affordability or negotiating prices.

Scholarship and expert guidance on HTA have so far consisted of non-legal or policy recommendations which, contrary to the framework in this book, are not formally authoritative (from a State's position) and would not primarily contribute to global health governance grounded in human rights. Frameworks derived from HTA implementation, organisational guidelines and policy research may be too constrained by their common terminology and traditional non-human rights focus – HTA guidance works around "good practices" or concepts of cost-effectiveness, value or even financial sustainability.[9]

These notions are not enough to incorporate human rights-centred perspectives, including affordability and progressive realisation as State-binding obligations.[10] Value and cost-effectiveness are not the indicators generally overseen in measures of State compliance to progressive realisation. Thus, traditional HTA standards advanced elsewhere would not permit HTA to be reviewed systematically by monitoring mechanisms available in HR systems as treaty obligations in order to pursue maximum available resources. By working with HR principles as part of a legally authoritative and globally consolidated framework, HTA institutions could gain legitimacy and be taken into consideration through HR reports and complaints methods. Human rights measuring and compliance could be enhanced by evaluating the HTA influence over resource mobilisation in non-monetary terms by State powers, such as market regulation or adequate procurement mechanisms. HTA bodies would then become a good source of information of whether a State is committed to organising a health system according to human rights principles and whether it has in place targeted policies to mobilise resources by restricting unaffordability of healthcare, where achievable, before rationing is the standard response.

Furthermore, the proposed framework can be extended to resource allocation beyond HTA to address any resource-dependent healthcare policymaking. During the COVID-19 pandemic, the CESCR brought attention to

9 See e.g.: Francesca Iandolo and others, 'From Health Technology Assessment to Health Technology Sustainability' (2018) 10 Sustainability 4748; Finn Børlum Kristensen and Don Husereau, 'Identifying the Need for Good Practices in Health Technology Assessment: Summary of the ISPOR HTA Council Working Group Report on Good Practices in HTA (Online Appendix)' 46; Darius N Lakdawalla and others, 'Defining Elements of Value in Health Care – A Health Economics Approach: An ISPOR Special Task Force Report [3]' (2018) 21 Value in Health 131.

10 See chapter 7, pp. 176–180.

"an extraordinary resource mobilisation" for long-term human rights concretisation, in times when many countries were presented with extraordinary rationing dilemmas.[11] In its statement, the Committee held that States parties must "adopt appropriate regulatory measures to ensure that health-care resources in both the public and the private sectors are mobilised and shared among the whole population to ensure a comprehensive, coordinated health-care response to the crisis". Thus, not only are States expected to devote their highest capacity of resources, they must "make every effort to mobilize the necessary resources to combat COVID-19 in the most equitable manner".[12] The recommendations, similar to what has been identified as a positive step in HTA, give some insights into which policies could be in place alongside priority-setting (debt relief, intellectual property flexibilities, market control for affordability such as anti-competition regulation, subsidies, tax relief, and international assistance and cooperation).[13]

However, as it has been developed on a principled basis, this framework could be further modified by future human rights practice as norms could be more clearly defined in terms of the entire range of resources to be mobilised and a reasonable time for progressive realisation could be allowed. So far, as commented by this author elsewhere, these notions still suffer from considerable uncertainty as to the precise immediate obligations during acute scarcity for unpredictable crises or catastrophes, a problem that is impossible to address in the short term.[14]

3 Towards a Full HRBA across Other Human Rights in HTA

The model of HRBA, as developed in this book, is solely grounded in the right to health and the general implementation obligations for economic and social rights. But a real engagement with rights beyond A4R may merit moving towards other human rights under international law to provide substantive standards for HTA institutionalisation. In terms of priority-setting criteria, a lingering question is what the interdependency and indivisibility of human

11 CESCR, 'Statement on the Coronavirus Disease (COVID-19) Pandemic and Economic, Social and Cultural Rights', 2020 (Pub. L. No. E/C.12/2020/1) 13.

12 Ibid, arts. 17, 19, 21.

13 Ibid.

14 Luciano Bottini Filho, 'State Positive Obligations and the International Right to Health in Epidemics: How Much Should Be Enough?' in Shinya Murase and Suzane Zhou (eds), *Epidemics and International Law*, International Relation Series, vol 22 (Brill 2021) 404–405.

rights mean and how progressive realisation and resource allocation would be delivered for competing needs and obligations across multiple human rights (civil and political as well).[15] As it stands, applying the full spectrum of rights to HTA requires a much more detailed doctrinal interpretation. Such an approach could also be tested in relation to the decision-making of the entire governmental budget in broader policies, not limited to healthcare. Considering the foregoing analysis of coupling resource prioritisation with mobilisation, two rights come to the fore as useful sources of HTA standards: the right to development and the right to access to science.

First, the burgeoning right to development (under a treaty proposal) is a plausible step in connecting substantive policies, market regulation and HTA institutionalisation.[16] Health and human rights scholars have also defended adopting a right to development framework to address public health policies and global health governance.[17] This book has shown how the UHC discourse has dominated global health relations, but the way in which HTA international cooperation could be interpreted under the right to development would turn the focus towards infrastructure and political power to invest in resilience and social transformation, as opposed to health systems being viewed as resource wasters that need to be educated in good habits. It seems fairly unlikely that the right to development would be compatible with HTA institutionalisation dissociated from increasing governmental bargaining powers and contractual terms of healthcare supply (instead of strict sustainable spending by excluding services). Second, HTA depends on scien-

15 See e.g. James W Nickel, 'Rethinking Indivisibility: Towards a Theory of Supporting Relations between Human Rights' (2008) 30 Human Rights Quarterly 984; Ida Elisabeth Koch, 'The Justifiability of Indivisible Rights' (2003) 72 Nordic Journal of International Law 3; Lanse Minkler and Shawna Sweeney, 'On the Indivisibility and Interdependence of Basic Rights in Developing Countries' (2011) 33 Human Rights Quarterly 351; Alberto Quintavalla and Klaus Heine, 'Priorities and Human Rights' (2019) 23 The International Journal of Human Rights 679.

16 HRC, "Draft Convention on the Right to Development, with commentaries" 20 January 2020 (A/HRC/WG.2/21/2/Add.1).

17 See e.g. Ashley M Fox and Benjamin Mason Meier, 'Health as Freedom: Addressing Social Determinants of Global Health Inequities through the Human Right to Development' (2009) 23 Bioethics 112; Benjamin Mason Meier and Ashley M Fox, 'Development as Health: Employing the Collective Right to Development to Achieve the Goals of the Individual Right to Health' (2008) 30 Hum. Rts. Q. 259; Stephen P Marks, 'Integrating a Human Rights-Based Approach to Development and the Right to Development into Global Governance for Health' in Lawrence Gostin and Benjamin Manson Meier (eds), *Human Rights in Global Health: Rights-Based Governance for a Globalizing World* (Oxford University Press 2018); Stephen Marks, 'Health, Development, and Human Rights' in Anna Gatti and Andrea Boggio (eds), *Health and Development* (Springer 2009).

tific knowledge, evidence-making and interdisciplinary analysis, all unquestionably falling under the remit of the right to access to science (which has addressed only IP laws as legal determinants of scarcity).[18]

In light of parallel human rights standards, a clear limitation of this research was its exclusive focus on the right to health. Future studies could fruitfully explore the implications of interpreting the entire spectrum of international human rights obligations within HTA. Such an inquiry would open valuable perspectives on the repercussions for priority-setting if policies were required to account for a wider range of substantive rights – such as education or work – whose fulfilment may hinge on access to new healthcare technologies (for example, assistive devices). New methodologies could be established by ensuring that patient values and the perspectives of vulnerable groups, in relation to those rights, are meaningfully included in the generation of evidence on quality of life and healthcare outcomes (as discussed in Chapter 5). In this way, HTA could move beyond a narrow health focus towards a rights-sensitive framework that embeds human rights aspirations as intrinsic to healthcare decision-making.[19]

18 CESCR, "General Comment No. 25" (chapter 6, n 70).

19 See chapter 5, pp. 136–141.

Bibliography

Abbott FM, 'Excessive Pharmaceutical Prices and Competition Law: Doctrinal Development to Protect Public Health' 6 UC Irvine Law Review 281

Abbott FM and Reichman JH, 'Facilitating Access to Cross-Border Supplies of Patented Pharmaceuticals: The Case of the COVID-19 Pandemic' (2020) 23 Journal of International Economic Law 535

Abelson J and others, 'Bringing "the Public" into Health Technology Assessment and Coverage Policy Decisions: From Principles to Practice' (2007) 82 Health Policy 37

Abrishami P, Oortwijn W and Hofmann B, 'Ethics in HTA: Examining the "Need for Expansion"' (2017) 6 International Journal of Health Policy and Management 551

Aceves WJ, 'Cost-Benefit Analysis and Human Rights' (2018) 92 St. John's Law Review 431

Aceves WJ, 'Valuing Life: A Human Rights Perspective on the Calculus of Regulation' (2018) 36 Law and Inequality: A Journal of Theory and Practice 1

Ago R, 'Document A/CN.4/302 AND ADD.1-3 (Sixth Report on State Responsibility)' (1977) II Yearbook of the International Law Commission 3

Ahlert M, Breyer F and Schwettmann L, 'How You Ask Is What You Get: Framing Effects in Willingness-to-Pay for a QALY' (2016) 150 Social Science & Medicine 40

Akehurst RL and others, 'Variation in Health Technology Assessment and Reimbursement Processes in Europe' (2017) 20 Value in Health 67

Akobeng AK, 'Understanding Randomised Controlled Trials' (2005) 90 Archives of disease in childhood 840

Aleman A and Galan AP, 'Impact of Health Technology Assessment in Litigation Concerning Access to High-Cost Drugs' (2017) 33 International Journal of Technology Assessment in Health Care 411

Al-Janabi H and others, 'An Investigation of the Construct Validity of the ICECAP-A Capability Measure' (2013) 22 Quality of Life Research 1831

Alston P, 'Out of the Abyss: The Challenges Confronting the New U.N. Committee on Economic, Social and Cultural Rights' (1987) 9 Human Rights Quarterly 332

Alston P and Quinn G, 'The Nature and Scope of States Parties' Obligations under the International Covenant on Economic, Social and Cultural Rights' (1987) 9 Human Rights Quarterly 156

Alves ISC, 'JUDICIALIZAÇÃO DO DIREITO À SAÚDE OU SAUDICIALIZAÇÃO DO JUDICIÁRIO: uma análise da audiência pública n° 4 do STF' (Sociedade Brasileira de Direito Público)

Andersen H, 'Mechanisms: What Are They Evidence for in Evidence-Based Medicine?: Mechanisms Evidence for What?' (2012) 18 Journal of Evaluation in Clinical Practice 992

 | HTTPS://DOI.ORG/10.1163/9789004730311-011

Andreassen B-A and others, 'Assessing Human Rights Performance in Developing Countries: The Case for a Minimal Threshold Approach to the Economic and Social Rights' (1987) 1997–1998 Yearbook of Human Rights in Developing Countries 333

Arambulo K, *Strengthening the Supervision of the International Covenant on Economic, Social and Cultural Rights: Theoretical and Procedural Aspects* (Intersentia 1999)

Arduin S, 'Article 3: General Principles' in Ilias Bantekas, Michael Ashley Stein and Dimitris Anastasiou (eds), *The Convention on the Rights of Persons with Disabilities: A Commentary* (Oxford University Press 2018)

Argyrou A, 'Making the Case for Case Studies in Empirical Legal Research' (2017) 13 Utrecht Law Review 19

Arickx F and others, 'Public Tendering for off Patent Medicines in Belgium: The Simvastatin Case' (National Institute for Health and Disability Insurance 2009)

Arndt C and others, 'A Human Rights-Consistent Approach to Multidimensional Welfare Measurement Applied to Sub-Saharan Africa' (2018) 108 World Development 181

Arora P and others, 'The Inflation Reduction Act: An Opportunity to Accelerate Confidence in Real-World Evidence in the United States' (2024) 27 Value in Health 999

Arosemena G, *Rights, Scarcity, and Justice: An Analytical Inquiry Into the Adjudication of the Welfare Aspects of Human Rights* (Intersentia 2014)

Arras JD and Fenton EM, 'Access to Health-Related Goods' (2009) 39 Hastings Center Report 27

Arzymanow B and Manning J, 'Value-Based Pricing: The Wrong Medicine for the Nation?' (20/20health 2014) <https://2020health.org/publication/value-based-pricing-the-wrong-medicine-for-the-nation/> accessed 21 January 2020

Ashcroft R, 'Fair Process and the Redundancy of Bioethics: A Polemic' (2008) 1 Public Health Ethics 3

Ashcroft R, 'Current Epistemological Problems in Evidence Based Medicine' (2004) 30 Journal of Medical Ethics 131

Aust A, 'The Theory and Practice of Informal International Instruments' (1986) 35 International & Comparative Law Quarterly 787

Aydin U, 'Competition Law & Policy in Developing Countries: Explaining Variations in Outcomes; Exploring Possibilities and Limits' (2016) 79 Law and Contemporary Problems 1

Bae J-M, 'Value-Based Medicine: Concepts and Application' (2015) 37 Epidemiology and Health

Baillie R, 'Judicial Restraint When Reviewing Heath Care Rationing Decisions: A Healthy Approach' (2012) 18 Auckland UL Rev. 137

Bakhoum M, 'The Interface between Intellectual Property Rights and Competition Law: Implications for Public Health in Sub-Saharan Africa' in Deborah Healey, Michael Jacobs and Rhonda L. Smith (eds), *Research Handbook on Methods and Models of Competition Law* (Edward Elgar Publishing 2020)

Bala MV, Mauskopf JA and Wood LL, 'Willingness to Pay as a Measure of Health Benefits' (1999) 15 Pharmacoeconomics 9

Balakrishnan R and Douglass College, 'Maximum Available Resources and Human Rights: Analytical Report' (Center for Women's Global Leadership 2011)

Balakrishnan R, Heintz J and Elson D, *Rethinking Economic Policy for Social Justice: The Radical Potential of Human Rights* (Routledge 2016)

Baldi S and Vannoni D, 'The Impact of Centralization on Pharmaceutical Procurement Prices: The Role of Institutional Quality and Corruption' (2017) 51 Regional Studies 426

Baltussen R and others, 'Priority Setting for Universal Health Coverage: We Need Evidence-Informed Deliberative Processes, Not Just More Evidence on Cost-Effectiveness' (2016) 5 International Journal of Health Policy and Management 615

Baltussen R and others, 'Value Assessment Frameworks for HTA Agencies: The Organization of Evidence-Informed Deliberative Processes' (2017) 20 Value in Health 256

Baltussen R and others, 'Progressive Realisation of Universal Health Coverage: What Are the Required Processes and Evidence?' (2017) 2 BMJ Global Health e000342

Baltussen R, Jansen M and Oortwijn W, 'Evidence-Informed Deliberative Processes for Legitimate Health Benefit Package Design – Part I: Conceptual Framework' [2021] International Journal of Health Policy and Management 1

Banta D, 'The Development of Health Technology Assessment' (2003) 63 Health Policy 121

Banta D, 'What Is Technology Assessment?' (2009) 25 International Journal of Technology Assessment in Health Care 7

Banta D and Almeida RT, 'The Development of Health Technology Assessment in Brazil' (2009) 25 International Journal of Technology Assessment in Health Care 255

Banta D, Jonsson E and Childs P, 'History of the International Societies in Health Technology Assessment: International Society for Technology Assessment in Health Care and Health Technology Assessment International' (2009) 25 International Journal of Technology Assessment in Health Care

Beall RF, Kuhn R and Attaran A, 'Compulsory Licensing Often Did Not Produce Lower Prices for Antiretrovirals Compared to International Procurement' (2015) 34 Health Affairs 493 <https://doi.org/10.1377/hlthaff.2014.0658>

Beetham D, 'What Future for Economic and Social Rights?' (1995) 43 Political Studies 41

Beneluxa, 'The Beneluxa Initiative on Pharmaceutical Policy: Terms of Reference' <https://beneluxa.org/sites/beneluxa.org/files/2018-10/180622%20Terms%20of%20Reference%20Beneluxa%20Initiative.pdf> accessed 5 May 2020

Berger J, 'Advancing Public Health by Other Means: Using Competition Policy' in P Roffe and DV Eugui (eds), *Negotiating Health: Intellectual Property and Access to Medicines* (Taylor & Francis 2012)

Bergner M and Rothman ML, 'Health Status Measures: An Overview and Guide for Selection' (1987) 8 Annual Review of Public Health 191

Bernier L and others, 'Legal Governance in HTA: Environment, Health and Safety Issues / Ethical, Legal and Social Issues (EHSI/ELSI), the Ongoing Debate' (2020) 3 Canadian Journal of Bioethics / Revue canadienne de bioéthique <https://doi.org/10.7202/1070226ar> accessed 30 July 2020

Bertram M, Dhaene G and Tan-Torres Edejer T (eds), *Institutionalizing Health Technology Assessments: A How to Guide* (World Health Organization 2021)

Berwick DM, Nolan TW and Whittington J, 'The Triple Aim: Care, Health, and Cost' (2008) 27 Health affairs 759

Betancourt JR, 'In Pursuit of High-Value Healthcare: The Case for Improving Quality and Achieving Equity in a Time of Healthcare Transformation' (2014) 30 Frontiers of health services management 16

Biehl J and others, 'Between the Court and the Clinic: Lawsuits for Medicines and the Right to Health in Brazil' (2012) 14 Health and Human Rights 36

Bilchitz D, 'Socio-Economic Rights, Economic Crisis, and Legal Doctrine' (2014) 12 International Journal of Constitutional Law 710

Birchall D, 'Human Rights and Political Economy: Violations and Realization Under Global Capitalism' [2021] SSRN Electronic Journal <http://dx.doi.org/10.2139/ssrn.3780591> accessed 5 May 2021

Blyberg A and Hofbauer H, *Article 2 and Governments' Budgets* (International Budget Partnership 2014) <https://www.internationalbudget.org/publications/escrarticle2/> accessed 21 February 2021

Bódig M, 'Soft Law, Doctrinal Development, and the General Comments of the UN Committee on Economic, Social and Cultural Rights' in Stéphanie Lagoutte, Thomas Gammeltoft-Hansen and John Cerone (eds), *Tracing the Roles of Soft Law in Human Rights* (Oxford University Press 2016)

Bogecho D and Upreti M, 'The Global Gag Rule: An Antithesis to the Rights-Based Approach to Health' (2006) 9 Health and Human Rights 17

Bognar G, 'Does Cost Effectiveness Analysis Unfairly Discriminate against People with Disabilities?: Cost Effectiveness Analysis and People with Disabilities' (2010) 27 Journal of Applied Philosophy 394

Bognar G, 'Impartiality and Disability Discrimination' (2011) 21 Kennedy Institute of Ethics Journal 1

Bognar G and Hirose I, *The Ethics of Health Care Rationing: An Introduction* (Routledge 2014)

Bombard Y and others, 'Eliciting Ethical and Social Values in Health Technology Assessment: A Participatory Approach' (2011) 73 Social Science & Medicine 135

Borges D da CL, 'Individual Inputs and Collective Outputs: Understanding the Structural Benefits of Individual Litigation on Healthcare in Brazil' in Marlies Hesselman, Antenor Hallo de Wolf and Brigit Toebes (eds), *Socio-Economic Human Rights in Essential Public Services Provision* (Routledge 2016)

Borges D da CL, 'Individual Health Care Litigation in Brazil through a Different Lens: Strengthening Health Technology Assessment and New Models of Health Care Governance' (2018) 20 Health and Human Rights 147

Bottini Filho L, 'State Positive Obligations and the International Right to Health in Epidemics: How Much Should Be Enough?' in Shinya Murase and Suzane Zhou (eds), *Epidemics and International Law*, vol 22 (Brill 2021)

Braunack-Mayer A, 'Health Technology Assessment: Ethical, Legal and Social Issues' in Stella R Quah (ed), *International Encyclopedia of Public Health (Second Edition)* (Academic Press 2017)

Brazier JE and others, 'Future Directions in Valuing Benefits for Estimating QALYs: Is Time Up for the EQ-5D?' (2019) 22 Value in Health 62

Brekke KR, Grasdal AL and Holmås TH, 'Regulation and Pricing of Pharmaceuticals: Reference Pricing or Price Cap Regulation?' (2009) 53 European Economic Review 170

Brekke KR, Königbauer I and Straume OR, 'Reference Pricing of Pharmaceuticals' (2007) 26 Journal of Health Economics 613

Brems E, 'Human Rights: Minimum and Maximum Perspectives' (2009) 9 Human Rights Law Review 349

Brems E and Lavrysen L, 'Procedural Justice in Human Rights Adjudication: The European Court of Human Rights' (2013) 35 Human Rights Quarterly 176

Breslau RM and others, 'A Review of HTA Guidelines on Societal and Novel Value Elements' (2023) 39 International Journal of Technology Assessment in Health Care e31

Brock DW, 'Broadening the Bioethics Agenda' (2000) 10 Kennedy Institute of Ethics Journal 21

Brody BA, 'Why the Right to Health Care Is Not a Useful Concept for Policy Debates' *Rights to health care* (Springer 1991)

Brolan CE and others, 'The Right to Health of Non-nationals and Displaced Persons in the Sustainable Development Goals Era: Challenges for Equity in Universal Health Care' (2017) 16 International Journal for Equity in Health 14

Brolan CE, Hill PS and Ooms G, '"Everywhere but Not Specifically Somewhere": A Qualitative Study on Why the Right to Health Is Not Explicit in the Post-2015 Negotiations' (2015) 15 BMC International Health and Human Rights

Bronfenbrenner M, 'The Scarcity Hypothesis in Modern Economics' (1962) 21 The American Journal of Economics and Sociology 265

Brouwer WBF and others, 'Welfarism vs. Extra-Welfarism' (2008) 27 Journal of Health Economics 325

Brouwer WBF and Rutten FFH, 'The Efficiency Frontier Approach to Economic Evaluation: Will It Help German Policy Making?' (2010) 19 Health Economics 1128

Brown MM and others, 'Evidence-Based Medicine, Utilities, and Quality of Life': (1999) 10 Current Opinion in Ophthalmology 221

Browne J and Cryer D, 'Is the QALY Fit for Purpose?' (2021) 9 The American Journal of Accountable Care 8

Buchanan AE, 'The Right to a Decent Minimum of Health Care' (1984) 13 Philosophy & Public Affairs 55

Burci GL, 'Global Health Law: Present and Future' in Gian Luca Burci and Brigit Toebes (eds), *Research Handbook on Global Health Law* (Edward Elgar Publishing 2018)

Byskov J and others, 'The Need for Global Application of the Accountability for Reasonableness Approach to Support Sustainable Outcomes Comment on "Expanded HTA: Enhancing Fairness and Legitimacy"' (2016) 6 International Journal of Health Policy and Management 115

Caetano R and others, 'Incorporação de Novos Medicamentos Pela Comissão Nacional de Incorporação de Tecnologias Do SUS, 2012 a Junho de 2016' (2017) 22 Ciência & Saúde Coletiva 2513

Calabresi G and Bobbitt P, *Tragic Choices* (Norton 1978)

Calcagno C, Chapsal A and White J, 'Economics of Excessive Pricing: An Application to the Pharmaceutical Industry' (2019) 10 Journal of European Competition Law & Practice 166

Callahan D, 'Reasonableness and Politics' in Akira Akabayashi (ed), *The Future of Bioethics: International Dialogues* (1st ed, Oxford University Press 2014)

Campillo-Artero C and others, 'Price Models for Multi-indication Drugs: A Systematic Review' (2020) 18 Applied Health Economics and Health Policy 47

Carlson JJ and others, 'Alternative Approaches to Quality-Adjusted Life-Year Estimation within Standard Cost-Effectiveness Models: Literature Review, Feasibility Assessment, and Impact Evaluation' (2020) 23 Value in Health 1523

Carmona MS, 'The Obligations of "International Assistance and Cooperation" under the International Covenant on Economic, Social and Cultural Rights. A Possible Entry Point to a Human Rights Based Approach to Millennium Development Goal 8' (2009) 13 The International Journal of Human Rights 86

Carmona MS, 'Alternatives to Austerity: A Human Rights Framework for Economic Recovery' in Aoife Nolan (ed), *Economic and Social Rights after the Global Financial Crisis* (Cambridge University Press 2014)

Caro JJ and others, 'The Efficiency Frontier Approach to Economic Evaluation of Health-Care Interventions' (2010) 19 Health economics 1117

Cenci A and Hussain MA, 'Epistemic and Non-epistemic Values in Economic Evaluations of Public Health' (2020) 27 Journal of Economic Methodology 66

Černič JL, 'The European Court of Human Rights, Rule of Law and Socio-economic Rights in Times of Crises' (2016) 8 Hague Journal on the Rule of Law 227

Chalkidou K and others, 'Health Technology Assessment in Universal Health Coverage' (2013) 382 The Lancet e48

Chalkidou K and others, 'Health Technology Assessment: Global Advocacy and Local Realities Comment on "Priority Setting for Universal Health Coverage: We Need Evidence-Informed Deliberative Processes, Not Just More Evidence on Cost-Effectiveness"' (2016) 6 International Journal of Health Policy and Management 233

Chapman A, 'The Foundations of a Human Right to Health: Human Rights and Bioethics in Dialogue.' (2015) 17 Health and Human Rights

Chapman AR, 'A Violations Approach for Monitoring the International Covenant on Economic, Social and Cultural Rights' (1996) 18 Human Rights Quarterly 23

Chapman AR, 'Core Obligations Related to the Right to Health' in Sage Russell and Audrey R Chapman (eds), *Core Obligations: Building a Framework for Economic, Social and Cultural Rights* (Intersentia 2002)

Chapman AR, *Global Health, Human Rights and the Challenge of Neoliberal Policies* (Cambridge University Press 2016)

Chapman AR, 'Assessing the Universal Health Coverage Target in the Sustainable Development Goals from a Human Rights Perspective' (2016) 16 BMC International Health and Human Rights

Charles Foster, 'Simple Rationality? The Law of Healthcare Resource Allocation in England' (2007) 33 Journal of Medical Ethics 404

Charlton V, 'NICE and Fair? Health Technology Assessment Policy Under the UK's National Institute for Health and Care Excellence, 1999–2018' (2020) 28 Health Care Analysis 193

Charlton V, 'Cost Effective but Unaffordable: An Emerging Challenge for Health Systems' [2017] BMJ j1402

Charlton V, 'We Need to Talk about Values: A Proposed Framework for the Articulation of Normative Reasoning in Health Technology Assessment' [2023] Health Economics, Policy and Law 1

Charvel S and others, 'Challenges in Priority Setting from a Legal Perspective in Brazil, Costa Rica, Chile, and Mexico' (2018) 20 Health and Human Rights 173

Chen S and others, 'Fangcang Shelter Hospitals: A Novel Concept for Responding to Public Health Emergencies' (2020) 395 The Lancet 1305

Choi Y, Fabic MS and Adetunji J, 'Measuring Access to Family Planning: Conceptual Frameworks and DHS Data' (2016) 47 Studies in Family Planning 145

Chopra NS and Muthappa D, 'The Curious Case of Compulsory Licensing in India' (2012) 8 Competition Law International 34

Cinaroglu S and Baser O, 'Network among HTA Ecosystem' (2019) 9 Health and Technology 153

Clarke D, 'Law, Regulation and Strategizing for Health' in Gerard Schmets and others (eds), *Strategizing national health in the 21st century: a handbook* (World Health Organization 2016)

Clarke D, Dhaene G and Lisman J, 'Legal Considerations: Reviewing or Establishing the Legal Framework.' in Melanie Bertram, Gwenaël Dhaene and Tessa Tan-Torres Edejer (eds), *Institutionalizing health technology assessment mechanisms: a how to guide* (World Health Organization 2021)

Coast J, 'Is Economic Evaluation in Touch with Society's Health Values?' (2004) 329 BMJ 1233

Coast J, Smith RD and Lorgelly P, 'Welfarism, Extra-Welfarism and Capability: The Spread of Ideas in Health Economics' (2008) 67 Social Science and Medicine 1190

Cochrane AL, *Effectiveness and Efficiency: Random Reflections on Health Services*, vol 900574178 (Nuffield Provincial Hospitals Trust London 1972)

Committee on Economic, Social and Cultural Rights, 'General Comment No. 20, Non-discrimination in Economic, Social and Cultural Rights (Art. 2, Para. 2, of the International Covenant on Economic, Social and Cultural Rights)' (2009) E/C.12/GC/20

Committee on Economic, Social and Cultural Rights, 'General Comment No. 22 (2016) on the Right to Sexual and Reproductive Health (Article 12 of the International Covenant on Economic, Social and Cultural Rights)' (2016) E/C.12/GC/22

Conitec, 'Medicamentos Biológicos (Infliximabe, Etanercepte, Adalimumabe Eustequinumabe) Para o Tratamento Da Psoríase Moderada a Grave Em Adultos' (Conitec 2012) 13

Conitec, 'Inibidores de Protease (Boceprevir e Telaprevir) Para o Tratamento Da Hepatite Crônica C' (Conitec 2012) 01

Conitec, 'Medicamentos Biológicos (Infliximabe, Etanercepte, Adalimumabe, Rituximabe, Abatacepte, Tocilizumabe, Golimumabe e Certolizumabe Pegol) Para o Tratamento Da Artrite Reumatóide' (Conitec 2012) 12

Conitec, 'Trastuzumabe Para Tratamento Do Câncer de Mama Avançado' (Conitec 2012) 08

Conitec, 'Maraviroque Para Pacientes Em Terapia Antirretroviral' (Conitec 2012) 14

Conitec, 'Fator VIII de Origem Recombinante Para Profilaxia Primária e Tratamento de Pacientes Com Hemofilia A' (Conitec 2012) 48

Conitec, 'Brometo de Tiotrópio Para Tratamento Da Doença Pulmonar Obstrutiva Crônica' (Conitec 2013) 68

Conitec, 'Cadeira de Rodas Motorizada Na Tabela de Órteses, Proteses e Materiais Especiais Nao Relacionados Ao Ato Cirurgico Do SUS' (Conitec 2013) 50

Conitec, 'Cadeira de Rodas Tipo Monobloco e Cadeira de Rodas (Acima de 90 Kg) Na Tabela de Órteses, Proteses e Materiais Especiais Nao Relacionados Ao Ato Cirurgico Do SUS' (Conitec 2013) 52

Conitec, 'Canaquinumabe- Síndromes Periódicas Associadas à Criopirina(CAPS)' (Conitec 2013) 76

Conitec, 'Sistema Intrauterino Liberador de Levonorgestrel Para o Tratamento Da Menorragia Idiopática' (Conitec 2013) 60

Conitec, 'Vacina Tetraviral (Sarampo, Caxumba, Rubéola e Varicela)' (Conitec 2013) 21

Conitec, 'Cadeira de Rodas Para Banho Em Concha Infantil, Cadeira de Rodas Para Banho Com Encosto Reclinável e Cadeira de Rodas Para Banho Com Aro de Propulsão Na Tabela de Órteses, Próteses e Materiais Especiais Não Relacionados Ao Ato Cirúrgico Do SUS' (Conitec 2013) 53

Conitec, 'Adaptação Postural Em Cadeira de Rodas Na Tabela de Órteses, Próteses e Materiais Especiais Do SUS' (Conitec 2013) 51

Conitec, 'Vacina Contra HPV Na Prevenção de Câncer de Colo Do Útero' (Conitec 2013) 83

Conitec, 'Procedimento Bengala de 4 Pontas Na Tabela de Órteses, Proteses e Materiais Especiais Nao Relacionados Ao Ato Cirurgico Do SUS' (Conitec 2013) 83

Conitec, 'Ambrisentana e Bosentana Para o Tratamento Da Hipertensão Arterial Pulmonar' (Conitec 2013) 90

Conitec, 'Erlotinibe Para Câncer de Pulmão de Células Não Pequenas' (Conitec 2013) 63

Conitec, 'Gefitinibe Para Câncer de Pulmão de Células Não Pequenas Em Primeira Linha' (Conitec 2013) 62

Conitec, 'Everolimo Para Tratamento Do Câncer de Mama Avançado Na Pós-Menopausa' (Conitec 2013) 91

Conitec, 'Implante de Válvulas Endobronquiais Unidirecionais Para Tratamento Do Enfisema Pulmonar Heterogêneo' (Conitec 2014) 122

Conitec, 'Procedimenots Relativos à Assistência à Saúde Auditiva Hospitalar Na Tabela Do SUS' (Conitec 2014) 99

Conitec, 'Teste Do Coraçãozinho (Oximetria de Pulso) Na Triagem NeoNatal' (Conitec 2014) 115

Conitec, 'Fingolimode Para o Tratamento Da Esclerose Múltipla' (Conitec 2014) 113

Conitec;, 'Stent Farmacológico Para o Tratamento Da Doença Arterial Coronariana (DAC)' (Conitec 2014) 111

Conitec, 'Alfataliglicerase Para o Tratamento Da Doença de Gaucher' (Conitec 2014) 124

Conitec, 'Talidomida Para Tratamento Da Síndrome Mielodisplásica' (Conitec 2014) 134

Conitec, 'Cipionato de Hidrocortisona, Comprimidos de 10 Mg e 20 Mg, Para Tratamento de Hiperplasia Adrenal Congênita de Recém-Nascidos Diagnosticados No Programa Nacional de Triagem Neonatal- PNTN' (Conitec 2015) 146

Conitec, 'Simeprevir, Sofosbuvir e Daclatasvir No Tratamento Da Hepatite Crônica Tipo C e Coinfecções' (Conitec 2015) 164

Conitec, 'Abatacepte Para o Tratamento Da Artrite Reumatoide Moderada a Grave' (Conitec 2015) 133

Conitec, 'Clozapina, Lamotrigina, Olanzapina, Quetiapina e Risperidona Para o Tratamento Do Transtorno Afetivo Bipolar' (Conitec 2015) 140

Conitec, 'Cinacalcete e Paricalcitol Para o Tratamento de Pacientes Com Hiperparatireoidismo Secundário à Doença Renal (HPTS), Em Diálise e Refratários à Terapia Convenciona' (Conitec 2015) 176

Conitec, 'Everolimo Para Imunossupressão Em Transplante Hepático Em Adultos' (Conitec 2015) 174

Conitec, 'Veruprevir, Ritonavir, Ombitasvir e Dasabuvir Para o Tratamento de Hepatite C Crônica Causada Por Infecção Pelo Genótipo 1 Do HCV' (Conitec 2015) 197

Conitec, 'Tofacitinibe Para o Tratamento de Pacientes Adultos Com Artrite Reumatoide Ativa Moderada a Grave Com Resposta Inadequada a Um Ou Mais Medicamentos Modificadores Do Curso Da Doença' (Conitec 2016) 241

Conitec, 'Apixabana, Rivoraxabana e Dabigratana Em Pacientes Com Fibrilação Atrial Não Valvar' (Conitec 2016) 195

Conitec, 'Implante Subdérmico Liberador de Etonogestrel 68 Mg Para Anticoncepção Em Mulheres de 15 a 19 Anos de Idade.' (Conitec 2016) 208

Conitec, 'Antibiótico Inalatório (Tobramicina) Para Colonização Das Vias Aéreas Em Pacientes Com Fibrose Cística' (Conitec 2016) 217

Conitec, 'Veruprevir, Ritonavir, Ombitasvir e Dasabuvir Para o Tratamento de Hepatite C Crônica Causada Por Infecção Pelo Genótipo 1 Do HCV' (Conitec 2016) 233

Conitec, 'Teriflunomida Para Primeira Linha de Tratamento Da Esclerose Múltipla Remitente Recorrente' (Conitec 2017) 259

Conitec, 'Fumarato de Dimetila No Tratamento Da Esclerose Múltipla Remitente-Recorrente Após Falha Com Betainterferona Ou Glatirâmer' (Conitec 2017) 286

Conitec, 'Pertuzumabe Para o Tratamento Do Câncer de Mama HER2-Positivo Metastático Em Primeira Linha de Tratamento Associado Ao Trastuzumabe e Docetaxel' (Conitec 2017) 319

Conti RM, Nguyen KH and Rosenthal MB, 'Generic Prescription Drug Price Increases: Which Products Will Be Affected by Proposed Anti-Gouging Legislation?' (2018) 11 Journal of Pharmaceutical Policy and Practice 29

Cookson R, 'Willingness to Pay Methods in Health Care: A Sceptical View' (2003) 12 Health Economics 891

Cookson R, 'QALYs and the Capability Approach' (2005) 14 Health economics 817

Cookson R, 'Using Cost-Effectiveness Analysis to Address Health Equity Concerns' (2017) 20 Value in Health 206

Corten O, 'Reasonableness in International Law' *Max Planck Encyclopedias of International Law* (Oxford University Press) <https://www.oxfordbibliographies.com/view/document/obo-9780199796953/obo-9780199796953-0127.xml> accessed 27 July 2019

Craven MCR, *The International Covenant on Economic, Social, and Cultural Rights: A Perspective on Its Development* (Clarendon Press 1998)

Crowther H, Lipworth W and Kerridge I, 'Evidence-Based Medicine and Epistemological Imperialism: Narrowing the Divide between Evidence and Illness: EBM and Epistemological Imperialism' (2011) 17 Journal of Evaluation in Clinical Practice 868

Cubillos L and others, 'Universal Health Coverage and Litigation in Latin America' (2012) 26 Journal of Health Organization and Management 390

Culyer AJ, 'Four Issues in Cost-Effectiveness Analysis and Health Technology Assessment: A View from the Touch-Line' in Juan E del Llano-Señarís and Carlos Campillo-Artero (eds), *Health Technology Assessment and Health Policy Today: A Multifaceted View of their Unstable Crossroads* (Springer International Publishing 2015)

Culyer AJ, 'HTA – Algorithm or Process?: Comment on "Expanded HTA: Enhancing Fairness and Legitimacy"' (2016) 5 International Journal of Health Policy and Management 501

Culyer AJ and Bombard Y, 'An Equity Framework for Health Technology Assessments' (2012) 32 Medical Decision Making 428

Culyer AJ, Podhisita C and Santatiwongchai B, *A Start in the East – A Short History of HITAP* (Health Intervention and Technology Assessment Program (HITAP) 2016)

Cupples LM, 'Disability, Epistemic Harms, and the Quality-Adjusted Life Year' (2020) 13 IJFAB: International Journal of Feminist Approaches to Bioethics 45

Da P and S R, 'The Limitations of QALY: A Literature Review' (2016) 06 Journal of Stem Cell Research & Therapy

Dabak SV and others, 'Budgeting for a Billion: Applying Health Technology Assessment (HTA) for Universal Health Coverage in India' (2018) 16 Health Research Policy and Systems 115

Danguole J, 'Development of Health Technology Assessment in Lithuania' (2009) 25 International Journal of Technology Assessment in Health Care 140

Daniels N, 'Rights to Health Care and Distributive Justice: Programmatic Worries' (1979) 4 Journal of Medicine and Philosophy 174

Daniels N, 'Health-Care Needs and Distributive Justice' (1981) 10 Philosophy & Public Affairs 146

DANIELS N, 'Normal Functioning and the Treatment-Enhancement Distinction' (2000) 9 Cambridge Quarterly of Healthcare Ethics 309

Daniels N, *Just Health: Meeting Health Needs Fairly* (Cambridge University Press 2007)

Daniels N, 'Some Remarks on Accountability for Reasonableness' (2018) 18 The American Journal of Bioethics 42

Daniels N, 'Role of the Courts in the Progressive Realization of the Right to Health: Between the Threat and the Promise of Judicialization in Mexico' (2015) 1 Health Systems & Reform 229

Daniels N, Porteny T and Urritia J, 'Expanded HTA: Enhancing Fairness and Legitimacy' (2015) 5 International Journal of Health Policy and Management 1

Daniels N and Sabin JE, 'Limits to Health Care: Fair Procedures, Democratic Deliberation, and the Legitimacy Problem for Insurers' (1997) 26 Philosophy & Public Affairs 303

Daniels N and Sabin JE, *Setting Limits Fairly: Learning to Share Resources for Health* (Oxford University Press 2008)

Daniels N and Sabin JE, *Setting Limits Fairly: Learning to Share Resources for Health* (2nd edn, Oxford University Press 2008)

Daniels N and Sabin J, 'Accountability for Priority Setting' in A den Exter and M Buijsen (eds), *Rationing Health Care: Hard Choices and Unavoidable Trade-Offs* (Maklu 2012)

Danzon PM, 'Affordability Challenges to Value-Based Pricing: Mass Diseases, Orphan Diseases, and Cures' (2018) 21 Value in Health 252

Danzon PM and Kim JD, 'International Price Comparisons for Pharmaceuticals: Measurement and Policy Issues' (1998) 14 PharmacoEconomics 115

Daoud A, 'Scarcity and Artificial Scarcity' in Daniel Thomas Cook and J Michael Ryan (eds), *The Wiley Blackwell Encyclopedia of Consumption and Consumer Studies* (John Wiley & Sons, Ltd 2015)

Darr A, 'Competition Law and Human Rights: A Complex Relationship' [2021] Wirtschaft und Wettbewerb 388-392

Davis SLM, *The Uncounted: Politics of Data in Global Health* (1st edn, Cambridge University Press 2020)

Day S, 'Evidence-Based Medicine and Rare Diseases' in Manuel Posada de la Paz, Domenica Taruscio and Stephen C Groft (eds), *Rare Diseases Epidemiology: Update and Overview* (Springer International Publishing 2017)

de Beco G, 'Human Rights Indicators for Assessing State Compliance with International Human Rights' (2008) 77 Nordic Journal of International Law 23

de Londras F and others, 'Integrating Rights and Evidence: A Technical Advance in Abortion Guideline Development' (2021) 6 BMJ Global Health e004141

de Mesquita JB, Hunt P and Khosla R, 'The Human Rights Responsibility of International Assistance and Cooperation in Health' *Universal human rights and extraterritorial obligations* (University of Pennsylvania Press 2012)

De Schutter O and others, 'Commentary to the Maastricht Principles on Extraterritorial Obligations of States in the Area of Economic, Social and Cultural Rights' (2012) 34 Human Rights Quarterly 1084

Decide, 'All You Need Is Law' (*Decide Health Decision Hub*) <https://decidehealth.world/en/law> accessed 5 May 2020

Decide – Health Decision, 'Welcome to Decide' (*Decide Health Decision Hub*) <https://decidehealth.world/en/where> accessed 10 September 2021

Dehm J, 'Righting Inequality: Human Rights Responses to Economic Inequality in the United Nations' (2019) 10 Humanity: An International Journal of Human Rights, Humanitarianism, and Development 443

den Exter A, 'Cost-Effectiveness: What's Law Got to Do with It?' [2014] Journal of the International Institute for Law and Medicine 285

den Exter A, 'Fighting Excessive Pharmaceutical Prices: Evaluating the Options' (2020) 28 European Journal of Health Law 68

Den Heijer M and Lawson R, 'Extraterritorial Human Rights and the Concept of "jurisdiction" [2013] *Global Justice, State Duties: The Extraterritorial Scope of Economic, Social, and Cultural Rights in International Law* 153

Denier Y, *Efficiency, Justice and Care: Philosophical Reflections on Scarcity in Health Care* (Springer Netherlands 2007)

Denzin NK and Lincoln YS, *The SAGE Handbook of Qualitative Research* (SAGE Publications 2011)

Devlin N, '"Preference-Based Measure" Is Misleading: Can We Agree on Something Better? The Academic Health Economists' Blog' (*The Academic Health Economists' Blog*) <https://aheblog.com/2020/08/12/preference-based-measure-is-misleading-can-we-agree-on-something-better/> accessed 16 April 2021

Dickinson H and others, 'Resource Scarcity and Priority-Setting: From Management to Leadership in the Rationing of Health Care?' (2011) 31 Public Money & Management 363

Diller JM, 'Economic, Social and Cultural Human Rights: The Journey towards Peremptory Norms in International Law' (2018) 36 Nordic Journal of Human Rights 19

Directorate-General for Health and Food Safety (European Commission), 'Defining Value in Value-Based Healthcare: Report of the Expert Panel on Effective Ways of Investing in Health (EXPH)' <https://op.europa.eu/en/publication-detail/-/publication/beaebce1-ac29-11e9-9d01-01aa75ed71a1> accessed 1 January 2021

DiStefano MJ and Krubiner CB, 'Beyond the Numbers: A Critique of Quantitative Multi-criteria Decision Analysis' (2020) 36 International Journal of Technology Assessment in Health Care 292

Dittrich R and others, 'The International Right to Health: What Does It Mean in Legal Practice and How Can It Affect Priority Setting for Universal Health Coverage?' (2016) 2 Health Systems & Reform 23

Doherty JE and others, 'Strengthening Expertise for Health Technology Assessment and Priority-Setting in Africa' (2017) 10 Global Health Action 1370194

Dolan P, 'Developing Methods That Really Do Value the "Q" in the QALY' (2008) 3 Health Economics, Policy and Law 69

Domingues R and others, 'Strategies to Deal with Drug Lawsuits in the State of São Paulo' (2017) 6 Cadernos Ibero-Americanos de Direito Sanitário 35

Draborg E and others, 'International Comparison of the Definition and the Practical Application of Health Technology Assessment' (2005) 21 International Journal of Technology Assessment in Health Care 89

Dreyfuss RC, 'Patents and Human Rights: Where Is the Paradox' in Willem Grosheide (ed), *Intellectual Property and Human Rights: A Paradox* (Edward Elgar 2010)

Drisko JW and Maschi T, *Content Analysis* (Oxford University Press 2015)

Drummond M and others, 'Reimbursement of Pharmaceuticals: Reference Pricing versus Health Technology Assessment' (2011) 12 The European Journal of Health Economics 263

Drummond M and Rutten F, 'New Guidelines for Economic Evaluation in Germany and the United Kingdom Are We Any Closer to Developing International Standards?' [2008] OHE briefing

Drummond M and Sorenson C, 'Nasty or Nice? A Perspective on the Use of Health Technology Assessment in the United Kingdom' (2009) 12 Value in Health S8

Dunlop WCN and others, 'Benefits, Challenges and Potential Strategies of Open Source Health Economic Models' (2017) 35 PharmacoEconomics 125

Durand B, 'Competition Law and Pharma: An Economic Perspective' in Pablo Figueroa and Alejandro Guerrero, *EU Law of Competition and Trade in the Pharmaceutical Sector* (Edward Elgar Publishing 2019)

Durojaye E, *Litigating the Right to Health in Africa: Challenges and Prospects* (Taylor & Francis 2016)

Duthie K and Bond K, 'Improving Ethics Analysis in Health Technology Assessment' (2011) 27 International Journal of Technology Assessment in Health Care 64

Eatwell E and Swierczyna A, 'Emerging Voluntary Cooperation between European Healthcare Systems: Are We Facing a New Future?' (2019) 3 Medicine Access @ Point of Care 239920261985231

EBDR, '2017-18 Public-Private Partnership Assessment' (EBDR 2018) <https://www.ebrd.com/cs/Satellite?c=Content&cid=1395278802473&d=&pagename=EBRD%2FContent%2FDownloadDocument> accessed 20 November 2020

Eddy D, 'Health Technology Assessment and Evidence-Based Medicine: What Are We Talking About?' (2009) 12 Value in Health S6

Edgar A, *The Ethical QALY: Ethical Issues in Health Care Resource Allocations* (Euromed Communications Limited 1998)

Edlin R and others, *Cost Effectiveness Modelling for Health Technology Assessment: A Practical Course* (Springer International Publishing 2015)

Elias FTS and Araújo DV, 'How Health Economic Evaluation (HEE) Contributes to Decision-Making in Public Health Care: The Case of Brazil' (2014) 108 Zeitschrift für Evidenz, Fortbildung und Qualität im Gesundheitswesen 405

Elif A, 'Economic and Social Rights, Extraterritorial Application' in Askin Elif, *Max Planck Encyclopedia of Public International Law* (Oxford University Press 2019) <https://doi.org/10.1093/law-epil/9780199231690/e2213> accessed 17 April 2021

Emanuel EJ and others, 'Fair Allocation of Scarce Medical Resources in the Time of Covid-19' (2020) 382 New England Journal of Medicine 2049

EUnetHTA, 'EUnetHTA Handbook on Health Technology Assessment Capacity Building' <http://eunethta.eu/eunethta-handbook-on-hta-capacity-building/> accessed 5 May 2020

EUnetHTA Joint Action 2, Work Package 8, 'HTA Core Model ® Version 3.0 (Pdf)' <www.htacoremodel.info/BrowseModel.aspx> accessed 11 February 2018

European Commission, 'HTA Sharing Experiences from the Regional Cooperations' <https://ec.europa.eu/health/sites/health/files/technology_assessment/docs/2018_regional_hta_reportsum_en.pdf> accessed 5 May 2020

European Commission, 'Competition Enforcement in the Pharmaceutical Sector (2009-2017)' (European Union 2019) <https://op.europa.eu/en/publication-detail/-/publication/9cb466c8-7b71-11e9-9f05-01aa75ed71a1> accessed 1 October 2020

Every-Palmer S and Howick J, 'How Evidence-based Medicine Is Failing Due to Biased Trials and Selective Publication' (2014) 20 Journal of Evaluation in Clinical Practice 908

Faulkner A, '7."Strange Bedfellows" in the Laboratory of the NHS? An Analysis of the New Science of Health Technology Assessment in the United Kingdom' (1997) 19 Sociology of Health & Illness 183

Ferrario A and Kanavos P, 'Dealing with Uncertainty and High Prices of New Medicines: A Comparative Analysis of the Use of Managed Entry Agreements in Belgium, England, the Netherlands and Sweden' (2015) 124 Social Science & Medicine 39

Ferraz OLM (ed), 'The Judicialisation of the Right to Health' *Health as a Human Right: The Politics and Judicialisation of Health in Brazil* (Cambridge University Press 2020)

Fierlbeck K, Gardner W and Levy A, 'New Public Governance in Health Care: Health Technology Assessment for Canadian Pharmaceuticals: NEW PUBLIC GOVERNANCE AND HTA' (2018) 61 Canadian Public Administration 45

Fine B, 'Economics and Scarcity: With Amartya Sen as Point of Departure' in Lyla Mehta (ed), *The Limits to Scarcity: Contesting the Politics of Allocation* (Routledge 2013)

FINOSE, 'Memorandum of Understanding' <https://www.fimea.fi/documents/160140/1454518/yhteisymm%C3%A4rrysp%C3%B6yt%C3%A4kirja.pdf/b5134913-8064-c224-270d-d23cd2c68e37> accessed 8 April 2020

Fish J and Bewley S, 'Using Human Rights-Based Approaches to Conceptualise Lesbian and Bisexual Women's Health Inequalities' (2010) 18 Health & social care in the community 355

FitzGerald P, 'State Regulation of Generic Drug Price Gouging' (2019) 2 Belmont Health Law Journal 100

Fleck LM, 'Just Health Care Rationing: A Democratic Decisionmaking Approach' (1992) 140 University of Pennsylvania Law Review 1597

Fleck LM, *Just Caring : Health Care Rationing and Democratic Deliberation* (Oxford University Press 2009)

Fleck LM, 'Just Solidarity: The Key to Fair Health Care Rationing' [2015] Diametros 44

Fleck LM, 'Just Caring: Do We Need Philosophical Foundations?' (2017) 3 Ethics, Medicine and Public Health 221

Flinterman C, '"Limburg Principles on the Implementation of the International Covenant on Economic, Social and Cultural Rights"(1987)' 9 Human Rights Quarterly 122

Flood CM and Gross A, 'Litigating the Right to Health: What Can We Learn from a Comparative Law and Health Care Systems Approach' (2014) 16 Health and Human Rights 62

Flood CM and Gross A, *The Right to Health at the Public/Private Divide: A Global Comparative Study* (Cambridge University Press 2014)

FM't Hoen E and others, 'Medicine Procurement and the Use of Flexibilities in the Agreement on Trade-Related Aspects of Intellectual Property Rights, 2001–2016' (2018) 96 Bulletin of the World Health Organization 185

Fontrier A-M, Kamphuis B and Kanavos P, 'How Can Health Technology Assessment Be Improved to Optimise Access to Medicines? Results from a Delphi Study in Europe: Better Access to Medicines through HTA' (2024) 25 The European Journal of Health Economics 935

Ford A, 'Accountability for Reasonableness: The Relevance, or Not, of Exceptionality in Resource Allocation' (2015) 18 Medicine, Health Care and Philosophy 217

Forman L, 'Trade Rules, Intellectual Property, and the Right to Health' (2007) 21 Ethics & International Affairs 337

Forman L, 'What Future for the Minimum Core? Contextualizing the Implications of South African Socioeconomic Rights Jurisprudence for the International Human Right to Health' in John Harrington and Maria Stuttaford (eds), *Global Health and Human Rights: Legal and Philosophical Perspectives* (Taylor & Francis 2010)

Forman L, 'Decoding the Right to Health: What Could It Offer to Global Health?' (2015) 8 Bioethica Forum 7

Forman L, 'Can Minimum Core Obligations Survive a Reasonableness Standard of Review under the Optional Protocol to the International Covenant on Economic, Social and Cultural Rights?' (2016) 47 Ottawa Law Review 557

Forman L, 'What Do Core Obligations under the Right to Health Bring to Universal Health Coverage?' (2016) 18 Health and Human Rights 23

Forman L, 'Conceptualising Minimum Core Obligations under the Right to Health: How Should We Define and Implement the "Morality of the Depths"' (2016) 20 The International Journal of Human Rights 531

Forman L and Kohler JC, *Access to Medicines as a Human Right: Implications for Pharmaceutical Industry Responsibility* (University of Toronto Press 2012)

Fox AM and Meier BM, 'Health as Freedom: Addressing Social Determinants of Global Health Inequities through the Human Right to Development' (2009) 23 Bioethics 112

Francke R and Hart D, 'HTA in den Entscheidungsprozessen des IQWiG und G-BA: Bestandsaufnahme und aktuelle Fragen der gesundheitsrechtlichen Regulierung' (2006) 49 Bundesgesundheitsblatt – Gesundheitsforschung – Gesundheitsschutz 241

Francke R and Hart D, 'Introduction to the Legal Aspects of HTAs' (2008) 102 Zeitschrift für Evidenz, Fortbildung und Qualität im Gesundheitswesen 63

Frank RG and Nichols LM, 'Medicare Drug-Price Negotiation – Why Now … and How' (2019) 381 New England Journal of Medicine 1404

Frank RH, 'Why Is Cost-Benefit Analysis so Controversial?' (2000) 29 The Journal of Legal Studies 913

Franklin D, 'Calibrating QALYs to Respect Equality of Persons' (2017) 29 Utilitas 65

Franzen N and others, 'Evidence Underlying Policy Proposals for Sustainable Anticancer Drug Prices: A Systematic Review' (2020) 6 JAMA Oncology 909

Fredman S, 'Substantive Equality Revisited' (2016) 14 International Journal of Constitutional Law 712

Freedman LP, 'Achieving the MDGs: Health Systems as Core Social Institutions' (2005) 48 Development 19

Freeman M, 'The Right to Health' in Rhiannon Morgan and Bryan Turner (eds), *Interpreting Human Rights: Social Science Perspectives* (Routledge 2009)

Fricker M, *Epistemic Injustice: Power and the Ethics of Knowing* (Oxford University Press 2007)

Friedman A, 'Beyond Accountability for Reasonableness' (2008) 22 Bioethics 101

Fritze J, 'Is Healthcare Budgeting Ethically Justifiable?' (2001) 2 The European Journal of Health Economics (HEPAC) 26

Fukuda-Parr S, Lawson-Remer T and Randolph S, *Fulfilling Social and Economic Rights* (Oxford University Press 2015)

Fundytus A, Sullivan R and Booth CM, 'Toward Affordable Cancer Drugs: Do We Need Firmer Price Negotiation, Me-Too Drugs, or a Biosimilar Silver Bullet?' (2020) 47 Seminars in Oncology 353

Gable L, 'The Proliferation of Human Rights in Global Health Governance' (2007) 35 The Journal of Law, Medicine & Ethics 534

Gaeta R and Gentile N, 'Evidence, Discovery and Justification: The Case of Evidence-Based Medicine: Evidence, Discovery and Justification' (2016) 22 Journal of Evaluation in Clinical Practice 550

Gallo P, 'Integrating Ethical Enquiry and Health Technology Assessment: Limits and Opportunities for Efficiency and Equity' (2004) 2 Poiesis & Praxis 103

Gandjour A, 'Reference Pricing and Price Negotiations for Innovative New Drugs: Viable Policies in the Long Term?' (2013) 31 PharmacoEconomics 11

Garattini L and Padula A, 'Pharmaceutical Pricing Conundrum: Time to Get Rid of It?' (2018) 19 The European Journal of Health Economics 1035

Garattini L and Padula A, 'HTA for Pharmaceuticals in Europe: Will the Mountain Deliver a Mouse?' (2020) 21 The European Journal of Health Economics 1

Garau M and others, 'Using QALYs in Cancer: A Review of the Methodological Limitations' (2011) 29 PharmacoEconomics 673

García-Mochón L and others, 'HTA and Decision-Making Processes in Central, Eastern and South Eastern Europe: Results from a Survey' (2019) 123 Health Policy 182

Garner S, Rintoul A and Hill SR, 'Value-Based Pricing: L'Enfant Terrible?' (2018) 36 PharmacoEconomics 5

Garrett Z, Imaz-Iglesia I and Willemsen A, 'Building a Model of Health Technology Assessment Cooperation: Lessons Learned from EUnetHTA Joint Action 3' (2022) 38 International Journal of Technology Assessment in Health Care

Garrison LP and others, 'Performance-Based Risk-Sharing Arrangements: Good Practices for Design, Implementation, and Evaluation: Report of the ISPOR Good Practices for Performance-Based Risk-Sharing Arrangements Task Force' (2013) 16 Value in Health 703

Gauvin F-P and others, '"It All Depends": Conceptualizing Public Involvement in the Context of Health Technology Assessment Agencies' (2010) 70 Social Science & Medicine 1518

'Generic Drugs | pCPA' <https://www.pcpacanada.ca/generic-drug-framework> accessed 9 March 2021

Gerber-Grote A and others, 'Decision Making in Germany: Is Health Economic Evaluation as a Supporting Tool a Sleeping Beauty?' (2014) 108 Zeitschrift für Evidenz, Fortbildung und Qualität im Gesundheitswesen 390

Gertner A, 'Health Technology Assessment and Incorporation in Brazil: Critical Reflections on an Emerging Public-Private Field' (2009) 2 Jornal Brasileiro de Economia da Saúde. 57

Gervais DJ, 'Patentability Criteria as TRIPS Flexibilities: The Examples of China and India' *Patent Law in Global Perspective*, (Oxford University Press 2014)

Giacomini M, 'One of These Things Is Not like the Others: The Idea of Precedence in Health Technology Assessment and Coverage Decisions' (2005) 83 The Milbank Quarterly 193

Giacomini M, Winsor S and Abelson J, 'Ethics in Health Technology Assessment: Understanding Health Technologies as Policies' (2013) 26 Healthcare Management Forum 72

Gilardino RE and others, 'Implementing Health Technology Assessments in Latin America: Looking at the Past, Mirroring the Future. A Perspective from the ISPOR Health Technology Assessment Roundtable in Latin America' (2020) 23 Value in Health Regional Issues 6

Giorgi MS, *The Human Right to Equal Access to Health Care* (Intersentia 2012)

Glassman A and others (eds), *What's in, What's out: Designing Benefits for Universal Health Coverage* (Center for Global Development 2017)

Glassman A, Fan V and Over M, 'More Health for the Money: Putting Incentives to Work for the Global Fund and Its Partners' (Center for Global Development 2013)

'Global Forum on Fair Drug Pricing and Access to Medicines' (2019) 826 PharmacoEconomics and Outcomes News 1

Gloppen S, 'Litigation as a Strategy to Hold Governments Accountable for Implementing the Right to Health.' (2008) 10 Health and Human Rights 21

Gloppen S, 'Right to Health in Contexts of Resource Scarcity: Towards Judicial Enforcement of the Right to a Fair Share' [2015] SSRN Electronic Journal <https://doi.org/10.2139/ssrn.2622779> accessed 28 October 2018

Godlee F, 'Effective, Safe, and a Good Patient Experience' (2009) 339 BMJ b4346

Gold MR, Stevenson D and Fryback DG, 'HALYs and QALYs and DALYs, Oh My: Similarities and Differences in Summary Measures of Population Health' (2002) 23 Annual Review of Public Health 115

Goldmann M, 'Contesting Austerity: Genealogies of Human Rights Discourse' [2020] Max Planck Institute for Comparative Public Law & International Law (MPIL) Research Paper

Goodman T, 'Is There a Right to Health?' (2005) 30 The Journal of Medicine and Philosophy 643

Goodwin-Gill GS, 'Obligations of Conduct and Result' in Paul Alston and Katarina Tomasevski (eds), *The Right to Food* (Martinus Nijhoff 1984)

Gostin L, 'The Ideology of Entitlement: The Contemporary Function of Law and Its Application to Psychiatry' *Psychiatry: Law and Ethics* (Springer 1986)

Gostin L, 'Health and Human Rights Working Paper Series 2 -The Domains of Health Responsiveness – A Human Rights Analysis' (World Health Organization 2003)

Gostin L, *Global Health Law* (Harvard University Press 2014)

Gostin L, '70 Years of Human Rights in Global Health: Drawing on a Contentious Past to Secure a Hopeful Future' (2018) 392 The Lancet 2731 <https://doi.org/10.1016/S0140-6736(18)32997-0>

Gostin L and Taylor AL, 'Global Health Law: A Definition and Grand Challenges' (2008) 1 Public Health Ethics 53 <https://doi.org/10.1093/phe/phn005>

Gostin LO, 'Public Health, Ethics, and Human Rights: A Tribute to the Late Jonathan Mann' (2001) 29 The Journal of law, medicine & ethics 121

Gostin LO, 'The next WHO Director-General's Highest Priority: A Global Treaty on the Human Right to Health' (2016) 4 The Lancet Global Health e890

Gostin LO, 'The Legal Determinants of Health: Harnessing the Power of Law for Global Health and Sustainable Development' (2019) 393 The Lancet 1857

Gray M, 'Value Based Healthcare' (2017) 356 BMJ: British Medical Journal (Online)

Gready P and Vandenhole W, *Human Rights and Development in the New Millennium: Towards a Theory of Change* (Routledge 2013)

Greenberg Traurig, LLP, 'Lessons from China's Negotiation of Drug Prices in 2020' (*The National Law Review*) <https://www.natlawreview.com/article/china-move-lesson-china-s-national-negotiation-drug-prices-2020> accessed 11 April 2021

Greenhalgh T and others, 'Evidence Based Medicine: A Movement in Crisis?' (2014) 348 BMJ g3725

Greenhalgh T and others, 'Six "Biases" against Patients and Carers in Evidence-Based Medicine' (2015) 13 BMC Medicine 200

Greiner W and von der Schulenburg J-MG, 'HTA in Germany: Very Special and Specific' (2010) 11 The European Journal of Health Economics 1

Griffey B, 'The "Reasonableness" Test: Assessing Violations of State Obligations under the Optional Protocol to the International Covenant on Economic, Social and Cultural Rights' (2011) 11 Human Rights Law Review 275

Griffin F, 'Fighting Overcharged Bills from Predatory Hospitals' (2019) 51 Arizona State Law Journal 1003

Gronde T van der, Uyl-de Groot CA and Pieters T, 'Addressing the Challenge of High-Priced Prescription Drugs in the Era of Precision Medicine: A Systematic Review of Drug Life Cycles, Therapeutic Drug Markets and Regulatory Frameworks' (2017) 12 PLOS ONE e0182613

Gruskin S, 'Rights-Based Approaches to Health: Something for Everyone' (2006) 9 Health and Human Rights 5

Gruskin S, 'Human Rights in Health Systems Frameworks: What Is There, What Is Missing and Why Does It Matter?' (2012) 7 Global Public Health 337

Gruskin S, Bogecho D and Ferguson L, '"Rights-Based Approaches" to Health Policies and Programs: Articulations, Ambiguities, and Assessment' (2010) 31 Journal of Public Health Policy 129

Gruskin S and Daniels N, 'Process Is the Point: Justice and Human Rights: Priority Setting and Fair Deliberative Process' (2008) 98 American Journal of Public Health 1573

Gu Y and others, 'Attributes and Weights in Health Care Priority Setting: A Systematic Review of What Counts and to What Extent' (2015) 146 Social Science & Medicine 41 <https://doi.org/10.1016/j.socscimed.2015.10.005>

Guennif S, 'Is Compulsory Licensing Bad for Public Health? Some Critical Comments on Drug Accessibility in Developing Countries' (2017) 15 Applied Health Economics and Health Policy 557

Guerra-Júnior AA and others, 'Health Technology Performance Assessment: Real-World Evidence for Public Healthcare Sustainability' (2017) 33 International Journal of Technology Assessment in Health Care 279

Gutmann A, *Why Deliberative Democracy?* (Princeton University Press 2004)

Gyrd-Hansen D, 'Willingness to Pay for a QALY' (2003) 12 Health Economics 1049

Hailey D, 'Development of the International Network of Agencies for Health Technology Assessment' (2009) 25 International Journal of Technology Assessment in Health Care 24

Hailey D and Alberta Heritage Foundation for Medical Research, *Elements of Effectiveness for Health Technology Assessment Programs* (Alberta Heritage Foundation for Medical Research 2003)

Hailey DM, Cowley DE and Dankiw W, 'The Impact of Health Technology Assessment' (1990) 14 Community Health Studies 223

Hall MA and Wright RF, 'Systematic Content Analysis of Judicial Opinions' (2008) 96 California Law Review 63

Hamlin R and Sala G, *The Judicialization of Politics Disentangled* (Interactive Factory 2018)

Hammonds R, Ooms G and Vandenhole W, 'Under the (Legal) Radar Screen: Global Health Initiatives and International Human Rights Obligations' (2012) 12 BMC International Health and Human Rights 31

Hancher L and Moran M, 'Organizing Regulatory Space' in Robert Baldwin, Colin Scott and Christopher Hood (eds), *A Reader on Regulation* (Oxford University Press 1998)

Harris J, 'QALYfying the Value of Life.' (1987) 13 Journal of medical ethics 117

Harris J, 'It's Not NICE to Discriminate' (2005) 31 Journal of Medical Ethics 373

Harris J, 'Taking the "Human" out of Human Rights' (2011) 20 Cambridge Quarterly of Healthcare Ethics 9

Hart HL, 'Between Utility and Rights' (1979) 79 Columbia Law Review 828

Harteloh PPM, 'The Meaning of Quality in Health Care: A Conceptual Analysis' (2003) 11 Health Care Analysis 259

Harteloh PPM, 'Understanding the Quality Concept in Health Care' (2004) 9 Accreditation and Quality Assurance 92

Hasman A and Holm S, 'Accountability for Reasonableness: Opening the Black Box of Process' (2005) 13 Health Care Analysis 261

Hassoun N, 'The Human Right to Health' (2015) 10 Philosophy Compass 275

Hassoun N, 'The Human Right to Health: A Defense' (2020) 51 Journal of Social Philosophy 158

Hausman DM, 'Valuing Health' (2006) 34 Philosophy & Public Affairs 246

Hausman DM, 'Can Health Be Measured?' in Nir Eyal and others (eds), *Measuring the Global Burden of Disease: Philosophical Dimensions* (Oxford University Press 2020)

Hawkins B and Alvarez Rosete A, 'Judicialization and Health Policy in Colombia: The Implications for Evidence-Informed Policymaking' (2019) 47 Policy Studies Journal 953

Health AGD of, 'Pharmaceutical Benefits Scheme (PBS) | Fact Sheet – Setting an Approved Ex-Manufacturer Price for New or Extended Listings' <https://www.pbs.gov.au/info/industry/pricing/pbs-items/fact-sheet-setting-an-approved-ex-manufacturer-price> accessed 9 March 2021

Helfer LR, 'Pharmaceutical Patents and the Human Right to Health' in Terence C Halliday and Gregory Shaffer (eds), *Transnational Legal Orders* (Cambridge University Press 2015)

Hemminki E, Hailey D and Koivusalo M, 'The Courts – A Challenge to Health Technology Assessment' (1999) 285 Science 203

Henshall C and others, 'Interactions between Health Technology Assessment, Coverage, and Regulatory Processes: Emerging Issues, Goals, and Opportunities' (2011) 27 International Journal of Technology Assessment in Health Care 253

Hertel S and Minkler L, 'Economic Rights: The Terrain' in Shareen Hertel and Lanse Minkler (eds), *Economic Rights: Conceptual measurement and policy issues* (Cambridge University Press 2007)

Hessler K, 'Exploring the Philosophical Foundations of the Human Rights Approach to International Public Health Ethics' in Michael Boylan (ed), *International Public Health Policy and Ethics* (Springer 2008)

Hessler K and Buchanan A, 'Specifying the Content of the Human Right to Health Care' in Rosamond Rhodes, Margaret Battin and Anita Silvers (eds), *Medicine and Social Justice: essays on the distribution of health care* (Oxford University Press 2002)

Heymann J and others, 'Constitutional Rights to Health, Public Health and Medical Care: The Status of Health Protections in 191 Countries' (2013) 8 Global Public Health 639

Hoffmann FF and Bentes FRNM, 'Accountability for Social and Economic Rights in Brazil' in Varun Gauri and Daniel M Brinks (eds), *Courting Social Justice* (Cambridge University Press 2008)

Hofmann B, 'Health Technology Assessment–Science or Art?' (2013) 9 GMS Health Technology Assessment

Hofmann B, 'Harmonization of Ethics in Health Technology Assessment: A Revision of the Socratic Approach' (2014) 30 International Journal of Technology Assessment in Health Care 3

Hofmann B, Bond K and Sandman L, 'Evaluating Facts and Facting Evaluations: On the Fact-Value Relationship in HTA' (2018) 24 Journal of Evaluation in Clinical Practice 957

Holdcroft A, 'Gender Bias in Research: How Does It Affect Evidence Based Medicine?' (2007) 100 Journal of the Royal Society of Medicine 2

Hollingworth S and others, 'Implementing Health Technology Assessment in Ghana to Support Universal Health Coverage: Building Relationships That Focus on People, Policy, and Process' (2020) 36 International Journal of Technology Assessment in Health Care 8

Hollingworth SA and others, 'What Do We Need to Know? Data Sources to Support Evidence-Based Decisions Using Health Technology Assessment in Ghana' (2020) 18 Health Research Policy and Systems 1

Holm S, 'Natural Talent, Fair Equality of Opportunity, and Therapeutic Use Exemptions' (2018) 18 The American Journal of Bioethics 18

Holtorf A-P and others, 'Pilot Approach to Analyzing Patient and Citizen Involvement in Health Technology Assessment in Four Diverse Low-and Middle-Income Countries' (2021) 37 International Journal of Technology Assessment in Health Care

Hopkins RB and Goeree R, *Health Technology Assessment: Using Biostatistics to Break the Barriers of Adopting New Medicines* (CRC Press 2015)

Huić M and others, 'Collaboration In Health Technology Assessment (EUNET_HTA Joint-Action, 2010–2012): Four Case Studies' (2013) 29 International Journal of Technology Assessment in Health Care 323

Hunt P, 'Interpreting the International Right to Health in a Human Rights-Based Approach to Health' (2016) 18 Health and Human Rights 109

Hunt P, 'The Right to the Highest Attainable Standard of Health' in Roger Detels and others (eds), *Oxford Textbook of Public Health* (2009)

Hunt P and Backman G, 'Health Systems and the Right to the Highest Attainable Standard of Health' (2008) 10 Health and Human Rights 81

Hunt P, Bhalotra S and Williams C, 'The Role and Impact of the Right to Health: Evidence from Brazil's Family Health Program' (2022) 44 Human Rights Quarterly 111

Hunt P and MacNaughton G, 'A Human Rights-Based Approach to Health Indicators' in Mashood Baderin and Robert McCorquodale (eds), *Economic, Social, and Cultural Rights in Action* (Oxford University Press 2007)

Hunt P, Yamin AE and Bustreo F, 'Making the Case: What Is the Evidence of Impact of Applying Human Rights-Based Approaches to Health?' (2015) 17 Health and Human Rights 1

Hunter DJ and others, 'Public Involvement in Health Priority Setting: Future Challenges for Policy, Research and Society' (2016) 30 Journal of Health Organization and Management 796

Hurwitz B, 'Clinical Guidelines: Legal and Political Considerations of Clinical Practice Guidelines' (1999) 318 BMJ 661

Hutton J, '"Health Economics" and the Evolution of Economic Evaluation of Health Technologies: EVOLUTION OF ECONOMIC EVALUATION OF HEALTH TECHNOLOGIES' (2012) 21 Health Economics 13

Hyry HI and others, 'Limits on Use of Health Economic Assessments for Rare Diseases' (2014) 107 241

Iandolo F and others, 'From Health Technology Assessment to Health Technology Sustainability' (2018) 10 Sustainability 4748

Ido VHP, 'Designing Pro-Health Competition Policies in Developing Countries' (South Center 2020) 125

International Decision Support Initiative (iDSI), 'About Us' (*iDSI*, 2020) <https://www.idsihealth.org/who-we-are/about-us/> accessed 22 August 2021

Ioannidis JP, 'The Mass Production of Redundant, Misleading, and Conflicted Systematic Reviews and Meta-analyses' (2016) 94 The Milbank Quarterly 485

IQWiG, 'Scientific Reply to Comments Regarding the "Methods for Assessment of the Relation of Benefits to Costs in the German Statutory Health Care System Version

1.0'" <https://www.iqwig.de/download/08-10-14_Scientific_Reply_to_Comments_v_1_0.pdf> accessed 3 December 2020

Ivandic V, 'Requirements for Benefit Assessment in Germany and England – Overview and Comparison' (2014) 4 Health Economics Review 12 <https://doi.org/10.1186/s13561-014-0012-8>

Jabbal J and Lewis M, 'Approaches to Better Value in the NHS: Improving Quality and Cost: CEBM Report' (Centre for Evidence-Based Medicine 2018) <https://www.cebm.net/2019/04/defining-value-based-healthcare-in-the-nhs> accessed 1 January 2021

Jacobs LA, 'Adapting Locally to International Health and Human Rights Standards: An Alternative Theoretical Framework for Progressive Realisation' in Mikael Rask Madsen and Gert Verschraegen (eds), *Making Human Rights Intelligible: Towards a Sociology of Human Rights* (Hart 2013)

Jan S, 'Proceduralism and Its Role in Economic Evaluation and Priority Setting in Health' (2014) 108 Social Science & Medicine 257

Jansen MPM, Baltussen R and Bærøe K, 'Stakeholder Participation for Legitimate Priority Setting: A Checklist' (2018) 7 International Journal of Health Policy and Management 973

Johnson FR, 'Editorial: Moving the QALY Forward or Just Stuck in Traffic?' (2009) 12 Value in Health S38

Johri M and Norheim O, 'Can Cost-Effectiveness Analysis Integrate Concerns for Equity?' (2012) 28 International Journal of Technology Assessment in Health Care 125

Jones GW and Sagar SM, 'No Guidance Is Provided for Situations for Which Evidence Is Lacking' (1995) 311 BMJ 258

Jonsson E, 'History of Health Technology Assessment in Sweden' (2009) 25 International Journal of Technology Assessment in Health Care 42

Jost TS, 'Health Care Rationing in the Courts: A Comparative Study' in Frances H Miller (ed), *Rights and Resources* (Routledge 2018)

Jost TS, 'The Role of the Courts in Health Care Rationing: The German Model' 18 Journal of Contemporary Health Law and Policy 7

Juškevičius J and Balsienė J, 'On Human Rights in Healthcare: Some Remarks on Limits of the Right to Healthcare' (2010) 122 Jurisprudencija: Mokslo darbu žurnalas 95

Kanavos P and others, 'Short-and Long-Term Effects of Value-Based Pricing vs. External Price Referencing' [2010] Eminet. LSE

Kapczynski A, 'The Right to Medicines in an Age of Neoliberalism' (2019) 10 Humanity: An International Journal of Human Rights, Humanitarianism, and Development 79

Karimi M and Brazier J, 'Health, Health-Related Quality of Life, and Quality of Life: What Is the Difference?' (2016) 34 PharmacoEconomics 645

Karimova T, 'The Nature and Meaning of "International Assistance and Cooperation" under the International Covenant on Economic, Social and Cultural Rights' in Eibe Riedel, Gilles Giacca and Christophe Golay (eds), *Economic, Social, and Cultural Rights in International Law* (Oxford University Press 2014)

Keliddar I, Mosadeghrad AM and Jafari-Sirizi M, 'Rationing in Health Systems: A Critical Review' (2017) 31 Medical Journal of the Islamic Republic of Iran 271

Kelly MP and others, 'The Importance of Values in Evidence-Based Medicine' (2015) 16 BMC medical ethics 1

Kelly MP and Moore TA, 'The Judgement Process in Evidence-Based Medicine and Health Technology Assessment' (2012) 10 Social Theory & Health 1

Kendrick A, 'Measuring Compliance: Social Rights and the Maximum Available Resources Dilemma' (2017) 39 Human Rights Quarterly 657

Khalfan A, 'Division of Responsibility amongst States' in Malcolm Langford and others (eds), *Global Justice, State Duties: The Extraterritorial Scope of Economic, Social, and Cultural Rights in International Law* (Cambridge University Press 2012)

Kieslich K and Littlejohns P, 'Does Accountability for Reasonableness Work? A Protocol for a Mixed Methods Study Using an Audit Tool to Evaluate the Decision-Making of Clinical Commissioning Groups in England: Table 1' (2015) 5 BMJ Open e007908

Kirkdale R and others, 'The Cost of a QALY' (2010) 103 QJM: An International Journal of Medicine 715

Klemp M, Frønsdal KB and Facey K, 'What Principles Should Govern the Use of Managed Entry Agreements?' (2011) 27 International Journal of Technology Assessment in Health Care 77

Klingler C and others, 'Regulatory Space and the Contextual Mediation of Common Functional Pressures: Analyzing the Factors That Led to the German Efficiency Frontier Approach' (2013) 109 Health Policy 270

Klonschinski A, '"Economic Imperialism" in Health Care Resource Allocation – How Can Equity Considerations Be Incorporated into Economic Evaluation?' (2014) 21 Journal of Economic Methodology 158

Klonschinski A, *The Economics of Resource Allocation in Health Care: Cost-Utility, Social Value, and Fairness* (Routledge 2016)

Kluger S and others, 'Is QALY-Based Rationing Illegal in Countries with a Natural-Law-Constitution? A Multidisciplinary Systematic Review' (2020) 14 Ethics, Medicine and Public Health 100484

Koch IE, 'The Justifiability of Indivisible Rights' (2003) 72 Nordic Journal of International Law 3

Kondowe GJ, 'Implementing Economic and Social Rights in "Domestic" Jurisdictions: Understanding the Minimum Core Obligations Approach' (2020) 46 Commonwealth Law Bulletin 314

Kostyak L and others, 'A Means of Improving Public Health in Low- and Middle-Income Countries? Benefits and Challenges of International Public–Private Partnerships' (2017) 149 Public Health 120

Krajewski M, 'Human Rights and Austerity Programmes' in Christian Tietje, Rosa M Lastra and Thomas Cottier (eds), *The Rule of Law in Monetary Affairs: World Trade Forum* (Cambridge University Press 2014)

Kravitz RL, Duan N and Braslow J, 'Evidence-Based Medicine, Heterogeneity of Treatment Effects, and the Trouble with Averages' (2004) 82 The Milbank Quarterly 661

Kristensen FB and others, 'The HTA Core Model®: 10 Years of Developing an International Framework to Share Multidimensional Value Assessment' (2017) 20 Value in Health 244

Kristensen FB and Husereau D, 'Identifying the Need for Good Practices in Health Technology Assessment: Summary of the ISPOR HTA Council Working Group Report on Good Practices in HTA (Online Appendix)' 46

Kumar R and Singh J, 'Biosimilar Drugs: Current Status' (2014) 4 International Journal of Applied & Basic Medical Research 63

Kuosmanen J, 'Towards "Human Rights Compatible" Public Budgets: An Account of Institutional Virtues' (2016) 64 Political Studies 683

Lakdawalla DN and others, 'Defining Elements of Value in Health Care – A Health Economics Approach: An ISPOR Special Task Force Report [3]' (2018) 21 Value in Health 131

Lamprea E, 'Colombia's Right-to-Health Litigation in a Context of Health Care Reform' in Colleen M Flood and Aeyal Gross (eds), *The Right to Health at the Public/Private Divide* (Cambridge University Press 2014)

Lancsar E and others, 'The Relative Value of Different QALY Types' (2020) 70 Journal of Health Economics 102303

Landman T, 'The Scope of Human Rights: From Background Concepts to Indicators' (2006) 2 Revista Iberoamericana de Derechos Humanos 109

Landman T, 'Measuring Human Rights: Principle, Practice, and Policy'(2004)' 26 Human Rights Quarterly 906

Landwehr C, 'Procedural Justice and Democratic Institutional Design in Health-Care Priority-Setting' (2013) 12 Contemporary Political Theory 296

Langford M, Coomans F and Gómez Isa F, 'Extraterritorial Duties in International Law' in Malcolm Langford and others (eds), *Global Justice, State Duties* (Cambridge University Press 2012)

Langford M and Fukuda-Parr S, ‘The Turn to Metrics’ (2012) 30 Nordic Journal of Human Rights 222

Langford M and King JA, ‘Committee on Economic, Social and Cultural Rights’ in Malcolm Langford (ed), *Social Rights Jurisprudence* (Cambridge University Press 2009)

Langley PC, ‘Great Expectations: Cost-Utility Models as Decision Criteria’ (2016) 7 Innovations in Pharmacy 1

Lenaghan J, *Rationing and Rights in Health Care* (Institute for Public Policy Research 1996)

Leon Kershaw A and Izmirlieva M, ‘Rapid Increase of Health Litigation as a Means of Market Access for Innovative Medicines in Colombia and the Potential Role of Health Technology Assessment’ (2015) 18 Value in Health A810

Li KK and others, ‘Conceptualizing the Use of Public Involvement in Health Policy Decision-Making’ (2015) 138 Social Science & Medicine 14

Liang BA and Mackey T, ‘Public-Private Partnerships to Promote Biosimilar Access, Affordability, and Patient Safety in Emerging Markets’ (2014) 7 Stanford Journal of Law, Science and Policy 1

Liddell K and others, ‘Who Gets the Ventilator? Important Legal Rights in a Pandemic’ (2020) 46 Journal of Medical Ethics 421

Lie RK, ‘Health, Human Rights and Mobilization of Resources for Health’ (2004) 4 BMC International Health and Human Rights

Lile HS, ‘Lost in Operationalisation: Developing Legally Relevant Indicators, Questions and Benchmarks’ (2017) 21 The International Journal of Human Rights 1378

Linarelli J, Salomon ME and Sornarajah M, *The Misery of International Law: Confrontations with Injustice in the Global Economy* (Oxford University Press 2018)

Lindor RA, ‘Advancing Evidence-Based Medicine by Expanding Coverage with Evidence Development Comment’ (2011) 52 Jurimetrics [i]

Littlejohns P and others, ‘Creating Sustainable Health Care Systems: Agreeing Social (Societal) Priorities through Public Participation’ (2019) 33 Journal of Health Organization and Management 18

Liu Y and Yang J, ‘A Study of Legal Framework of National Drug Price Negotiations in China’ (2017) 10 Chinese Journal of Health Policy 20

London L, *Can Human Rights Serve as a Tool for Equity?* (Regional Network for Equity in Health in Southern Africa (EQUINET) and the University of Cape Town School of Public Health and Family Medicine 2003) <http://www.equinetafrica.org/bibl/docs/POL14rights.pdf> accessed 28 June 2021

London L, ‘What Is a Human-Rights Based Approach to Health and Does It Matter?’ (2008) 10 Health and Human Rights 65

Lopes E and others, 'Involving Patients in Health Technology Funding Decisions: Stakeholder Perspectives on Processes Used in Australia' (2016) 19 Health Expectations 331

López-Casasnovas G and Pellisé-Urquiza L, 'Resource Allocation and Priority-Setting in Health Care Systems' in RM Scheffler (ed), *World Scientific Handbook of Global Health Economics and Public Policy (A 3-volume Set)*

López-Gómez C and others, 'COVID-19 Critical Supplies: The Manufacturing Repurposing Challenge' (*UNIDO*, 2020)

Luce BR and others, 'EBM, HTA, and CER: Clearing the Confusion' (2010) 88 The Milbank Quarterly 256

Lysdahl K and others, 'Guidance for Assessing Effectiveness, Economic Aspects, Ethical Aspects, Socio-Cultural Aspects and Legal Aspects in Complex Technologies' (Integrated Health Technology Assessment for Evaluating Complex Technologies (INTEGRATE-HTA) 2016) <Available from: http://www.integrate-hta.eu/downloads/> accessed 21 August 2021

'Maastricht Principles on Extraterritorial Obligations of States in the Area of Economic, Social and Cultural Rights' (2011) 29 Netherlands Quarterly of Human Rights 578

MacKinnon CA, 'Substantive Equality Revisited: A Reply to Sandra Fredman' (2016) 14 International Journal of Constitutional Law 739

MacNaughton G, 'Untangling Equality and Non-discrimination to Promote the Right to Health Care for All' (2009) 11 Health and Human Rights 47

MacNaughton G, 'Healthcare Systems and Equality Rights' (2011) 6 The Equal Rights Review 61

Mahajan M, 'The Right to Health as the Right to Treatment: Shifting Conceptions of Public Health' (2012) 79 Social Research: An International Quarterly 819

Mahendraratnam N and others, 'Understanding Use of Real-world Data and Real-world Evidence to Support Regulatory Decisions on Medical Product Effectiveness' (2022) 111 Clinical Pharmacology & Therapeutics 150

Mahfood TC, 'Sovaldi: The High Price for a Cure' (2018) 27 Annals of Health Law 37

Mahlich J and others, 'Cultural Beliefs, Utility Values, and Health Technology Assessment' (2018) 16 Cost Effectiveness and Resource Allocation 1

Maluka S and others, 'Implementing Accountability for Reasonableness Framework at District Level in Tanzania: A Realist Evaluation' (2011) 6 Implementation Science 11

Mamiya H, 'Update of Drug Pricing System in Japan' (Ministry of Health, Welfare, Japan 2018)

Maniadakis N and others, 'Comprehensive Taxonomy and Worldwide Trends in Pharmaceutical Policies in Relation to Country Income Status' (2017) 17 BMC Health Services Research 371

Maniadakis N and others, 'Shaping Pharmaceutical Tenders for Effectiveness and Sustainability in Countries with Expanding Healthcare Coverage' (2018) 16 Applied Health Economics and Health Policy 591

Mann JM and others, 'Health and Human Rights' (1994) 1 Health and Human Rights 6

Marks JH, 'Toward a Systemic Ethics of Public–Private Partnerships Related to Food and Health' (2014) 24 Kennedy Institute of Ethics Journal 267

Marks S, 'Health, Development, and Human Rights' in Anna Gatti and Andrea Boggio (eds), *Health and Development* (Springer 2009)

Marks SP, 'Normative Expansion of the Right to Health and the Proliferation of Human Rights' (2016) 49 George Washington International Law Review. 97

Marks SP, 'Integrating a Human Rights-Based Approach to Development and the Right to Development into Global Governance for Health' in Lawrence Gostin and Benjamin Manson Meier (eds), *Human Rights in Global Health: Rights-Based Governance for a Globalizing World* (Oxford University Press 2018)

Martelli F and others, 'Health Technology Assessment Agencies: An International Overview of Organizational Aspects' (2007) 23 International Journal of Technology Assessment in Health Care 414

Martin-Ortega O and O'Brien CM, 'Public Procurement and Human Rights: Interrogating the Role of the State as Buyer' in Olga Martin-Ortega and Claire Methven O'Brien (eds), *Public Procurement and Human Rights* (Edward Elgar Publishing 2019)

Maru V, 'Allies Unknown: Social Accountability and Legal Empowermen' in Stephen Golub and Thomas McInerney (eds), *Legal Empowerment: Practitioners' Perspectives* (International Development Law Organization 2010)

Matthews D, 'Right to Health and Patents' in Christophe Geiger (ed), *Research Handbook on Human Rights and Intellectual Property* (Edward Elgar Publishing 2015)

McKenna J and Smith W, 'The Legality of QALY under the ADA' (Pioneer Institute 2020)

Mégret F, 'Nature of Obligations' in Sangeeta Shah and others (eds), *International Human Rights Law* (3rd edn, Oxford University Press 2017)

Meier BM, 'Organization, the Evolution of Human Rights, and the Failure to Achieve Health for All' in John Harrington and Maria Stuttaford (eds), *Global Health and Human Rights* (2010)

Meier BM and Fox AM, 'Development as Health: Employing the Collective Right to Development to Achieve the Goals of the Individual Right to Health' (2008) 30 Hum. Rts. Q. 259

Meier BM and Fox AM, 'International Obligations through Collective Rights: Moving from Foreign Health Assistance to Global Health Governance' (2010) 12 Health and Human Rights 61

Meier BM and Kastler F, 'Development of Human Rights through WHO' in Lawrence Gostin and Benjamin Mason Meier (eds), *Human Rights in Global Health*, vol 1 (Oxford University Press 2018)

Meier BM and Onzivu W, 'The Evolution of Human Rights in World Health Organization Policy and the Future of Human Rights through Global Health Governance' (2014) 128 Public Health 179

Meneu R, 'The Wisdom Tooth of Health Technology Assessment' in Juan E Llano-Señarís and Carlos Campillo-Artero (eds), *Health Technology Assessment and Health Policy Today: A Multifaceted View of Their Unstable Crossroads* (Springer International Publishing 2015)

Menon D and Marshall D, 'The Internationalization of Health Technology Assessment' (1996) 12 International Journal of Technology Assessment in Health Care 45

Meregaglia M and others, '"Mapping" Health State Utility Values from Non-preference-Based Measures: A Systematic Literature Review in Rare Diseases' (2020) 38 PharmacoEconomics 557

Merlin T and others, 'What's in a Name? Developing Definitions for Common Health Technology Assessment Product Types of the International Network of Agencies for Health Technology Assessment (INAHTA)' (2014) 30 International Journal of Technology Assessment in Health Care 430

Merry SE, 'Measuring the World: Indicators, Human Rights, and Global Governance' (2011) 52 Current Anthropology S83

Merry SE, *The Seductions of Quantification: Measuring Human Rights, Gender Violence, and Sex Trafficking* (University of Chicago Press 2016)

Mestre Ferrandiz J and others, 'Multi-indication Pricing: Nice in Theory but Can It Work in Practice?' (2018) 36 PharmacoEconomics 1407

Michaels JA, 'Potential for Epistemic Injustice in Evidence-Based Healthcare Policy and Guidance' (2021) 47 Journal of Medical Ethics 417

Mielke D and Rohde V, 'Randomized Controlled Trials: A Critical Re-appraisal' [2020] Neurosurgical Review

Milewa T and Barry C, 'Health Policy and the Politics of Evidence' (2005) 39 Social Policy & Administration 498

Miller H, 'Human Rights and Development: The Advancement of New Campaign Strategies' (2019) 23 The International Journal of Human Rights 719

Miller H and Redhead R, 'Beyond "Rights-Based Approaches"? Employing a Process and Outcomes Framework' (2019) 23 The International Journal of Human Rights 699

Millington KA and Bhardwaj M, 'Evidence and Experience of Procurement in Health Sector Decentralisation' (Institute of Development Studies 2017)

Minkler L, 'Introduction: Why Economic and Social Human Rights?' in Lanse Minkler (ed), *The State of Economic and Social Human Rights: A Global Overview* (Cambridge University Press 2013)

Minkler L and Sweeney S, 'On the Indivisibility and Interdependence of Basic Rights in Developing Countries' (2011) 33 Human Rights Quarterly 351

Moeckli D, 'Equality and Non-discrimination' in Daniel Moeckli and others (eds), *International Human Rights Law* (Oxford University Press 2010)

Mohammad Mosadeghrad A, 'Healthcare Service Quality: Towards a Broad Definition' (2013) 26 International Journal of Health Care Quality Assurance 203

Mok EA, 'International Assistance and Cooperation for Access to Essential Medicines' (2010) 12 Health and Human Rights 73

Montel L and others, 'The Right to Health in Times of Pandemic: What Can We Learn from the UK's Response to the COVID-19 Outbreak?' (2020) 22 Health and Human Rights 227

Moon S, 'Respecting the Right to Access to Medicines: Implications of the UN Guiding Principles on Business and Human Rights for the Pharmaceutical Industry' (2013) 15 Health and Human Rights 13

Moon S, 'Global Health Law and Governance: Concepts, Tools, Actors and Power' in Gian Luca Burci and Brigit Toebes (eds), *Research Handbook on Global Health Law* (Edward Elgar Publishing 2018)

Moon S, 'Defining the Concept of Fair Pricing for Medicines' [2020] BMJ l4726

Moran V and Fidler AH, 'Health Technology Assessment in Europe: Communicating and Applying Lessons Learned from High-Income Countries to Middle-Income Countries' (2010) 3 Journal of Management & Marketing in Healthcare 141

Morawa AH, 'Vulnerability as a Concept of International Human Rights Law' (2003) 6 Journal of International Relations and Development 139

Morel T and others, 'Reconciling Uncertainty of Costs and Outcomes with the Need for Access to Orphan Medicinal Products: A Comparative Study of Managed Entry Agreements across Seven European Countries' (2013) 8 Orphanet Journal of Rare Diseases 198

Morgan SG, Bathula HS and Moon S, 'Pricing of Pharmaceuticals Is Becoming a Major Challenge for Health Systems' [2020] BMJ l4627

Mortimer D and Segal L, 'Comparing the Incomparable? A Systematic Review of Competing Techniques for Converting Descriptive Measures of Health Status into QALY-Weights' (2008) 28 Medical Decision Making 66

Moyn S, 'A Powerless Companion: Human Rights in the Age of Neoliberalism' (2014) 77 Law & Contemporary Problems. 147

Mueller D, Tivey D and Croce D, 'Health-Technology Assessment: Its Role in Strengthening Health Systems in Developing Countries' (2017) 2 Southern African Journal of Public Health 6

Mulholland LA, 'Rights, Utilitarianism, and the Conflation of Persons' (1986) 83 The Journal of Philosophy 323

Mullainathan S and Shafir E, *Scarcity: Why Having Too Little Means so Much* (Macmillan 2013)

Müller A, 'The Minimum Core Approach to the Right to Health Progress and Remaining Challenges' in Sabine Klotz and others (eds), *Healthcare as a Human Rights Issue* (transcript Verlag 2017)

Murphy T, *Health and Human Rights* (Bloomsbury Publishing 2014)

Mykhalovskiy E and Weir L, 'The Problem of Evidence-Based Medicine: Directions for Social Science' (2004) 59 Social Science & Medicine 1059

Neumann PJ and Cohen JT, 'QALYs in 2018: Advantages and Concerns' (2018) 319 JAMA 2473

Neumann PJ, Goldie SJ and Weinstein MC, 'Preference-Based Measures in Economic Evaluation in Health Care' (2000) 21 Annual Review of Public Health 587

Nevo I and Slonim-Nevo V, 'The Myth of Evidence-Based Practice: Towards Evidence-Informed Practice' (2011) 41 British Journal of Social Work 1176

Newdick C, 'Health Care Rights and NHS Rationing: Turning Theory into Practice' (2014) 32 Revista Portuguesa de Saúde Pública 151

Neyt M, 'Value-Based Pricing: Do Not Throw Away the Baby with the Bath Water' (2018) 36 PharmacoEconomics 1

Ngorsuraches S, 'Defining Types of Economic Evaluation.' (2008) 91 Journal of the Medical Association of Thailand= Chotmaihet thangphaet S21

NHS England, '013/14 NHS Standard Contract for Cryopyrin Associated Periodic Syndrome (All Ages)' <https://www.england.nhs.uk/wp-content/uploads/2013/06/e13-cryopyrin-ass-periodic-syn.pdf>

Niada-Avshalom L, 'Some Scepticism on the Right to Health: The Case of the Provision of Medicines' (2015) 19 The International Journal of Human Rights 527

NICE Board Meeting, 'Value Based Assessment. Item 4' (Nice 2014) <http://www.pruceconsulting.co.uk/ITEM%2004%20-%20Value%20Based%20Assessment%20of%20Health%20Technologies.pdf?attredirects=0> accessed 15 January 2020

Nickel JW, 'Rethinking Indivisibility: Towards a Theory of Supporting Relations between Human Rights' (2008) 30 Human Rights Quarterly 984

Nolan A, 'Putting ESR-Based Budget Analysis into Practice: Addressing the Conceptual Challenges' in Aoife Nolan (ed), *Human Rights and Public Finance: Budgets and the Promotion of Economic and Social Rights* (2013)

Nolan A (ed), *Economic and Social Rights after the Global Financial Crisis* (Cambridge University Press 2014)

Nolan A , 'Not Fit for Purpose? Human Rights in Times of Financial and Economic Crisis'(2015)' 4 European Human Rights Law Review 358

Nord E, 'The Person-Trade-off Approach to Valuing Health Care Programs' (1995) 15 Medical Decision Making 201

Norheim O, 'Healthcare Rationing – Are Additional Criteria Needed for Assessing Evidence Based Clinical Practice Guidelines?' (1999) 319 BMJ 1426

Norheim O and Gloppen S, 'Litigating for Medicines. How Can We Assess Impact on Health Outcomes?' in Alicia Ely Yamin and Siri Gloppen (eds), *Litigating health rights: Can courts bring more justice to health?* (Harvard University Press)

Norheim OF and Wilson BM, 'Health Rights Litigation and Access to Medicines: Priority Classification of Successful Cases from Costa Rica's Constitutional Chamber of the Supreme Court' (2014) 16 Health and Human Rights 47

Novaes HMD and Soárez PC de, 'Health Technology Assessment (HTA) Organizations: Dimensions of the Institutional and Political Framework' (2016) 32 Cadernos de Saúde Pública

Nuijten MJC and Dubois DJ, 'Cost-Utility Analysis: Current Methodological Issues and Future Perspectives' (2011) 2 Frontiers in pharmacology 29

Nunes R, 'Evidence-Based Medicine: A New Tool for Resource Allocation?' (2003) 6 Medicine, Health Care and Philosophy 297

Nunes R, Nunes SB and Rego G, 'Health Care as a Universal Right' (2017) 25 Journal of Public Health 1

Nyak N, 'Advancing Competition Frameworks in the Low- and Middle-Income Country Context' in Frederick M Abbott and others (eds), *Using Competition Laws to Promote Access to Medicines: A Guidebook for Low- and Middle- Income Countries* (United Nations Development Programme 2014)

Odello M and Seatzu F, *The UN Committee on Economic, Social and Cultural Rights: The Law, Process and Practice* (Taylor & Francis 2013)

OECD, *OECD Health Policy Studies Value for Money in Health Spending* (OECD Publishing 2010)

Office of the High Commissioner for Human Rights, *Realizing Human Rights through Government Budgets* (United Nations, 2017)

Office of the High Commissioner for Human Rights, 'Report on Indicators for Monitoring Compliance with International Human Rights Instruments' (2006) HRI/MC/2006/7

Ognyanova D, Zentner A and Busse R, 'Pharmaceutical Reform 2010 in Germany' (2011) 17 Eurohealth 11

Okuda T, 'Deliberation, Fair Outcome, and Empirical Evidence: An Analogy with Archives' in Akira Akabayashi (ed), *The Future of Bioethics: International Dialogues* (Oxford University Press 2014)

Oliver K and Pearce W, 'Three Lessons from Evidence-Based Medicine and Policy: Increase Transparency, Balance Inputs and Understand Power' (2017) 3 Palgrave Communications 1

O'Mahony JF, 'Beneluxa: What Are the Prospects for Collective Bargaining on Pharmaceutical Prices Given Diverse Health Technology Assessment Processes?' (2019) 37 PharmacoEconomics 627

Ooms G and others, 'Could International Compulsory Licensing Reconcile Tiered Pricing of Pharmaceuticals with the Right to Health?' (2014) 14 BMC International Health and Human Rights 37

Ooms G and Hanefeld J, 'Threat of Compulsory Licences Could Increase Access to Essential Medicines' [2019] BMJ l2098

Ooms G, Keygnaert I and Hammonds R, 'The Right to Health: From Citizen's Right to Human Right (and Back)' (2019) 172 Public Health 99

Oortwijn W, Jansen M and Baltussen R, *Evidence-Informed Deliberative Processes Version 2.0* (Radboud University Medical Center 2021)

Oortwijn W, Jansen M and Baltussen R, 'Evidence-Informed Deliberative Processes for Health Benefit Package Design – Part II: A Practical Guide' [2021] International Journal of Health Policy and Management 1

Oortwijn W, Sampietro-Colom L and Trowman R, 'How to Deal with the Inevitable: Generating Real-World Data and Using Real-World Evidence for HTA Purposes – From Theory to Action' (2019) 35 International Journal of Technology Assessment in Health Care 346

O'Rourke B and others, 'The New Definition of Health Technology Assessment: A Milestone in International Collaboration' (2020) 36 International Journal of Technology Assessment in Health Care 187

O'Rourke B, Oortwijn W and Schuller T, 'The New Definition of Health Technology Assessment: A Milestone in International Collaboration' (2020) 36 International Journal of Technology Assessment in Health Care 187

Ortenzi F and others, 'Whole of Government and Whole of Society Approaches: Call for Further Research to Improve Population Health and Health Equity' (2022) 7 BMJ Global Health e009972

Osiatynski W, *Human Rights and Their Limits* (Cambridge University Press 2009)

Ozsu U, 'Neoliberalism and Human Rights: The Brandt Commission and the Struggle for a New World' (2018) 81 Law & Contemporary Problems 139

P. Janecka I, 'Quality vs. Value' (2009) 339 BMJ b4346

Padula WV, 'State and Federal Policy Solutions to Rising Prescriptions Drug Prices in the U.S. Symposium' (2019) 22 Journal of Health Care Law and Policy 15

Paolucci F and others, 'Decision Making and Priority Setting: The Evolving Path towards Universal Health Coverage' (2017) 15 Applied Health Economics and Health Policy 697

Parisi TJ, 'How Much Did You Pay for Your Heart: Is a Centralized Entity Performing Health Technology Assessment with Cost-Effectiveness Analysis the Answer to the Rising Costs of Health Care?' [2009] Jurimetrics 285

Parker-Lue S, Santoro M and Koski G, 'The Ethics and Economics of Pharmaceutical Pricing' (2015) 55 Annual Review of Pharmacology and Toxicology 191

Paulden M, 'Recent Amendments to NICE's Value-Based Assessment of Health Technologies: Implicitly Inequitable?' (2017) 17 Expert Review of Pharmacoeconomics & Outcomes Research 239

Pavel CE, 'Healthcare: Between a Human and a Conventional Right' (2019) 35 Economics & Philosophy 499

Pavlos Eleftheriadis, 'A Right to Health Care' (2012) 40 The Journal of Law, Medicine & Ethics 268

Pearce W, Raman S and Turner A, 'Randomised Trials in Context: Practical Problems and Social Aspects of Evidence-Based Medicine and Policy' (2015) 16 Trials 1

Pearson SD, 'Why the Coming Debate Over the QALY and Disability Will Be Different' (2019) 47 The Journal of Law, Medicine & Ethics 304

Penchansky R and Thomas JW, 'The Concept of Access: Definition and Relationship to Consumer Satisfaction' [1981] Medical care 127

Perehudoff K, 'Health, Human Rights and National Constitutions' [2008] WHO (July 31, 2008)

Perehudoff K and Forman L, 'What Constitutes "Reasonable" State Action on Core Obligations? Considering a Right to Health Framework to Provide Essential Medicines' (2019) 11 Journal of Human Rights Practice 1

Perehudoff K, Toebes B and Hogerzeil H, 'Essential Medicines in National Constitutions: Progress since 2008' (2016) 18 Health and Human Rights 141

Perlingeiro R, 'Procedural and Substantive Judicial Review of the Right to Health in Brazil' [2014] SSRN Electronic Journal <https://doi.org/10.2139/ssrn.2481539> accessed 5 April 2018

Persson Å, Weitz N and Nilsson M, 'Follow-Up and Review of the Sustainable Development Goals: Alignment vs. Internalization' (2016) 25 Review of European, Comparative & International Environmental Law 59

Pharmaceutical Benefits Advisory Committee, 'Public Summary Document: Erenumab (Aimovig®)' (July 2018) <https://www.pbs.gov.au/info/industry/listing/elements/pbac-meetings/psd accessed 16 September 2025>

Pharmaceutical Benefits Advisory Committee, 'Public Summary Document: Fremanezumab (Ajovy®)' (March 2020) https://www.pbs.gov.au/info/industry/listing/elements/pbac-meetings/psd accessed 16 September 2025

Pharmaceutical Benefits Advisory Committee, 'Public Summary Document: Galcanezumab (Emgality®)' (July 2019) https://www.pbs.gov.au/info/industry/listing/elements/pbac-meetings/psd accessed 16 September 2025

Pichon-Riviere A and others, 'Stakeholder Involvement in the Health Technology Assessment Process in Latin America' (2018) 34 International Journal of Technology Assessment in Health Care 248

Pickard AS, 'Is It Time to Update Societal Value Sets for Preference-Based Measures of Health?' (2015) 33 PharmacoEconomics 191

Pieterse M, 'Eating Socioeconomic Rights: The Usefulness of Rights Talk in Alleviating Social Hardship Revisited' (2007) 29 Human Rights Quarterly 796

Pinto-Prades J-L and others, 'Valuing QALYs at the End of Life' (2014) 113 Social Science & Medicine 5

Plomer A, 'The Human Rights Paradox: Intellectual Property Rights and Rights of Access to Science' (2013) 35 Human Rights Quarterly 143

Porter B, 'Rethinking Progressive Realization: How Should It Be Implemented in Canada?' <http://www.socialrights.ca/documents/publications/Porter%20Progressive%20Implementation.pdf> accessed 21 November 2019

Potter H, 'Participation and the Right to the Highest Attainable Standard of Health' (Human Rights Centre, University of Essex 2003)

Poudel RS, Shrestha S and Poudel A, 'Immense Price Variation of Branded Generic Medicines in Low-Income Countries: The Need for an Inclusive Price Control Policy' (2020) 16 Research in Social & Administrative Pharmacy: RSAP 1326

Powers M, 'Health Care as a Human Right: The Problem of Indeterminate Content' (2015) 6 Jurisprudence 138

Pribytkova E, 'What Global Human Rights Obligations Do We Have?' (2019) 20 Chicago Journal of International Law 384

Puras D, 'Universal Health Coverage: A Return to Alma-Ata and Ottawa' (2016) 18 Health and Human Rights 7

Pūras D and others, 'The Right to Health Must Guide Responses to COVID-19' (2020) 395 The Lancet 1888

Qadeer I and Reddy S, 'Medical Care in the Shadow of Public Private Partnership' (2006) 34 Social Scientist 4

Queiroz C and Martinez AL, 'Legal Frameworks for Successful Public–Private Partnerships' in Piet De Vries and Yehoue Etienne B. (eds), *The Routledge Companion to Public-Private Partnerships* (Routledge 2010)

Quintavalla A and Heine K, 'Priorities and Human Rights' (2019) 23 The International Journal of Human Rights 679

Rabeharisoa V, Moreira T and Akrich M, 'Evidence-Based Activism: Patients', Users' and Activists' Groups in Knowledge Society.' (2014) 9 BioSocieties 111

Raftery J, 'Value Based Pricing: Can It Work?' (2013) 347 BMJ f5941

Raimond VC and others, 'Why France Spends Less Than the United States on Drugs: A Comparative Study of Drug Pricing and Pricing Regulation' (2021) 99 The Milbank Quarterly 240

Ramani SV and Urias E, 'Access to Critical Medicines: When Are Compulsory Licenses Effective in Price Negotiations?' (2015) 135 Social Science & Medicine 75

Rand L, 'Legitimate Priority-Setting: Refining Accountability for Reasonableness and Its Application within NICE' (PhD Thesis, 2016)

Rand LZ and Kesselheim AS, 'Controversy Over Using Quality-Adjusted Life-Years In Cost-Effectiveness Analyses: A Systematic Literature Review' (2021) 40 Health Affairs 1402

Ransom ER (ed), *The Healthcare Quality Book: Vision, Strategy, and Tools* (2nd ed, Health Administration Press 2008)

Raustiala K, 'The Architecture of International Cooperation: Transgovernmental Networks and the Future of International Law' (2002) 43 Virginia Journal of International Law 1

Rawles J, 'Castigating QALYs.' (1989) 15 Journal of Medical Ethics 143

Rawlins MD, 'Pharmacopolitics and Deliberative Democracy' (2005) 5 Clinical Medicine 471

Rawls J, *A Theory of Justice* (Oxford University Press 1999)

RedETSA, 'What Is RedETSA?' (*RedETSA*) <http://redetsa.org/wp/?page_id=3952> accessed 5 May 2020

Rehfuess EA and others, 'The WHO-INTEGRATE Evidence to Decision Framework Version 1.0: Integrating WHO Norms and Values and a Complexity Perspective' (2019) 4 BMJ Global Health

Reich MR and others, 'Workshop on Public Health Law and Ethics I & II: The Challenge of Public/Private Partnerships (PPPs)' (2003) 31 Journal of Law, Medicine & Ethics 90

Resnik DB, MacDougall DR and Smith EM, 'Ethical Dilemmas in Protecting Susceptible Subpopulations from Environmental Health Risks: Liberty, Utility, Fairness, and Accountability for Reasonableness' (2018) 18 The American Journal of Bioethics 29

Reveiz L and others, 'Litigios por derecho a la salud en tres países de América Latina: revisión sistemática de la literatura' (2013) 33 Revista Panamericana de Salud Pública 213

Rida NA and Ibrahim MIM, 'Medicines Pricing Policy and Strategies in Developing Countries: A Review' in Mohamed Izham Mohamed Ibrahim, Zaheer-Ud-Din Babar and Albert I Weirtheimer (eds), *Social and Administrative Aspects of Pharmacy in Low-and Middle-Income Countries* (Elsevier 2018)

Riedel E, Giacca G and Golay C, 'The Development of Economic, Social, and Cultural Rights in International Law' in Eibe Riedel, Gilles Giacca and Christophe Golay (eds), *Economic, Social, and Cultural Rights in International Law: Contemporary Issues and Challenges* (Oxford University Press 2014)

Roberts MJ and Reich MR, 'Ethical Analysis in Public Health' (2002) 359 The Lancet 1055

Robertson RE, 'Measuring State Compliance with the Obligation to Devote the Maximum Available Resources to Realizing Economic, Social, and Cultural Rights' (1994) 16 Human Rights Quarterly 693

Rogers W, 'Does Evidence-Based Medicine Offer Fair Benefits for All?' (2004) 6 AMA Journal of Ethics

Rogers W, Degeling C and Townley C, 'Equity under the Knife: Justice and Evidence in Surgery: Equity under the Knife: Justice and Evidence in Surgery' (2014) 28 Bioethics 119

Rose N, 'Unreasonable Rights: Mental Illness and the Limits of the Law' (1985) 12 Journal of Law and Society 199

Rosga A and Satterthwaite M, 'Measuring Human Rights: UN Indicators in Critical Perspective' in Kevin Davis and others (eds), *Governance by indicators: Global power through classification and rankings* (Oxford University Press 2012)

Rosga A and Satterthwaite ML, 'The Trust in Indicators: Measuring Human Rights' (2009) 27 Berkeley Journal of International Law 253

Rosselli D and others, 'HTA Implementation in Latin American Countries: Comparison of Current and Preferred Status' (2017) 14 Value in Health Regional Issues 20

Rothstein MA, 'Rethinking the Meaning of Public Health' (2002) 30 The Journal of Law, Medicine and Ethics 144

Rouse WB, 'Impacts of Healthcare Price Controls: Potential Unintended Consequences of Firms' Responses to Price Policies' (2010) 4 IEEE Systems Journal 34

Royo-Bordonada MÁ and Román-Maestre B, 'Towards Public Health Ethics' (2015) 36 Public Health Reviews

Ruger JP, 'Toward a Theory of a Right to Health: Capability and Incompletely Theorized Agreements' (2006) 18 Yale Journal of Law and the Humanities 273

Rumbold B and others, 'Universal Health Coverage, Priority Setting, and the Human Right to Health' (2017) 390 The Lancet 712

Rumbold BE, 'Review Article: The Moral Right to Health: A Survey of Available Conceptions' (2017) 20 Critical Review of International Social and Political Philosophy 508

Saarni SL, 'Evidence Based Medicine Guidelines: A Solution to Rationing or Politics Disguised as Science?' (2004) 30 Journal of Medical Ethics 171

Sabik LM and Lie RK, 'Principles versus Procedures in Making Health Care Coverage Decisions: Addressing Inevitable Conflicts' (2008) 29 Theoretical Medicine and Bioethics 73

Sackett DL and others, 'Evidence Based Medicine: What It Is and What It Isn't' (1996) 312 British Medical Journal 71

Safaei J, 'Deliberative Democracy in Health Care: Current Challenges and Future Prospects' (2015) 7 Journal of healthcare leadership 123

Sahoo M and Pradhan J, 'Sustainable Development Goals and Reproductive Healthcare Rights of Internally Displaced Persons in India' (2019) 12 International Journal of Human Rights in Healthcare 38

Salomon ME, 'Deprivation, Causation and the Law of International Cooperation' in Malcolm Langford and others (eds), *Global Justice, State Duties* (Cambridge University Press 2012)

Salomon ME and Seiderman I, 'Human Rights Norms for a Globalized World: The Maastricht Principles on Extraterritorial Obligations of States in the Area of Economic, Social and Cultural Rights: The Maastricht Principles on Extraterritorial Obligations' (2012) 3 Global Policy 458

Santos L, 'Judicialization of Health: The Theses of the STF' (2021) 45 Saúde em Debate 807

Scheinin M, 'Just Another Word?: Jurisdiction in the Roadmaps of State Responsibility and Human Rights' in Malcolm Langford and others (eds), *Global Justice, State Duties : The Extraterritorial Scope of Economic, Social, and Cultural Rights in International Law* (Cambridge University Press 2013)

Schlegl E, Ducournau P and Ruof J, 'Different Weights of the Evidence-Based Medicine Triad in Regulatory, Health Technology Assessment, and Clinical Decision Making' (2017) 31 Pharmaceutical Medicine 213

Schneider P and Vogler S, 'Practice of External Price Referencing' *Medicine Price Surveys, Analyses and Comparisons* (Elsevier 2019)

Schokkaert E, 'Philosophers and Taboo Trade-Offs in Health Care' in A Gosseries and Y Vanderborght (eds), *Arguing about Justice: Essays for Philippe Van Parijs* (Presses universitaires de Louvain 2011)

Schokkaert E, 'How to Introduce More (Or Better) Ethical Arguments in HTA?' (2015) 31 International Journal of Technology Assessment in Health Care 111

Schrecker T, 'Denaturalizing Scarcity: A Strategy of Enquiry for Public-Health Ethics' (2008) 86 Bulletin of the World Health Organization 600

Schrecker T, 'Priority Setting: Right Answer to a Far Too Narrow Question? Comment on "Global Developments in Priority Setting in Health"' (2017) 7 International Journal of Health Policy and Management 86

Schulte M-C, *Evidence-Based Medicine: A Paradigm Ready to Be Challenged?: How Scientific Evidence Shapes Our Understanding and Use of Medicine* (JB Metzler 2020)

Schwarzer R and Siebert U, 'Methods, Procedures, and Contextual Characteristics of Health Technology Assessment and Health Policy Decision Making: Comparison of Health Technology Assessment Agencies in Germany, United Kingdom,

France, and Sweden' (2009) 25 International Journal of Technology Assessment in Health Care 305

Scott A and Kernick D, 'Understanding Healthcare Delivery: The Economic Contribution' *Getting Health Economics into Practice* (CRC Press 2018)

Scott C, 'Analysing Regulatory Space: Fragmented Resources and Institutional Design' [2001] Public law 283

Sekalala S, Masud H and Bosco RT, 'Human Rights Mechanisms for Anti-corruption, Transparency and Accountability: Enabling the Right to Health' (2020) 13 Global Health Action 1699343

Sen A, 'Why Health Equity?' (2002) 11 Health Economics 659

Sen A, 'Elements of a Theory of Human Rights' (2004) 32 Philosophy & Public Affairs 315

Sepúlveda Carmona M, *The Nature of the Obligations Under the International Covenant on Economic, Social and Cultural Rights* (Intersentia 2003)

Sepúlveda M, 'Obligations of 'International Assistance and Cooperation'in an Optional Protocol to the International Covenant on Economic, Social and Cultural Rights' (2006) 24 Netherlands Quarterly of Human Rights 271

Shadlen KC, Sampat BN and Kapczynski A, 'Patents, Trade and Medicines: Past, Present and Future' (2019) 27 Review of International Political Economy 1

Shah SMB and others, 'A Regulatory Governance Perspective on Health Technology Assessment (HTA) in Sweden' (2014) 116 Health Policy 27

Shelton D and Gould A, 'Positive and Negative Obligations' in Dinah Shelton (ed), *The Oxford Handbook of International Human Rights Law* (OUP 2013)

Shields K, 'The Minimum Core Obligations of Economic, Social and Cultural Rights: The Rights to Health and Education' (World Bank 2017)

Siems M and Nelken D, 'Global Social Indicators and the Concept of Legitimacy' (2017) 13 International Journal of Law in Context 436

Sievers H, Joos A and Hiligsmann M, 'Real-World Evidence: Perspectives on Challenges, Value, and Alignment of Regulatory and National Health Technology Assessment Data Collection Requirements' (2021) 37 International Journal of Technology Assessment in Health Care

Simabuku EMG and others, 'Comissão Nacional de Incorporação de Tecnologias No SUS e a Judicialização Do Acesso à Saúde' (2015) 6 Revista Eletronica Gestão & Saúde 3024

Simoens S, 'Health Technology Assessment and Economic Evaluation across Jurisdictions' (2010) 13 Value in Health 857

Skogly S, *Beyond National Borders: States' Human Rights Obligations in International Cooperation* (Intersentia 2006)

Slaughter JR, 'Hijacking Human Rights: Neoliberalism, the New Historiography, and the End of the Third World' (2018) 40 Human Rights Quarterly 735

Smith GP, 'Aspirational, Paradoxical, or Oxymoronic?' in Belinda Bennett, Sarah Hawkes and Michael Freeman (eds), *Law and Global Health: Current Legal Issues* (Oxford University Press 2014)

Smith PC, 'Measuring Value for Money in Healthcare: Concepts and Tools' (Centre for Health Economics, University of York 2009)

Smith WR, 'Saving Environmental Justice from Proceduralism' (2018) 18 The American Journal of Bioethics 55

Smith WR, 'Legitimacy in Bioethics: Challenging the Orthodoxy' (2018) 44 Journal of Medical Ethics 416

Solomon M, *Making Medical Knowledge* (Oxford University Press 2015)

Sorenson C, Drummond M and Kanavos P, *Ensuring Value for Money in Health Care: The Role of Health Technology Assessment in the European Union* (WHO Regional Office Europe 2008)

Souza KA de O and Souza LEPF de, 'Incorporação de Tecnologias No Sistema Único de Saúde: As Racionalidades Do Processo de Decisão Da Comissão Nacional de Incorporação de Tecnologias No Sistema Único de Saúde' (2018) 42 Saúde em Debate 48

Sparer EV, 'The Legal Right to Health Care: Public Policy and Equal Access' (1976) 6 The Hastings Center Report 39

Sparke M, 'Neoliberal Regime Change and the Remaking of Global Health: From Rollback Disinvestment to Rollout Reinvestment and Reterritorialization' (2020) 27 Review of International Political Economy 48

Sreenivasan G, 'II – Gopal Sreenivasan: A Human Right to Health? Some Inconclusive Scepticism' (2012) 86 Aristotelian Society Supplementary Volume 239

Ssenyonjo M, 'Reflections on State Obligations with Respect to Economic, Social and Cultural Rights in International Human Rights Law' (2011) 15 The International Journal of Human Rights 969

Stafinski T and others, 'Health Technology Funding Decision-Making Processes Around the World: The Same, Yet Different' (2011) 29 PharmacoEconomics 475

Staley LB, 'A Drug's Worth: Why Federal Makes It Hard to Pay for Pharmaceutical Performance' (2018) 98 Boston University Law Review 303

Stanak M, 'Nudging in Neonatology: Practical Wisdom and Accountability for Reasonableness' (2019) 35 International Journal of Technology Assessment in Health Care 5

Staniszewska S and Werkö S, 'Patient-Based Evidence in HTA' *Patient involvement in health technology assessment* (Springer 2017)

Staniszewska S and Werkö SS, 'Mind the Evidence Gap: The Use of Patient-Based Evidence to Create "Complete HTA" in the Twenty-First Century' (2021) 37 International Journal of Technology Assessment in Health Care

STAP, 'Theory of Change: A Short Literature Review and Annotated Bibliography' (Scientific and Technical Advisory Panel (STAP), United Nations Global Environment Facility (GEF)) GEF/STAP/C.57/Inf.05 <https://www.thegef.org/council-meeting-documents/theory-change-short-literature-review-and-annotated-bibliography> accessed 3 April 2022

Starmer K, 'Positive Obligations under the ECHR in the Area of Medical Negligence' in Jeffrey Lowell and Jonathan Cooper (eds), *Understanding Human Rights Principles* (Hart Publishing)

Steffen GE, 'Quality Medical Care: A Definition' (1988) 260 Journal of the American Medical Association 56

Stein D and Valters C, 'Understanding Theory of Change in International Development' (Justice and Security Research Programme, International Development Department, LSE 2012) JSRP Paper 1

Stevens A, Milne R and Burls A, 'Health Technology Assessment: History and Demand' (2003) 25 Journal of Public Health 98

Stewart R, 'NICE Guidelines and the Treatment of Alzheimer's Disease: Evidence-Based Medicine May Be Discriminatory' (2001) 179 British Journal of Psychiatry 367

Stratil JM and others, 'Advancing the WHO-INTEGRATE Framework as a Tool for Evidence-Informed, Deliberative Decision-Making Processes: Exploring the Views of Developers and Users of WHO Guidelines' (2020) 11. International Journal of Health Policy and Management

Stratil JM and others, 'Development of the WHO-INTEGRATE Evidence-to-Decision Framework: An Overview of Systematic Reviews of Decision Criteria for Health Decision-Making' (2020) 18 Cost Effectiveness and Resource Allocation

Stühlinger V, 'Health Technology Assessment (HTA) and Access Policies' (2020) 27 European Journal of Health Law 274

Supply MD, 'Managing Access to Medicines and Health Technologies' [2012] Management Sciences for Health. Available at: www.mds-online.org

Surgey G and others, 'Introducing Health Technology Assessment in Tanzania' [2019] International Journal of Technology Assessment in Health Care 1

Suri A and others, 'Values and Global Health' in Paul Farmer and others (eds), *Reimagining Global Health* (University of California Press 2013)

Sweatman LR and Woollard D, 'Resource Allocation Decisions in Canada's Health Care System: Can These Decisions Be Challenged in a Court of Law' (2002) 62 Health Policy 275

Syrett K, 'Revisiting the Judicial Role in the Allocation of Healthcare Resources: On Deference, Democratic Dialogue and Deliberation' (2005) 30 Journal for Juridical Science 1

Syrett K, 'Priority-Setting and Public Law: Potential Realised or Unfulfilled?' (2006) 7 Medical Law International 265

Syrett K, 'Health Technology Appraisal and the Courts: Accountability for Reasonableness and the Judicial Model of Procedural Justice' (2011) 6 Health Economics, Policy and Law 469

Syrett K, 'Courts, Expertise and Resource Allocation: Is There a Judicial "Legitimacy Problem"?' (2014) 7 Public Health Ethics 112

Syrett K, 'Evolving the Right to Health: Rethinking the Normative Response to Problems of Judicialization' (2018) 20 Health and Human Rights 121

Taggart CP, 'Fairness Versus Welfare: The Limits of Kaplow and Shavell's Pareto Argument' (2016) 99 Marquette Law Review 662

Tantivess S and others, 'Health Technology Assessment Capacity Development in Low- and Middle-Income Countries: Experiences from the International Units of HITAP and NICE' (2017) 6

Taplin DH and Clark H, 'Theory of Change Basics: A Primer on Theory of Change' [2012] New York NY: ActKnowledge

Tasioulas J, *Minimum Core Obligations: Human Rights in the Here and Now* (World Bank 2017)

Tasioulas J, 'The Minimum Core of the Human Right to Health' (World Bank 2017)

Tasioulas J, 'Capabilities, Development and Human Rights: A Conversation with Amartya Sen' (*ABC Religion & Ethics*) <https://www.abc.net.au/religion/conversation-with-amartya-sen/10599038> accessed 16 April 2021

Tasioulas J and Vayena E, 'Getting Human Rights Right in Global Health Policy' (2015) 385 The Lancet e42

Teerawattananon Y and others, 'Historical Development of the HTAsiaLink Network and Its Key Determinants of Success' (2018) 34 International Journal of Technology Assessment in Health Care 260

Teerawattananon Y and Luz A, 'Health Technology Assessment as a Priority-Setting Tool for Universal Health Coverage: The Call for Global Action at the Prince Mahidol Award Conference 2016' (2016) 34 PharmacoEconomics1

Teixeira C, 'Priority, Agency and Cooperation: How International Human Rights Law Helps Fulfil the Economic and Social Rights of the Most Vulnerable' (2019) 24 The International Journal of Human Rights 1031

Thacher D, 'The Normative Case Study' (2006) 111 American Journal of Sociology 1631

Thatcher M, 'Governance Structures and Health Technology Assessment Agencies: A Comparative Approach' (Department of Government, London School of Economics and Political Science 2010)

'The ASSESS Project FAQ' (*The ASSESS Project*) <https://assessproject.org/faq> accessed 29 March 2022

Tobin J, *The Right to Health in International Law* (Oxford University Press 2011)

Toebes B, 'International Health Law: An Emerging Field of Public International Law' (2015) 55 Indian Journal of International Law 299

Toebes B, 'Global Health Law: Defining the Field' in Gian Luca Burci and Brigit Toebes (eds), *Research Handbook on Global Health Law* (Edward Elgar Publishing 2018)

Toebes B, *The Right to Health: A Multi-country Study of Law, Policy and Practice* (TMC Asser Press 2014)

Toebes B, Hesselman M and de Wolf AH, 'International Guideposts for Essential Public Services Provisions and Socio-Economic Rights' in Marlies Hesselman, Antenor Hallo de Wolf and Brigit Toebes (eds), *Socio-economic Human Rights in Essential Public Services Provision* (Taylor & Francis 2016)

Tomsons KA, 'Denying Medical Treatment: The Right to Health Care and the "Quality-Adjusted Life-Year" (QALY)' (Queen's University: PhD Thesis 1998)

Torchia M, Calabrò A and Morner M, 'Public–Private Partnerships in the Health Care Sector: A Systematic Review of the Literature' (2015) 17 Public Management Review 236

Tumilty E, Walker S and Tumilty S, 'Tainting by Numbers: How the Disadvantaged Become Invisible within Evidence-Based Medicine' (2014) 19 Physical Therapy Reviews 367

Tyler TR and Mentovich A, 'Mechanisms of Legal Effect: Theories of Procedural Justice' [2011] PHLR Methods Monograph Series

Uezono D and others, 'Review of Philippine Health Laws and Its Implication to HTA Institutionalization' (2020) 30 European Journal of Public Health v748

Ujewe SJ and van Staden WC, 'Inequitable Access to Healthcare in Africa: Reconceptualising the "Accountability for Reasonableness Framework" to Reflect Indigenous Principles' (2021) 20 International Journal for Equity in Health 1

UNCTAD, *Tool Box for Policy Coherence in Access to Medicines and Local Pharmaceutical Production* (UNCTAD 2018)

United Nations, 'The Human Rights-Based Approach to Development Cooperation towards a Common Understanding among the UN Agencies (UN Common Understanding)' (Workshop on a human rights-based approach in the context of UN reform, 3-5 May 2003 2003) <http://www.undp.org/governance/docs/HR_Guides_CommonUnderstanding.pdf> accessed 1 May 2020

United Nations and Department of Economic and Social Affairs, *Disability and Development Report: Realizing the Sustainable Development Goals by, for and with Persons with Disabilities : 2018* (2019)

Uprimny R, Chaparro Hernández S and Araújo AC, 'Bridging the Gap: The Evolving Doctrine on ESCR and "Maximum Available Resources"' in Katharine G Young (ed), *The Future of Economic and Social Rights* (Cambridge University Press 2019)

Urias E and Ramani SV, 'Access to Medicines after TRIPS: Is Compulsory Licensing an Effective Mechanism to Lower Drug Prices? A Review of the Existing Evidence' (2020) 3 Journal of International Business Policy 367

Urias EMP, *Improving Access to HIV/AIDS Treatment in Brazil: When Are Compulsory Licenses Effective in Price Negotiations?* (Datawyse/Universitaire Pers Maastricht 2015)

van der Wilt GJ, Rüther A and Trowman R, 'Scientific Development of HTA: A Proposal by the Health Technology Assessment International Scientific Development and Capacity Building Committee' (2019) 35 International Journal of Technology Assessment in Health Care 263

Vandenhole W and Gready P, 'Failures and Successes of Human Rights-Based Approaches to Development: Towards a Change Perspective' (2014) 32 Nordic Journal of Human Rights 291

Viens AM, 'Interdependence, Human Rights and Global Health Law' (2015) 23 Health Care Analysis 401

Vinogradov D, Shadrina E and Kokareva L, 'Public Procurement Mechanisms for Public-Private Partnerships' (2014) 14 Journal of Public Procurement 538

Vogler S, 'Access to High-Cost Medicines in Europe' in Zaheer-Ud-Din Babar (ed), *Equitable Access to High-Cost Pharmaceuticals* (Academic Press 2018)

Vogler S, 'Fair Prices for Medicines? Exploring Competent Authorities' and Public Payers' Preferences on Pharmaceutical Policies' (2019) 46 Empirica 443

Vogler S, 'How Can Pricing and Reimbursement Policies Improve Affordable Access to Medicines? Lessons Learned from European Countries' (2017) 15 Applied Health Economics and Health Policy 307

Vogler S, Paris V and Panteli D, 'Ensuring Access to Medicines: How to Redesign Pricing, Reimbursement and Procurement?' (European Observatory on Health Systems and Policies)

Vogler S and Paterson KR, 'Can Price Transparency Contribute to More Affordable Patient Access to Medicines?' (2017) 1 PharmacoEconomics: Open 145

Vogler S, Schneider P and Zimmermann N, 'Evolution of Average European Medicine Prices: Implications for the Methodology of External Price Referencing' (2019) 3 PharmacoEconomics: Open 303

Vreman RA and others, 'Differences in Health Technology Assessment Recommendations among European Jurisdictions: The Role of Practice Variations' (2020) 23 Value in Health 10

Wale J and others, 'Why Patients Should Be Involved in Health Technology Assessment' (2017) 33 International Journal of Technology Assessment in Health Care 1

Walker S, 'Challenges of Human Rights Measurement' in Bård Andreassen, Hans-Otto Sano and Siobhán McInerney-Lankford (eds), *Research Methods in Human Rights* (Edward Elgar Publishing 2017)

Wang D, 'Courts and Health Care Rationing: The Case of the Brazilian Federal Supreme Court' (2013) 8 Health Economics, Policy and Law 75

Wang D, 'Right to Health Litigation in Brazil: The Problem and the Institutional Responses' (2015) 15 Human Rights Law Review 617

Wang D, 'From Wednesbury Unreasonableness to Accountability for Reasonableness' (2017) 76 The Cambridge Law Journal 642

Wang D, 'Health Technology Assessment and Judicial Deference to Priority-Setting Decisions in Healthcare: Quasi-Experimental Analysis of Right-to-Health Litigation in Brazil' (2020) 265 Social Science & Medicine 113401

Wang D and Rumbold B, 'Priority Setting, Judicial Review, and Procedural Justice' in Andelka M Phillips, Thana C De Campos and Jonathan Herring (eds), *Philosophical Foundations of Medical Law* (1st edn, Oxford University PressOxford 2019)

Warwick BT, 'Socio-economic Rights during Economic Crises: A Changed Approach to Non-retrogression' (2016) 65 International and Comparative Law Quarterly 249

Warwick BT, 'Unwinding Retrogression: Examining the Practice of the Committee on Economic, Social and Cultural Rights' (2019) 19 Human Rights Law Review 467

Warwick BTC, 'A Hierarchy of Comfort? The CESCR's Approach to the 2008 Economic Crisis' in Gillian MacNaughton and Diane F Frey (eds), *Economic and Social Rights in a Neoliberal World* (1st edn, Cambridge University Press 2018)

Watt A and others, 'Rapid versus Full Systematic Reviews: Validity in Clinical Practice?' (2008) 78 ANZ Journal of Surgery 1037

Watt A and others, 'Rapid versus Full Systematic Reviews: Validity in Clinical Practice?' (2008) 78 ANZ Journal of Surgery 1037

Weale A, 'The Right to Health versus Good Medical Care?' (2012) 15 Critical Review of International Social and Political Philosophy 473

Weinstein MC, 'A QALY Is a QALY Is a QALY: Or Is It?' (1988) 7 Journal of Health Economics 289

Westendorp I, *Maastricht Guidelines on Violations of Economic, Social and Cultural Rights: Proceedings of the Workshop of Experts Organised by the International Commission of Jurists (Geneva, Switzerland), the Urban Morgan Institute on Human Rights (Cincinnati, USA) and the Maastricht Centre for Human Rights of Maastricht University 22-26 January 1997* (SIM 1998)

Whitehead SJ and Ali S, 'Health Outcomes in Economic Evaluation: The QALY and Utilities' (2010) 96 British Medical Bulletin 5>

Whitelaw S, Fiorentino N and O'Leary J, 'Drug Pricing-The Next Compliance Waterloo' (2018) 44 Mitchell Hamline Law Review 1165

Whittal A and others, 'Facilitating More Efficient Negotiations for Innovative Therapies: A Value-Based Negotiation Framework' (2022) 38 International Journal of Technology Assessment in Health Care e23

Whitty JA, 'Health Technology Assessment' in Zaheer-Ud-Din Babar (ed), *Equitable Access to High-Cost Pharmaceuticals* (Elsevier 2018)

'WHO | HTA Definitions' (*WHO*) <https://www.who.int/health-technology-assessment/about/Defining/en/> accessed 5 March 2021

Whoqol Group, 'Measuring Quality of Life' [1997] Geneva: The World Health Organization 1

Whyte J, *The Morals of the Market: Human Rights and the Rise of Neoliberalism* (Verso Books 2019)

Wichmann AB and others, 'The Use of Quality-Adjusted Life Years in Cost-Effectiveness Analyses in Palliative Care: Mapping the Debate through an Integrative Review' (2017) 31 Palliative Medicine 306

Widrig D and Tag B, 'HTA and Its Legal Issues: A Framework for Identifying Legal Issues in Health Technology Assessments' (2014) 30 International Journal of Technology Assessment in Health Care

Wiktor SZ and Scott JD, 'What Is the Impact of Treatment for Hepatitis C Virus Infection?' (2017) 390 The Lancet 107

Wild C, 'Austria: History of Health Technology Assessment during the Past 20 Years' (2009) 25 International Journal of Technology Assessment in Health Care 74

Wilde R, 'Dilemmas in Promoting Global Economic Justice through Human Rights Law' in Nehal Bhuta (ed), *The Frontiers of Human Rights* (Oxford University Press 2016)

Wilde R, 'Socioeconomic Rights, Extraterritorially' in Eyal Benvenisti and George Nolte (eds), *Community Interests Across International Law* (Oxford University Press 2018)

Wilkinson T and others, 'The International Decision Support Initiative Reference Case for Economic Evaluation: An Aid to Thought' (2016) 19 Value in Health 921

Wilkinson T and Chalkidou K, 'Improving the Quality of Economic Evaluation in Health in Low- and Middle-Income Countries: Where Are We Now?' (2019) 8 Journal of Comparative Effectiveness Research 1041

Willen SS and others, 'Syndemic Vulnerability and the Right to Health' (2017) 389 The Lancet 964

Williams AH and Cookson RA, 'Equity–Efficiency Trade-Offs in Health Technology Assessment' (2006) 22 International Journal of Technology Assessment in Health Care 1

Wilson S and Dugard J, 'Constitutional Jurisprudence' in Malcolm Langford and others (eds), *Socio-economic Rights in South Africa* (Cambridge University Press 2013)

Winkler IT, Satterthwaite ML and De Albuquerque C, 'Treasuring What We Measure and Measuring What We Treasure: Post-2015 Monitoring for the Promotion of Equality in the Water, Sanitation, and Hygiene Sector' (2014) 32 Wisconsin International Law Journal 547

Wolfrum R, 'Obligations of Result Versus Obligations of Conduct' in Mahnoush H Arsanjani and W Michael Reisman (eds), *Looking to the Future: Essays on International Law in Honor of W. Michael Reisman* (Martinus Nijhoff Publishers 2011)

Wolfson PJ, 'The Development and Use of Extracorporeal Membrane Oxygenation in Neonates' (2003) 76 The Annals of thoracic surgery S2224

Wong J, 'The History of Technology Assessment and Comparative Effectiveness Research for Drugs and Medical Devices and the Role of the Federal Government' (2014) 33 Biotechnology Law Report 221

World Health Organization, 'Making Fair Choices on the Path to Universal Health Coverage: Final Report of the WHO Consultative Group on Equity and Universal Health Coverage' (World Health Organization 2014)

World Health Organization, 'Advancing the Right to Health: The Vital Role of Law' (World Health Organization 2017)

World Health Organization, *Technical Report: Pricing of Cancer Medicines and Its Impacts: A Comprehensive Technical Report for the World Health Assembly Resolution 70.12: Operative Paragraph 2.9 on Pricing Approaches and Their Impacts on Availability and Affordability of Medicines for the Prevention and Treatment of Cancer* (World Health Organization 2018)

World Health Organization, 'Current Status of Health Intervention and Technology Assessment in the Balkan Region' (World Health Organization Regional Office for Europe 2020)

World Health Organization, 'Web Annex A. Systematic Reviews for the Update of the WHO Guideline on Country Pharmaceutical Pricing Policies. In' *WHO Guideline on Country Pharmaceutical Pricing Policies* (2nd edn, 2020)

World Health Organization, 'WHO Director-General's Opening Remarks at the Mission Briefing on COVID-19-9 April 2020' [2020] Geneva, Switzerland: WHO 1502

World Health Organization, *WHO Guideline on Country Pharmaceutical Pricing Policies* (2nd ed, World Health Organization 2020)

World Health Organization, 'What Are the Legal Considerations Reviewing or Establishing the Legal Framework' *Guidance for institutionalising HTA mechanisms for reimbursement* <https://decidehealth.world/en/node/7066> accessed 5 May 2020

World Health Organization and United Nations Children's Fund, 'Report of the International Conference on Primary Health Care, Alma-Ata, USSR, 6-12 September 1978' (World Health Organization 1978)

World Health Organization. Regional Office for Europe and others, *Building on Value-Based Health Care: Towards a Health System Perspective* (World Health Organization Regional Office for Europe 2020)

Xenos N, *Scarcity and Modernity* (Taylor & Francis 2017)

Yamin AE, *Power, Suffering, and the Struggle for Dignity: Human Rights Frameworks for Health and Why They Matter* (University of Pennsylvania Press 2015)

Yamin AE, 'Taking the Right to Health Seriously: Implications for Health Systems, Courts, and Achieving Universal Health Coverage' (2017) 39 Human Rights Quarterly 341

Yamin AE, 'Democracy, Health Systems, and the Right to Health: Narratives of Charity, Markets, and Citizenship' in Silja Voeneky and Gerald L Neuman (eds), *Human Rights, Democracy, and Legitimacy in a World of Disorder* (Cambridge University Press 2018)

Yamin AE and Boghosian T, 'Democracy and Health: Situating Health Rights within a Republic of Reasons' (2020) 19 Yale Journal of Health Policy, Law, and Ethics 96

Yamin AE and Cantor R, 'Between Insurrectional Discourse and Operational Guidance: Challenges and Dilemmas in Implementing Human Rights-Based Approaches to Health' (2014) 6 Journal of Human Rights Practice 451

Yamin AE and Frisancho A, 'Human-Rights-Based Approaches to Health in Latin America' (2015) 385 The Lancet e26

Yamin AE and Gloppen S (eds), *Litigating Health Rights: Can Courts Bring More Justice to Health?* (Harvard University Press 2011)

Yamin AE and Lander F, 'Implementing a Circle of Accountability: A Proposed Framework for Judiciaries and Other Actors in Enforcing Health-Related Rights' (2015) 14 Journal of Human Rights 312

Yamin AE and Lander F, 'Implementing a Circle of Accountability: A Proposed Framework for Judiciaries and Other Actors in Enforcing Health-Related Rights' (2015) 14 Journal of Human Rights 312

Yamin AE and Norheim O, 'Taking Equality Seriously: Applying Human Rights Frameworks to Priority Setting in Health' (2014) 36 Human Rights Quarterly 296

Yamin AE and Parra-Vera O, 'How Do Courts Set Health Policy? The Case of the Colombian Constitutional Court' (2009) 6 PLoS Medicine e1000032

Yepes RU and Hernández SC, 'Inequality, Human Rights, and Social Rights: Tensions and Complementarities' (2019) 10 Humanity: An International Journal of Human Rights, Humanitarianism, and Development 376

Yin RK, *Case Study Research and Applications: Design and Methods* (6th ed., SAGE Publications 2019)

Yoo K, 'Interaction of Human Rights Law and Competition Law: The Right to Access to Medicine and Consumer Welfare in the U.S. Pharmaceutical Sector' (2018) 43 Vermont Law Review 30

Young KG, 'The Minimum Core of Economic and Social Rights: A Concept in Search of Content' (2008) 33 Yale International Law Journal 64

Young KG, *Constituting Economic and Social Rights* (Oxford University Press 2012)

Young KG, 'The Immediacy of Economic and Social Rights' (*Jamesg Stewart*, 23 May 2018) <http://jamesgstewart.com/the-immediacy-of-economic-and-social-rights/> accessed 15 June 2020

Young KG, 'Waiting for Rights: Progressive Realization and Lost Time' in Katharine G Young (ed), *The Future of Economic and Social Rights* (Cambridge University Press 2019)

Yuasa A and others, 'Investigation of Factors Considered by Health Technology Assessment Agencies in Eight Countries' (2021) 5 PharmacoEconomics-open 57

Yuba TY, Novaes HMD and de Soárez PC, 'Challenges to Decision-Making Processes in the National HTA Agency in Brazil: Operational Procedures, Evidence Use and Recommendations' (2018) 16 Health Research Policy and Systems 1

Zaprutko T and others, 'Affordability of Medicines in the European Union' (2017) 12 PLOS ONE e0172753

Zechmeister-Koss I, Schnell-Inderst P and Zauner G, 'Appropriate Evidence Sources for Populating Decision Analytic Models within Health Technology Assessment (HTA): A Systematic Review of HTA Manuals and Health Economic Guidelines' (2013) 16 Value in Health A591

Zerbe Jr RO, 'The Legal Foundation of Cost-Benefit Analysis' (2007) 2 Charleston L. Rcv. 93

Zerbe Jr RO, 'Cost–Benefit Analysis in Legal Decision-Making' in Francesco Parisi (ed), *Oxford Handbook of Law and Economics Methodology and Concepts* (Oxford University Press 2017)

International Law Sources and Treaties

CESCR, "An Evaluation of the Obligation to Take Steps to the "Maximum Available Resources" under an Optional Protocol to the Covenant" 10 May 2007 ((E/C.12/2007/1).

CESCR, "An Open Letter" 16 May 2012 (CESCR/48th/SP/MAB/SW).

CESCR, "Concluding observations on the combined 5th and 6th periodic reports of the Philippines" 26 October 2016 (E/C.12/PHL/CO/5-6), paras 53–4.

CESCR, "Concluding observations on the combined second to fourth periodic reports of Egypt"13 December 2013 (E/C.12/EGY/CO/2-4).

CESCR, "Concluding observations on the combined third, fourth and fifth periodic reports of El Salvador", 19 June 2014 (E/C.12/SLV/CO/3-5).

CESCR, "Concluding observations on the sixth periodic report of Colombia" 19 October 2017 (E/C.12/COL/CO/6).

CESCR, "Concluding observations: Angola", 1 December 2008 (E/C.12/AGO/CO3.

CESCR, "General Comment No. 12: The Right to Adequate Food (Art. 11 of the Covenant)" 12 May 1999 (E/C.12/1999/5).

CESCR, "General Comment No. 13: The Right to Education (Art. 13)" 8 December 1999 (E/C.12/1999/10).

CESCR. "General Comment No. 14. The Right to the Highest Attainable Standard of Health (GC 14)." 12 August 2000 (E/C.12/2000/4).

CESCR, "General Comment No. 15: The Right to Water" 20 January 2003 (E/C.12/2002/11).

CESCR, "General Comment No. 19: The Right to Social Security" 4 February 2008 (E/C.12/GC/19).

CESCR, "General Comment No. 20: Non-Discrimination in Economic, Social and Cultural Rights (Art. 2, Para. 2, of the International Covenant on Economic, Social and Cultural Rights)" 2 July 2009 (E/C.12/GC/20).

CESCR, "General Comment No. 22 on the Right to Sexual and Reproductive Health (Article 12 of the International Covenant on Economic, Social and Cultural Rights)" 2 May 2016 (E/C.12/GC/22).

CESCR, "General comment No. 24 (2017) on State obligations under the International Covenant on Economic, Social and Cultural Rights in the context of business activities" 10 August 2017 (E/C.12/GC/24).

CESCR, "General Comment No. 25: Science and economic, social and cultural rights (article 15 (1) (b), (2), (3) and (4) of the International Covenant on Economic, Social and Cultural Rights)", 30 April 2020 (E/C.12/GC/25).

CESCR, "General Comment No. 3: "The nature of States parties" obligations" (GC 3)" 14 December 1990 (E/1991/23).

 | HTTPS://DOI.ORG/10.1163/9789004730311-012

CESCR, "General Comment No. 4: The Right to Adequate Housing" 13 December 1991 (E/1992/23).

CESCR, "General Comment No. 9, The domestic application of the Covenant", 3 December 1998 (E/C.12/1998/24).

CESCR, "Statement on the Coronavirus Disease (COVID-19) Pandemic and Economic, Social and Cultural Rights", 6 April 2020 (E/C.12/2020/1).

Commission on Human Rights, Preliminary report of the Special Rapporteur on the right to education, Ms. Katarina Tomasevski, submitted in accordance with Commission on Human Rights resolution 1998/33, 13 January1990 (E/CN.4/1999/49).

Conference of the State Parties of the CRPD "Improvement of disability data and statistics: objectives and challenges" 1 April 2015 (CRPD/CSP/2015/3).

Convention concerning Discrimination in Respect of Employment and Occupation (ILO Convention No. 111) (adopted 25 June 1958, entered into force 15 June 1960) 362 U.N.T.S. 31.

Convention on the Elimination of All Forms of Discrimination against Women (adopted 18 December 1979, entered into force 3 September 1981) 1249 UNTS 13.

Convention on the Rights of Persons with Disabilities (adopted 13 December 2006, entered into force 3 May 2008) 49 UNTS 2.

Convention on the Rights of the Child (adopted 20 November 1989, entered into force 2 September 1990) UN GAORes 44/25 (1989).

Convention relating to the Status of Refugees (adopted 28 July 1951, entered into force 22 April. 1954) 189 UNTS 137.

CRC, Day of General Discussion on "Resources for the Rights of the Child – Responsibility of States", 46th session, 21 September 2007 (CRC/C/46/CRP.1).

CRPD "Concluding observations on the initial report of Seychelles" (16 April 2018) CRPD/C/SYC/CO/1, paras 53–54.

HRC "Follow-up on the application of the technical guidance on the application of a human rights-based approach to the implementation of policies and programmes to reduce preventable maternal mortality and morbidity" (29 June 2018) A/HRC/39/26.

HRC, "The impact of the Agreement on Trade-related Aspects of Intellectual Property Rights on human rights, report of the High Commissioner" 27 June 2001 (E/CN.4/Sub.2/2001/13).

HRC, "Draft Convention on the Right to Development, with commentaries" 20 January 2020 (A/HRC/WG.2/21/2/Add.1).

HRC, "Draft guidelines for States on the effective implementation of the right to participate in public affairs", 20 July 2018 (A/HRC/39/28).

HRC, "Good practices and challenges to respecting, protecting and fulfilling all human rights in the elimination of preventable maternal mortality and morbidity" 13 July 2020 (A/HRC/45/19).
HRC, "Guiding principles on human rights impact assessments of economic reforms" (19 December 2018) paras 17.1–2.
HRC, "Human Rights of Older People: The Data Gap" 9 July 2020 (A/HRC/45/14).
HRC, "Report of the Independent Expert on the enjoyment of all human rights by older persons" 10 July 2018 (A/HRC/39/50.
HRC, "Report of the Open-ended Working Group to Consider Options Regarding the Elaboration of an Optional Protocol to the International Covenant on Economic, Social and Cultural Rights on its Second Session", 23 May 2008 (E/CN.4/2005/52).
HRC, "Report of the Special Rapporteur on E/CN.4/Sub.2/2001/13 on the right of everyone to the enjoyment of the highest attainable standard of physical and mental health, Anand Grover" 31 March 2009 (A/HRC/11/12).
HRC, "Report of the Special Rapporteur on the right of everyone to the enjoyment of the highest attainable standard of physical and mental health, Dainius Pūras" 2 April 2015 (A/HRC/29/33).
HRC, "Report of the Special Rapporteur on the right of everyone to the enjoyment of the highest attainable standard of physical and mental health", 5 March 2008 (A/HRC/7/11/Add.2).
HRC, "Report of the Special Rapporteur on the right of everyone to the enjoyment of the highest attainable standard of physical and mental health" 15 April 2020 (A/HRC/44/48).
HRC, "Report of the Special Rapporteur on the right of everyone to the enjoyment of the highest attainable standard of physical and mental health, Anand Grover, on access to medicines", 1 May 2013 (A/HRC/23/42).
HRC, "Report of the United Nations High Commissioner for Human Rights" (20 April 2018) A/HRC/38/37.
HRC, Resolution 32/15 1 July 2016 (A/HRC/RES/32/15).
HRC, Resolution 41/10 19 July 2019 (A/HRC/RES/41/10).
HRC, "Technical guidance on the application of a human rights-based approach to the implementation of policies and programmes to reduce preventable maternal morbidity and mortality", 12 July 2012 (A/HRC/21/22 2012)
International Covenant on Civil and Political Rights (ICCPR) (adopted 16 December. 1966, entered into force 23 March 1976) 999 UNTS 171.
International Covenant on Economic, Social and Cultural Rights (adopted 16 December 1966, entered into force 3 January 1976) 993 UNTS 3.
International Convention on the Elimination of All Forms of Racial Discrimination (adopted 21 December 1965, entered into force 4 January 1969) 660 UNTS 195.

International Convention on the Protection of the Rights of All Migrant Workers and Members of Their Families (adopted 18 December 1990, entered into force 1 July 2003) 2220 UNTS 3.

OHCHR, "Human Rights Indicators: A Guide to Measurement and Implementation", 2012 (HR/PUB/12/5).

Pan-American Sanitary Conference (PASC), "Health Technology Assessment and Incorporation into Health Systems", 16 July 2012 (CSP28/11).

Pan-American Sanitary Conference (PASC), "HTA and Incorporation into Health Systems, 28th Pan American Sanitarian Conference, Pan-American Health Organization", 19 September 2012 (CSP28.R9).

UN Sub-Commission on the Promotion and Protection of Human Rights, "Intellectual property rights and human rights", 23 November 2000 (E/CN.4/2001/2).

UN, "Report of the Second World Assembly on Ageing" 8–12 April 2002 (A/CONF.197/9).

UNGA "Human rights to safe drinking water and sanitation" 16 July 2018 (A/73/162).

UNGA, "Format and organizational aspects of the high-level political forum on sustainable development (Resolution 67/290) 23 August 2013 (A/RES/67/290).

UNGA, "Report of the Special Rapporteur on the right to development" (30 July 2018) A/73/271.

UNGA, "Follow-up and review of the 2030 Agenda for Sustainable Development at the global level(Resolution 70/299), 18 August 2016 (A/RES/70/299).

UNGA, "Optional Protocol to the International Covenant on Economic, Social and Cultural Rights'. 10 December 2008 (A/RES/63/117).

UNGA, "Report of the Special Rapporteur on the rights of persons with disabilities" 16 July 2018 (A/73/161).

UNGA, "Universal Declaration of Human Rights", 10 December 1948 (UNGA Res 217 A(III) (UDHR)).

United Nations and Department of Economic and Social Affairs, Disability and Development Report: Realizing the Sustainable Development Goals by, for and with Persons with Disabilities : 2018 (2019) 275–83, Statistical Commission " Joint report of the Secretary-General, the Washington Group on Disability Statistics and international agencies" 20 December 2019 (E/CN.3/2020/34).

United Nations, Charter of the United Nations, 24 October 1945, 1 UNTS XV.

WHO, Constitution of the World Health Organization. World Health Organization; 1948.

World Health Assembly, Health intervention and technology assessment in support of universal health coverage, 24 May 2014 (WHA67.23).

Index

 | HTTPS://DOI.ORG/10.1163/9789004730311-013